Letts

GCSE Success

Revision Guide

AQA Science Foundation

Brian Arnold • Hannah Kingston • Emma Poole

Contents

SCIENCE SUCCESS

Contents

Biology

Chemistry

Physics

The nervous system

The nervous system is in charge. It *controls and co-ordinates* the parts of your body so that they work together at the right time. The nervous system co-ordinates things you do not even think about, like breathing and blinking.

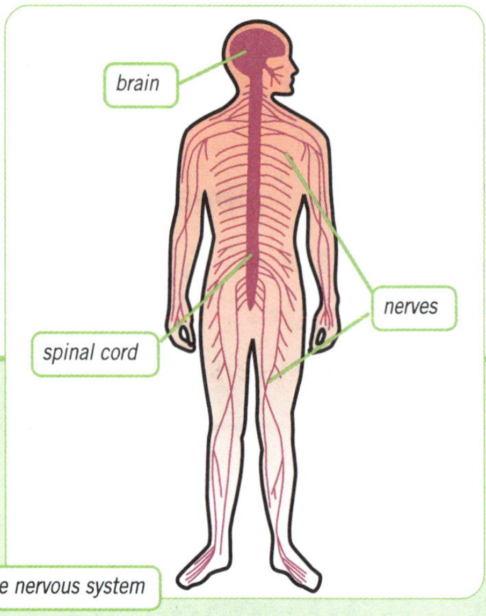

The nervous system

The central nervous system

The central nervous system (**CNS**) consists of the brain and spinal cord connected to different parts of the body by **nerves**. Your body's sense organs contain **receptors**. Receptors detect changes in the environment called stimuli.

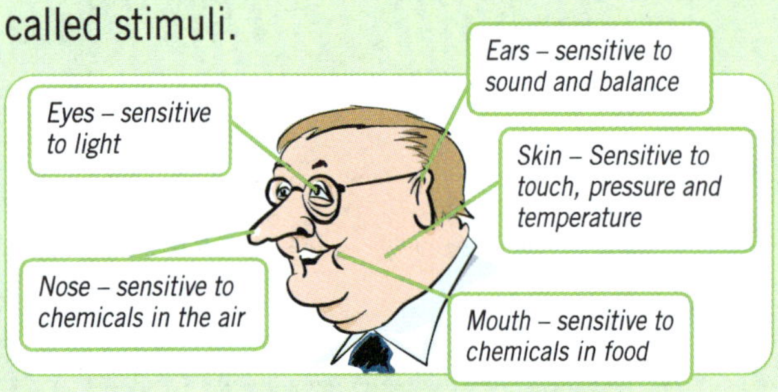

The receptors send messages along nerves to the brain and spinal cord in response to stimuli from the environment. The messages are called **nerve impulses**. The CNS send nerve impulses back along nerves to **effectors**, which bring about a response. Effectors are muscles that bring about movement, or glands that secrete hormones.

Nerves 1

Nerves are made up of nerve cells or **neurones**. There are three types of neurone.

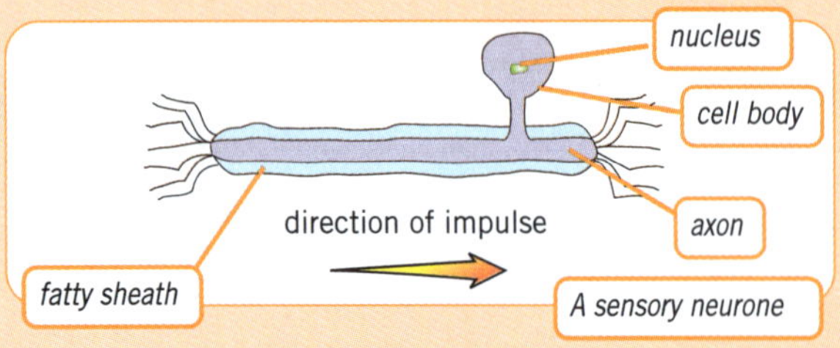

A sensory neurone

The **sensory neurones** receive messages from the receptors and send them to the CNS.

The **motor neurones** send messages from the CNS to the effectors telling them what to do. Nerve impulses travel in one direction only. A **relay neurone** connects the sensory neurone to the motor neurone in the CNS. In between the neurones there is a gap called a **synapse**.

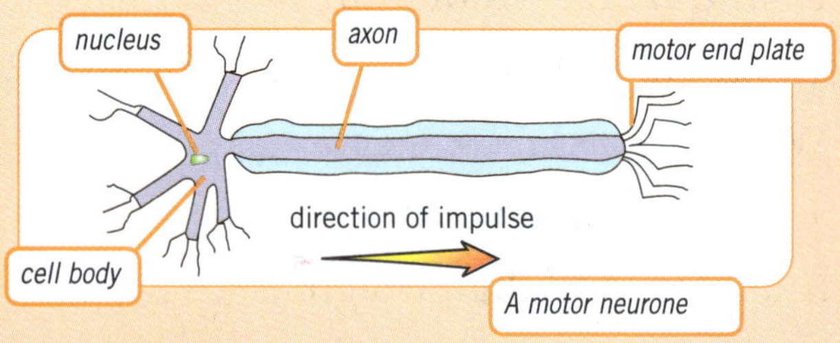

A motor neurone

The reflex arc

The reflex response to your CNS and back again can be shown in a diagram called the **reflex arc**:

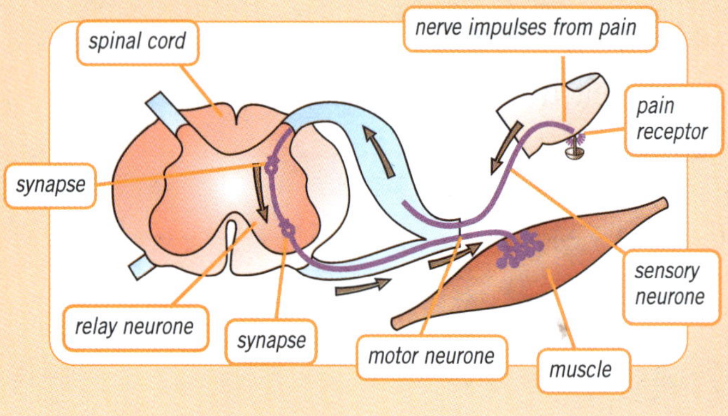

Nerves 2

1 The stimulus in this example is a sharp object.
2 The receptor is the pain sensor in the skin which detects the sharpness as pain and generates a nerve impulse.
3 The nerve impulse travels along the sensory neurone towards the relay neurone.
4 The impulse is passed across a synapse to the relay neurone, which carries the impulse towards the motor neurone.
5 The impulse is passed across a synapse to the motor neurone.
6 The impulse is passed along a synapse to the muscle effector in the arm.
7 You move your hand away.

Block diagram

The reflex arc can also be shown as a block diagram, see below.

stimulus → receptor → sensory neurone → relay neurone → motor neurone → effector → response

Reflex and voluntary actions

- **Voluntary actions** are things you have to think about: they are under your control. They have to be learned, like talking or writing.
- **Reflex actions** produce quick responses. They often protect us and other animals from harm. Examples include the reflex actions of a newborn baby, the pupils' response to light, the knee jerk reflex, and blinking.

Learn examples that follow the reflex arc, for example touching a hot object or dust in the eye.

Scientific concept

What is a synapse? It is a gap between neurones. A chemical is released across the synapse that starts the impulse in the next neurone. Drugs and alcohol affect synapses and slow down nervous reactions.

KEY TERMS

Make sure you understand these terms before moving on!

- CNS
- receptors
- nerve impulse
- effectors
- sensory neurone
- motor neurone
- relay neurone
- synapse
- reflex arc
- reflex action

QUICK TEST

1. Name the five sense organs.
2. What is CNS an abbreviation for?
3. What does the CNS consist of?
4. Name the three types of neurone.
5. Which neurone is connected to the receptors?
6. Which neurone is connected to the effectors?
7. Which neurone connects the sensory neurone and the motor neurone?
8. Nerve impulses can only travel in one direction – true or false?
9. Why are reflex actions useful?
10. What is the difference between a reflex action and a voluntary action?

Hormones and the menstrual cycle

***Hormones* are chemicals released from glands in the body straight into the blood stream to the target organs. The effects of hormones are slower than nervous messages but are longer lasting. They control things that need constant adjustment.**

An example is the menstrual cycle in women where several hormones are involved.

Homeostasis

The nervous system and hormones enable us to respond to changes in the environment by making slight adjustments inside our bodies to our internal environment. Our internal environment changes very little. It remains at a safe level through a process called homeostasis. This is all controlled by nerves and hormones.

Internal conditions controlled by homeostasis include:

- The water content of the body. We drink to replace the water lost through sweating and breathing. Any excess is lost in urine.
- The ion content of the body. We lose ions such as salt when we sweat. Any excess is lost in the urine.
- The temperature of the body, which must be maintained to enable enzymes to work effectively.
- Blood sugar levels, which are monitored by hormones to ensure that our cells receive a constant supply of energy.

The menstrual cycle

A sequence of events that occurs each month in females is called the menstrual cycle.

The menstrual cycle lasts approximately **28 days.**

It consists of a **menstrual bleed lasting 4–7 days and ovulation** – the release of an egg.

Ovaries secrete the hormones **progesterone** and **oestrogen**.

The stages of the menstrual cycle

Day 1–5, a menstrual bleed (a period) occurs the lining of the uterus breaks down. Caused by **lack of progesterone**.

Day 5–14, oestrogen is released from the ovaries and the uterus lining builds up again.

Oestrogen also stimulates egg development and release of the egg from the ovaries – called ovulation.

The 28-day menstrual cycle

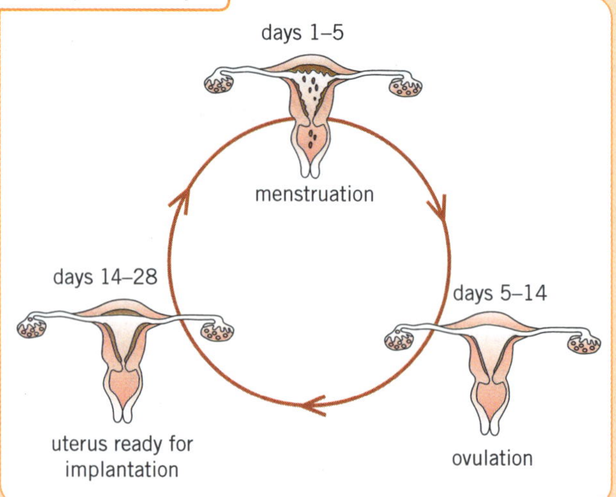

Day 14–28, progesterone is released which maintains the uterus lining.

If no fertilisation occurs then progesterone production stops.

Day 28–5, cycle begins again.

The pituitary gland

The two hormones released from the ovaries are in fact controlled by the **pituitary gland** situated at the base of the brain.

The pituitary gland secretes two more hormones, the follicle stimulating hormone (**FSH**) and the luteinising hormone (**LH**).

Progesterone is released which maintains the uterus lining.

Oestrogen also keeps the uterus lining thick ready for pregnancy.

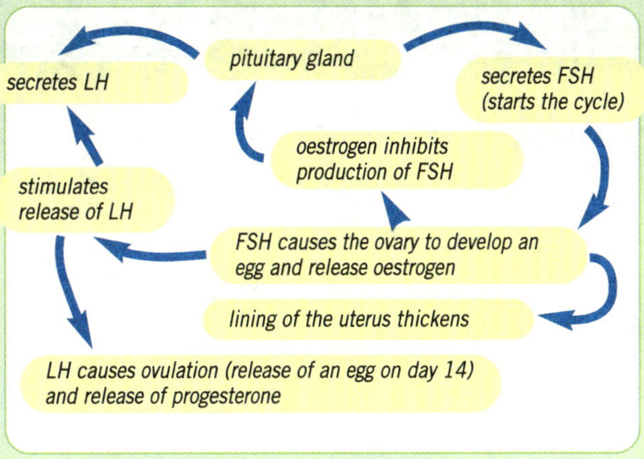

If no pregnancy occurs then progesterone production stops and the cycle begins again.

Controlling fertility

Fertility in women can be controlled in two ways.

- FSH can be administered as a '**fertility drug**' to women whose own production is too low to stimulate eggs to mature. This can result in multiple births.
- Oestrogen can be used as an **oral contraceptive** to inhibit FSH so that no eggs mature.

IVF

In vitro fertilisation (**IVF**) is a treatment for infertile couples. It involves extracting the eggs and sperm and fertilising them outside the body. The cells that develop are then implanted in the womb for growth and development into an embryo.

FSH is the hormone used to stimulate egg production.

Be prepared to evaluate the benefits and problems associated with the use of hormones to control fertility. For example, do they interfere with nature? Or are the possible side effects they may cause a risk worth taking?

The role of the hormones in controlling the menstrual cycle is a favourite for the exam.

KEY TERMS

- hormones
- ovulation
- progesterone
- oestrogen
- pituitary gland
- FSH
- LH
- fertility drugs
- IVF

QUICK TEST

1. How are hormones transported around the body?
2. What causes the uterus lining to break down?
3. Where are the hormones oestrogen and progesterone made?
4. From where are the eggs released?
5. Which hormone is used in IVF?
6. Which two hormones are produced by the pituitary gland?
7. What two things does the follicle stimulating hormone do?
8. Which two hormones maintain the uterus lining?
9. What is ovulation?
10. What is IVF an abbreviation for?

A balanced diet

The seven nutritional groups are: *carbohydrates, proteins, fat, vitamins and minerals, fibre and water.*

A balanced diet is made up of all of the above nutrients.

A total lack of any one important nutrient will cause illness and even death which is why they are called *essential nutrients.*

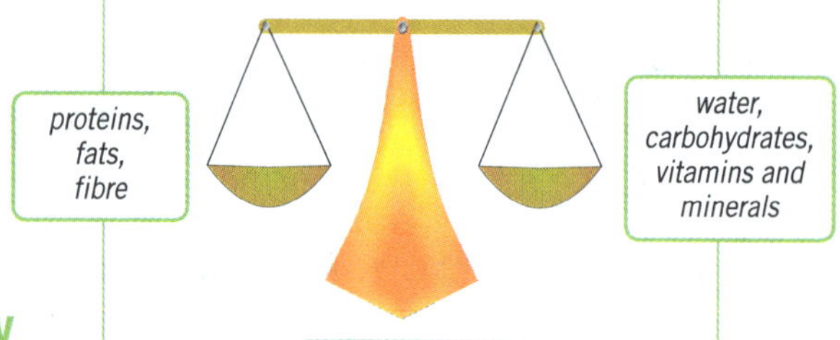

A balanced diet

Carbohydrates

Carbohydrates consist of starch and different types of sugar e.g. glucose (the sugar our bodies use for respiration) and lactose (the sugar in milk).

We need carbohydrates to **give us energy**.

Starch is actually made up of smaller glucose molecules joined together. Which means it has to broken down first to give us energy. Starch is a slow release energy source whereas glucose is more immediate.

These are foods containing a lot of carbohydrate

Protein

Your body cells are made of mostly protein.

Proteins are made up of lots of amino acids.

We need protein to **repair and replace damaged cells** or to **make new cells during growth**.

These are foods containing a lot of protein

Fats

Fats are made from fatty acids and glycerol.

We need fats for a **store of energy**, to **make cell membranes** and for **warmth** (**insulation**).

Fat can also be bad for us. **Cholesterol** is a fatty deposit that can narrow the arteries and can contribute to heart disease.

These are foods containing a lot of fat

Fibre

Fibre or roughage comes from plants.

Fibre is not actually digested it just keeps food moving smoothly through your system.

Fibre provides something for your gut muscles to push against. It's a bit like squeezing toothpaste through a tube.

It prevents constipation.

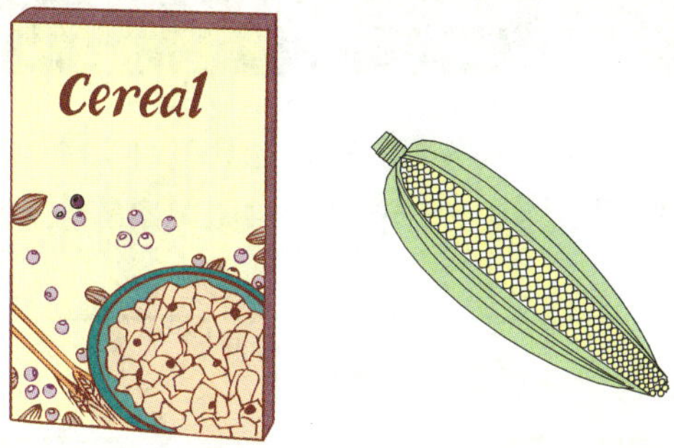

These are foods containing a lot of fibre

Water

Water makes up approximately 65% of your body weight.

Water is important because:

- Our blood plasma is mainly water.
- Water is in sweat that cools us down.
- Chemical reactions in our cells take place in water.
- Waste products are removed from our bodies in water.

Food and drink contain water.

Vitamins and minerals

We only need these in small amounts but they are essential for good health.

Your body turns everything you eat into body tissue by billions of reactions that occur in your body. Vitamins and minerals are essential to this process. They also make up cells and tissue in your body.

These are foods containing a lot of vitamins and minerals

Vitamins and minerals are found in fruit, vegetables and cereals.

Remember that carbohydrates are for energy, proteins are for growth and repair and fats are for energy store and insulation. But do not forget the other important food groups.

KEY TERMS

- carbohydrate
- fats
- protein
- vitamins and minerals
- fibre
- water
- energy
- growth and repair
- insulation

QUICK TEST

1. What do we use carbohydrates for?
2. Name the two main carbohydrates.
3. What type of carbohydrate would long distance runners need to eat before a race?
4. In cold countries, what nutritional group is particularly important?
5. Why do we need fat in our diets?
6. Why is protein important to our cells?
7. How does fibre prevent constipation?
8. Which carbohydrate would give you energy quickly?
9. Which food groups are only needed in small amounts?
10. What type of fat contributes to heart disease?

Nutrition and health

A combination of a balanced diet and exercise is needed to keep the body healthy.

A healthy diet

A healthy diet contains the right balance of the different foods you need and the right amount of energy. The amount of energy a person needs in their diet depends on **age**, **gender** and the **amount of activity** they do. If a person takes in a larger amount of energy than they use up exercising, the excess is stored as fat.

If a person becomes overweight, they are more likely to suffer health problems such as arthritis, diabetes, **heart disease**, high blood pressure, stress and anxiety.

Occasionally a person can become so worried about being overweight that they develop an eating disorder such as **anorexia nervosa**. This can lead to health problems such as reduced resistance to infection, pale, papery skin and in women, irregular periods or periods that stop altogether.

In the developing world, lack of food is linked to health problems such as reduced resistance to infection from diseases.

Healthy foods

Deficiency diseases are caused by lack of vitamins and minerals, or any other essential nutrient.

Metabolic rate

Your **metabolic rate** (MR) is the rate at which your body burns calories or uses up energy to carry out all the chemical reactions that take place in your cells. Genetics affect a person's metabolic rate, as do various other factors. Metabolic rates vary: activity will increase your MR and it usually stays at a higher level for some time after exercise is finished. People who exercise are usually fitter than people who don't exercise.

The proportion of muscle to fat ratio is also important. People with more muscle than fat have a higher MR than those with more fat than muscle.

Other factors that will increase your metabolic rate are eating smaller, regular meals, pregnancy and the cold weather (when we tend to move around more).

Factors that lower your MR are age (younger people tend to have a lower rate) and crash dieting.

Cholesterol

Cholesterol is made in the liver and found in the blood. The level of cholesterol in the blood is influenced by the amount and type of fat in your diet.

Cholesterol is carried in the blood by lipoproteins. There are two types of lipoproteins. Low-density lipoproteins (LDLs) are classed as 'bad' cholesterol and high-density lipoproteins (HDLs) are 'good' cholesterol. It is important to get the balance between the two types right to avoid heart and blood vessel disease.

Saturated fats increase blood cholesterol.

Monounsaturated fats have little effect on blood cholesterol. **Polyunsaturated fats**, however, may help reduce blood cholesterol and improve the balance between LDLs and HDLs.

Genetic factors, smoking and alcohol can also contribute to the effects of cholesterol and increase the risk of heart disease.

Statins are drugs that can be used to lower levels of cholesterol in the blood. They are used to treat atherosclerosis and heart disease as they reduce the formation of plaque and any inflammation in the arteries.

Salt

Salt is needed in small amounts in our diets. An adult needs, on average, about 6 grams per day but is actually consuming 60% more. Salt contains sodium, which is linked to heart disease, high blood pressure and strokes. It is found in high quantities in processed food from cereals to biscuits and soups.

0.5 g of sodium in food is considered to be a lot, whereas 0.1 g is a small amount.

Remember, each individual's diet reflects their personal choice, which may be influenced by their medical requirements or their religion.

KEY TERMS

- heart disease
- metabolic rate
- cholesterol
- saturated fat
- polyunsaturated fats

QUICK TEST

1. What would you be at risk of if your diet is high in saturated fats?
2. What type of fat can lower cholesterol?
3. How much salt should an average person eat per day?
4. When you read food labels, what amount of sodium is considered to be a little?
5. Is a person who exercises regularly likely to have a high or a low metabolic rate?
6. Where is cholesterol made?
7. What health problems are associated with being overweight?
8. Does exercise increase or lower your metabolic rate?

Causes of disease

Microbes are *bacteria*, fungi and *viruses*.
Not all microbes cause disease, some are useful.
Microbes that get inside you and make you feel ill are called *pathogens* or germs.
Pathogens rapidly reproduce in warm conditions and with plenty of food.

How are diseases spread?

- **Contact** with infected people, animals or objects used by infected people e.g. athlete's foot, chicken pox, measles and HIV through infected blood.
- Through the **air** e.g. flu, colds and pneumonia.
- Through infected **food and drink** e.g. cholera from infected drinking water and salmonella food poisoning.

Disease can be non infectious and caused by vitamin deficiencies such as scurvy (lack of vitamin C), mineral deficiencies such as anaemia (lack of iron) or body disorders like cancer or diabetes. Other disorders can be inherited, like red-green colour blindness or diabetes.

Bacteria

- Bacteria are living organisms that feed, move and carry out respiration.
- Bacteria reproduce rapidly and produce exact copies.
- Bacteria are good at surviving in unfavorable conditions such as extreme temperatures.

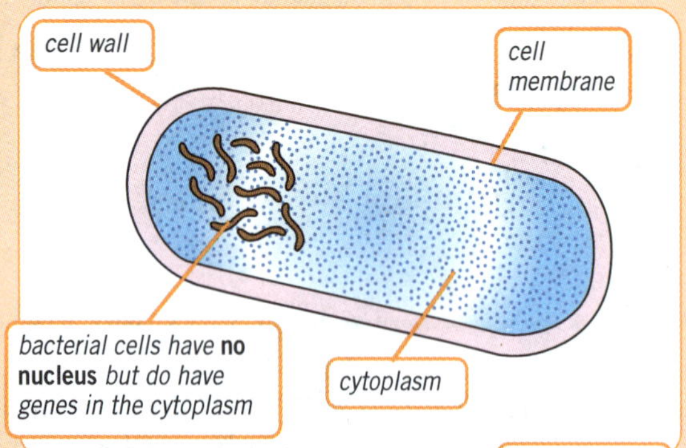

A bacterium

Bacterial cells have **no nucleus** but do have genes in the cytoplasm.

Some bacteria have circular DNA called **plasmids**; these are useful in genetic engineering, as you will read about later on the genetic engineering pages.

How they cause disease

1 Bacteria **destroy living tissue**. For example, tuberculosis destroys lung tissue.

2 Bacteria can produce poisons, called **toxins**. For example, food poisoning is caused by bacteria releasing toxins.

Viruses

Viruses are much smaller than bacteria.

Viruses don't feed, move, respire or grow they just reproduce. Viruses can only survive inside the cells of a living organism.

They **reproduce inside the cells** and release thousands of new viruses to infect new cells.

They **kill the cell** in the process.

Examples of viruses causing disease are HIV, flu, chicken pox and measles.

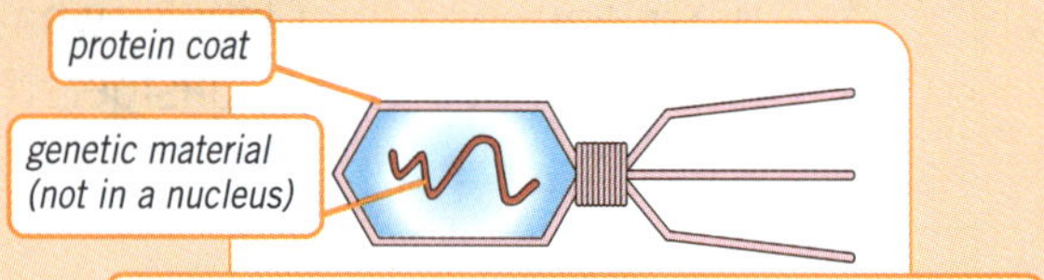

*Viruses consist of a **protein coat** surrounding a few **genes***

Fungi

Fungi cause athlete's foot and ringworm.

Fungi reproduce by **making spores** that can be carried from person to person.

Most fungi are useful as decomposers and yeast is a fungus that is used in bread, beer and wine making.

Vectors

Some pathogens rely on **vectors** to transfer them from one organism to another. A vector is an organism that transports a pathogen. An example would be a **mosquito**.

A mosquito that is carrying the bacteria that causes malaria may infect another person by injecting the bacteria into the person's bloodstream when it bites them.

KEY TERMS

Make sure you understand these terms before moving on!

- microbes
- bacteria
- virus
- pathogens
- toxins
- vectors

How do pathogens get in?

Pathogens have to enter our body before they can do any harm.

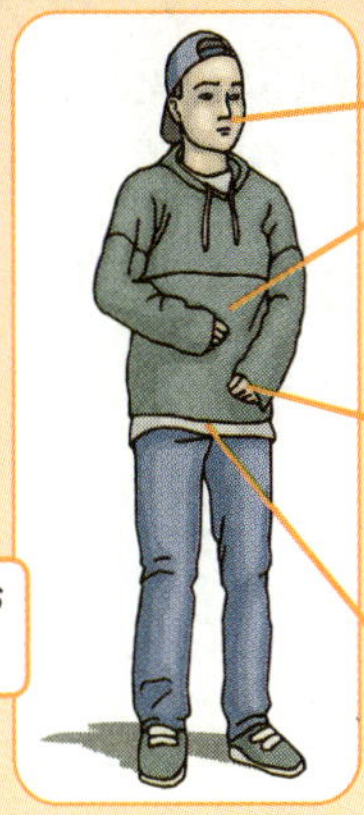

Routes for microbes to enter the body

Symptoms of infection

Symptoms are the effects diseases have on the body; the symptoms are usually caused by the toxins releases by the pathogens.

Symptoms include a high temperature, headache, loss of appetite and sickness.

Remember that not all microbes are harmful and cause disease.

Learn the structure of a bacterium and a virus; notice the similarities and differences between them.

QUICK TEST

1. Name the three types of microbes.
2. What do we call microbes that cause disease?
3. Why should you be careful in countries that have mosquitoes?
4. How do viruses cause disease?
5. Give two examples of diseases caused by fungi.
6. What is a vector? Give an example.
7. Name three ways in which pathogens can enter the body.
8. Name two diseases caused by bacteria.

Defence against disease

The human body has many methods of *preventing pathogens* from entering the body.

If pathogens do get in the body, then your *immune system* goes into action.

Prevention is better than cure

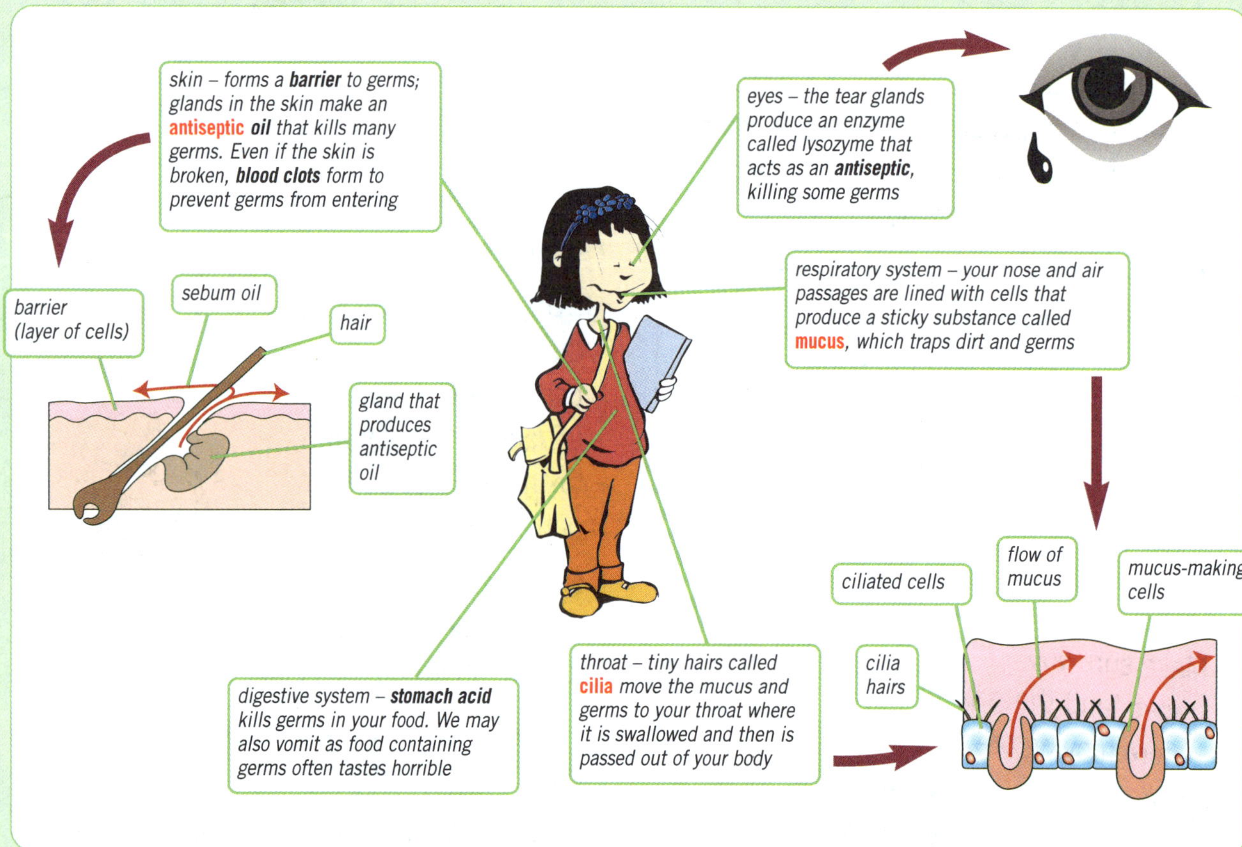

The human body has several ways of preventing disease causing microbes from entering. They are our natural defences.

Preventing the spread of germs

We can **sterilise** equipment used in food preparation or in operating theatres by heating them to a temperature of 120°C.

We can use **disinfectants** on work surfaces and areas where germs thrive such as toilets.

Antiseptics can kill germs on living tissue if we cut ourselves.

General good hygiene is important in preventing the spread of disease. Examples include washing hands after going to the toilet, cooking food thoroughly and keeping food in the fridge or freezer. These methods prevent bacteria from multiplying and causing disease.

The immune system response

If the pathogens get into the body, then the **white blood cells** travelling around in your blood spring into action.

1 White blood cells can make chemicals called **antitoxins** that destroy the toxins produced by bacteria.

2 White blood cells called **phagocytes** engulf the odd bacteria or viruses before they have a chance to do any harm.

3 However, if they are in large numbers then the other type of white blood cell is involved, called **lymphocytes**.

All germs have chemicals on their surface called **antigens**.

Lymphocytes recognise these antigens as foreign.

Lymphocytes produce chemicals called antibodies that attach to these antigens and clump them together. **Phagocytes** can then engulf and destroy the bacteria and viruses.

Natural immunity

Making antibodies takes time which is why you feel ill at first, and then get better as the disease is destroyed by the white blood cells.

Once a particular antibody is made, it stays in your body. If the same disease enters your body, the antibodies are much quicker at destroying it and you feel no symptoms. **You are now immune to that disease.**

Ways of preventing infection comes up often in the exam so make sure you are clear how the body prevents infection from getting in and causing disease.

KEY TERMS

Make sure you understand these terms before moving on!

- pathogen
- immune system
- antiseptic
- mucus
- cilia
- phagocyte
- lymphocyte
- natural immunity

QUICK TEST

1. How does the skin protect against disease?
2. What is the job of mucus?
3. Name four ways of preventing the spread of germs.
4. Name the two types of white blood cell that are involved in the immune response.
5. How do phagocytes kill germs?
6. What chemicals do white blood cells produce?
7. What do antitoxins do?
8. What is the role of antibodies?
9. What are cilia?
10. How does the body recognise foreign bacteria and viruses?

Treatment of disease

There are various ways of treating disease and infection once they get past the body's natural defenses.

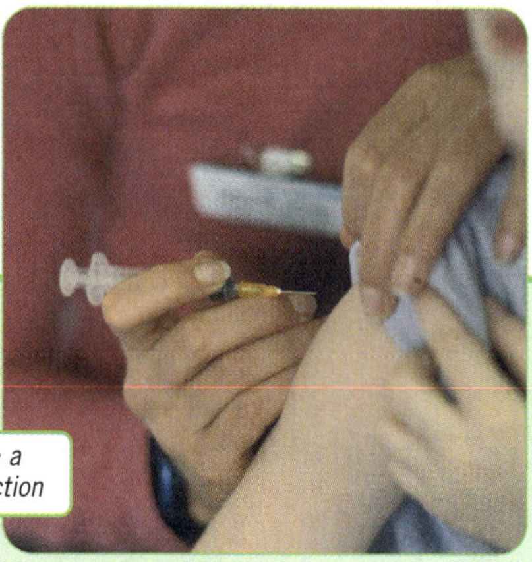

Artificial immunity: a shield against infection

Artificial immunity

Artificial immunity involves the use of **vaccines**.

A vaccine contains dead or harmless germs.

These germs still have antigens on them and your white blood cells respond to them as if they were alive by multiplying and producing antibodies.

A vaccine is an advanced warning so that if the person is infected by the germ, the white blood cells can **respond immediately** and kill them.

Vaccines help prevent the spread of disease and epidemics, but it is a person's choice to decide on vaccinations for themselves or their children.

Some people argue that improved sanitation and hygiene have led to the decrease of some diseases and not vaccinations.

The vaccine to treat MMR (measles, mumps and rubella) is a viral vaccine and is causing controversy because of its possible side effects.

Antibiotics

Sometimes bacteria get through the body's defenses. In this case, outside help is needed to kill the germs in the form of **antibiotics**.

Antibiotics kill the germs without harming the body cells.

Penicillin was the first form of antibiotic. It is made from a mould called *penicillium notatum*.

Antibiotics cannot treat infections caused by viruses. The body has to fight them on its own.

Mutations

Antibiotics can kill most bacteria, but as we continue to use them, bacteria are becoming **resistant** to them.

New antibiotics are constantly needed to fight the battle against bacteria.

There is a need for careful use of antibiotics as overuse has led to the highly resistant MRSA developing. MRSA is a 'superbug' that thrives in unhygienic conditions and is highly contagious. Places such as hospitals need scrupulous hygiene to try and prevent it developing and spreading.

Bird Flu or Avian flu is causing concern and there are worries that it may become a pandemic affecting many areas of the world.

The main concern is if the Bird Flu infects humans that have the human flu virus, it may mutate into a new strain. This new strain may then be easily transmitted from human to human.

Drug testing

New drugs and medical treatments have to be extensively tested and trialled before being used. They are tested in the laboratory before being tested on human volunteers.

They are first tested on healthy volunteers to test for safety and then people with the illness to test for effectiveness.

The tests are normally blind or double blind where neither the patients nor the doctors know which are being treated. The patients still receive normal treatment for their disease. Placebos (a dummy drug that will not have any affect) are not often used as patients must still receive treatment.

Sometimes the tests fail, as in the case of **thalidomide**, a drug developed as a sleeping pill. It was found to be effective at treating morning sickness; however it had not been tested for this use. This drug caused severe limb abnormalities in babies born to mothers taking the drug and was then banned. It is now more recently being used to treat leprosy and some forms of cancer.

Scientific concept

In 1847, a Dr Semmelweiss suggested that washing hands prevents infection. He discovered this while delivering babies. There seemed to be a spread of childhood fever that was significantly reduced when hands were washed between patients. He suggested the modern day idea of disinfecting hands and instruments.

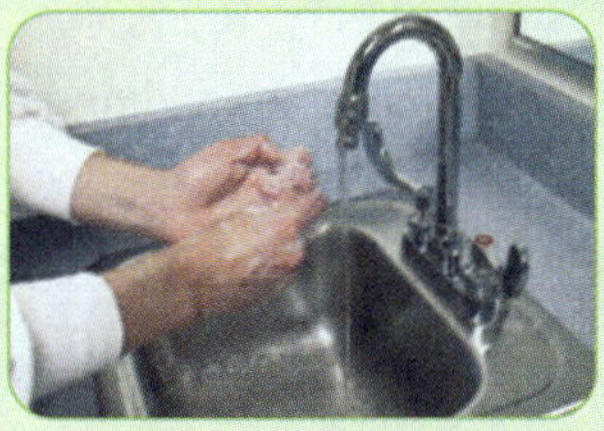

KEY TERMS

Make sure you understand these terms before moving on!

- artificial immunity
- vaccine
- antibiotics
- penicillin
- drug testing

QUICK TEST

1. What does MMR stand for?
2. Who first suggested that washing hands would help prevent infection?
3. What was the first form of antibiotic called?
4. How do bacteria and viruses become resistant to antibiotics?
5. Why do we not use antibiotics for virus infections?
6. What do vaccines contain?
7. What does the term 'double blind' mean?
8. What is a placebo?
9. Why was thalidomide banned?
10. Why is it important not to overuse antibiotics?

Drugs

There is no doubt that smoking and solvents damage health. Alcohol and drugs are also dangerous if misused for either recreational or pharmaceutical purposes.

Drugs – why are they dangerous?

Drugs are powerful chemicals: they alter the way the body works, often without you realising it. Drugs can become quickly **addictive**: people become dependent on them and suffer from withdrawal symptoms.

Drugs affect the brain and nervous system. Some drugs are taken for recreational purposes and are illegal: others are legal, such as alcohol and smoking. The overall impact on health of legal drugs is often greater as more people take them than the illegal drugs.

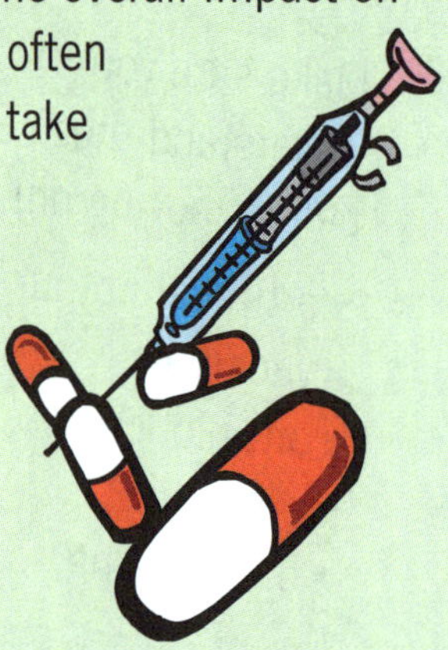

A drug alters, or inhibits, the way the body works

Drugs fall into four main groups:

Sedatives
These drugs **slow down the brain** and make you feel sleepy. Examples are tranquillisers and sleeping pills.

Painkillers
These drugs **suppress the pain sensors in the brain**. Examples are aspirin, heroin and morphine.

Hallucinogens
These drugs **make you see or hear things that don't exist**. These are called hallucinations. Ecstasy, LSD and cannabis are examples.

Stimulants
These drugs **speed up the brain and nervous system**: they make you feel more alert and awake. Amphetamines, cocaine, and the less harmful caffeine in tea and coffee, are examples.

Drugs and the law

Drugs are classified in law as class A, class B and class C. Class A drugs, such as heroin, carry the most severe penalties if you are caught with it in your possession. Supplying the drug to someone else can lead to life imprisonment. Recently, cannabis has become a class C drug, carrying less harsh penalties.

The debate still continues about whether cannabis is harmful and addictive or whether it leads on to harder drugs such as heroin. At present, health professionals cannot agree. It is said to be psychologically addictive, however, and if taken with nicotine, the nicotine makes it physically addictive. Some people argue that it is a useful pain relief drug for the terminally ill but medical opinion fluctuates.

Solvents

Solvents include everyday products like glue and aerosols. Solvent fumes are inhaled and are absorbed by the lungs. They soon reach the brain and **slow down breathing and heart rates**. Solvents also damage the **kidneys and liver**. Repeated inhalation can cause loss of control and unconsciousness. Many first time inhalers die from heart failure, or suffocation if using aerosols.

Solvents, like glue and aerosols, reach the brain

Smoking

Without a doubt, tobacco causes health problems. It contains many harmful chemicals: **nicotine** is an addictive substance and a mild stimulant, **tar** is known to contain carcinogens that contribute to cancer, and **carbon monoxide** prevents the red blood cells from carrying oxygen. If pregnant women smoke, **carbon monoxide** deprives the foetus of oxygen and can lead to a low birth mass. Some of the diseases aggravated by smoking include **emphysema, bronchitis, heart and blood vessel problems** and **lung cancer**.

Smoking: a proven cause of health problems

Alcohol

Alcohol is a **depressant** and reduces the activity of the brain and nervous system. It is absorbed through the gut and taken up to the brain in the blood. Alcohol damages neurones in the brain and can cause irreversible brain damage. The liver breaks down alcohol at rate of one unit an hour but an excess of alcohol has a very **damaging effect on the liver, called cirrhosis**.

Increasing amounts of alcohol causes people to lose control and slur their words. In this state, accidents are more likely to happen.

Scientific concept

The link between smoking and lung cancer is now widely accepted. According to Cancer Research UK, it causes 9 out of 10 lung cancers.

KEY TERMS

- addictive
- depressant
- cirrhosis
- carbon monoxide
- lung cancer

QUICK TEST

1. Which parts of the body are affected by alcohol?
2. What class of drug is cannabis?
3. Name three chemicals contained in tobacco.
4. What disease does smoking cause?
5. What is the name of the disease of the liver?

Adaptation and competition

- A *habitat* is where an organism lives: it provides the conditions needed for that organism to survive.
- A *community* consists of living things in the *habitat*.
- Each *community* is made up of different *populations of animals and plants*.
- Each *population* is adapted to live in that particular *habitat*.

The camel: ideally suited to living in hot, dry deserts

Adaptation

You never see a polar bear in the desert or a camel at the North Pole. This is because they have not **adapted** to live there.

The polar bear: adapted to deal with arctic conditions

A polar bear lives in cold, arctic regions of the world. It has many features that enable it to survive:

- It has a **thick coat** to keep in body heat, as well as a **layer of blubber** for insulation.
- Its coat is **white** so that it can blend into its surroundings.
- A polar bear has **big feet** to spread its weight on snow and ice: it also has big, **sharp claws** to catch fish.
- It is a **good swimmer** and **runner** in order to catch prey.
- The shape of a polar bear is **compact** even though it is large. This keeps its surface area to a minimum to reduce loss of body heat.

A camel has features that enable it to survive in the hot deserts of the world:

- The camel has an ability to **drink** a lot of water and **store** it.
- It loses very little water as it produces **little urine** and can cope with big changes in temperature, so there **is no need for sweating**.
- All its fat is stored in the humps, so there is **no insulation layer**.
- Its **sandy** colour provides **camouflage**.
- It has a **large surface area** to enable it to lose heat effectively.

Competition 1

Population numbers cannot keep growing out of control. The factors that affect the size of a population are:

- the amount of food and water available
- predators or grazing – who may eat the animal or plant
- disease
- climate, temperature, floods, droughts and storms
- human activity such as pollution or destruction of habitats.

As populations grow, there may be overcrowding and limited resources to support the growing numbers. Animals have to compete in their struggle to survive.

Competition 2

Only the strongest will live, leading to the survival of the fittest. Even plants compete for space, light, water and nutrients.

Resources vary with time of day and time of year: they help explain why organisms vary from place to place and are restricted to certain habitats. Organisms have adapted to live in certain areas.

Predator/prey graphs

In a community, the number of animals stays fairly constant. A **predator** is an animal that hunts and kills another animal. The **prey** is the hunted animal. Populations of predator and prey go in cycles.

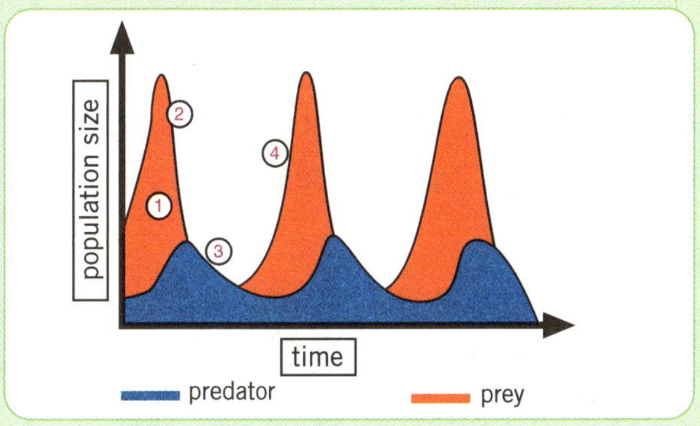

Follow the graph to see how the numbers of prey affect the numbers of predators and vice versa.

1. If the population of prey increases, there is more food for the predator, so its numbers increase.
2. This causes the number of prey to decrease as they are eaten.
3. This, in turn, causes the number of predators to decrease, as there is not enough food to support the increased numbers of predators and they must compete for one another for food.
4. If the predator numbers fall, the prey numbers can increase again, as they are no longer being eaten, and so on.

The adaptations of a camel and polar bear are just two popular exam examples. Don't forget that other animals and plants show adaptations to their environment.

KEY TERMS

Make sure you understand these terms before moving on!

- habitat
- community
- populations
- adaptation
- competition
- predator/prey graph

QUICK TEST

1. What is a habitat?
2. Define the word 'community'.
3. What makes up a population?
4. What things do animals compete for?
5. What things do plants compete for?
6. If the numbers of prey increase, what will happen to the number of predators?
7. Why do the numbers of prey and predators in a community stay fairly constant?
8. How does the polar bear's coat help it survive in the Arctic?
9. How does the camel's large surface area help it survive in the desert?
10. What factor determines whether animals or plants survive in their environments?

Genes and chromosomes

Genes

The relationship between genes, chromosomes and DNA

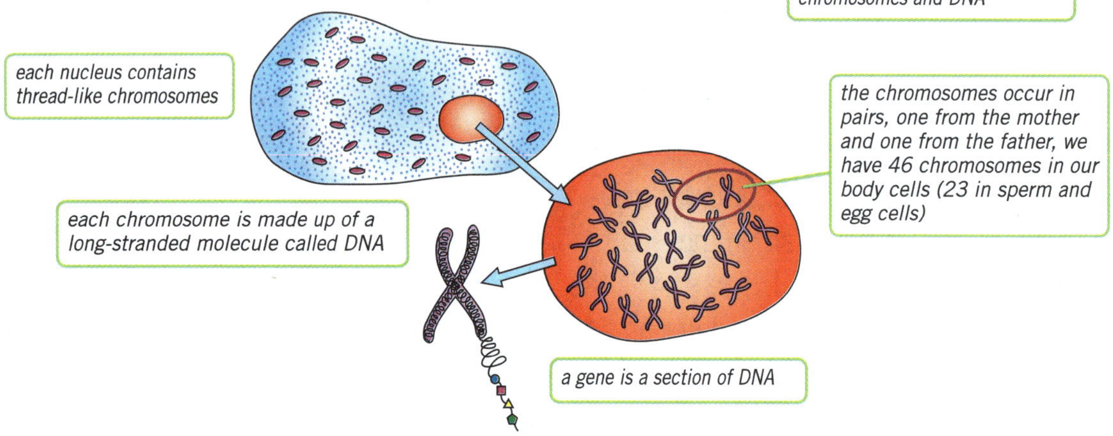

Inside nearly all cells is a **nucleus**.

The nucleus **contains instructions** that control all your characteristics. The instructions are carried on **chromosomes**.

Genes on the chromosome control each particular **characteristic**. Different genes control the development of different characteristics.

Inside human cells there are **46 chromosomes or 23 pairs**. The cell is called a **diploid cell**. Other animals have different numbers of chromosomes.

Proteins and enzymes control all our characteristics, genes are chemical instructions that code for a particular protein or enzyme, and therefore our characteristics.

There is a **pair of genes** for each feature. We call the different versions of a gene **alleles**.

Inheritance

To inherit characteristics from parents, **DNA**, some form of reproduction needs to take place. There are two forms:

- **Asexual reproduction** involves only one parent; the offspring have exact copies of the parental genes. There is no fusing (joining) of the parental **gametes** (sperm and eggs).

  Asexual reproduction produces clones, there is no variation.
- **Sexual reproduction** involves fertilisation and two parents. The gametes' nuclei do fuse and the genes are passed on to the offspring. The offspring are not genetically identical.

Sexual reproduction leads to variation, not only between different species of plants and animals, but also between individuals of the same species.

The differences are partly due to the **inheritance** of genes from the parents but also the **environments** in which the offspring live and grow.

DNA molecule

A coiled up DNA molecule makes up the arms of a chromosome.

A DNA molecule is joined together by chemical bases like rungs in a ladder.

The two rungs of the ladder are coiled together to form a **double helix**.

DNA has the ability to copy itself exactly so that any new cells made have exactly the same genetic information.

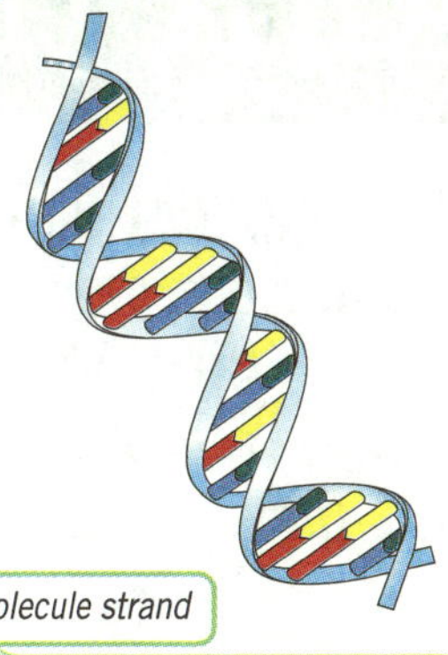

DNA molecule strand

Mutations

DNA is a very stable molecule, but occasionally things can go wrong in the copying process.

A mutation is a change in the chemical structure of a gene or chromosome, which alters the way an organism develops.

The change may happen for no reason or there might be a definite cause.

Mutations occur naturally in the environment, for example, new strains of the flu virus are always appearing.

Mutations that occur to body cells are not inherited; they are only harmful to the person whose body cells are altered.

Mutations that occur in reproductive cells are inherited; the child will develop abnormally or die at an early age.

Some mutations that are inherited are beneficial and form the basis of evolution.

There are lots of key words on this page that are new, learn their definitions.

KEY TERMS

Make sure you understand these terms before moving on!

- nucleus
- chromosomes
- genes
- DNA
- asexual reproduction
- gametes
- sexual reproduction

QUICK TEST

1. What are the thread-like features contained in the nucleus called?
2. What actually controls all our characteristics?
3. What are genes?
4. Where are genes found?
5. In what circumstances are mutations inherited?
6. How many chromosomes does a human body cell have and where are they found?
7. How many genes are there for each feature?
8. What are the human gametes?
9. Which type of reproduction produces clones?
10. Which type of reproduction formed you? What else has an effect on how you look and behave?

Genetic engineering

Genetic engineering is the process by which genes from one organism are removed and inserted into the cells of another organism. Scientists can now genetically modify plants and animals by adding, removing or changing genes to produce the plants and animals they want.

Manipulating genes

It is our genes code for a particular protein that enables all our life processes to function normally. **Many diseases are caused when the body cannot make a particular protein.**

Genetic engineering has been used to treat people with diabetes through the production of the protein, insulin.

The gene that codes for **insulin** can be found in the human pancreas cells.

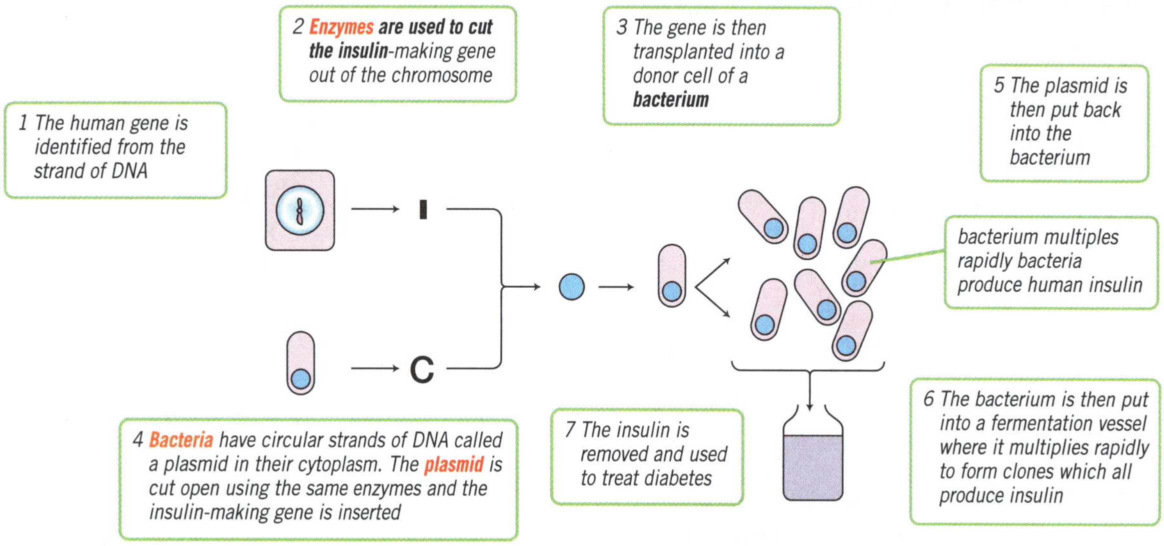

GM crops

There are, at present, no genetically modified crops grown in the UK and there are no plans to grow them until 2008. They have, however, been grown for research and development purposes.

Countries that do grow **GM crops** include the USA, Argentina, Canada, and China. What they grow, and how much, varies from country to country but the crops often include corn, cotton and soybean.

The benefits of genetic engineering 1

Genetic engineering benefits industry, medicine and agriculture in many ways. We have developed plants that are resistant to pests and diseases, and plants that can grow in less desirable conditions. Wheat and other crops have been developed that can take nitrogen directly from the air and produce proteins without the need for costly fertilisers.

The benefits of genetic engineering 2

Tomatoes and other sorts of fruit are now able to stay fresh for longer.

Animals are engineered to produce chemicals in their milk such as drugs and human antibodies. The list seems endless and there is no doubt as to the benefits of genetic engineering, now and in the future. There are also, however, many risks and moral issues associated with this relatively modern technology.

Tomatos can be genetically engineered to stay fresh for longer by inserting a gene from fish into their cells. Would you eat one?

Risks of genetic engineering

Manipulating bacteria for use in producing proteins could result in previously harmful bacteria mutating into disease-causing bacteria. There is also concern about the potential damage to human health GM crops could cause. Are they responsible for causing allergies, and will the nutritional quality of the food remain identical? The notion of eating 'foreign' DNA is also worrying for many.

There is also concern about the damage to the environment, crops may cross pollinate with weeds and transfer the gene that gives resistance to herbicides and pesticides.

Genetic engineering is seen by many as manipulating the 'stuff of life'. Is it morally and ethically wrong to interfere with nature? There is still a lot of unease about the methods used as nobody can be completely sure what the results will be.

You may be asked to provide arguments for and against the use of genetic engineering, so be prepared to discuss the benefits and risks involved.

KEY TERMS

Make sure you understand these terms before moving on!

- insulin
- enzymes
- bacteria
- plasmids
- GM crops

QUICK TEST

1. What is the circular DNA of a bacterium called?
2. What does the GM stand for in GM crops?
3. How are human genes 'cut out'?
4. How could weeds benefit from GM crops?
5. Name a disease that has the potential to be treated using genetic engineering.
6. What are the benefits of developing crops that are resistant to frost?
7. Where is the insulin gene found in humans?
8. Give an example of the use of bacteria to treat a disease.
9. What are the risks associated with using bacteria to produce human proteins?

Selective breeding

Selective breeding **is the process by which humans breed the features that they want into a plant or animal, and breed out features that they don't want. Since humans do the selecting, as opposed to nature, we call it *artificial selection*.**

Artificial selection

We are always trying to breed animals and plants with special characteristics: for example, a faster racehorse or a cow that produces more milk. Breeding must be carried out between members of the same species. Different species cannot breed together.

The procedures involved in **artificial selection** are as follows:

- Select the individuals with the best characteristics.
- Breed them together using sexual reproduction.
- Some of the offspring will have inherited some of the desirable features: the best offspring are selected and are bred together.
- This process is repeated over generations until any offspring have all the desired characteristics.

Selective breeding in animals

Cows have been selectively bred to produce a greater quality of milk. Beef cattle have been bred to produce better meat. The problem with only breeding from the best cows and bulls is that cows can only give birth once a year. As a consequence, new **selective breeding** techniques have been developed.

Embryo transfer

The process is as follows:

1. The sperm is taken from the best bull.
2. The best cow is given hormones to produce lots of eggs.
3. The eggs are removed from the cow and are fertilised in a petri dish.
4. The embryos are allowed to develop, but are then split apart to form **clones** before they become specialised.
5. The embryos are implanted into other cows called 'surrogates', where they grow into the desired offspring.

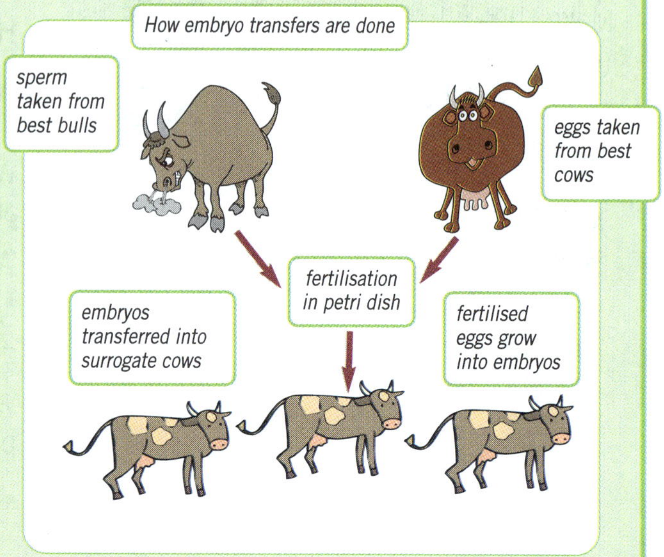

Selective breeding in plants

Selectively bred individuals will not always produce offspring with the desired characteristics, as sexual reproduction always produces variation. With plants, this can be overcome by producing clones. Clones are genetically identical individuals. To produce clones, asexual reproduction is needed. Many plants reproduce asexually on their own: strawberry plants, for example, produce runners.

Tissue culture

Gardeners can produce new, identical plants by taking **cuttings** from the original parent plant. The plants are dipped in a rooting powder, containing hormones and kept in a damp atmosphere where they grow into new plants. New plants grown in this way are clones.

Tissue culture is a technique used by commercial plant breeders. They take just a few plant cells and grow a complete new plant from them, using a special growth medium containing hormones. The advantage of this method is that new plants can be grown quickly and cheaply all year round. They can also be grown with special properties, such as resistance to diseases.

Problems with selective breeding

If animals or plants are continually bred from the same, best parent animals or plants, then all offspring animals and plants will be very similar. Certain genetic characteristics will have been bred out. A change in the environment could leave the new offspring unable to adapt. Characteristics that were once thought unimportant could be an advantage in a different environment, but there would be no animals or plants with these characteristics left. It is, therefore, important to keep wild varieties alive, just in case.

Make sure you can list the advantages and disadvantages of the various methods of selective breeding.

KEY TERMS

- artificial selection
- selective breeding
- embryo transfer
- clones
- cuttings
- tissue culture

QUICK TEST

1. What is selective breeding?
2. What are clones?
3. Name a technique used in the selective breeding of animals.
4. Name two methods of selective breeding in plants.
5. What is the main disadvantage of selective breeding?

Evolution

Evolution **is all about change and improvement from simple life forms.**

The *theory of evolution* states that all living things that exist today or once existed, evolved from simple life forms three billion years ago.

Natural selection **is the process that causes *evolution*.**

The theory of evolution

Religious theories are based on the need for a 'creator' for all life to exist on earth, but there are other theories.

Charles Darwin, a British naturalist first put forward his theory about 140 years ago.

Charles visited the Galapagos Islands off the coast of South America and made a number of observations that led to his theory of **evolution**.

They were:

- Organisms produce more offspring than could possibly survive.
- Population numbers remain fairly constant despite this.
- All organisms in a **species** show **variation**.
- Some of these variations are inherited.

He also concluded from these observations that since there were more offspring produced that could survive; there must be a struggle for existence.

This led to the strongest and fittest offspring surviving and passing on their genes to their offspring.

This is sometimes called the '**survival of the fittest**' or **natural selection**.

The combined effects of natural selection, selective breeding, genetic engineering and mutations may lead to a new species forming.

Other theories

In the 17th Century, an Archbishop called James Usher said that God created all life forms from the simple to the complex, he thought that life began on Monday October 3rd 4004 BC

Then in the 18th century Conte De Buffon, a French zoologist thought that living things do change over time due to the environment or chance. He also thought that humans and apes were related.

Erasmus Darwin (father to Charles) believed in evolution but did not know what caused it.

Natural selection

Darwin stated that the process of natural selection was the basis for evolution.

A species is defined as a group of living things that are able to breed together and produce fertile offspring. Within a species there is variation between individuals.

Changes in the environment may affect some individuals and not others.

Only those who can adapt to suit their new environment survive to breed and pass on their advantageous genes.

Other factors that tend to prevent all offspring surviving are:

- **competition for food**
- **predators**
- **disease.**

Eventually it seems that nature has decided which individuals should survive and breed.

There is a **'survival of the fittest'**.

Scientific concept

Darwin's theory became widely accepted eventually, but a man called **Lamarck** suggested that animals evolved features according to how much they used them. For example giraffes grew longer necks because they needed to reach food.

KEY TERMS

Make sure you understand these terms before moving on!

- evolution
- Charles Darwin
- Lamarck
- species
- natural selection

QUICK TEST

1. When did life forms first exist?
2. Whose theory of evolution was gradually accepted?
3. What prevents all the organisms in a species surviving?
4. Which individuals would survive a change in the environment?
5. What process causes evolution?
6. Where in the world did Darwin make observations that led to his theory?
7. What does the word species mean?
8. What was Darwin's observation when he looked at the individuals in a species?
9. Why was there a struggle for existence within a population?
10. Does evolution happen gradually or does it occur suddenly?

Evidence for evolution

Fossils

Fossils are the remains of dead organisms that lived millions of years ago. They are found in rocks.

Most dead organisms decay and disintegrate, but the following are ways that fossils can be formed:

- The hard parts of animals that don't decay and form into a rock.
- Minerals which preserve their shape gradually replace the softer parts of animals that decay very slowly.
- In areas where one or more of the conditions needed for decay are absent, for example areas where there is **no oxygen, moisture or warmth**.

Fossils provide **evidence** for evolution.

They are preserved in rock with generally the younger fossils being found near the surface

The evolution of the horse is clearly shown by fossils.

Look at the changes in their size and feet caused by the changes in the environment over the years.

Natural selection has operated to produce the modern horse.

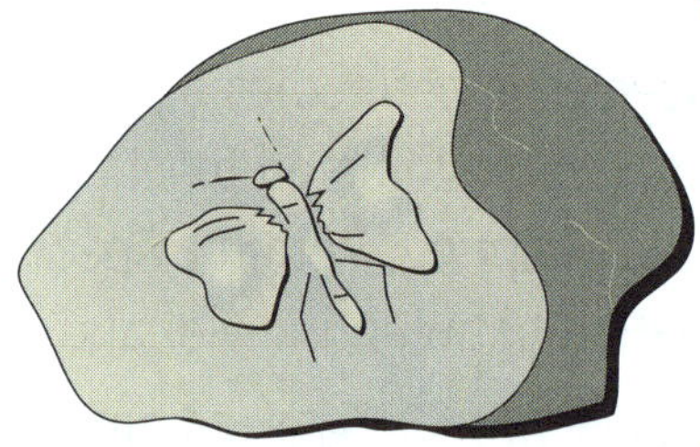

fossil in rock

The modern horse: an example of natural selection

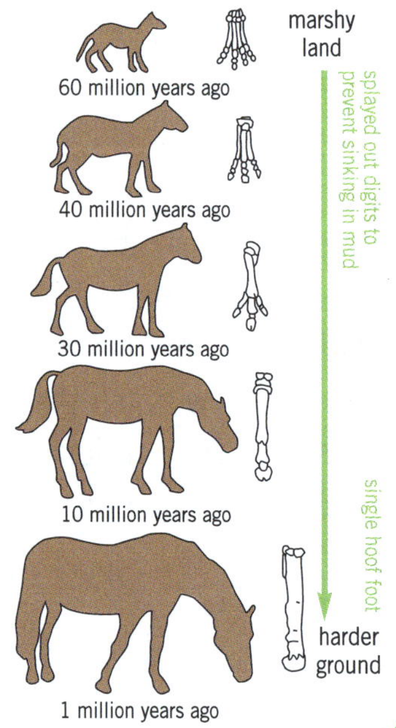

Natural selection in action

An example of the environment causing changes in a species is the **peppered moth**.

They live in woodlands on lichen covered trees

There are two types of peppered moth: a light, speckled form and a dark form.

Pollution played a key role in the 'survival of the fittest' for these peppered moths

dark-coloured moth against a soot-covered tree

the pale moth is at a disadvantage in polluted areas

The dark coloured moth was caused by a mutation and was usually eaten by predators.

In the 1850s the dark type of moth was rare, but pollution from factories started to blacken tree trunks.

The dark moth was then at an advantage because it was camouflaged.

In 1895 most of the population of moths was dark.

In cleaner areas the light moth had an advantage against predators so it survived to breed.

Mutations

Mutations that occur in genes are usually harmful, but in the case of the peppered moth it turned out to be useful when the environment changed.

Over a long period of time, gradual changes (mutations) may result in totally new species being formed.

This brings us back to the theory of evolution that all species evolved from a common ancestor that existed billions of years ago.

Those species that were unable to adapt to their surroundings became extinct.

Extinction

Species that are unable to adapt to their surroundings become extinct.

Examples include the mammoth, the dodo, and sabre-toothed tiger.

Extinction can also be caused by changes in the environment, new predators, new disease, new competition, or human activity e.g. hunting, pollution or habitat destruction.

The peppered moth and the evolution of the horse are popular examples to demonstrate evolution by natural selection.

KEY TERMS

Make sure you understand these terms before moving on!

- fossils
- evidence
- natural selection in action
- peppered moth
- mutations
- extinction

QUICK TEST

1. Why did the feet of the modern horse change?
2. Which type of peppered moth would survive in industrial regions and why?
3. What conditions need to be **absent** for fossils to be formed?
4. What is the prime reason why organisms become extinct?
5. What are fossils?
6. Is it possible for fossils to be formed in the Arctic?
7. What caused the light-peppered moth to change colour?
8. How could humans cause a species to become extinct?
9. Where are young fossils found in relation to older fossils?
10. What process has led to produce the modern day horse?

Environmental damage

Improvements in agriculture, health and medicine have led to a dramatic rise *in the human population*. An increase in population size also leads to an increase in *pollution* and increased demands on the Earth's resources.

Intensive farming

Farming has had to become more intensive to try and provide more food from a given area of land. **Intensive farming** can produce more food but it has its problems. Many people regard the intensive farming of animals as cruel and in order to produce more food from the land, **fertilisers and pesticides** are needed.

Learn the arguments for and against intensive farming.

Pesticides

Pesticides are used to kill the insects that damage crops. They also kill harmless insects, however, which can cause a shortage of food for insect-eating birds. There is always the danger that pesticides can get washed into rivers and lakes and **end up in our food chains**. This was the case in the 1960s, when a pesticide called DDT got into the food chain and threatened whole populations of animals.

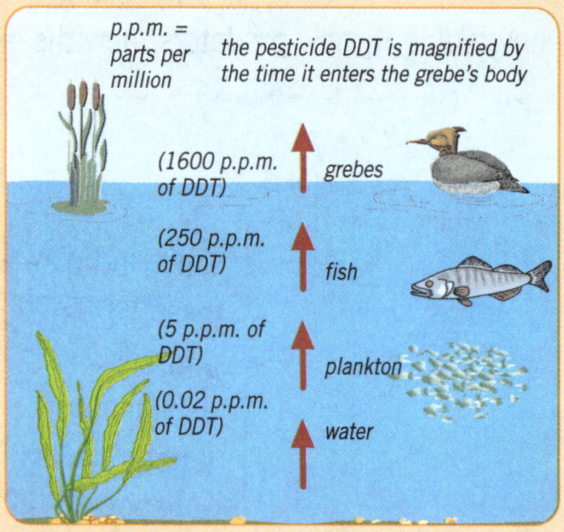

Fertilisers

Plants need nutrients to grow, which they take up from the soil. With intensive farming methods, nutrients are quickly used up, and so the farmer has to replace them with artificial fertilisers. **Fertilisers** enable farmers to produce more crops in a smaller area of land, and can reduce the need to destroy the countryside to gain extra farming land.

There are, however, problems – in particular eutrophication – associated with the use of fertilisers.

Eutrophication

If too much fertiliser is added to the soil and it rains soon afterwards, then the fertiliser finds its way into rivers and lakes. This causes the water plants to grow more quickly and cover the surface of the water. More water plants means more competition for light, and some plants die. Microbes (bacteria and fungi) break down the dead plants and use up oxygen for respiration. This reduces the amount of oxygen available for animals and they die of suffocation. **Untreated sewage** pumped into rivers and streams also causes **eutrophication**.

Destruction of the land and seas

An increase in industry has resulted in the need to take over more land, which destroys wildlife and cause further **pollution**. Many kilometres of wetlands have also been drained for agriculture. Coral reefs have been destroyed by pollution and over fishing.

Fish is a major source of the world's protein but many fisheries are at the point of collapse. Fishing for tuna can also trap and drown dolphins.

we use land for building

dumping our rubbish

getting raw materials

farming to feed the world

Deforestation

In the UK there are not many forests left. In other under-developed countries, people are **chopping down forests** to provide timber or space for agriculture, to try to provide for the growing numbers of people. **Deforestation**, with no replacing or trees causes several problems for the environment.

Burning timber increases the levels of carbon dioxide in the air. Forests absorb the carbon dioxide in the air and provide us with oxygen. Chopping down trees leads to soil erosion, as the soil is exposed to rain and wind. The trees evaporate water into the air and without them there will be a decrease in rainfall. Destroying forests also destroys the habitats of many different animals and plants.

Other pollutants

Industrial waste is a problem as many chemicals are toxic, long lasting and gradually accumulate in living things. Oil spills kill sea birds and wildlife, and the smoke and fumes from power stations, vehicles and homes pollute the air, causing acid rain and global warming.

KEY TERMS

Make sure you understand these terms before moving on!

- pollution
- intensive farming
- pesticides
- fertilisers
- eutrophication
- deforestation

QUICK TEST

1. Why has the human population increased in last few hundred years?
2. What problems can the use of pesticides cause?
3. How do fertilisers get into rivers and lakes?
4. What is the name of the process whereby fertilisers lead to the death of animals and plants in water?
5. Name four ways that humans reduce the amount of land.
6. What is deforestation?
7. What problems does deforestation cause?

How can we help?

Humans are using up the Earth's resources, including fossil fuels, at an alarming rate. Burning fossil fuels contributes to *acid rain* and the *greenhouse effect* by releasing harmful gases into the air.

If the destruction of our planet continues, we will only be left with a few species of animals and plants. Large areas of land will become deserts and the polluted lakes, rivers and the sea will contain little life. The air we breathe will no longer be clean, our drinking water will also be polluted and the land will no longer be fertile enough to grow crops.

What can be done?

Up to 60% of the energy we get from fossil fuels is lost as heat. Burning fossil fuels also give off pollutant gases.

We can look for **alternative energy sources**, such as solar power and wind energy. These are clean energy sources that do not contribute to **pollution**.

We can also make our homes more energy efficient by insulating roofs, walls and windows, and buying more energy efficient products. This would also help to conserve the world's rapidly diminishing supply of fossil fuel.

Using **unleaded petrol** and **catalytic converters** in our cars would help to reduce the emissions of harmful gases. Further research into designing more efficient engines could also cut down pollution, as would reducing the need for cars by running a public transport that could carry more people.

We must also halt **large-scale deforestation** as it is trees that absorb carbon dioxide.

Conservation and sustainable development

With the human population increasing and using up resources, we need to find a way of maintaining a quality of life for future generations. This is known as **sustainable development**.

It is important to protect our food supply, maintain biodiversity and conserve resources, as we do not know what the future may hold. Many species of animal have already become extinct and many more are in danger, such as the red squirrel, osprey and the whale. **Endangered organism like these and many others may be of use to us in the future, so it is important to protect and save them.** We need to look at ways of protecting habitats, breeding in captivity to increase numbers, and providing endangered species with legal protection.

A good way to maintain fish stocks and our woodland is to introduce quotas and replant woodland. Sustainable development requires a lot of planning and co-operation at every level or our valuable resources will run out and many more species will become extinct.

These problems will continue to get worse, unless people can learn to limit their needs and so prevent the destruction of our planet.

Organic farming

Intensive farming does produce quality food, more than enough to supply people's needs in Europe, but it also creates many problems. A possible solution to some of the problems is **organic farming**.

Harvesting corn

Organic farming produces less food per area of land and can be expensive, but it attempts to leave the countryside as it is, and is kinder to animals. Organic farming **uses manure as a fertiliser**, **sets aside land** to allow wild plants and animals to flourish and utilizes **biological control of pests**. Biological control of pests is the use of other natural predators to eat pests or the breeding of sterile male pests. It is not as effective as some pesticides but it produces no harmful effects.

Greenhouse production

Another way of reducing harm to the environment is the use of **greenhouses** to grow food efficiently and out of season.

KEY TERMS

Make sure you understand these terms before moving on!

- alternative energy sources
- pollution
- sustainable development
- organic farming
- biological control

QUICK TEST

1. How can we maintain fish stocks?
2. Chopping down trees may be necessary, but what can be done to minimise the effects of deforestation?
3. What could be used as an alternative to pesticides?
4. What is set-aside land?
5. How can we increase the surviving numbers of endangered species?
6. How could we reduce the amount of pollution produced by cars?
7. How would insulating our roofs reduce pollution?
8. What could be used as an alternative to fertilisers?

Practice questions

Use the questions to test your progress. Check your answers on page 110.

1. What are pathogens?

2. What was Thalidomide first used for?

3. What does the technique embryo transfer involve?

4. What is the difference between artificial selection and natural selection?

5. What is a foreign antigen?

6. Smoking during pregnancy is harmful to the foetus but in what particular way?

7. Where can the animal, the dodo be found?

8. What are alternative energy sources?

9. If you were to eat a diet rich in saturated fats what would the effects be?

10. What do the letters 'CNS' stand for and what does it consist of?

11. Name the three types of neurone.

12. If you were prescribed a statin drug what would be your problem?

13. When cuttings are taken and grown is it asexual or sexual reproduction?

14. Is measles caused by a bacterium or virus?

15. Which are smaller, bacteria or viruses?

16. Explain what a vector is and give an example.

17. Name the two types of white blood cell that protect us from disease.

18. Explain the term 'natural immunity'.

19. Define the word homeostasis.

20. How long ago was the theory of evolution first stated?

21. What are the advantages of intensive farming?

22. Which hormones are involved in the menstrual cycle?

23. What type of organisms do we use for genetic engineering?

24. Can Penicillin be used to treat measles?

25. Who developed the theory of evolution that we use today?

26. Who developed an alternative theory of evolution based on observations of giraffes?

27. A hospital patient develops MRSA, what type of drug could be used to treat it?

28. The nervous system responds to stimuli. What are stimuli?

29. What is an alternative to intensive farming?

30. Where in your body would you find the chemical DNA?

Atoms and elements

***Elements* are made of only one type of atom.**

What's in an atom?

An atom consists of a central nucleus (containing protons and neurons) surrounded by shells of electrons.

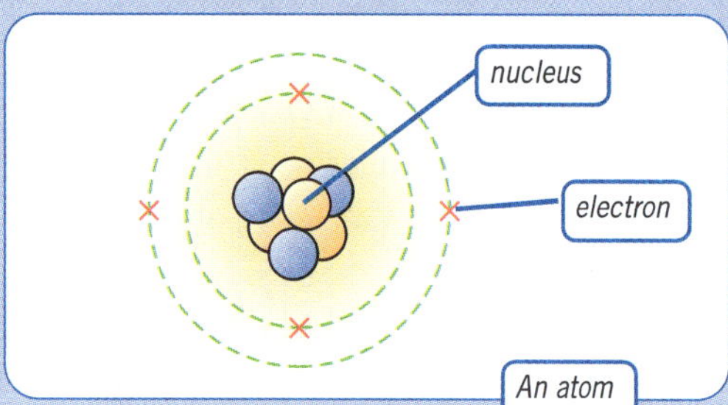

An atom

How can atoms join together?

Atoms can join together by:

- sharing electrons
- giving and taking electrons.

Compounds consist of two or more different types of atom that have been chemically combined.

The periodic table

Elements are often displayed in the **periodic table**, where elements with similar properties are found in the same vertical column. These columns are called groups.

Period \ Group	1	2											3	4	5	6	7	0
1	H Hydrogen																	He Helium
2	Li Lithium	Be Beryllium											B Boron	C Carbon	N Nitrogen	O Oxygen	F Fluorine	Ne Neon
3	Na Sodium	Mg Magnesium											Al Aluminium	Si Silicon	P Phosphorous	S Sulphur	Cl Chlorine	Ar Argon
4	K Potassium	Ca Calcium	Sc Scandium	Ti Titanium	V Vanadium	Cr Chromium	Mn Manganese	Fe Iron	Co Cobalt	Ni Nickel	Cu Copper	Zn Zinc	Ga Gallium	Ge Germanium	As Arsenic	Se Selenium	Br Bromine	Kr Krypton
5	Rb Rubidium	Sr Strontium	Y Yttrium	Zr Zirconium	Nb Niobium	Mo Molybdenum	Tc Technetium	Ru Ruthenium	Rh Rhodium	Pd Palladium	Ag Silver	Cd Cadmium	In Indium	Sn Tin	Sb Antimony	Te Tellurium	I Iodine	Xe Xenon
6	Cs Caesium	Ba Barium	La Lanthanum	Hf Hafnium	Ta Tantalum	W Tungsten	Re Rhenium	Os Osmium	Ir Iridium	Pt Platinum	Au Gold	Hg Mercury	Tl Thallium	Pb Lead	Bi Bismuth	Po Polonium	At Astatine	Rn Radon
7	Fr Francium	Ra Radium	Ac Actinium															

Symbols 1

In science, elements can be represented by **symbols**. Each element has its own unique symbol that is recognised all over the world. Each symbol consists of one or two letters and is much easier to read and write than the full name. In some cases the symbol for an element is simply the first letter of the element's name. This letter must be a capital letter.

Symbols 2

I

The element iodine is represented by the symbol I.

Sometimes several elements have names that start with the same letter. When this happens, we use the first letter of the element's name together with another letter from the name. The first letter is a capital, the second letter is lower case.

Mg

The element magnesium is represented by the symbol Mg.

Mn

The element manganese is represented by the symbol Mn.

Occasionally, an element may take its symbol from its old Latin name. When this happens, the first letter is a capital and the second letter, if there is one, is lower case.

Hg

The element mercury is represented by the symbol Hg. This comes from the Latin name for mercury which was hydrargyrum, or 'liquid silver'.

Chemical formula

A compound can be represented using a **chemical formula**.

The formula shows the type and ratio of the atoms that are joined together in the compound.

Ammonia has the chemical formula NH_3.

This shows that in ammonia, nitrogen and hydrogen atoms are joined together in the ratio of one nitrogen atom to three hydrogen atoms.

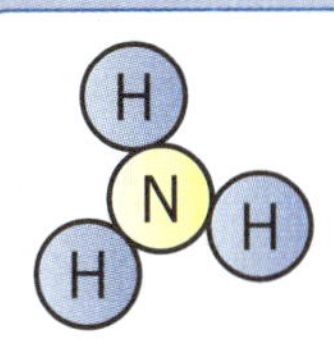

Chemical formula for ammonia NH_3

Chemical reactions

Symbol equations can be used to explain what happens during a chemical reaction.

When magnesium burns in air, the magnesium metal reacts with oxygen molecules to form the compound magnesium oxide. This reaction can be shown in a word equation:

magnesium + oxygen → magnesium oxide

Or by the symbol equation:

$$2Mg + O_2 \rightarrow 2MgO$$

KEY TERMS

- elements
- compounds
- periodic table
- symbols
- chemical formula

QUICK TEST

1. What is the centre of an atom called?
2. What is special about elements?
3. How can atoms join together?
4. Give the chemical symbol of the element oxygen.
5. Give the name of the element with the symbol Na.
6. Give the name of the element with the symbol Cr.
7. Water has the formula H_2O. Explain what this formula tells us.

Limestone

Limestone is a *sedimentary* rock. It is mainly composed of the chemical *calcium carbonate*. It can be *quarried* and cut into blocks that can be used for *building*.

If limestone is powdered, it can be used to *neutralise* the acidity in lakes caused by acid rain and to neutralise acidic soils.

Heating limestone

When **limestone** (calcium carbonate) is heated, it breaks down to form **quicklime** (calcium oxide) and **carbon dioxide**.

calcium carbonate	→	calcium oxide	+	carbon dioxide
$CaCO_{3(s)}$	→	$CaO_{(s)}$	+	$CO_{2(g)}$

This is an example of a **thermal decomposition** reaction.

Quicklime (calcium oxide) reacts with water to form **slaked lime** (**calcium hydroxide**).

A solution of slaked lime is known as limewater.

calcium oxide	+	water	→	calcium hydroxide
$CaO_{(s)}$	+	$H_2O_{(l)}$	→	$Ca(OH)_{2(s)}$

Calcium oxide and calcium hydroxide are both **bases** so they can be used to neutralise acidic lakes and soils.

The thermal decomposition of limestone is an example of a reaction that takes in heat. This is called an endothermic reaction.

Reaction summary

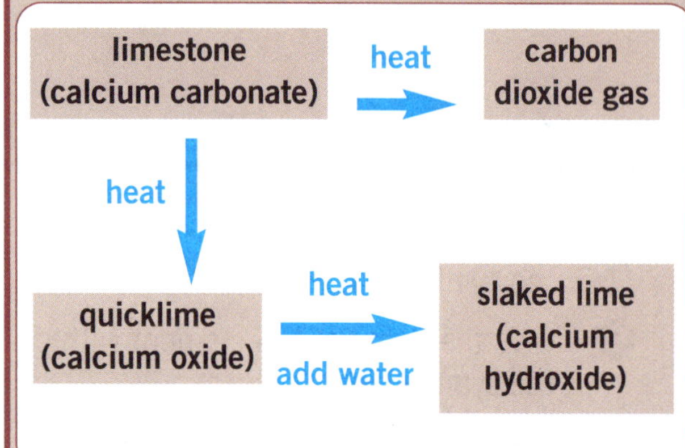

Similar thermal decomposition reactions

Other metal carbonates decompose in a **similar way** when they are heated.

When copper carbonate is heated it breaks down to give copper oxide and carbon dioxide.

copper carbonate	→	copper oxide	+	carbon dioxide
$CuCO_3$	→	CuO	+	CO_2

Other uses of limestone

Limestone can be used to make other useful materials.

Cement

Cement is produced by **roasting powdered clay with powdered limestone** in a rotating kiln. If water is mixed with it and the mixture is allowed to set, it forms the hard, stone-like material cement.

Mortar

When **water is mixed with cement and sand**, and then allowed to set, **mortar** is made.

Concrete

Concrete is made by **mixing cement, sand and rock chippings with water**. When water is added to cement it hydrates and binds together all the particles to form a material that is as hard as rock. Concrete is hard and cheap and is widely used in building.

Glass

Glass can be made by **heating up a mixture of limestone (calcium carbonate), sand (silicon dioxide) and soda (sodium carbonate)** until the mixture melts.

Heating baking powder

When **metal hydrogen carbonate compounds** are heated, they undergo thermal decomposition reactions to form **metal carbonates, carbon dioxide and water.**

The main chemical compound in baking powder is sodium hydrogen carbonate, $NaHCO_3$. When heated fiercely, it reacts to form sodium carbonate, carbon dioxide and water.

sodium hydrogen carbonate → sodium carbonate + carbon dioxide + water

KEY TERMS

- quicklime
- thermal decomposition
- slaked lime
- cement
- mortar
- concrete
- glass

QUICK TEST

1. What is the main chemical in limestone?
2. What type of rock is limestone?
3. What is the formula of calcium carbonate?
4. What is powdered limestone used for?
5. Give the word equation for the thermal decomposition of zinc carbonate.
6. What is the word equation for the thermal decomposition of magnesium carbonate?
7. How is cement made?
8. How is glass made?
9. Name the three products formed by the thermal decomposition of sodium hydrogen carbonate.
10. What is the word equation for the thermal decomposition of sodium hydrogen carbonate?

Fuels

Fuels are burnt to release energy. In this country, the fossil fuels *coal, oil and gas* are widely used. The burning of fuels is an exothermic reaction.

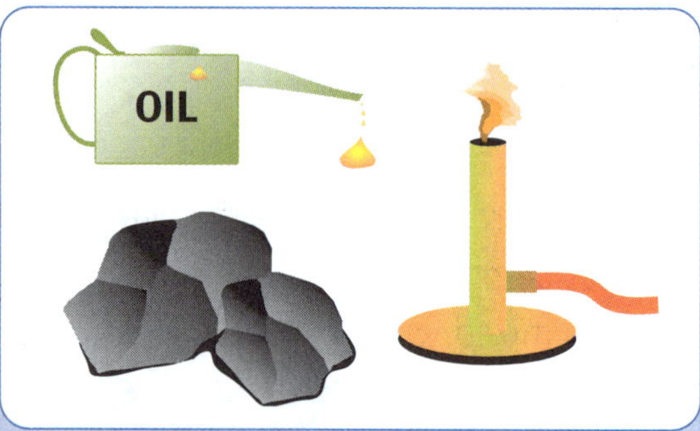

Crude oil

Like many natural substances, crude oil is a **mixture of many substances**, the most important of which are called **hydrocarbons**. Hydrocarbons are molecules that only contain carbon and hydrogen atoms.

Some of the hydrocarbons have very short chains of carbon atoms. These hydrocarbons:

- are runny
- are easy to ignite
- have low boiling points
- are valuable fuels.

Other hydrocarbon molecules have much longer chains of carbon atoms. These hydrocarbon molecules:

- are more **viscous** (less runny)
- are harder to ignite
- have higher boiling points.

These longer hydrocarbon molecules are less useful as fuels. Before any of these hydrocarbon molecules can be used, however, they must first be separated into groups of molecules with a similar number of carbon atoms called **fractions**.

Coal is mainly carbon. Petrol, diesel and oil are hydrocarbons.

Fractional distillation of crude oil 1

Crude oil can be separated by **fractional distillation**. First the crude oil is heated until it eventually evaporates. As the diagram of the fractionating column shows, the bottom of the column is much hotter than the top of the column. This means that short hydrocarbon molecules can reach the top of the column before they condense and are collected. Longer hydrocarbon molecules condense at higher temperatures and are collected at different points down the column.

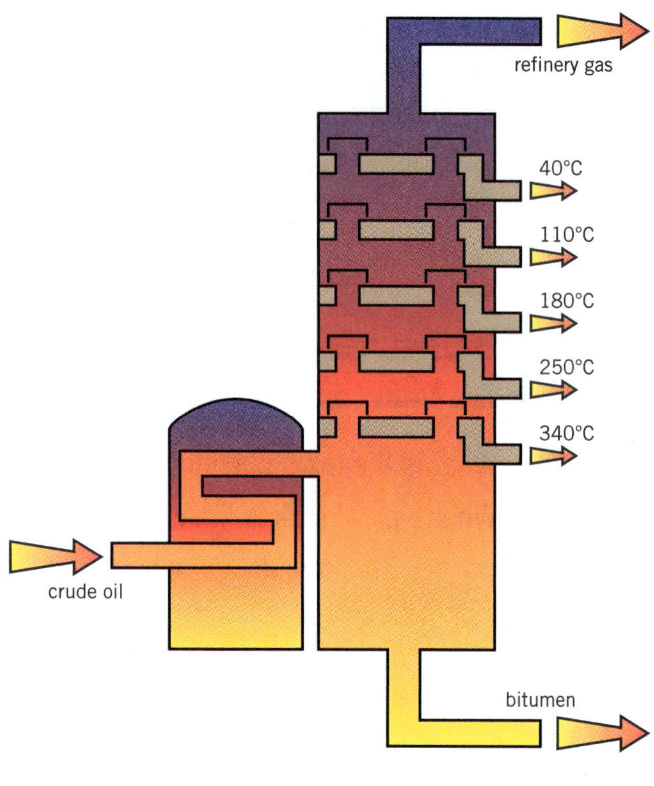

Fractionating column

Fractional distillation of crude oil 2

No. carbon atoms in hydrocarbon chain	Temperature	Fraction collected
3	less than 40°C	refinery gas
8	40°C	petrol
10	110°C	naphtha
15	180°C	kerosene
20	250°C	diesel
35	340°C	oil
50+	above 340°C	bitumen

How a fractionating column works

Cracking

decane $C_{10}H_{22}$ (from the naphtha fraction) → octane C_8H_{18} + ethene C_2H_4

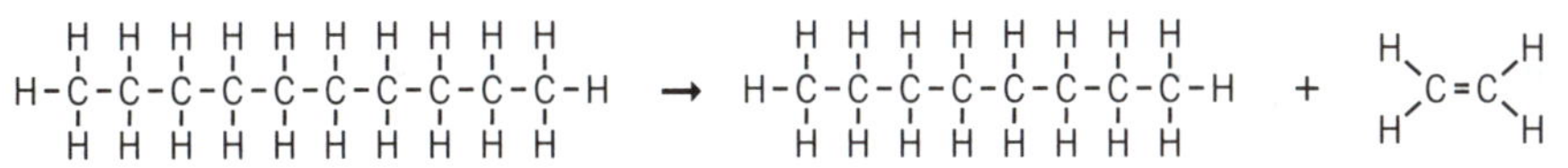

Cracking large hydrocarbon molecules can produce more useful products. Some of these molecules are used as fuels

The large hydrocarbon molecules separated during the fractional distillation of crude oil are not very useful. These hydrocarbon molecules, however, can be broken down into smaller, more useful and more valuable molecules by a process called **cracking**.

Octane is one of the hydrocarbon molecules found in petrol. **Ethene**, which is a member of the alkene family of hydrocarbons, is also produced. Ethene is used to make a range of new compounds including plastics.

Cracking is an example of a thermal decomposition reaction. Some of the products of the cracking are very useful fuels.

KEY TERMS

- hydrocarbons
- viscous
- fractions
- fractional distillation
- cracking

QUICK TEST

1. Name three fossil fuels.
2. Is crude oil a mixture or a compound?
3. Which elements are found in hydrocarbon molecules?
4. Give three properties of short chain hydrocarbon molecules.
5. Which hydrocarbons make the best fuels?
6. Where are the short chain hydrocarbon molecules collected in a fractionating column?
7. Why are long chain hydrocarbons cracked to form smaller ones?
8. What is a catalyst?
9. What family does ethene belong to?
10. What does a 'fraction' mean in this context?

Organic families

Carbon **atoms have the ability to form *four bonds* with other atoms. This means that carbon atoms can be made into a large range of compounds. These compounds are the basis of life and the chemistry of these compounds is called *organic chemistry*.**

Alkanes

The **alkanes** are a family of **hydrocarbon molecules**. This means that alkanes only contain hydrogen and carbon atoms. Scientists describe alkanes as **saturated** hydrocarbons because they contain no C=C bonds, so they already contain the maximum number of hydrogen atoms.

Alkanes are useful fuels, but as they do not contain C=C bonds, they do not react with bromine water.

Alkanes have the general formula C_nH_{2n+2}.

Name	methane	ethane	propane	butane
Chemical formula	CH_4	C_2H_6	C_3H_8	C_4H_{10}
Structure	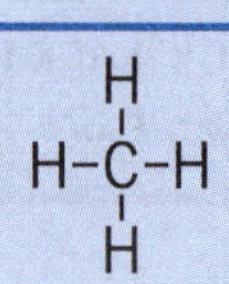	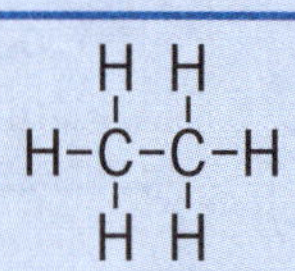	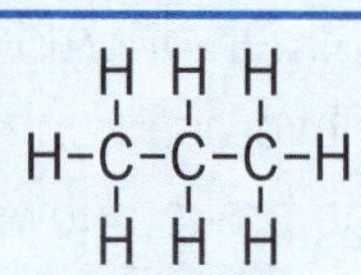	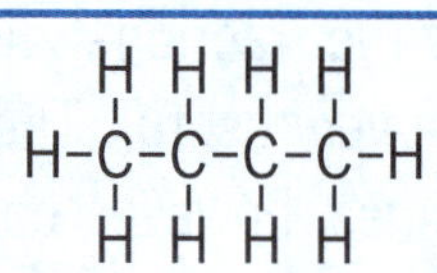

Alkenes

The **alkenes** are also hydrocarbon molecules. Scientists describe alkenes as **unsaturated** hydrocarbons because they all contain one or more C=C bond.

Alkenes are more reactive than alkanes due to the presence of C=C bonds. This means alkenes are more useful because they can be used to make new substances. Alkenes also react with **bromine water**, which decolourises in their presence.

Alkenes have the general formula C_nH_{2n}.

Name	ethene	propene
Chemical formula	C_2H_4	C_3H_6
Structure	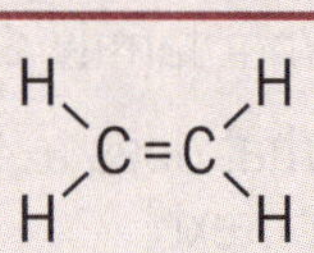	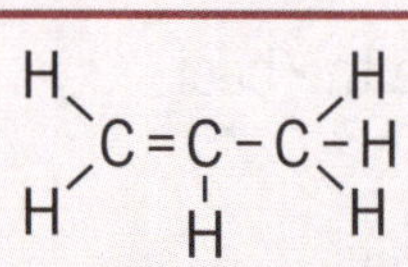

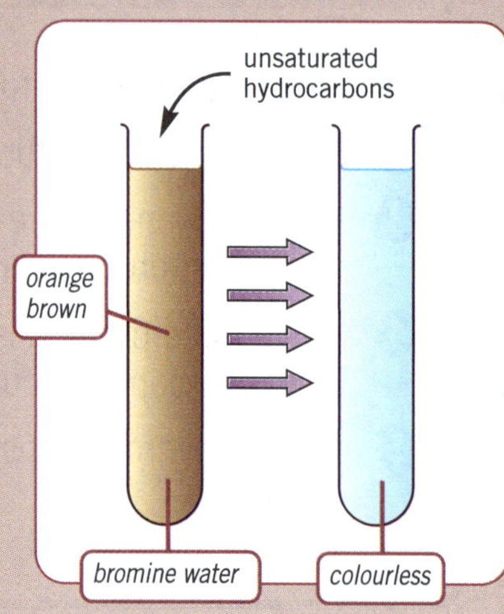

Alcohols

The term alcohol is often used for the compound **ethanol**. In fact, ethanol is just one member of a family of organic compounds called alcohols. All alcohols have an **–OH group**.

Each member of the family differs from the previous one by the addition of a CH_2 group.

Name	methanol	ethanol
Chemical formula	CH_3OH	C_2H_5OH
Structure	H H–C–O–H H	H H H–C–C–O–H H H

Covalent bonding

These compounds all contain covalent bonds.

Covalent bonding involves the sharing of electrons. The shared pairs of electrons hold the atoms together.

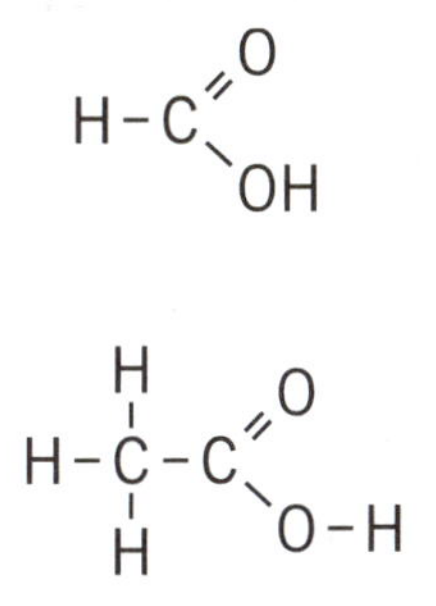

These molecules are carboxylic acids

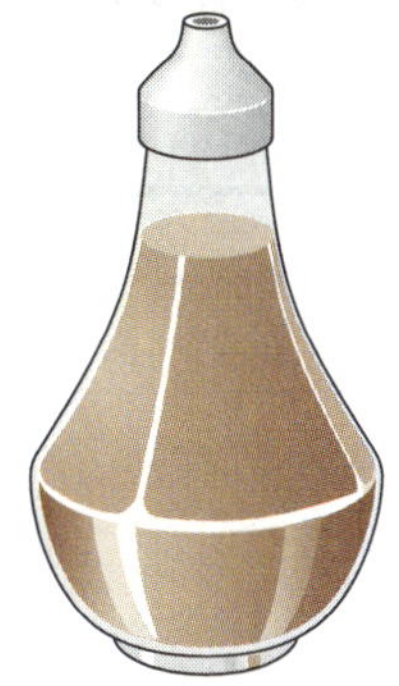

Vinegar contains carboxylic acids

KEY TERMS

Make sure you understand these terms before moving on!

- carbon
- alkanes
- saturated
- alkenes
- unsaturated

QUICK TEST

1. How many bonds do carbon atoms form?
2. Why are alkanes described as saturated hydrocarbons?
3. What is the name of the first member of the alkane family?
4. Draw the structure of the first four members of the alkane family.
5. Draw the structure of the first two members of the alkene family.
6. Which family does ethene belong to?
7. How could you differentiate between an alkane and an alkene?
8. What is the general formula for an alkane?
9. Which hydrocarbon family does the compound ethanol belong to?
10. What is the formula of ethanol?

Vegetable oils

Plant oils are a valuable source of *energy* in our diets. They are also essential sources of vitaminsA and D.

Vegetable oils can be extracted from the fruits, seeds and nuts of some plants. The oil is removed by crushing up the plant material and then collecting the oil

Vegetable oils

Vegetable oils can be produced from the **fruits, seeds or nuts** of some plants. Popular vegetable oils include olive oil and sunflower oil.

Fuels

When vegetable oils are burnt they release lots of energy. In fact, vegetable oils can be used in place of fossil fuels in the production of **bio-diesel**.

Using fats for cooking

Cooking food by frying is much faster than cooking food by boiling. In addition, frying foods produces interesting **new flavours** and **increases the energy content** of the food.

Frying potatoes to make chips

What is a fat molecule?

Fats and oils are complex molecules.

Saturated and unsaturated fats

Animal fats are usually **solid**, or nearly solid, at room temperature. A **saturated** fat contains many C–C bonds but **no C=C** bonds. Scientists believe that people who eat lots of saturated fats may develop raised blood cholesterol levels and this is linked with an increased risk of heart disease.

Most vegetable fats are liquids at room temperature and so are described as oils. Vegetable oils contain C=C bonds. Scientists describe these molecules as unsaturated. **Unsaturated** fats have **lower melting points** than saturated fats and, whilst most vegetable fats are **liquid at room temperature**, most animal fats are solids.

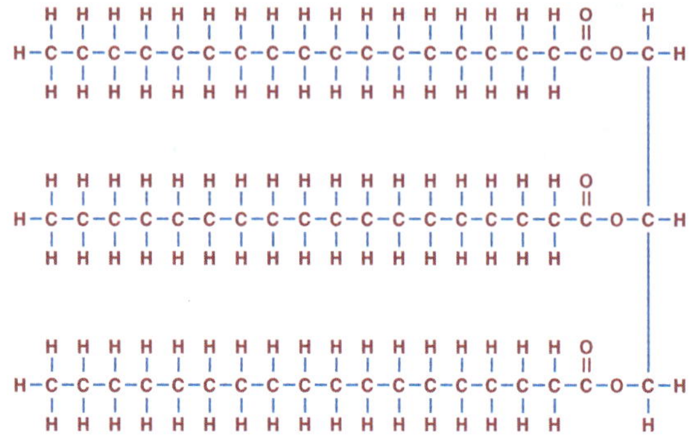

This is a molecule of a common animal fat

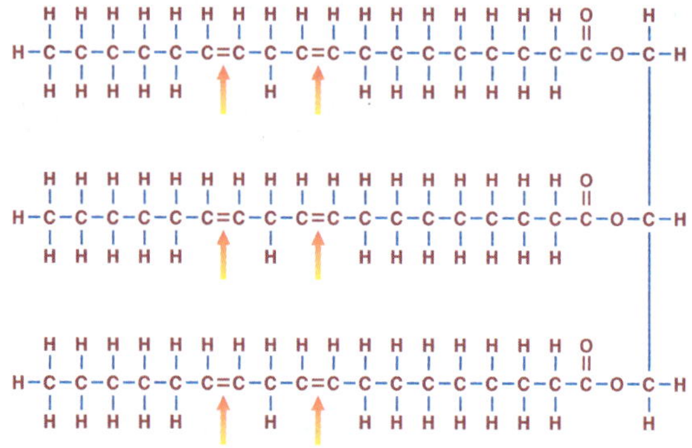

This is a molecule of a common vegetable oil

Polyunsaturated fats

Some unsaturated fats have just one C=C bond in the fatty acid chain. These are described as monounsaturated fats.

Other unsaturated fats have **many C=C bonds**. These are known as **polyunsaturated fats**.

Hydrogenated vegetable oils

Vegetable oils are often liquids at room temperature because they contain C=C bonds.

Margarine is one example of a hydrogenated vegetable oil

Vegetable oils can be made solid at room temperature by a process known as **hydrogenation**. The oils are heated with **hydrogen and a catalyst**.

Emulsions

Salad dressing is an example of a type of everyday mixture called an **emulsion**. It is a **mixture of two liquids**: oil and vinegar. Salad dressing is made by shaking oil and vinegar so that they mix together. After a short while, however, the oil and vinegar **separate out to form two distinct layers**. Many of the salad dressings bought from shops contain molecules called emulsifiers that help the oil and vinegar to mix together.

Emulsifiers are molecules that have two very different ends. One end is attracted to oil (hydrophobic), while the other end is attracted to the water in the vinegar (hydrophilic).

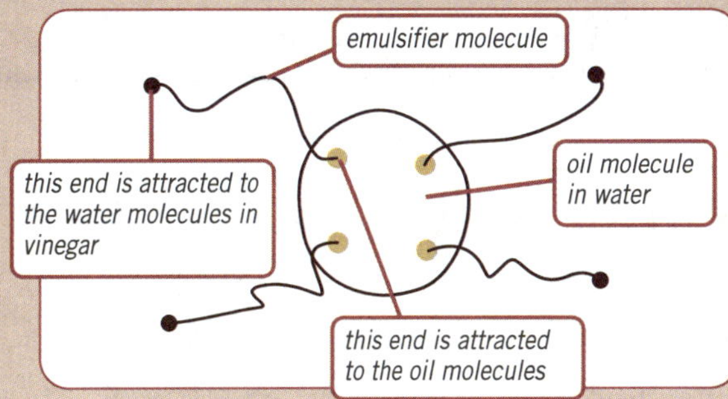

KEY TERMS

Make sure you understand these terms before moving on!

- bio-diesel
- saturated
- unsaturated
- hydrogenation
- emulsion

QUICK TEST

1. Which parts of plants can we obtain oils from?
2. Which part of a sunflower is used to obtain oil?
3. Which vitamins do we obtain from eating fats?
4. Why is frying food faster than boiling food?
5. Will a food that has been fried or boiled contain more energy?
6. If a fat is a solid at room temperature do you expect it to be saturated or unsaturated?
7. What do polyunsaturated fats have?

Plastics

Lots of small molecules can be joined together to make one big molecule.

Polymerisation

We have seen how the simplest alkene, **ethene**, can be formed by the cracking of large hydrocarbon molecules. If ethene is heated under pressure in the presence of a catalyst, many ethene molecules can join together to form a larger molecule called poly(ethene) or **polythene**. Here we can see how a large number of ethene molecules join together to form polythene.

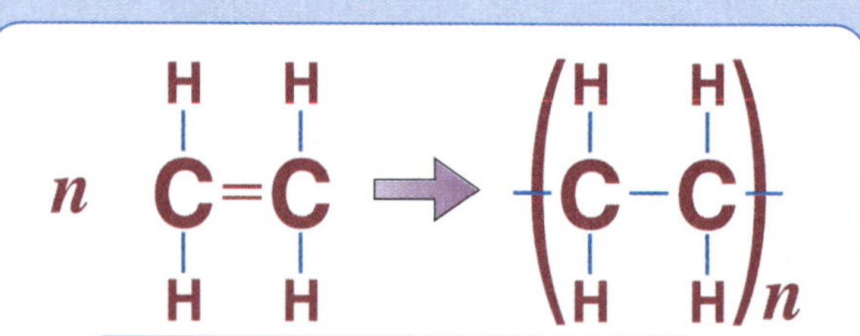

This is an example of an addition polymerisation reaction. Poly means 'lots'

The monomer ethene molecules have joined together to form the polymer poly(ethene) or 'polythene'.

Other polymers

Polymerisation reactions may involve other monomer units. The exact properties of the polymer formed depend upon:

- the monomers involved
- the conditions under which it was made.

Polypropene

Polypropene is made by an additional polymerisation reaction between **many propene** molecules.

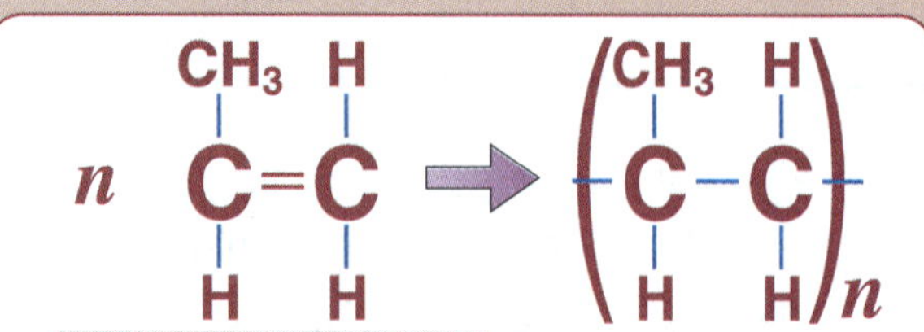

Many propene molecules join together to form polypropene

Poly vinyl chloride (PVC)

Poly vinyl chloride is made by an additional polymerisation reaction between **many chloroethene** molecules.

Chloroethene used to be called vinyl chloride.

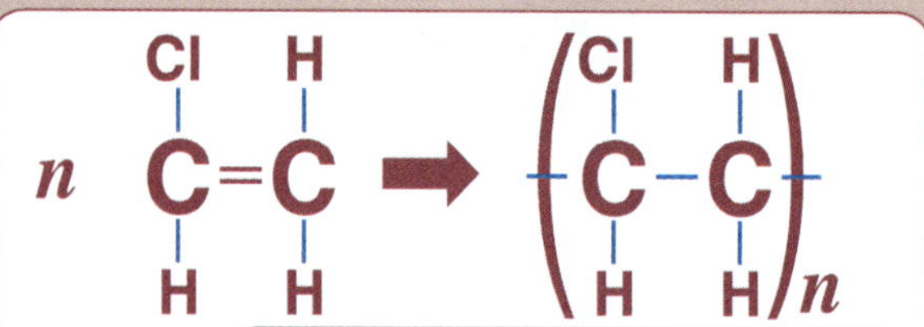

Many chloroethene (vinyl chloride) molecules join together to form poly vinyl chloride

Polytetrafluoroethene (PTFE or Teflon)

Polytetrafluoroethene is made by an additional polymerisation reaction between **many tetrafluoroethene** molecules.

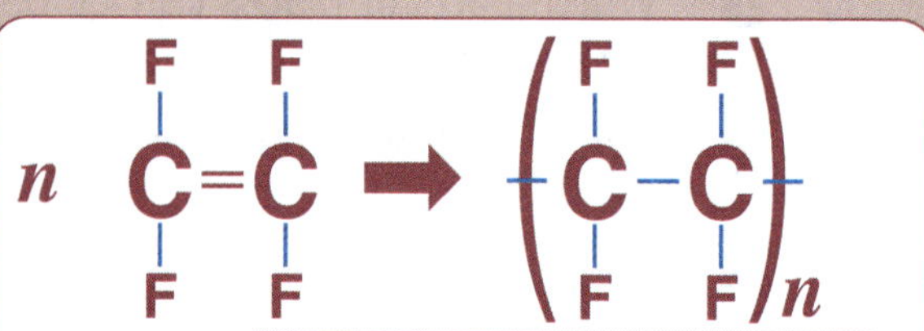

Many tetrafluoroethene molecules join together to form polytetrafluoroethene (PTFE)

New polymers

Scientists are **developing new and exciting polymers**.

Hydrogels are an example of these new types of polymers. They are able to bind water and are being used to make special wound dressings to help injured people. Hydrogels help to:

- stop fluid loss from the wound
- absorb bacteria and odour molecules
- cool and cushion the wound
- reduce the number of times the wound has to be disturbed. The hydrogel is transparent so doctors and nurses can monitor the wound without having to remove the dressing.

Uses of plastics

Polythene

Polythene is cheap and strong.

It is used to make plastic bags and bottles.

PVC

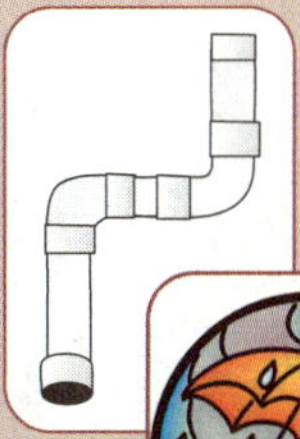

PVC is rigid and can be used to make building materials such as drainpipes.

Chemicals called plasticisers can be added to PVC to make products like Wellington boots and mackintoshes.

Polypropene

Polypropene is strong and has a high elasticity.

It is used for crates and ropes.

Polystyrene

Polystyrene is cheap and can be moulded into different shapes.

It is used for packaging and for plastic casings.

Know the properties and uses of different plastics.

Scientific process

The problems caused by plastics that do not breakdown in the environment have encouraged scientists to design new biodegradable plastics.

KEY TERMS

Make sure you understand these terms before moving on!

- ethene
- polythene
- hydrogels

QUICK TEST

1. Draw diagrams to show how polythene is formed from ethene.
2. Draw diagrams to show how polypropene is formed from propene.
3. What type of reaction is involved in the formation of polythene?
4. What is the name given to the small units that join together to form a polymer?
5. Name the monomer used to make PVC.
6. Name the monomer used to make PTFE.
7. How are hydrogels used?
8. Which plastic is cheap and strong?

Ethanol

Ethanol is a member of the alcohol family.

Uses of ethanol

Ethanol has the structure:

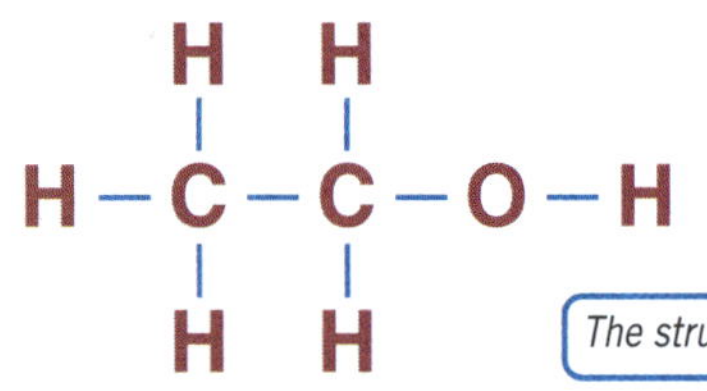

The structure of ethanol

Ethanol is found in drinks like beer and wine. In large amounts however, it is toxic. Ethanol has many useful properties. It is a **good solvent** and evaporates quickly. Many aftershaves contain ethanol. Ethanol is an important raw material and can also be used as a **fuel**.

Methanol is another member of the **alcohol** group and is even more toxic than ethanol.

Ethanol as a fuel

In some countries, alcohol made from sugar beet or sugar cane is made into alcohol. This alcohol can then be mixed with petrol to produce a fuel for vehicles like cars. Ethanol is a **renewable energy** resource that burns very cleanly. **Alcohols**, however, **release less energy** than petrol when they are burnt.

Sugar cane can be used to produce alcohol, which can be burnt as a fuel. In order to produce enough alcohol for fuel, large areas of fertile land would be required to grow the plants needed to produce the alcohol

Fermentation 1

Fermentation has been used to make alcohol for thousands of years. We use fermentation to make alcoholic drinks. Fruits, vegetables and cereals are all sources of the sugar, glucose.

During fermentation, **yeast** is used to catalyse (speed up) the reaction in which glucose is converted into ethanol and carbon dioxide.

$$\text{glucose} \xrightarrow{\text{yeast}} \text{ethanol} + \text{carbon dioxide}$$

Fermentation 2

The temperature of the reaction has to be carefully controlled. If the temperature falls too low, the yeast becomes inactive and the rate of the reaction slows down. If the temperature rises too high, the yeast is denatured and stops working altogether.

Ethanol produced by fermentation has a concentration of around 6 to 14%. There is a very strong link, however, between the consumption of alcohol and an increased risk of accidents and raised crime levels. Some religions prohibit the consumption of all alcoholic drinks altogether.

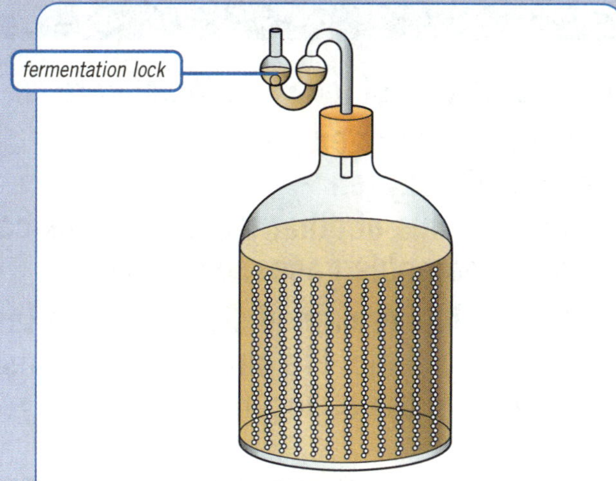

The fermentation lock allows carbon dioxide to escape, but stops oxygen in the air from reaching the alcohol. This is important, as ethanol can be easily oxidised to ethanoic acid, which would make the drink taste sour

Yeast is an enzyme or biological catalyst. It speeds up the conversion of sugar to alcohol and carbon dioxide, but is not itself used up in the process.

Industrial alcohol

There is another, more modern way, of producing vast amounts of alcohol. During this method, **ethene** is **reacted with steam to produce ethanol**.

ethene + steam → ethanol

A catalyst of **phosphoric acid and a temperature of 300°C** are needed.

This method of producing ethanol is much cheaper than fermentation. Our reserves of fossil fuels, however, are finite and will run out one day.

KEY TERMS

Make sure you understand these terms before moving on!

- solvent
- alcohol
- renewable
- fermentation
- yeast

QUICK TEST

1. What is the formula of ethanol?
2. Give three uses of ethanol.
3. What could happen to someone who drinks the alcohol methanol?
4. What is the catalyst used in fermentation?
5. What is glucose?
6. What happens to yeast if the temperature is too high?
7. What is the name of the gas produced during fermentation?
8. Give a word equation for the industrial production of ethanol.

Evolution of the atmosphere

The composition of today's *atmosphere* is:

- **about 80% nitrogen**
- **about 20% oxygen**
- **small amounts of other gases such as carbon dioxide, water vapour and noble gases, e.g. argon.**

Its make-up has remained stable for the last 200 million years. This has not always been the case. Over the history of the Earth, the composition of the atmosphere has changed and *evolved*.

Formation of the atmosphere

The first billion years

- During the first billion years of the Earth's life there was **enormous volcanic activity**.
- Volcanoes belched out carbon dioxide (CO_2), steam (H_2O), ammonia (NH_3) and methane (CH_4).
- The atmosphere was **mainly carbon dioxide** and there was very little oxygen. In fact, Earth's early atmosphere was very similar to the modern day atmospheres of the planets **Mars and Venus**.
- The steam cooled and turned to liquid to form the early oceans.

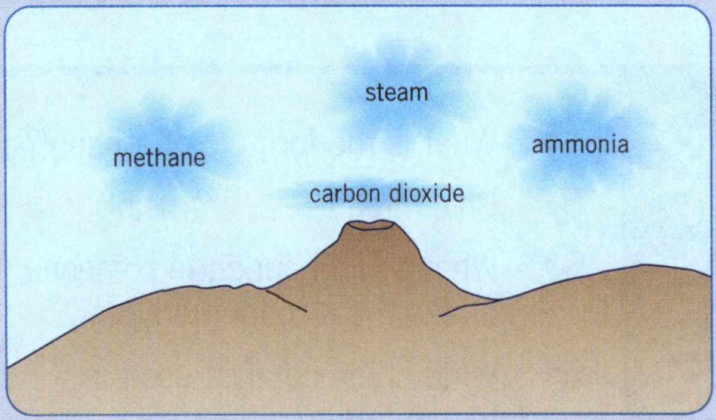

Later

- During the next two billion years **plants evolved** and began to cover the surface of the Earth.
- The plants grew very well in the carbon dioxide rich atmosphere. They steadily removed carbon dioxide and produced oxygen (O_2).

Later still

- Most of the carbon from the carbon dioxide in the early atmosphere gradually became **locked up** as carbonate minerals and fossil fuels in sedimentary rocks.
- The ammonia in the early atmosphere reacted with oxygen to release nitrogen.
- Living organisms, such as denitrifying bacteria, also produced nitrogen.
- As the amount of oxygen increased, an **ozone layer** (O_3) developed. This layer filtered out harmful ultraviolet radiation from the Sun, enabling new, more complex life forms to develop.

This limestone rock is rich in the chemical calcium carbonate

Is burning fossil fuel going to cause problems?

The level of carbon dioxide in our atmosphere has increased as we have burnt more fossil fuels. These fossil fuels had stored carbon dioxide from the Earth's early atmosphere for hundreds of millions of years.

Scientists believe that much of the carbon dioxide that is produced is removed from the atmosphere by the **reaction between carbon dioxide and seawater to form sediment**. However, not all of the carbon dioxide released by the burning of fossil fuels is removed in these ways. Many people are concerned about rising levels of carbon dioxide in the Earth's atmosphere and the possible link between these increased levels and **global warming**.

Scientific process

Our ideas about the evolution of the Earth's atmosphere have come from scientists' studies of rocks formed in the past. Our ideas have changed as more evidence has become available.

KEY TERMS

Make sure you understand these terms before moving on!

- atmosphere
- evolved
- volcanic
- ozone layer
- global warming

QUICK TEST

1. Roughly how much of today's atmosphere is made up of oxygen?
2. What is the main gas in the atmosphere today?
3. What other gases are present in small amounts in the Earth's atmosphere?
4. Which gases formed the Earth's early atmosphere?
5. Which was the main gas in the Earth's early atmosphere?
6. How did the evolution of plants affect the Earth's atmosphere?
7. What happened to most of the carbon dioxide in the Earth's early atmosphere?
8. What does the ozone layer do?
9. How did the development of the ozone layer affect life on Earth?
10. Why is the amount of carbon dioxide in the Earth's atmosphere increasing?

Pollution of the atmosphere

The atmosphere can be polluted in many ways.

Acid rain

Fossil fuels like coal, oil and gas often contain small amounts of **sulphur**. When these fuels are burnt, the gas **sulphur dioxide**, SO_2 is produced. This gas can dissolve in rainwater to form **acid rain**. Acid rain can affect the environment by damaging statues and buildings, as well as plant and aquatic life.

Reducing acid rain

The amount of acid rain produced can be reduced in several ways. The easiest way is simply to **use less electricity**, by turning off lights when they are not in use and not leaving everyday appliances on standby mode. Alternatively, sulphur compounds can be **removed directly from oil and gas** before they are burnt so that they do not produce sulphur dioxide as they burn. In addition, the sulphur that is removed is a valuable material that can be sold.

It is more difficult to remove sulphur from the fossil fuel coal. Instead, the sulphur dioxide produced can be **removed from the waste gases** before they are released into the atmosphere.

Carbon monoxide

The gas carbon monoxide (CO), can also cause problems. When fossil fuels containing carbon and hydrogen are burnt, the gases carbon dioxide and water vapour are produced. However, if carbon is burnt in a poor **supply of oxygen**, the gas carbon monoxide can also be produced.

Carbon monoxide is colourless, odourless and very poisonous. Faulty gas appliances can produce carbon monoxide, and so it is important that they are regularly serviced.

Incomplete combustion is undesirable in several ways:

- *Carbon monoxide is produced.*
- *Less heat than expected is given off when the fuel is burnt.*
- *Soot is produced which must then be cleaned. (A sooty flame has a yellow colour.)*

Global dimming

Global dimming is caused by **smoke particles** that are released into the atmosphere. Scientists believe that these smoke particles reduce the amount of sunlight that reaches the Earth's surface and may even affect weather patterns.

Carbon dioxide and the greenhouse effect

The **greenhouse effect** is slowly heating up the Earth. When fossil fuels are burnt, the gas carbon dioxide is produced. Although some of this carbon dioxide is removed from the atmosphere by the reaction between carbon dioxide and seawater, the overall amount of carbon dioxide in the atmosphere has increased over the last 200 years.

The carbon dioxide gas **traps the heat energy** that has reached the Earth from the Sun. **Global warming** may mean that the polar **icecaps** will eventually melt and this could cause massive flooding.

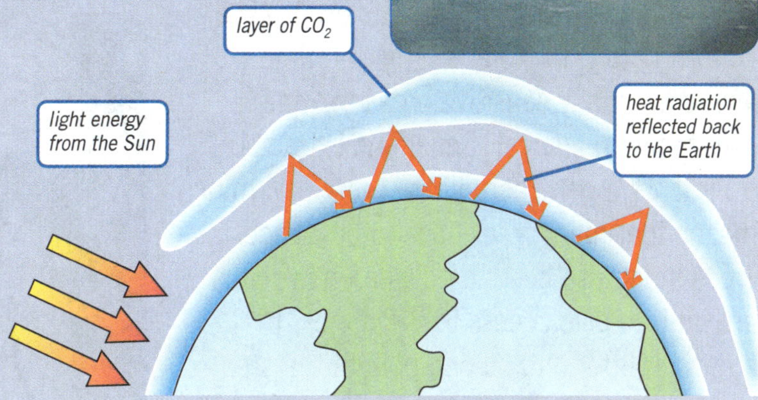

Carbon dioxide is the gas used by plants during photosynthesis.

Scientific theory

Not all scientists believe that human activity is causing global warming. Other factors may be more important. Until we have more evidence we will not really know. Do you think we should be careful about the amount of carbon dioxide we produce?

KEY TERMS

Make sure you understand these terms before moving on!

- acid rain
- global dimming
- global warming
- icecaps

QUICK TEST

1. What is the name of the gas produced when sulphur is burnt?
2. Which fossil fuel contains the most sulphur?
3. How can switching off lights prevent the formation of acid rain?
4. How can you tell if a fuel is being burnt in a poor supply of oxygen?
5. What gas is produced when carbon is burnt in an insufficient supply of oxygen?
6. What causes global dimming?
7. What are the problems associated with global dimming?
8. Which gas is linked to the greenhouse effect?

Pollution of the environment

All substances are obtained or made from matter from the Earth's crust, sea or atmosphere. It is vital, therefore, that we protect the environment from harmful *pollution*.

Problems with bauxite quarrying

Aluminium is extracted from its ore **bauxite**. Unfortunately, this ore is often found in environmentally sensitive areas like the Amazonian **rainforest**. Bauxite is extracted from large, open-cast mines: every new mine means that many trees have to be cut down. Trees must also be cleared when new roads are built to give access to the mines. In addition, litter and oil can pollute the area around the mine.

However, aluminium can be recycled. This cuts down on landfill here in Britain and helps to preserve the rainforests.

Aluminium drinks cans

Problems with limestone quarrying

Limestone is a very important raw material. The economic benefits of quarrying for limestone, however, must be balanced against the social and environmental consequences of quarrying. Limestone has to be blasted from hillsides in huge quantities. This **scars the landscape, causes noise pollution and dust, and affects local wildlife**.

Transporting limestone from the quarry can also cause problems, with **heavy lorries creating noise, congestion and damaging local roads**.

However, quarrying does create new **jobs** and bring new **money** into an area.

Problems disposing of plastic

Plastics are very useful materials. They are very stable and most plastics do not react with water, oxygen or other common chemicals. Plastics are also **non-biodegradable**, however, which means that microorganisms do not decompose them.

When plastic objects are no longer needed, they do not rot away. They remain in the environment and may cause problems. Plastic objects now fill many landfill sites.

We can get rid of plastics by burning them, but this solution can also cause problems. Although some plastics burn quite easily, they can give off **harmful** gases. The common plastic PVC releases the gas hydrogen chloride when it is burnt.

In response to these problems, scientists have developed new, **biodegradable** plastics, which will eventually rot away.

QUICK TEST

1. Name the main ore of aluminium.
2. Name one place where aluminium ore can be mined.
3. How can we help cut landfill and preserve rainforests?
4. How can limestone extraction affect the landscape?
5. What are the advantages of a new, local limestone quarry?
6. How can lorries cause problems near limestone quarries?
7. Where does rubbish end up?
8. What is the name used to describe materials that are not broken down by microorganisms?
9. What is the harmful gas produced when PVC is burnt?
10. Which plastics will breakdown in the environment?

KEY TERMS

Make sure you understand these terms before moving on!

- pollution
- bauxite
- non-biodegradable
- harmful
- biodegradable

Evidence for plate tectonics

Structure of the Earth

The elements silicon, oxygen and aluminium are all very common in the Earth's **crust**.

Scientists believe that the Earth has a layered structure.

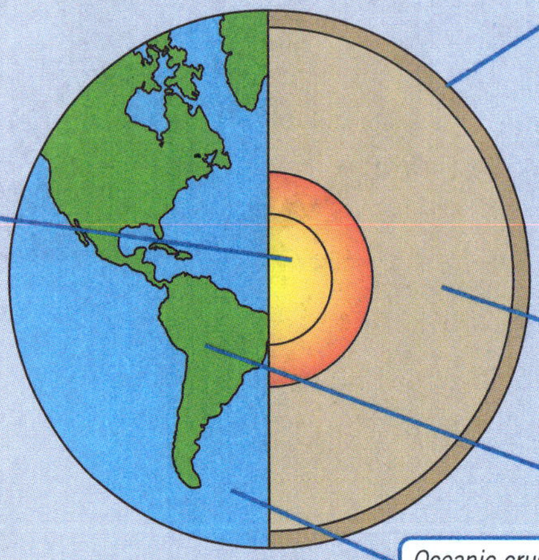

Evidence for the structure of the earth

Evidence for the layered structure of the Earth comes from studies of the way that **seismic waves** (the shock waves sent out by earthquakes) travel through the Earth. Scientists believe that the core is mainly made of **iron and nickel**.

Movement of the crust

People used to believe that the features of the Earth's surface, for example the mountain ranges, were formed as the surface of the Earth shrank as it cooled down. However, scientists now believe that the Earth's geological features can be explained using a single, unifying theory called **plate tectonics**.

The scientist, Alfred Wegener, first proposed the ideas involved in plate tectonics. At first his ideas were resisted, particularly by religious groups, but as more evidence emerged, the theory of plate tectonics was gradually accepted.

The main idea in plate tectonics is that the Earth's lithosphere (crust and upper mantle) is split up into about 12 large plates. Each of these plates moves slowly over the Earth's surface, at a rate of just a few centimetres a year. The movement of the plates is caused by **convection currents** in the mantle. These currents are caused by the **natural radioactive decay** of elements deep inside the Earth, which release heat energy.

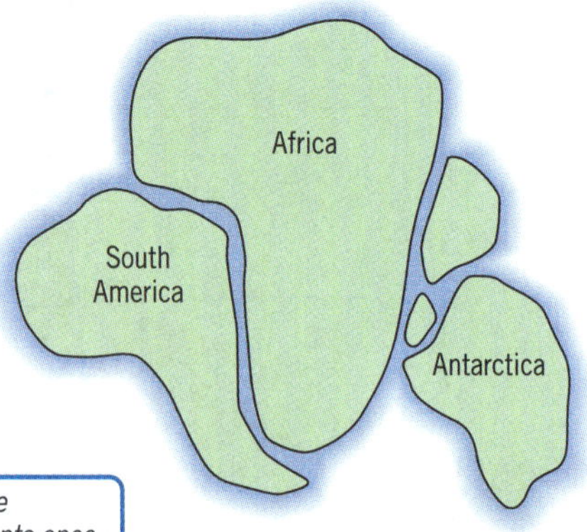

How the continents once looked

Evidence to support the theory of plate tectonics

There are many clues that support our ideas about plate tectonics:

- As soon as the South American coast was mapped, people began to notice how the east coast of South America and the west coast of Africa fitted together like pieces of an enormous jigsaw.

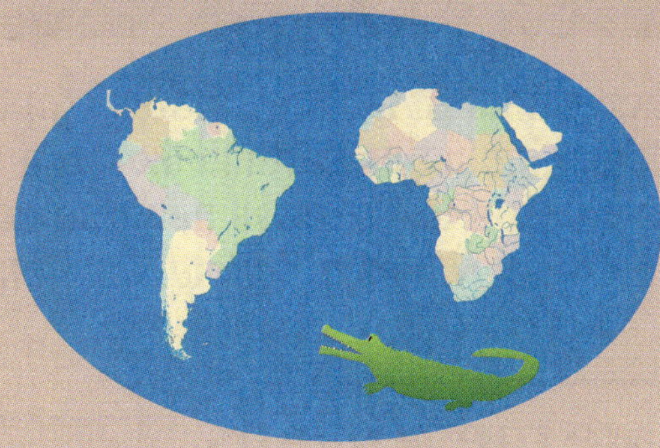

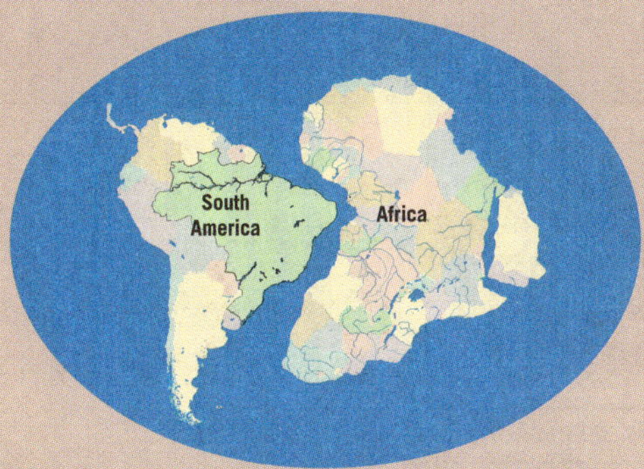

- Examination of **fossil remains** in South America and Africa showed that rocks of the same age contained the remains of an unusual, freshwater, crocodile-like creature.
- Further evidence that South America and Africa were once joined was found when scientists discovered that **rock strata** of the same age were strikingly similar on both sides of the Atlantic.

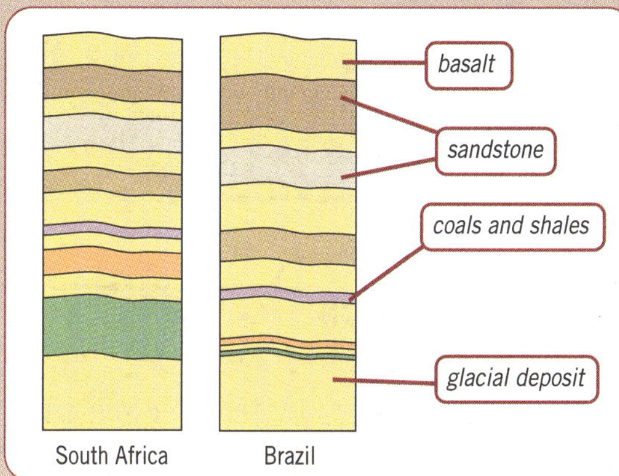

Scientific process

Our ideas about plate tectonics have changed over time. Scientists build a model that fits with the evidence that is available to them at any given time. When new evidence becomes available, scientists must re-evaluate existing models and, if necessary, change them to take in the new evidence.

KEY TERMS

Make sure you understand these terms before moving on!

- crust
- core
- mantle
- seismic waves
- plate tectonics
- convection currents

QUICK TEST

1. What name is given to the outer layer of the Earth?
2. In which state is the Earth's inner core?
3. Which elements are abundant in the Earth's crust?
4. Which elements are abundant in the Earth's core?
5. How fast do tectonic plates move?
6. What is the Earth's lithosphere?

Consequences of plate tectonics

The movement of tectonic plates can cause many problems, including earthquakes and volcanoes. These problems tend to be worse near the edges of plates. These are known as the *plate boundaries*.

Plate movements

The plates can move in three different ways:

1 They can slide past each other.

2 They can move towards each other.

3 They can move away from each other.

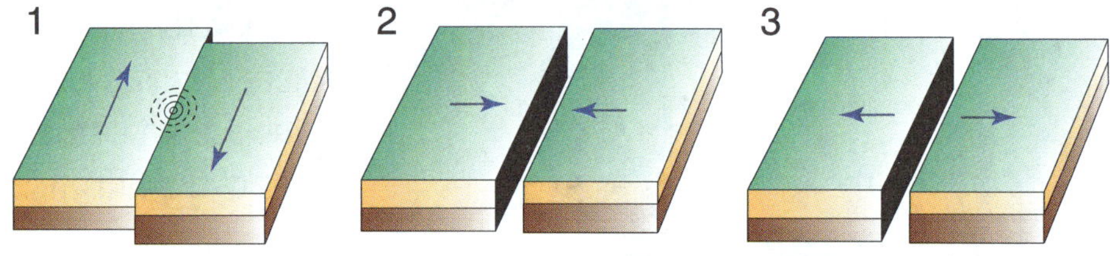

These diagrams show how the Earth's plates can move

Earthquakes

Earthquakes are caused by tectonic plates sliding past each other. The San Andreas Fault, in California, is a famous example of this occurring. The plates in this area have been fractured into a very complicated pattern. As the plates try to move past each other, they tend to stick together, rather than slide smoothly past each other. When the **plates stick together, forces build up**, until eventually the **plates move suddenly**. The strain that has built up is released as an earthquake. If this happens under the oceans, the result is catastrophic tsunami waves.

Earthquakes can cause enormous damage. This photograph was taken in Los Angeles after the 1994 earthquake

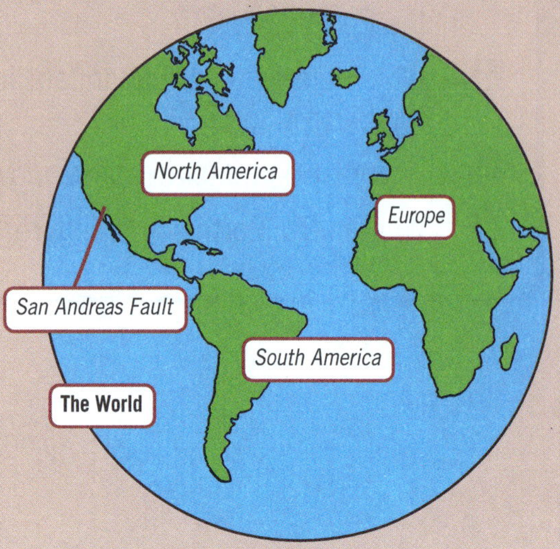

Scientists have studied earthquakes in an attempt to predict exactly when and where future earthquakes might occur, so that they can warn people to get away from the affected areas. However, with so many **factors** involved, it is not always possible to predict exactly when an earthquake will occur. When they do happen, they can cause massive destruction and loss of life.

Volcanoes

Volcanoes are found in locations around the Earth where two plates are moving towards each other.

- These convergent plate boundaries often involve a collision between an **oceanic and a continental plate**.
- **Oceanic plates** contain minerals that are rich in the elements iron and magnesium and are **denser** than **continental plates**.
- When an oceanic plate and a continental plate converge, the denser, oceanic plate is forced beneath the continental plate.
- The continental plate is stressed and the existing rocks are folded and metamorphosed (changed).
- As the oceanic plate is forced down below the continental plate, some rock may melt to form magma. This magma may rise up through cracks to form volcanoes.
- As the plates are moving past each other, earthquakes are also common in these areas.
- A convergent plate boundary along the western coast of South America resulted in the Andes mountain range.

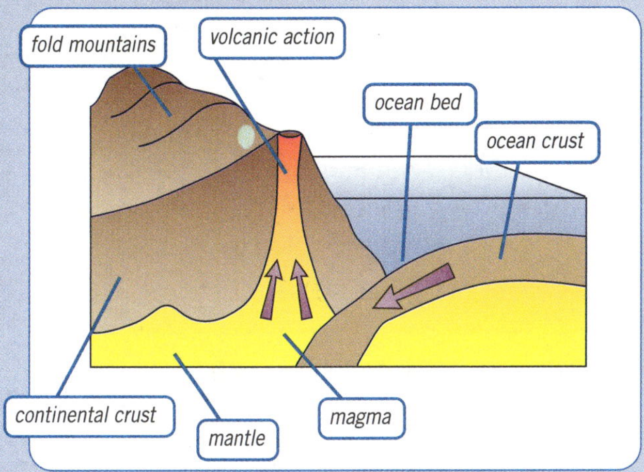

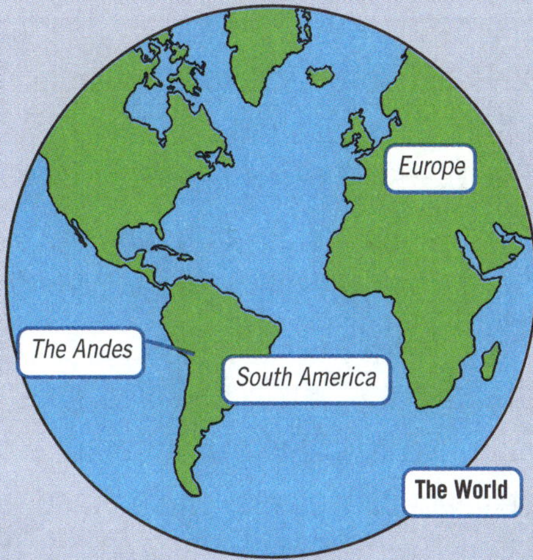

KEY TERMS

Make sure you understand these terms before moving on!

- plate boundaries
- earthquakes
- factors
- volcanoes
- oceanic plates
- continental plates

QUICK TEST

1. What are the three ways that plates can move?
2. How are earthquakes caused?
3. Why can't scientists predict the exact date of an earthquake?
4. Where is the San Andreas Fault?
5. Which type of plate is densest?
6. What is magma?
7. How is magma formed when two plates converge?
8. Why do earthquakes sometimes occur near volcanoes?
9. Where are the Andes?
10. What does 'metamorphosed' mean?

Extraction of iron

Iron is an element. Elements are substances that are made of only one type of atom.

There are only about 100 different elements. Elements are often displayed on the periodic table.

Iron is an extremely important metal. It is extracted from iron ore in the *blast furnace*.

Methods of extraction

The more reactive a metal is, the harder it is to remove from its compound. Gold is so unreactive that it is found uncombined. However, all other metals are found in compounds. Occasionally we may find rocks that contain metals in such high concentrations that it is economically worthwhile to extract the metal from the rock. Such rocks are called **ores**. The method chosen to extract the metal depends on the **reactivity** of the metal.

Iron is less reactive than carbon. Iron can be extracted from iron oxide by reducing the metal oxide with carbon.

potassium sodium calcium magnesium aluminium	**metals that are more reactive than carbon are extracted by electrolysis**
carbon zinc iron tin lead gold	**metals that are less reactive than carbon are extracted by reducing the metal oxide using carbon (or carbon monoxide)**

The solid raw materials

The solid raw materials in the blast furnace are:

- iron ore
- **coke** (which is a source of the element carbon)
- **limestone** (which reacts with impurities).

The main ore of iron is **haematite**. This ore contains the compound iron (III) oxide.

What happens in the blast furnace? 1

1 First hot air is blasted into the furnace. The oxygen in the air reacts with the carbon in the coke to form carbon dioxide and release energy.

carbon + oxygen → carbon dioxide

What happens in the blast furnace? 2

2 At the very high temperatures inside the blast furnace, carbon dioxide reacts with more carbon to form carbon monoxide.

carbon dioxide + carbon → carbon monoxide

3 The carbon monoxide reacts with iron oxide to form iron and carbon dioxide.

carbon monoxide + iron oxide → iron + carbon dioxide

During this reaction:

- **the iron oxide is reduced to iron**
- **the carbon monoxide is oxidised to carbon dioxide.**

Due to the high temperatures in the blast furnace, the iron that is made is in liquid form. This molten iron is **dense** (heavy for its size) and sinks to the bottom of the furnace, where it can be removed.

Iron ore is mainly reduced by the gas carbon monoxide.

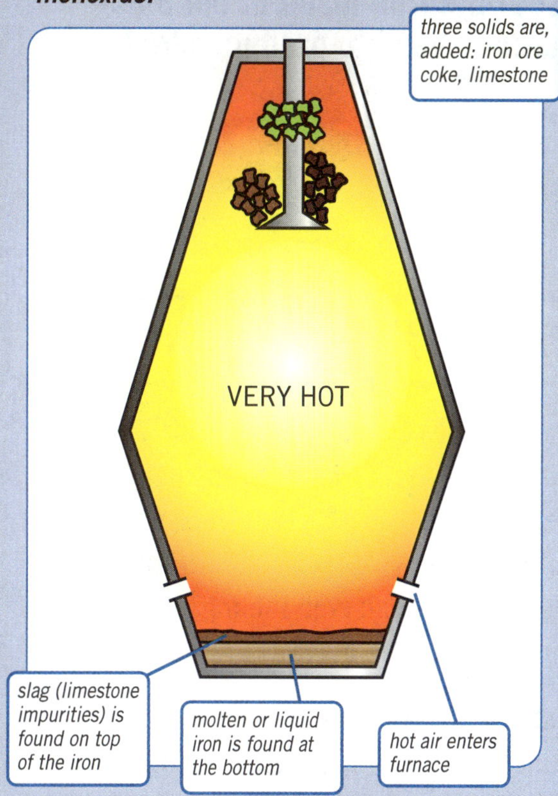

Removing impurities in the blast furnace

Haematite (iron ore) contains many impurities: most commonly, it contains substantial amounts of silicon dioxide or silica. Limestone is added to the blast furnace because it reacts with these silica impurities to form **slag**. Slag has a low density and so floats to the top of the iron ore where it can be removed.

KEY TERMS

Make sure you understand these terms before moving on!

- blast furnace
- ores
- reactivity
- coke
- limestone
- dense

QUICK TEST

1. Which element is so unreactive that it can be found uncombined?
2. Which method of extraction can be used for metals that are less reactive than carbon?
3. Which method of extraction can be used for metals that are more reactive than carbon?
4. What is the name of the main ore of iron?
5. What are the three solid raw materials added to the blast furnace?
6. What is the other raw material used in the blast furnace?
7. Which gas actually reduces iron oxide to iron?
8. Why does iron sink to the bottom of the furnace?
9. What does 'dense' mean?
10. What is the name of the substance formed when limestone reacts with silica?

Iron and steel

Most of the iron made in the blast furnace is used to produce steel.

Preventing iron rusting

Iron **corrodes** or 'rusts' faster than most transition metals. However, rusting requires the presence of both oxygen and water. If we can completely remove either of these chemicals we can stop the iron from **rusting**. This can be done in several ways.

Coating the iron

Painting or coating iron in plastic or oil can stop **oxygen and water** from reaching the metal and prevent it from rusting. However, as soon as the coating is damaged, the iron will start to rust.

Sacrificial protection

We can stop iron from rusting by placing it in contact with a more reactive metal like **zinc or magnesium**. The iron is protected because the zinc or magnesium reacts instead of the iron. This method is called **sacrificial protection**. Expensive objects made from iron, such as speedboat engines, are protected in this way.

Alloying the metal

Mixing the metal with other metals and carbon to form alloys, such as stainless steel, can also protect iron.

Cast iron

The iron that is made in the blast furnace contains large amounts of the element carbon. If this iron is allowed to cool down and solidify it forms **cast iron**. This metal can be used to make objects like drain covers. It:

- is hard
- is strong
- does not rust.

Cast iron does have one notable disadvantage: it is brittle and can easily crack.

Drain covers need to be strong and must not rust. They are made from cast iron

Wrought iron

Wrought iron is made by removing the impurities from cast iron. Wrought iron is much softer than cast iron and can be used to make objects like gates.

This beautiful gate is made from wrought iron. Wrought iron is much softer than cast iron

Wrought iron is softer than cast iron because of its structure. It is made from almost pure iron. This means that the iron atoms form a **very regular arrangement**. The layers of iron atoms are able to slip easily over each other. This makes wrought iron soft and easy to shape.

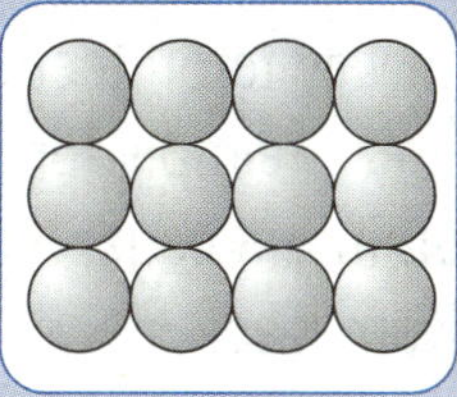

Steel

Most iron is made into steel. Most of the metal objects that we use today are made from steel.

- First, the carbon impurities are removed from iron to produce pure iron.
- Then other metals, and carefully controlled amounts of the non-metal element carbon, are added to the iron.

Steel is much harder than wrought iron because it consists of atoms of different elements. These atoms are different sizes. This means that the atoms in steel cannot pack together to form a regular structure. This irregular structure makes it **very difficult for the layers of atoms to slide** over each other and makes steel hard.

Stainless steel

Stainless steel is a very widely used **alloy.** It consists of:

- 70% iron
- 20% chromium
- 10% nickel.

Stainless steel is extremely resistant to corrosion.

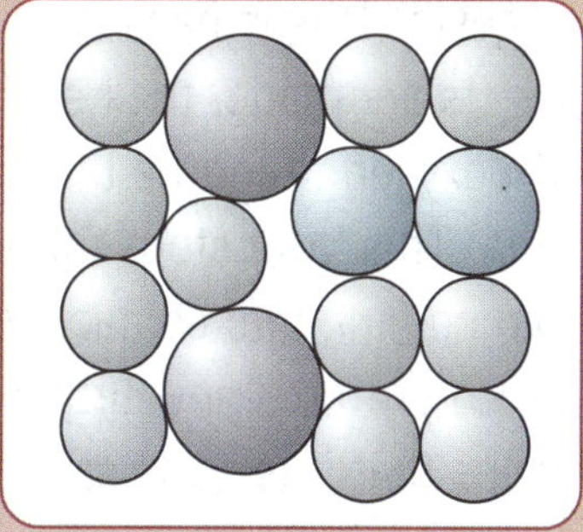

KEY TERMS

Make sure you understand these terms before moving on!

- corrodes
- rusting
- sacrificial protection
- cast iron
- wrought iron
- stainless steel

QUICK TEST

1. What is the main use of iron?
2. What must be present for iron to rust?
3. How does oiling an iron object stop it from rusting?
4. Name a metal that could be used in sacrificial protection to stop iron rusting.
5. Give four properties of cast iron.
6. What is the main impurity in cast iron?

Aluminium

Aluminium is abundant in the Earth's crust, but it is also very reactive. Consequently, aluminium is more expensive than iron.

Bauxite

The main ore of aluminium is called **bauxite**. Bauxite contains the compound aluminium oxide.

Properties of aluminium

Although pure aluminium is quite soft, it becomes much stronger when it is alloyed with other metals. **Aluminium alloys combine high strength with low density**. This makes aluminium a very useful metal for making objects like aeroplanes and mountain bikes.

Aluminium is quite a reactive metal and yet it is widely used to make drinks cans. In fact, aluminium appears to be much less reactive than its position in the reactivity series suggests. This is because when aluminium objects are made, their surfaces quickly react with oxygen to form a thin **layer of aluminium oxide**. This layer stops the aluminium metal from coming into contact with other chemicals and so prevents any further reaction. It also means that it is quite safe for us to drink fizzy, acidic drinks from aluminium cans.

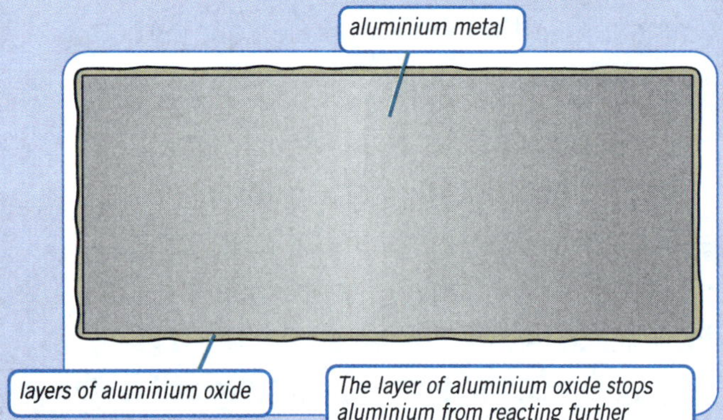

The layer of aluminium oxide stops aluminium from reacting further

Recycling aluminium

One way to protect the areas where bauxite is found is simply for people to recycle their old aluminium cans. **Recycling** has many advantages:

- We will not have to extract so much bauxite.
- Landfill sites will not be filled up with discarded aluminium cans.
- It uses much less energy than extracting aluminium straight from its ore.

The extraction of aluminium

Aluminium is more reactive than carbon so it is extracted using electrolysis, even though this is a very expensive method. The main ore of aluminium is bauxite, which contains aluminium oxide. For electrolysis to occur, the aluminium ions and oxide ions in bauxite must be able to move.

Bauxite has a very high melting point and heating the ore to this temperature would be very expensive. Fortunately, another ore of aluminium called **cryolite** has a much lower melting point. First, the cryolite is heated up until it melts and then the bauxite is dissolved in the molten cryolite.

Electrolysis

Aluminium can now be extracted by electrolysis.

1 By dissolving the aluminium oxide, both the aluminium Al^{3+} and the oxide O^{2-} ions can move.

2 During electrolysis the Al^{3+} ions are attracted to the negative electrode where they pick up electrons to form aluminium atoms. The aluminium metal accumulates at the bottom of the cell where it can be collected.

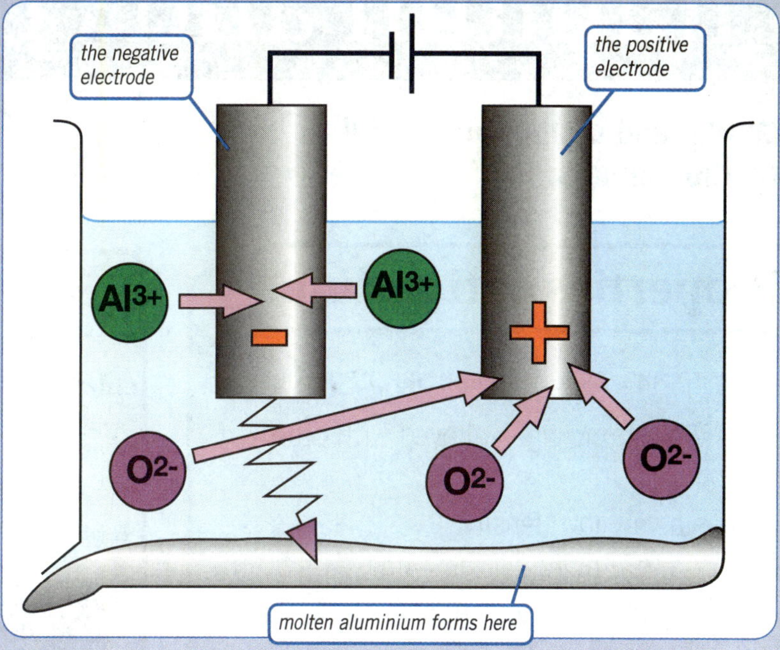

aluminium ions + electrons → aluminium atoms

The O^{2-} ions are attracted to the positive electrode where they deposit electrons to form oxygen molecules.

oxide ions – electrons → oxygen molecules

3 The oxygen that forms at the positive electrode readily reacts with the **carbon, graphite electrode** to form carbon dioxide. The electrodes, therefore, must be replaced periodically.

Oxidation and reduction

In the electrolysis of aluminium oxide:

- **Aluminium ions are reduced to aluminium atoms.**
- **Oxide ions are oxidised to oxygen molecules.**

KEY TERMS

Make sure you understand these terms before moving on!

- bauxite
- recycling
- density
- cryolite
- reduced
- oxidised

QUICK TEST

1. Name the main ore of aluminium.
2. Give two properties of pure aluminium.
3. What is a mixture of metals called?
4. Why is aluminium less reactive than expected?
5. What is the formula of aluminium oxide?
6. What is the name of the method used to extract aluminium from its ore?
7. During the electrolysis of aluminium oxide which ions are oxidised?
8. During the electrolysis of aluminium oxide which ions are reduced?

Titanium and copper

Titanium and copper are useful transition metals.

Properties of titanium

Titanium has some very special properties:

- It is very strong when alloyed with other metals.
- It has a very low density.
- It has a very high melting point.
- It is very resistant to corrosion.

Titanium appears to be **unreactive** because the surface of titanium objects quickly react with oxygen to form a **layer of titanium oxide**.

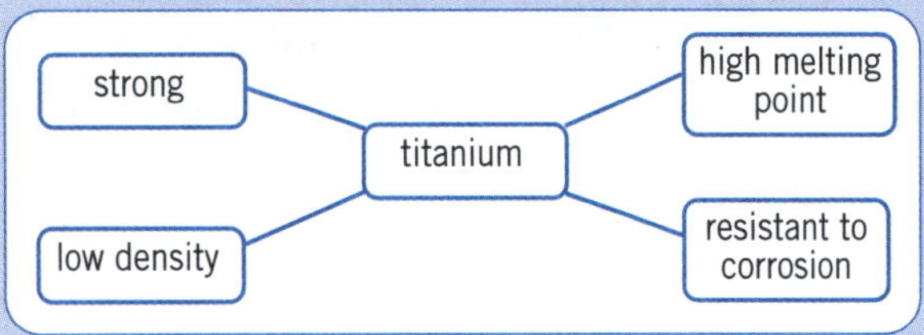

Uses of titanium

Titanium's properties make it a very useful metal. Titanium **alloys** are used to make:

- replacement hip and elbow joints
- aircraft.

The F22 fighter is made from a titanium alloy

Titanium ore

The main **ore** of titanium is rutile. Rutile contains the compound **titanium dioxide**.

It is a very hard mineral that is resistant to weathering and is found mixed amongst sand on certain beaches.

Extraction of titanium

Titanium is more reactive than carbon and so it cannot be extracted simply by heating titanium dioxide with carbon. The **extraction** of titanium is quite a complicated process involving several chemical reactions.

Smart alloys

Smart alloys are new materials with amazing properties. They have one or more property that can be dramatically altered by changes in the environment.

One famous example of a smart alloy is **nitinol**. Nitinol is an alloy of nickel and titanium that has a shape memory. When a force is applied to a smart alloy, it stretches. However, when a smart alloy is heated up it returns to its original shape.

Other smart alloys also have interesting properties.

Thermo-chromic materials change colour as the temperature changes, and can be used to make objects like mugs which reveal a new pattern when hot liquids are poured into them.

Copper

Copper has some very special properties:

This saucepan is made from copper. Copper is a good thermal conductor and does not contaminate the food that is being cooked

- It is a good **thermal conductor**.
- It is a good electrical conductor.
- It is easy to shape.
- It is very unreactive.
- It is very resistant to corrosion.

Purification of copper

Copper must be purified before it can be used for certain applications. Copper is purified using **electrolysis**.

Electrolysis involves passing an electrical current through a molten ionic substance or dissolved ionic substance to break down the substance into simpler parts.

KEY TERMS

Make sure you understand these terms before moving on!

- unreactive
- alloys
- ore
- extraction
- thermal conductor
- electrolysis

Uses of copper

Copper's properties make it a very useful metal. Copper is used to make:

- water pipes
- saucepans
- electrical wires.

Copper oxide

Copper can be extracted from copper oxide by removing the oxygen. This is called reduction.

Copper can be extracted from its ore, chalcopyrite

Copper alloys

Pure copper is too soft for many uses. In pure copper, the atoms are all the same size and so they form a regular arrangement. Copper is soft because the layers of atoms can pass easily over each other.

Copper is often mixed with other metals to form alloys such as:

- brass
- bronze.

bronze is an alloy of copper and tin

QUICK TEST

1. How can titanium be made stronger?
2. Why does titanium appear to be unreactive?
3. How is titanium used inside the human body?
4. What is the name of main ore of titanium?
5. What is the chemical name of the main ore of titanium?
6. How is copper purified?
7. What name is used to describe a mixture of metals?
8. Why is pure copper soft?
9. Name two alloys of copper.

Transition metals

Metals have a *giant structure*. In metals, the outer electrons are not bound to one atom, but are free to move through the whole structure. This means that metals consist of positive metal ions surrounded by negative electrons. *Metallic bonding is the attraction between these ions and the electrons.*

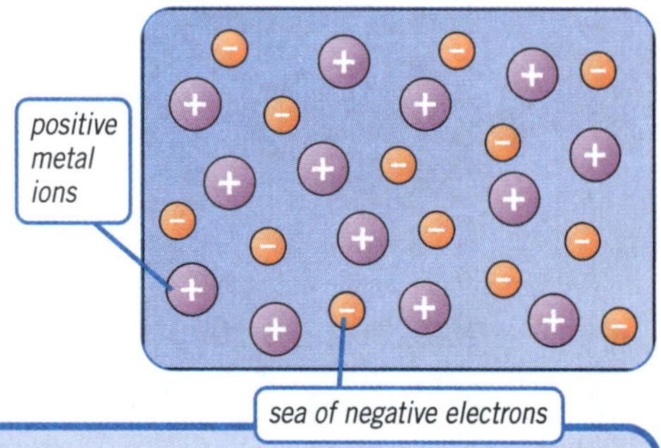

Properties of metals

Metallic bonding means that metals have several, very useful properties:

- They are **good electrical conductors**.
- They are **good thermal conductors**.
- They can be drawn into **wires**.
- They can also be **hammered into shape**.

The transition metals are found in the middle section of the **periodic table**. Copper, iron and nickel are examples are very useful transition metals. All transition metals have characteristic properties.

They:

- have **high melting points** (except for mercury which is a liquid at room temperature)
- are **high density**
- have coloured compounds
- are strong, tough and hard wearing
- are much less reactive than Group 1 metals
- react less vigorously with oxygen and water.

Many transition metals and their compounds are also useful catalysts.

Period	Group 1	2											3	4	5	6	7	0
1	H Hydrogen																	He Helium
2	Li Lithium	Be Beryllium											B Boron	C Carbon	N Nitrogen	O Oxygen	F Fluorine	Ne Neon
3	Na Sodium	Mg Magnesium											Al Aluminium	Si Silicon	P Phosphorous	S Sulphur	Cl Chlorine	Ar Argon
4	K Potassium	Ca Calcium	Sc Scandium	Ti Titanium	V Vanadium	Cr Chromium	Mn Manganese	Fe Iron	Co Cobalt	Ni Nickel	Cu Copper	Zn Zinc	Ga Gallium	Ge Germanium	As Arsenic	Se Selenium	Br Bromine	Kr Krypton
5	Rb Rubidium	Sr Strontium	Y Yttrium	Zr Zirconium	Nb Niobium	Mo Molybdenum	Tc Technetium	Ru Ruthenium	Rh Rhodium	Pd Palladium	Ag Silver	Cd Cadmium	In Indium	Sn Tin	Sb Antimony	Te Tellurium	I Iodine	Xe Xenon
6	Cs Caesium	Ba Barium	La Lanthanum	Hf Hafnium	Ta Tantalum	W Tungsten	Re Rhenium	Os Osmium	Ir Iridium	Pt Platinum	Au Gold	Hg Mercury	Tl Thallium	Pb Lead	Bi Bismuth	Po Polonium	At Astatine	Rn Radon
7	Fr Francium	Ra Radium	Ac Actinium															

Copper

- Copper is a good electrical and thermal conductor.
- It can be easily bent into new shapes and does not corrode.
- Copper is widely used in electrical wiring.
- It is also used to make water pipes.

Iron

- Iron made in the blast furnace is strong but brittle.
- Iron is often made into steel.

- Steel is strong and cheap, and is used in vast quantities. However, it is also heavy and may rust.
- Iron and steel are useful structural materials. They are used to make buildings, bridges, ships, cars and trains.
- Iron is used as a catalyst in the Haber process.

Gold

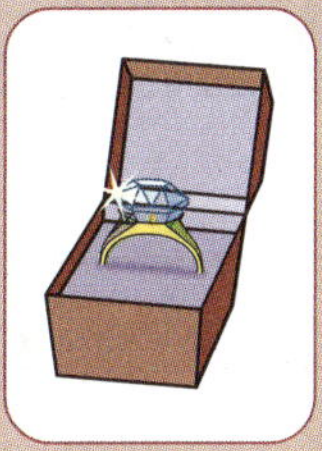

- Gold is rare and this makes it valuable.
- It is shiny and unreactive, but too soft for many uses.
- Gold can be mixed with other metals.
- It is widely used to make jewellery.

KEY TERMS

- giant structure
- electrical conductors
- thermal conductors
- periodic table
- density
- alloys

Nickel

- Nickel is hard, shiny and dense.
- It is widely used to make coins.

- Nickel is used as a catalyst in the manufacture of margarine.

Silver

- Silver is shiny and quite unreactive.
- It has the highest electrical and thermal conductivity of any metal.

- It is used to make coins, jewellery and cutlery.

Metal alloys

Alloys are made by mixing metals together. In fact, mixing metals with non-metals can occasionally make alloys.

Common alloys include:

- Amalgams, which are mainly mercury.
- Brass, which is made from copper and zinc.
- Bronze, which is made from copper and tin.
- Solder, which is made from lead and tin.
- Steel, which is mainly iron.

QUICK TEST

1. Why are metals able to conduct heat and electricity?
2. In which part of the periodic table are the transition metals found?
3. What are the characteristics of transition metals?
4. Which items can be made from steel?
5. In which process is iron used as a catalyst?
6. Which items can be made from nickel?

The noble gases

The noble gases are very unreactive. They are sometimes described as being *'inert'* because they do not react. This is because they have a full, *stable*, outer shell of electrons.

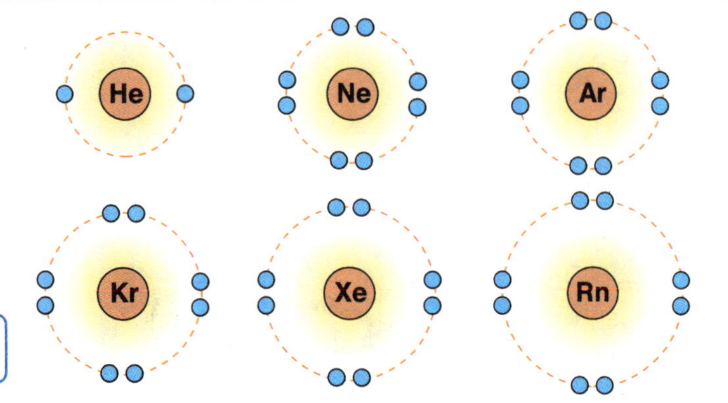

A model showing the outer shell of electrons

Characteristics of noble gases

- The noble gases are found on the far right-hand side of the periodic table.
- The noble gases are all colourless.
- They are **monatomic gases**. This means that they exist as single atoms rather than as diatomic molecules as other gases do.

Why do melting and boiling points increase down the group?

- Melting and boiling points increase down the group, as the atoms get larger and have more electrons.
- This means that the strength of the attraction between atoms increases.
- **The forces of attraction between atoms get stronger** down the group, and so it takes more energy to overcome these forces. As a consequence, noble gases will melt and boil at higher temperatures.

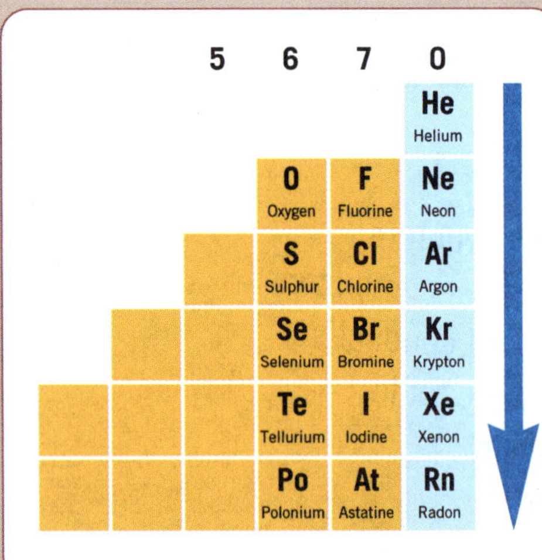

Why are noble gases so unreactive?

When atoms react, they share, gain or lose electrons in order to obtain a full outer shell of electrons. **Noble gases already have a full and stable outer shell so they do not react.** Noble gases are useful precisely because they do not react.

Uses of noble gases

Helium

- Helium is used in balloons and in airships.
- It is less dense than air.
- It is not **flammable**. (Early airships used hydrogen, which is flammable and this caused problems.)

Neon

- Neon is used in electrical discharge tubes in advertising signs.

Argon

- Argon is used in filament light bulbs.
- Surrounding the hot filament with argon stops the filament from burning away and breaking the bulb.

Krypton

- Krypton is used in lasers.

KEY TERMS

Make sure you understand these terms before moving on!

- inert
- stable
- monatomic
- flammable

QUICK TEST

1. Why are the noble gases so unreactive?
2. What is the trend in boiling point down the group?
3. Draw the (outer shell) electron shell of helium.
4. Draw the (outer shell) electron shell of argon.
5. What does 'monatomic' mean?
6. What is helium used for?
7. Why is it used?
8. What is neon used for?
9. What is argon used for?
10. What is krypton used for?

Practice questions

Use the questions to test your progress. Check your answers on page 111.

1. This table is about limestone and some of the substances that can be made from limestone.

Substance	Information about the substance
A	is made when limestone is heated with silica and soda
B	is made when water is added to calcium oxide
C	is a rock that contains large amounts of calcium carbonate
D	is formed when calcium carbonate is heated

a) What is the name of substance C? ....

b) What is the chemical name of substance D? ....

c) What is the name of substance B? ....

d) What is the name of substance A? ....

2. Atoms can join together to form molecules. Here are four diagrams of molecules.

A 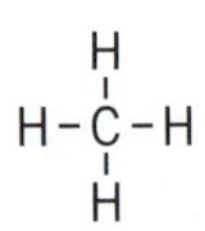

B 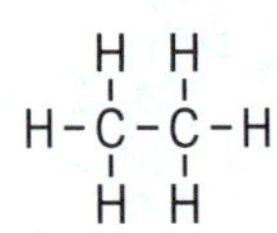

C 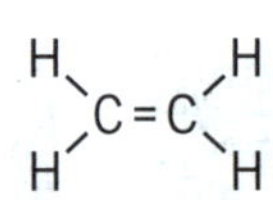

D 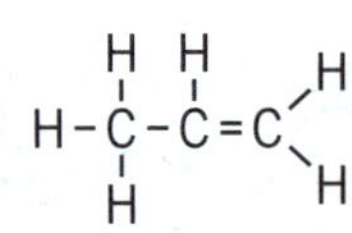

a) What is the formula of molecule A? ....

b) What is the name of molecule B? ....

c) What is the formula of substance C? ....

d) What is the name of substance D? ....

3. Crude oil can be separated into fractions.

a) What is the name of the process used to separate crude oil into fractions? ....

b) Molecules found in the diesel oil fraction contain about twenty carbon atoms. Molecules in the petrol fraction have about eight carbon atoms. Tick one box to show how petrol and diesel molecules compare.

Compared with diesel molecules, petrol molecules are:

- ❑ more flammable
- ❑ more viscous
- ❑ have a higher boiling point
- ❑ have more carbon atoms

c) Some long hydrocarbon molecules can be split into smaller, more useful molecules. What is the name of the process used to break up long hydrocarbon molecules into shorter more useful hydrocarbons?

....

4. Which of these diagrams represents a molecule of butane, C_4H_{10}?

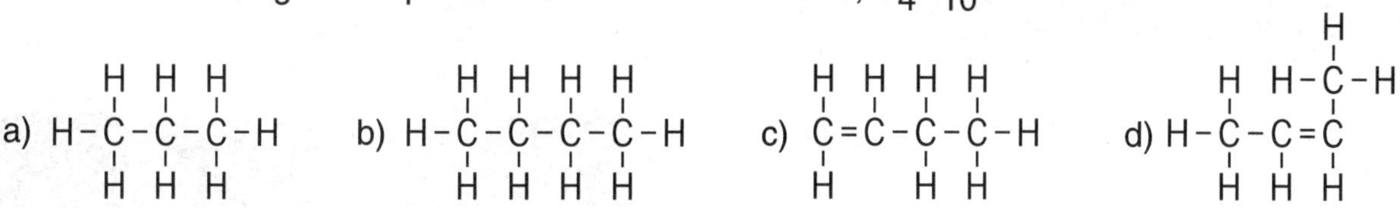

....

5. a) What is the name given to a mixture of metals? ....

b) Which non-metal element is often added to steel to make it harder? ....

6. Here is a sketch of the atoms in pure titanium.

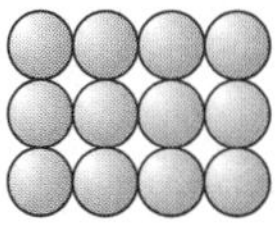

Here is a sketch of the atoms in a titanium alloy.

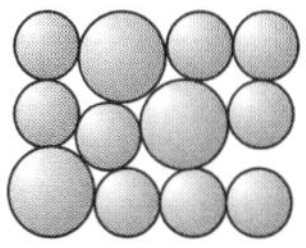

Explain why a titanium alloy is stronger than pure titanium.

7. Iron is produced in the blast furnace. Place these statements in order to show how iron is produced.

a) Carbon dioxide reacts with carbon to form carbon monoxide

b) The iron is dense and sinks to the bottom of the furnace where it can be removed.

c) Carbon reacts with oxygen to form carbon dioxide.

d) The carbon monoxide reacts with iron oxide to form iron and carbon dioxide.

....

8. This table shows the names of four different metals.

Name of metal
aluminium
iron
copper
gold

a) Which of these metals is more reactive than carbon? ....

b) Which of these metals is extracted from its ore bauxite? ....

c) Which metal can be alloyed to form steel? ....

d) Which of these metals is the least reactive? ....

Energy

We are using up our energy resources too quickly. If we continue they will soon disappear. Our high demand and use of energy may also be causing *drastic changes to our climate.* It is important that we look at these problems now and begin to find solutions before it is too late.

Cities like this need large amounts of energy

Types of energy

First, let us remind ourselves of the different **forms of energy**:

Types of energy	Sources
heat or thermal energy	hot objects, such as fires
light energy	the Sun, light bulbs, lamps, etc.
sound energy	loudspeakers, vibrating objects
electrical energy	this is carried around a circuit whenever a current flows
chemical energy	food, fuels and batteries
kinetic energy (the energy an object has because it is moving)	flowing water, wind, etc.
elastic or strain potential energy	objects such as springs and rubber bands that are stretched or twisted e.g. clockwork radio
gravitational potential energy	objects that have a high position and are able to fall e.g. water at the top of a waterfall
nuclear energy	reactions in the centre or nucleus of an atom

Energy transfer 1

When we use energy to do something for us **it does not disappear**. Energy cannot be created or destroyed. It is just **changed into other, different** forms of energy.

A **light bulb** changes **electrical energy** into **heat and light energy**.

The **motor** inside this locomotive changes **electrical energy** into **kinetic energy**.

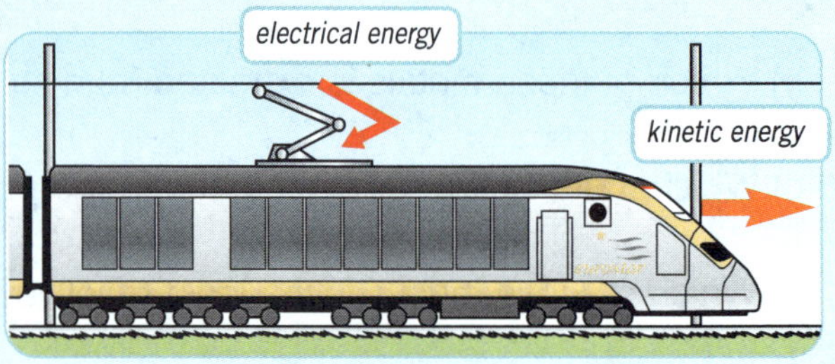

Energy transfer 2

A **loudspeaker** changes **electrical energy** into **sound energy**.

Here are some other examples of **energy changes**:

Energy in	Energy changer	Energy out
electrical	television	light, sound and heat
electrical	battery charger	chemical
electrical	electric fire	heat and light
chemical	firework	heat, light and sound
light	solar cell	electrical
kinetic	wind turbine	electrical
chemical	battery	electrical

We often use electrical devices because they will transfer energy at the flick of a switch. It is also easy to move electrical energy over large distances using wires and cables.

KEY TERMS

Make sure you understand these terms before moving on!

- energy resources
- forms of energy
- energy change
- electrical device

QUICK TEST

1. Name five different types of energy.
2. Name three devices that change electrical energy into other forms of energy.
3. Describe the energy changes which take place in the three devices you named in question 2.
4. Can you think of an electrical appliance in your house which changes electrical energy into heat, sound and kinetic energy?
5. Why is electrical energy a very convenient form of energy?
6. Give one example of where electrical energy is moved a distance of about a) 1 m, b) 10-20 m and c) more than 1 km.
7. Give two reasons why we need to reduce the amount of energy we are using.

Efficiency

Many devices take in one form of energy and transform (*change*) it into another. It is important that we know how efficiently they do this so that we can choose between them and, where possible, try to improve them.

Given the choice, most of us would probably choose the car on the left. Is it the most efficient or is just a 'gas guzzler' that wastes energy?

Energy transfer

Usually when an energy transfer takes place, only part of the energy is transformed into something useful. The remainder is **wasted**. The table below contains some examples.

The wasted energy is eventually transferred to the **surroundings**, which become warmer.

The greater the percentage of energy that is usefully transformed by a device, the more efficient the device is.

Energy input	Device	Useful energy output	Wasted energy
electrical	television	light and sound	heat
chemical	car	kinetic energy	heat and sound
electrical	electric motor	kinetic energy	heat and sound
chemical	candle	light	heat

Seeing the light 1

We use a large amount of energy to produce light at night-time. However, are the devices we are using efficient? Let us compare the **efficiency** of the traditional light bulbs with some more modern ones.

To calculate the efficiency of a transfer we use the equation:

$$\text{Efficiency} = \frac{\text{useful energy transferred by the device}}{\text{total energy supplied to the device}} \times 100\%$$

In this case, 200 J of electrical energy enter the bulb, of which 8 J is transferred into light energy and 192 J is transferred into heat.

$$\text{Efficiency} = \frac{\text{useful energy transferred by the device}}{\text{total energy supplied to the device}} \times 100\%$$

$$\text{The efficiency of the bulb} = \frac{8\text{ J}}{200\text{ J}} \times 100\% = 4\%.$$

Seeing the light 2

This is a very **inefficient energy transfer** and yet we use so many of them. Are there any alternatives? What about strip lights?

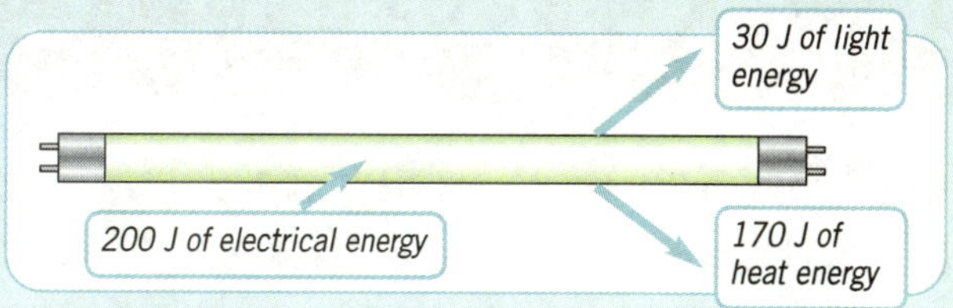

$$\text{Efficiency} = \frac{\text{useful energy transferred by the device}}{\text{total energy supplied to the device}} \times 100\%$$

$$\text{The efficiency of the fluorescent strip light} = \frac{\mathbf{30\ J}}{200\ \text{J}} \times 100\% = 15\%$$

We can see from these figures that a fluorescent strip light is much more efficient than a traditional light bulb. Nevertheless, it is still not very good and lots of work is being done to try and find better replacements. One example, which is now available in shops, is the **compact fluorescent bulb** shown below.

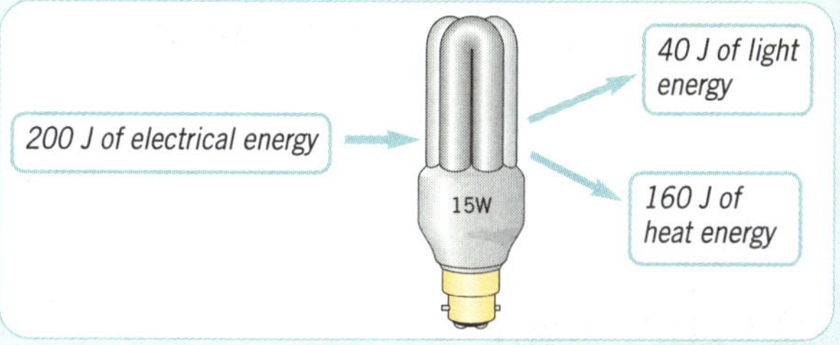

$$\text{Efficiency} = \frac{\textbf{useful energy transferred by the device}}{\text{total energy supplied to the device}} \times 100\%$$

$$\text{The efficiency of the compact fluorescent light} = \frac{\mathbf{40\ J}}{200\ \text{J}} \times 100\% = 20\%$$

Remember, an efficient device saves you money and helps protect the environment by reducing your energy consumption. An inefficient device wastes energy and helps use up our energy resources.

KEY TERMS

- wasted
- surroundings
- efficiency
- inefficient energy transfer

QUICK TEST

1. What energy transfers take place when you burn a candle? Which energy transfer wastes energy?
2. Suggest an energy transfer which takes place in an electric motor that will make it less than 100% efficient.
3. Why is it important for scientists to develop more efficient devices?
4. Calculate the efficiency of a radio that changes 200 J of electrical energy into 180 J of sound energy.
5. Calculate the efficiency of a battery charger which changes 500 J of electrical energy into 350 J of chemical energy.

Generating electricity

Most of the electrical energy we use at home is generated at *power stations*. There are several different types of power station including those that use *coal, oil or gas* as their *source of energy* (*fuel*).

Power stations

- The fuel is burned to release its **chemical energy**.
- The **heat energy released** is used to heat water and turn it into **steam**.
- The steam **turns turbines**.
- The turbines **turn large generators**.
- The **generators produce electrical energy**.
- The electrical energy is carried to our homes through the **National Grid**.

Before entering the National Grid, the electrical energy passes through step-up **transformers** which increase its voltage and decrease the current. These changes **reduce the energy losses in the cables and wires**.

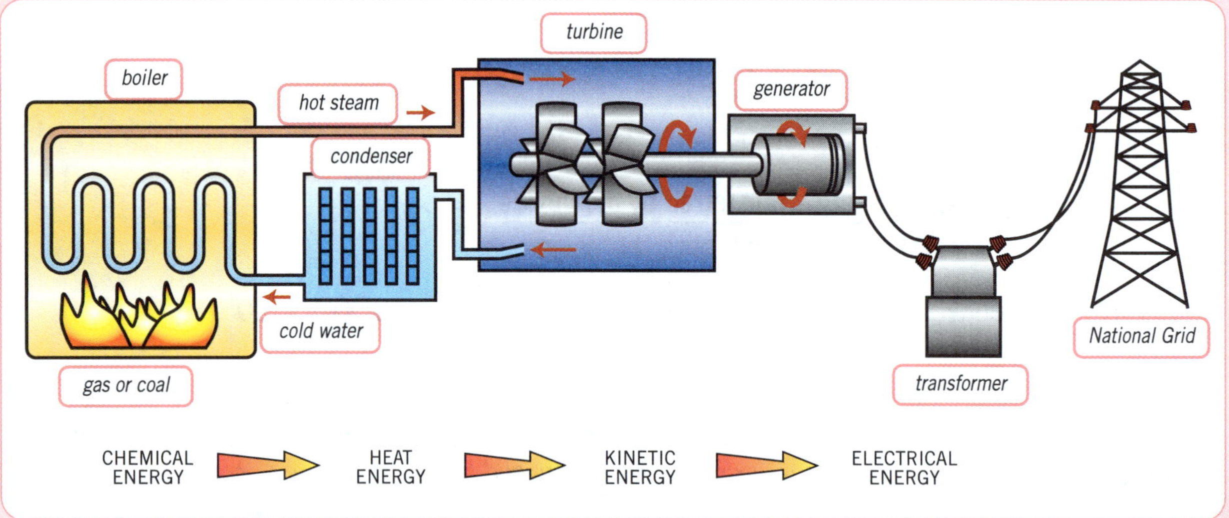

Fossil fuels 1

Coal, oil and gas are called **fossil fuels**. They are formed from **plants and animals** that died over 100 million years ago. Since they take **millions of years to form**, these fuels are called **non-renewable** fuels. Once they have been used up they **cannot be replaced**.

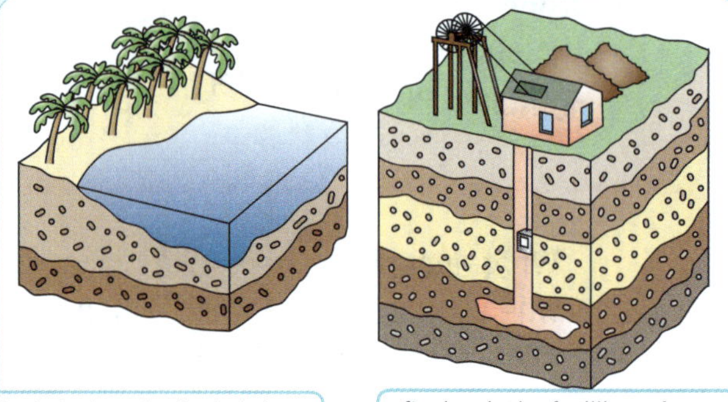

dead plants and animals being covered with mud and earth

after hundreds of millions of years they have changed into fossil fuels

The problems with fossil fuels

- When fossil fuels are burned they produce **carbon dioxide**. Increasing the amount of carbon dioxide in the atmosphere will cause the temperature of the Earth and its atmosphere to rise. **This is called the greenhouse effect and could lead to drastic changes in climate, flooding and drought.**

Fossil fuels 2

- When coal and oil are burned they produce gases that cause **acid rain**.
- **Environmental problems** are created by **mining** and **spillage of oil during transport**.
- We are using fossil fuels up very quickly and will soon have to find other sources of energy, but we need to start looking now.

The solutions

We need to slow down the rate at which we are using fossil fuels so that they will last longer. There are several ways in which we can do this:

- **Reduce petrol consumption** by driving smaller cars, using public transport or walking or cycling. We should also develop more efficient car engines.
- **Improve the insulation** to our homes and factories so less energy is wasted heating them.
- Use more **renewable sources of energy** (see page 82).

In the UK, some of our electricity is generated by nuclear power stations.

Here **uranium or plutonium** (**the fuel**) undergoes a kind of **nuclear reaction** called **fission** which releases large amounts of energy. This energy

is used to heat water, creating the steam needed to drive the turbines.

These power stations have the advantage of producing electrical energy without emitting greenhouse or other **polluting gases** and the actual cost of producing electricity is very low. There are, however, several very serious disadvantages which need to be considered:

- The building and **decommissioning** (taking out of use and demolishing) of nuclear power stations is very expensive.
- **Nuclear waste** material will remain dangerously radioactive for thousands of years.
- There is always the possibility of leaks into the atmosphere of radioactive materials.
- There is the risk of a nuclear explosion.

Be sure to mention that our society relies heavily on electricity. How we choose to generate it is important to the well being of our planet.

KEY TERMS

Make sure you understand these terms before moving on!

- source of energy
- turbine
- generator
- National Grid
- fossil fuel
- non-renewable
- greenhouse effect
- acid rain
- environmental problems
- polluting gases
- decommissioning
- nuclear waste

QUICK TEST

1. Name three fossil fuels.
2. Name a fuel which is used in some power stations but is not a fossil fuel.
3. Why are fossil fuels called non-renewable sources of energy?
4. Sweden generates most of its electricity using nuclear power stations. Give two reasons why Sweden has decided to do this even though it has fossil fuels.
5. What problems will Sweden have to deal with in the future because of this decision?

Renewable sources of energy

Unlike fossil fuels, there are some sources of energy which will not run out. They are continually being replaced. These are called *renewable sources of energy*. Each of these sources has advantages and disadvantages to their use. We need to consider all of these carefully before we make any choices.

Wind power

The **kinetic energy of the wind** is used to drive turbines and generators.

+ It is a **renewable** source of energy and therefore will not be exhausted.
+ **It has low level technology (i.e. is easy to build and fix) and therefore can be used by developing countries.**
+ **There is no atmospheric pollution.**
− **There is visual and noise pollution.**
− **They are limited to windy sites.**
− **It creates no energy if there is no wind.**

Hydroelectricity

The **kinetic energy of flowing water** is used to drive turbines and generators.

+ **It is a renewable source.**
+ Energy **can be stored** until required.
+ **There is no atmospheric pollution.**
− **There is high initial cost.**
− **There is high cost to environment**, i.e. flooding, loss of habitat.

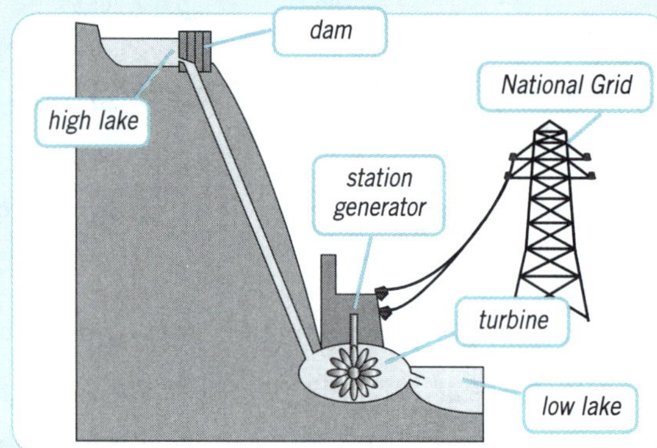

Wave power

The **rocking motion of the waves** is used to generate electricity.

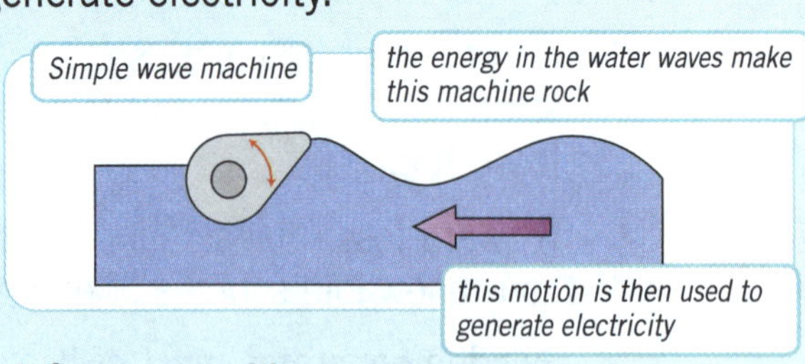

+ **It is a renewable source.**
+ **There is no atmospheric pollution.**
+ **It is useful for isolated islands.**
− **There is high initial cost.**
− **It creates visual pollution.**
− **There is poor energy capture.** Large area of machines needed even for small energy return.

Tidal power

At high tide, water is trapped behind a barrage or dam. When it is released at low tide the **gravitational potential energy of the water** changes into kinetic energy which then drives turbines and generates electricity.

+ **It is a renewable source.**
+ **It is reliable** – there are always two tides per day.
+ **There is no atmospheric pollution.**
+ **It has low running costs.**
− **There is high initial cost.**
− **It has the potential to damage the environment**, e.g. flooding.
− **It is an obstacle to water transport.**

Geothermal

In regions where the Earth's crust is thin, **hot rocks beneath the ground** can be used to heat water, turning it into steam. This steam is then used to drive turbines and generate electricity.

+ **It is a renewable source of energy.**
+ **There is no pollution and no environmental problems.**
- **There are very few suitable sites.**
- **There is a high cost of drilling deep** into the ground.

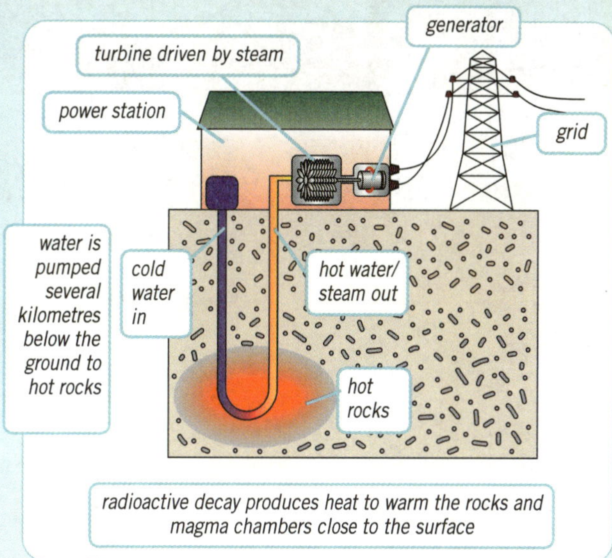

Biomass

The **chemical energy stored in 'things that have grown'**, e.g. wood, can be **released by burning** them in a power station. This energy source can be maintained by growing a succession of trees and then cropping them when they mature.

+ **It is a renewable source of energy.**
+ **It uses low level technology** and therefore useful in developing countries.
+ It does not add to the greenhouse effect as the carbon dioxide released when the trees are burned was taken from the atmosphere as they grew.
- **Large areas of land are needed** to grow sufficient numbers of trees.

Solar energy

The energy carried in the Sun's rays can be converted directly into electricity using solar cells.

The energy carried in the Sun's rays can be absorbed by dark coloured panels and used to heat water.

+ It is low maintenance.
+ There is no pollution from burning fuel.
+ There is no need for power cables.
- Initially it can be quite expensive.
- It may not be so useful in regions where there is limited sunshine.

KEY TERMS

Make sure you understand these terms before moving on!

- renewable source of energy
- wind power
- hydroelectricity
- wave power
- tidal power
- geothermal
- biomass
- solar energy

QUICK TEST

1. Name two energy resources which may pollute the environment visually.
2. Name two energy resources which could be easily used and maintained in developing countries.

Heat transfer – conduction

Heat will try to flow between two places that are at different temperatures. It will flow *from the hotter to the cooler place*. The bigger the *difference in temperature*, the faster the heat will flow.

***Conduction*, convection and radiation are three ways in which heat can move.**

Conduction is the movement of heat by passing on vibration energy.

Conduction through solids 1

After five or ten minutes, the whole length of this metal rod is hot.

Heat has been transferred along the rod by conduction.

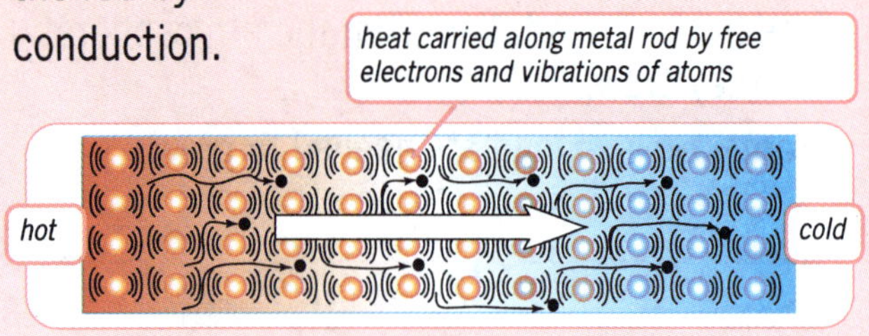

The atoms **at the hot end vibrate more violently as they gain energy from the fire. These vibrations transfer energy from the hot end to the cooler end of the rod.**

All metals are good **conductors** of heat because their particles are close together and can pass on their vibrations easily.

Non-metals are usually poor conductors of heat because their particles are unable to pass on their vibrations.

An **insulator** is a material which does not allow heat to travel through it easily. Insulators are used to prevent or reduce heat transfer.

Let us have a look at some examples of heat transfer in the home.

A good saucepan is made from materials that are **conductors** and **insulators**.

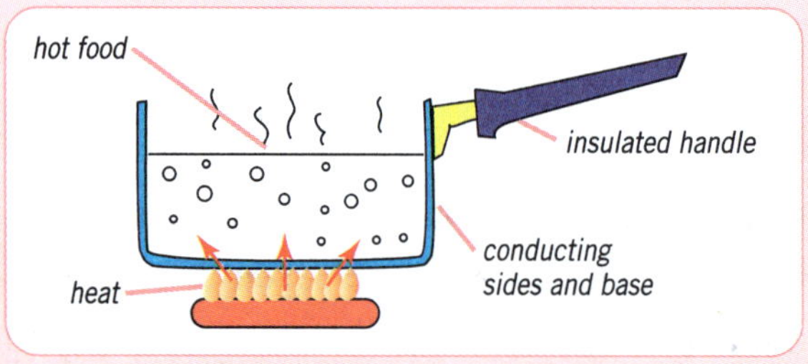

The base and sides of the pan are made of metal so that heat is easily conducted from the flame to the food. The handle is made from an insulator so that it does not become too hot to hold.

The particles in a gas are far apart. It is therefore very difficult for heat to pass through a gas by conduction. Gases are in fact excellent **insulators** and are often used in situations where we want to prevent the flow of heat.

From the above, you should also realise that it is impossible for heat to travel through a vacuum by conduction, as it contains no particles.

Woven materials, e.g. wool and cotton, contain lots of **trapped air** and so are excellent **insulators**. This is why they keep you warm.

Glass fibre is an excellent insulator because it contains large amounts of **trapped air**. It is placed in the loft to **reduce heat loss** through the roof.

Conduction through solids 2

It is the layer of air trapped between the two panes of glass that make **double glazing** an excellent method of reducing heat loss from a house.

Double glazing reduces heat loss from a house. It is the layer of air trapped between the two panes of glass that makes it difficult for the heat to escape

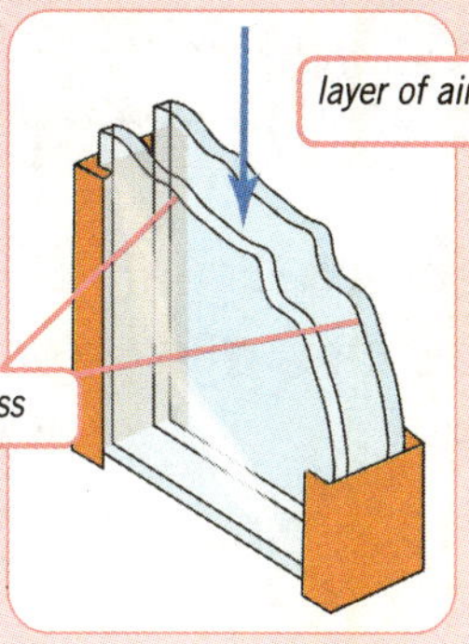

Insulating the home

This diagram shows how heat may escape from a house that has not been insulated.

The cost of insulating your home

The table on the right shows the cost of the different types of insulation that can be used in the home and the annual savings that might result from each.

Type of insulation	Typical cost (£s)	Typical annual saving (£s)	Payback time (years)
double glazing	3000	50	60
cavity wall	500	100	5
loft insulation	250	125	2
draft excluders	100	20	5

Make sure you understand the idea of cost effectiveness. A question about the cost effectiveness of different types of insulation is asking, 'How quickly will the savings pay for the extra insulation?' It is not asking which is the best insulator.

KEY TERMS

Make sure you understand these terms before moving on!

- temperature difference
- conduction
- conductor
- insulator
- double glazing
- cavity wall
- draught excluder
- cost effectiveness

QUICK TEST

1. What is a conductor?
2. Give one example and one use of a good conductor.
3. What is an insulator?
4. Give one example and one use of a good insulator.
5. What is double glazing?
6. Suggest five methods by which you could reduce the heat escaping from your house.

Heat transfer – convection

When we turn on the burners, the air inside a balloon is warmed and *expands*. As a result, it rises carrying its extra energy with it. If we turn the burners off, the air cools and *contracts*. It is now more *dense* and so begins to fall. This movement of air, because of its expansion and contraction, is called a *convection current* and can transfer energy from place to place.

Rising warm air will lift these balloons into the sky. But what will happen when the air cools?

Heating a room by convection

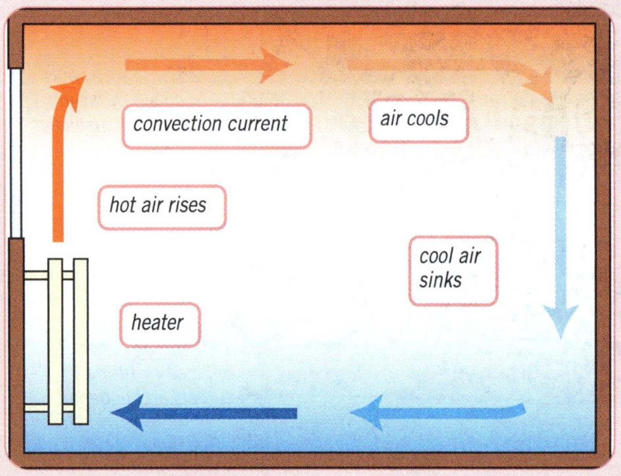

The energy is transferred to all parts of this room by convection.

The traditional open fire that we like to sit in front of is not very efficient at warming a room. It creates convection currents which transfer a lot of heat up the chimney and then it escapes to the surroundings. Modern gas fires and convector heaters are far more efficient.

Cavity walls 1

Many older homes have **cavity walls** which contain just air. Air is a good insulator and so reduces heat loss by conduction. However, heat can cross the gap if a convection current is set up.

To prevent this from happening, we can inject foam insulation into the cavity. The foam contains lots of trapped air which is unable to move and so cannot form a convection current.

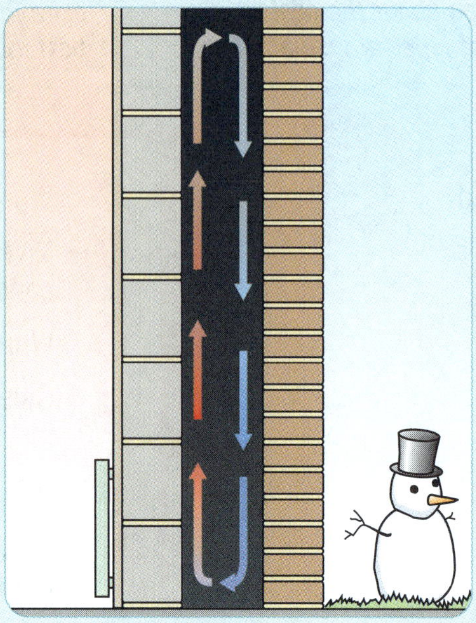

Injecting foam insulation into the cavity

Cavity walls 2

In modern houses, solid foam insulation boards are placed inside the cavity as the house is being built.

Solid insulation boards are now built in

Sea breezes

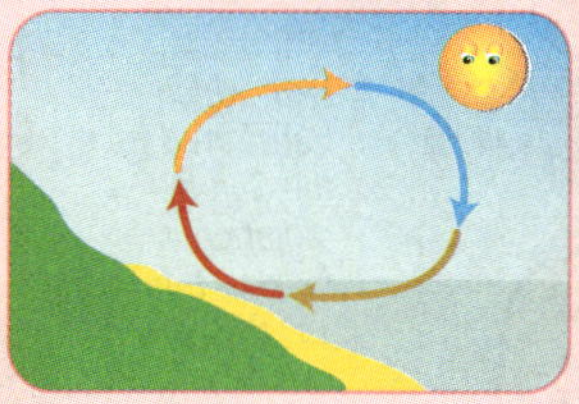

During the daytime, the land is hotter than the sea and an onshore breeze is set up

During the night, the sea is warmer than the land and an offshore breeze is set up

It is a common mistake to write that heat rises. It is better to say that, when warmed, a gas becomes less dense and rises, taking heat energy with it.

Convection currents in ovens and fridges

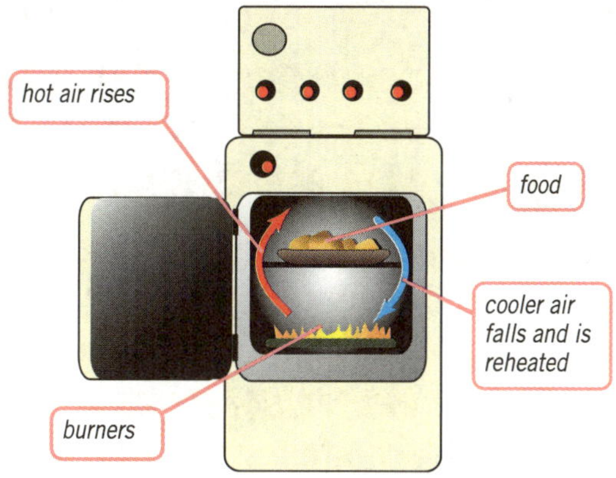

To heat the whole of an oven, the heat source must be at the bottom

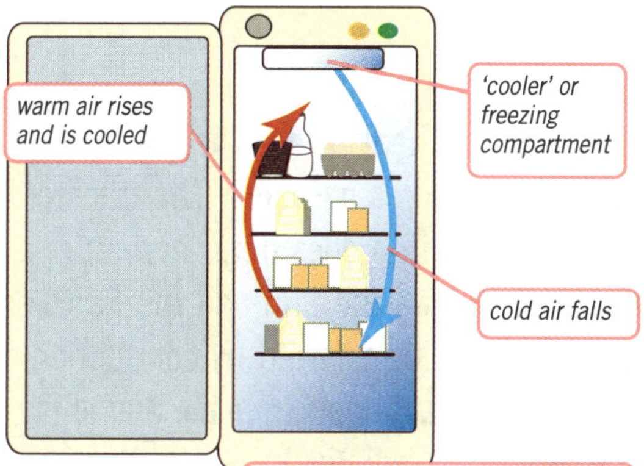

To cool the whole of a fridge, the cooler must be placed at the top

KEY TERMS

Make sure you understand these terms before moving on!

- expand
- contract
- dense
- convection current

QUICK TEST

1. Why are traditional open fires inefficient?
2. Why should foam be placed inside a cavity wall?
3. The diagram on the right shows some simple mine workings. It is important the miners get a good supply of fresh air but pumps have not yet been invented.

The mine owners solve this problem by lighting a fire under one of the shafts. Explain in your own words how this solves the problem.

HEAT TRANSFER – CONVECTION

Physics

Heat transfer – radiation

All bodies *emit* and absorb thermal *radiation*.

Thermal radiation is the transfer of heat by *electromagnetic waves* (infrared). The hotter the body, the more energy it *radiates*.

The photograph on the right is called a *thermogram*. It was taken using the radiation emitted by the building. The *different colours indicate different temperatures*. The lighter colours are the hottest parts of the building. The coldest parts are blue.

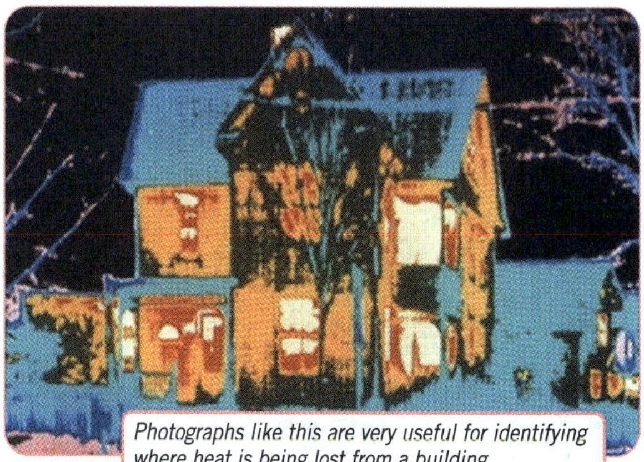

Photographs like this are very useful for identifying where heat is being lost from a building

Heat from the Sun

The transfer of heat by conduction or convection **requires particles**. The transfer of energy by radiation does not. There are no particles between the Sun and the Earth so heat cannot be transferred by conduction or convection. **Heat travels from the Sun to the Earth as waves (radiation).**

Heat which is transferred from the Sun by radiation is making this young girl too hot

Absorption or reflection

When radiation strikes an object, it can be a) **absorbed** or b) **reflected**. Which depends upon the nature of the surface of the object.

Radiation can be reflected back into a room by placing a sheet of aluminium foil behind the radiator

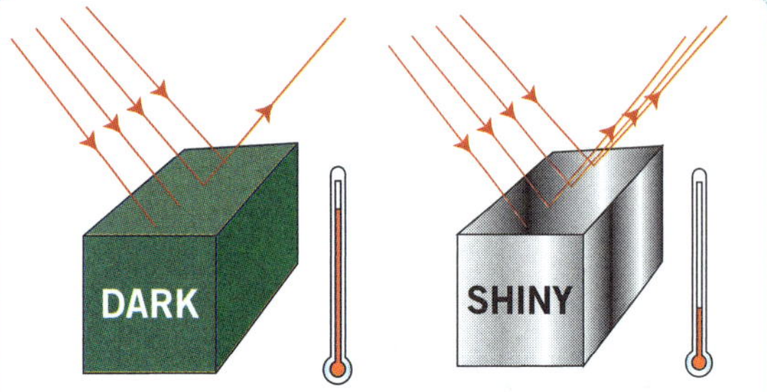

*Objects with **dark, rough surfaces** absorb most of the radiation and become warmer*

*Objects with **light-coloured, shiny surfaces** reflect most of the radiation and will remain cooler*

In hot countries where fuel is scarce, food can be cooked using a solar heater like the one shown below.

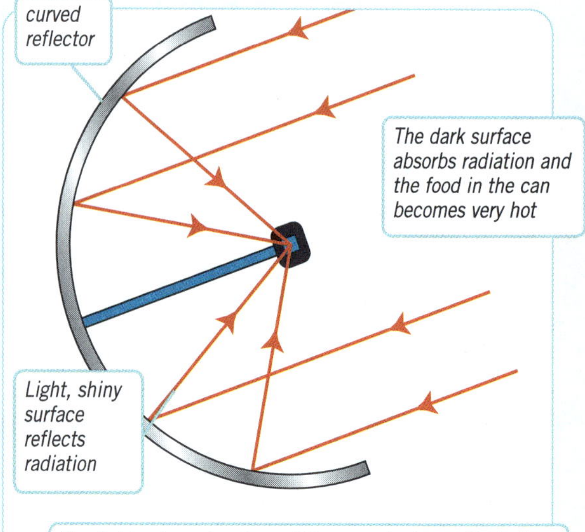

The light-coloured surface of the curved mirror reflects the heat. The dark matt surface of the can absorbs the heat

Emitting radiation

How much radiation an object emits depends upon a) its temperature and b) the nature of its surface.

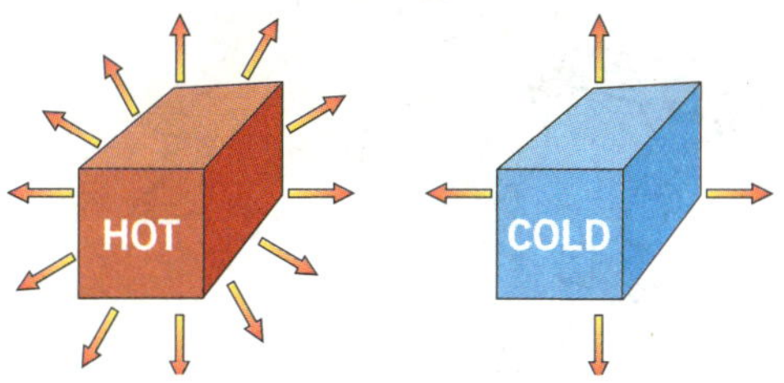

Warm objects give off (emit) heat radiation more than cold objects

Light shiny surfaces emit less radiation than dark surface as this simple experiment shows

After 20 minutes the water in the black teapot is cooler as it has emitted more radiation

When wrapped in these shiny space blankets athletes will emit less radiation and so will lose body heat more slowly

Heat transfer to and from bodies

The shape and size of a body affects the rate at which it gains or loses energy. The smaller the surface area, the lower the rate of heat transfer.

Remember that good emitters of radiation are also good absorbers of radiation.

When animals are cold, they try to curl up to reduce the surface area through which they are losing heat

KEY TERMS

Make sure you understand these terms before moving on!

- emit
- radiation
- radiates
- thermogram
- absorption
- reflection
- emitter
- absorber

QUICK TEST

1. What kind of radiation is emitted by a hot object?
2. How do we know that heat travels from the Sun to Earth by radiation?
3. What two things might happen when radiation strikes an object?
4. What kind of a surface should an object, which is a good absorber of radiation, have?
5. What kind of a surface should an object, which is a very poor absorber of radiation, have?
6. What is a thermogram?
7. Why might people in very hot sunny countries paint their houses white?

Electrical power

All *electrical appliances* transfer *electrical energy* into *other forms.*

- A *hairdryer* transfers *electrical energy* into *heat, kinetic and some sound energy.*
- A *radio* transfers *electrical energy* into *sound energy.*

The *power* of an appliance is a measure of how quickly these energy *changes take place*. This *power rating* is *measured in watts.*

The meaning of power

If a light bulb has a **power rating of 40 W**, it **transfers 40 J of electrical energy** into heat and light energy **every second**.

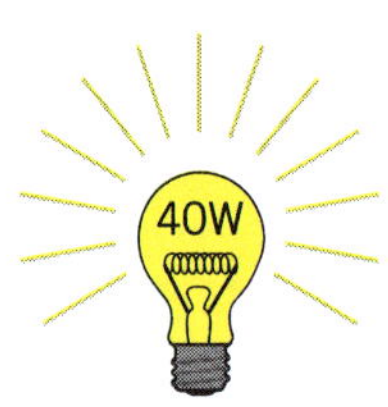

If an electrical fire has a **power rating of 2 kW** (2000 W) it **transfers 2000 J of electrical energy** into 2000 J of heat and light energy **every second**.

How many joules of energy have been changed?

To calculate the total amount of energy an appliance has changed we use the equation

Energy = Power x time (in seconds)

or **E = P x t**

Example

How much electrical energy is changed into heat and light energy when a 60 W bulb is turned on for 30 s?

E = P x t = 60 W x 30 s = 1800 J

Kilowatt-hours and units

The electricity board measures the energy we use in the home in **kilowatt-hours** or **units**.

They calculate this value using the formula:

Energy use in kilowatt-hours	**=**	**power in kilowatts x time in hours**

Example

Calculate the energy used when a 3 kW fire is turned on for 2 h.

E = P x t = 3 kW x 2 h = 6 kWh or 6 units

The meter and the bill

Somewhere in your house is a **meter** like the one shown above. It shows how many units of **electrical energy have been used**.

We usually pay our electricity bills every three months, i.e. every quarter.

By reading the meter at the beginning and end of the quarter we can calculate how many units of electrical energy have been used.

The bill shows the **number of units used** and **the cost per unit**.

By multiplying these two values together we can obtain the cost of the electrical energy used.

The electricity board will also add to your bill a **standing charge**. This pays for the equipment used by the electricity board in bringing the electricity into your home and its maintenance.

Example

The readings on an electricity meter at the beginning and end of a quarter show that a family has used 800 units. If the cost of one unit is 11p and the standing charge per quarter is £12, calculate the total bill for this household.

Cost of electricity = number of units used x cost per unit = 800 x 11p = £88.00
If the standing charge is £12 the total cost of the bill is £88.00 + £12 = £100

ELECTRICITY BILL

Charges for electricity used

Present reading	Previous reading	Units used	Pence per unit	Charge amount
80139	78579	800	11.00	£171.60
Quarterly standing charge				£12.00
Total				£183.60

KEY TERMS

Make sure you understand these terms before moving on!

- electrical appliance
- power
- joule (J)
- watt (W)
- kilowatt (kW)
- unit

QUICK TEST

1. How many kilowatt-hours (units) of electrical energy are converted into other forms in the following situations?
   a) 3 kW fire turned on for 3 hours
   b) 2 kW tumble dryer used for 30 minutes
   c) 1.5 kW water heater turned on for 2 hours
   d) 500 W TV turned on for 4 hours
   e) 100 W radio turned on for 10 hours.

Waves

Waves **transfer energy by vibrations. There are two main types of waves. These are** ***transverse waves*** **and** ***longitudinal waves*****.**

A transverse wave has vibrations across or at ***right angles*** **to the direction in which the wave is moving.**

Examples of transverse waves include light waves and surface water waves.

A ***longitudinal*** **wave has vibrations that are** ***along*** **the direction in which the wave is moving.**

A transverse wave

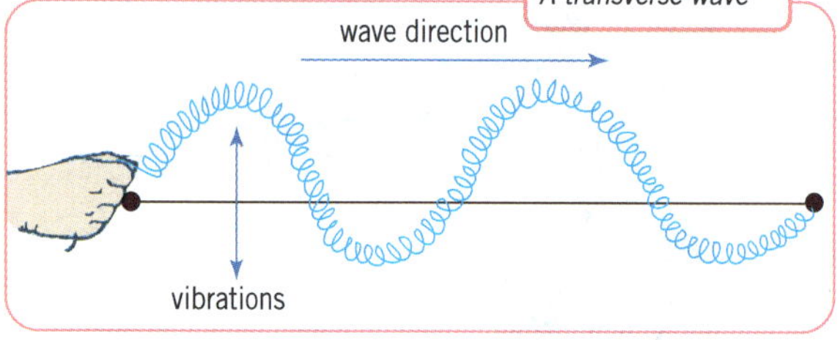

A longitudinal wave

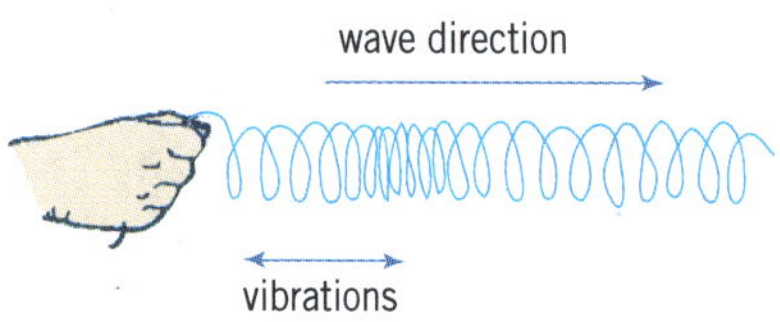

Properties of waves

The **amplitude** of a wave is the **height of a crest** or depth of a trough from the **undisturbed position**. The **wavelength** of a wave is the distance between successive crests.

A graph showing a current's wavelength and amplitude

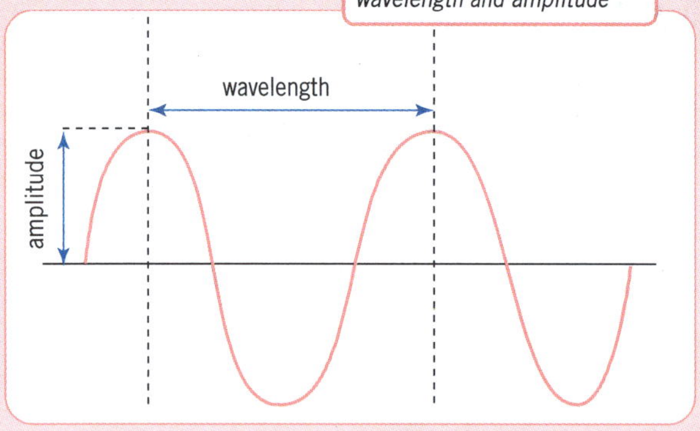

The **frequency** of a wave is the number of complete waves produced each second by the source. It is measured in hertz (**Hz**). A wave has a frequency of 200 Hz if the source is producing 200 waves each second.

The velocity of a wave (v), its frequency (f) and its wavelength (λ) are related by the equation

$$v = f \times \lambda$$

Example

A sound wave has a frequency of 170 Hz and a wavelength of 2 m. Calculate the velocity of this wave.

$$v = f \times \lambda = 170 \times 2 = 340 \text{ m/s}$$

The electromagnetic spectrum 1

Electromagnetic radiations are vibrations in an electric field. They travel as waves. This large **family of waves** has lots of **common properties**.

- They are all **able to travel through a vacuum**.
- They all **travel at the same speed** through a vacuum, i.e. the speed of light.
- They are all **transverse waves**.
- They all **transfer energy**.
- They can all be **reflected, absorbed, transmitted, refracted and diffracted**.

Some of the **properties** of these waves **change** as their **wavelength and frequency** change. The family is therefore divided into seven smaller groups.

The electromagnetic spectrum 2

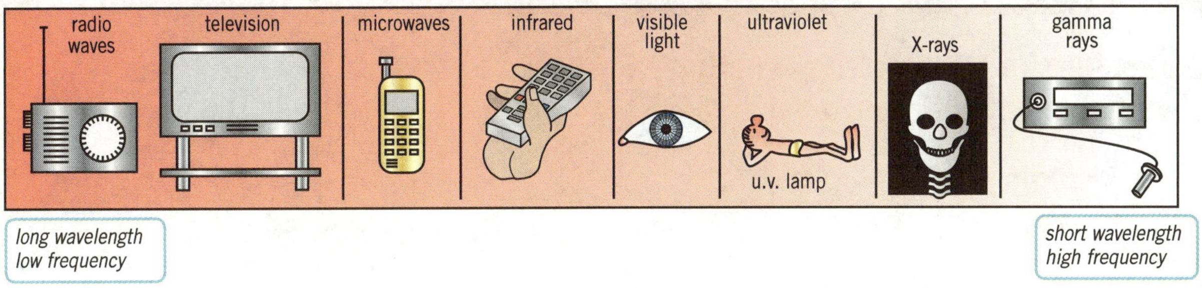

Biological effects of exposure to electromagnetic waves

Radio waves	No known effect
Microwaves	These are absorbed by water molecules causing body tissue to warm. Large doses can cause burns. The rapid increase in the usage of mobile phones and the erection of microwave transmitter masts close to communities is causing concern over the possible long term effects of **exposure** to microwaves.
Infrared	Overexposure can cause burning to the skin.
Visible light	This causes the chemical changes on the retina of the eye which makes vision possible. Overexposure, e.g. looking directly at the Sun, can cause damage to the retina resulting in impaired vision or blindness.
Ultra violet	These cause chemical changes in the skin resulting in tanning and premature aging. Excessive exposure will result in sunburn and possibly skin cancer. Sun blocks prevent all the radiation from reaching the skin.
X-rays	These are highly penetrating rays which can cause cancer and kill living cells. Workers exposed to X-rays, e.g. radiographers, wear lead aprons or stand behind lead screens, as X-rays cannot penetrate lead.
Gamma rays	Emitted by some radioactive materials, they are also very penetrating and can cause cancer and kill living cells.

Try to remember that the effect of exposure to radiation depends on the type of radiation and how much radiation is received.

KEY TERMS

Make sure you understand these terms before moving on!

- wave
- transverse wave
- longitudinal wave
- amplitude
- wavelength
- frequency
- electromagnetic spectrum
- transmission
- exposure

QUICK TEST

1. What do waves carry from place to place?
2. Explain the phrase, 'a wave has a frequency of 25 Hz'.
3. Give one example of a) a transverse wave and b) a longitudinal wave.
4. A water wave has a frequency of 5 Hz and a wavelength of 3 m. Calculate the velocity of this wave.
5. Name two properties all electromagnetic waves have in common.
6. Name two features of electromagnetic waves that change as we move from group to group.

The electromagnetic spectrum

The members of the electromagnetic spectrum are used in many different ways.

Radio waves

- Used for **communicating over large distances**.
- Short wavelength radio waves are used for television broadcasting and FM radio.
- Longer wavelength radio waves are used for traditional AM radio.

Infrared waves

Also known as heat radiation.

Infrared waves are **given out by all objects**. The hotter they are, the more radiation they emit.

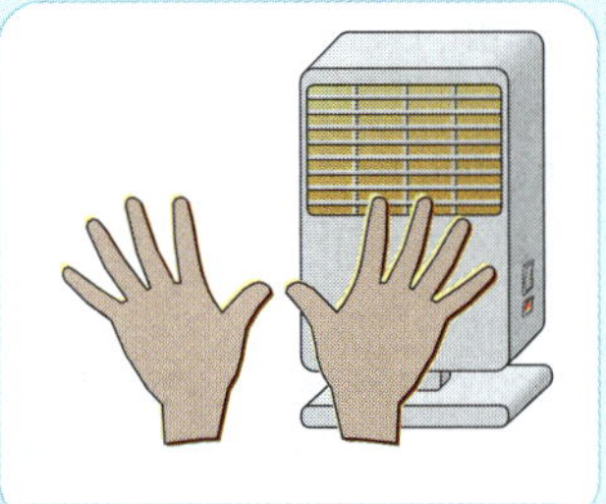

Warm objects give off infrared waves which our skin can detect

Our skin can sense or detect the infrared waves.

Over**exposure** causes **sunburn**, but not tanning.

Infrared waves are used to **'see in the dark'**. Special **'heat seeking'** cameras **create images** of objects **using the infrared waves they are emitting**. These are often used by the emergency services to detect people trapped in collapsed buildings or lost in mountains or on moors.

Remote controls for TVs, radios, etc. use infrared waves to carry instructions.

infrared waves carry the instructions from the remote to the TV

Microwaves

Some microwaves pass easily through the Earth's atmosphere and so are used for **communications via satellites**, e.g. **mobile phones**.

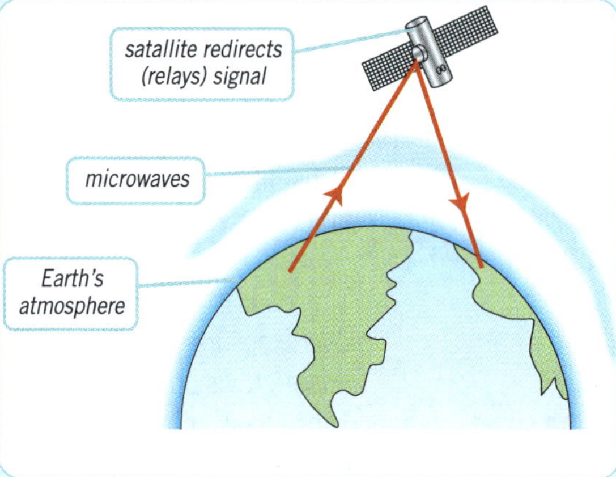

Some are used for **cooking**, e.g. **microwave ovens**.

food absorbs microwaves

Water molecules inside food absorb microwaves.

They become 'hot', cooking the food from the inside.

Microwaves can be dangerous if misused. They **can cause damage to living cells**.

Visible light

We use these waves **to see**.
It is the one part of the electromagnetic spectrum to which our **eyes are sensitive**.
Visible light is used to carry messages down **optical fibres**.

Ultraviolet

Ultraviolet waves are **emitted by the Sun**.

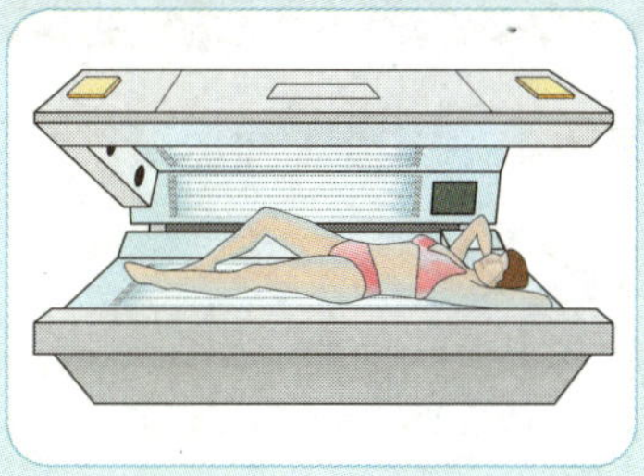

They **cause our skins to tan**.

Over exposure to ultraviolet waves **can lead to skin cancer**.

Certain chemicals when exposed to ultraviolet **fluoresce** (**glow**).

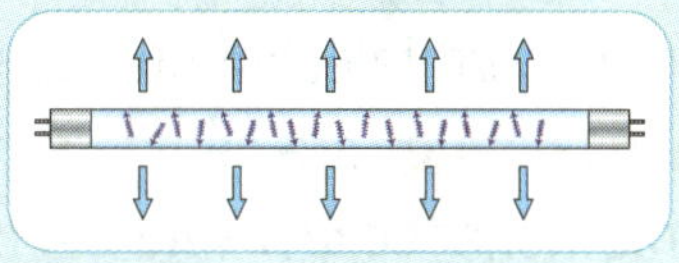

Words written with security markers are only visible in ultraviolet light.

Ultraviolet light can be used to detect forged banks notes by fluorescence.

X-rays

X-rays have a very **short wavelength** and a very **high frequency**.

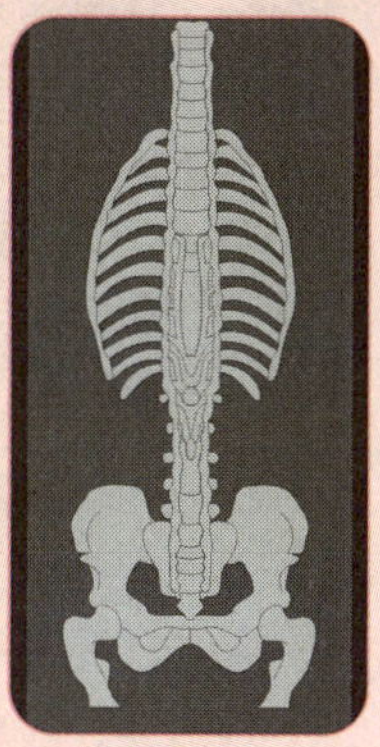

They are **highly penetrating**.

They are used to look for damaged bones inside the body.

Overexposure can cause cancer. Radiographers therefore **stand behind lead screens** or **wear lead aprons** to **prevent over exposure**.

They used to be used to **monitor the development of the foetus in the womb** during pregnancy, but **ultrasound** is used now as it is **less likely to cause any damage** to the unborn baby.

Gamma rays

These are **very penetrating waves** which are **emitted by some radioactive materials**.

They can be used to kill harmful bacteria, e.g. sterilise surgical equipment.

If used correctly they can be used to kill certain kinds of cancer (radiotherapy).

Incorrect exposure/**dosage** can **damage living cells and cause cancer**.

Try to remember at least one use for each of the groups of waves that make up the electromagnetic spectrum. Knowing a use will help you remember any special properties that a group of waves has. Also try to remember the possible dangers of overexposure associated with each.

QUICK TEST

1. Name three groups of waves that can be used for communications.
2. Name two groups of waves that can be used for cooking.
3. Name three groups of waves that might cause cancer.
4. Name one group of waves that can be used to treat cancer.
5. Name two types of waves we as human beings can sense.
6. Name one source of gamma waves.
7. Why are microwaves rather than radio waves used in satellite communication systems?
8. Why are X-rays no longer used to monitor the development of a foetus in the womb?

KEY TERMS

Make sure you understand these terms before moving on!

- exposure
- fluoresce
- highly penetrating
- dosage

Analogue and digital signals

This spread explains why in modern telecommunication systems:

a) optical fibres are replacing traditional copper wires and

b) information is now being transmitted as digital signals rather than *analogue signals.*

Total internal reflection and optical fibres

When a ray of light enters a glass block at an angle, it **slows down** and bends towards **the normal**. This change in direction is called **refraction**. When the ray emerges from the block it **speeds up** and bends **away from the normal**.

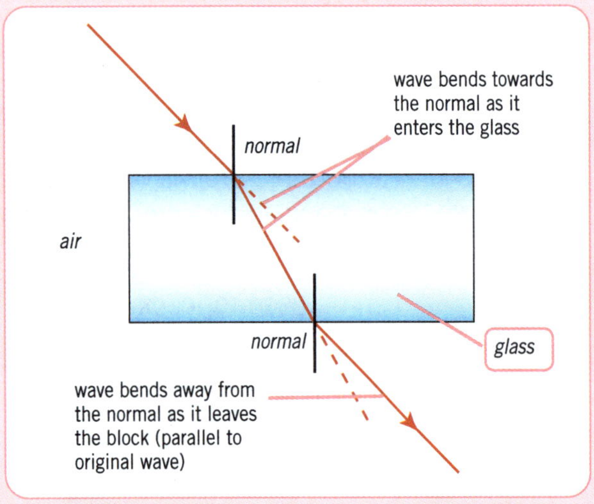

If a ray leaving a glass block strikes the boundary at an angle **greater than the critical angle, total internal reflection** takes place, i.e. the ray is not refracted but reflected.

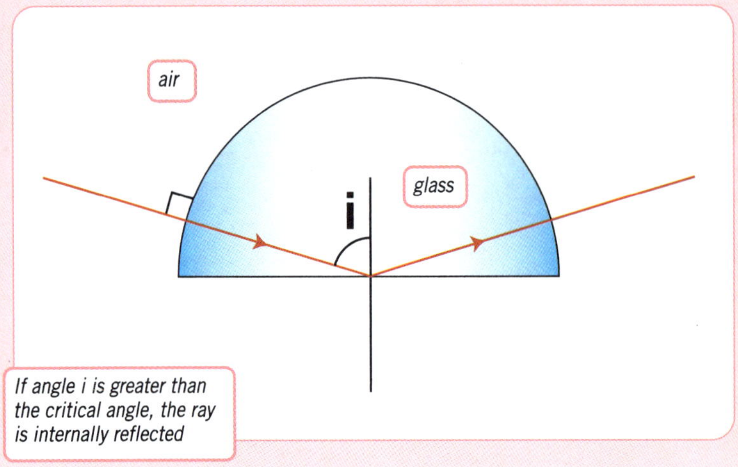

In modern telecommunications systems, **optical fibres** are being used to replace traditional **copper wires** to carry signals. The light signals in optical fibres undergo total internal reflection.

An optical fibre has a **high density glass for its core** and a **less dense glass as an outer coating**. The fibre is so narrow that light entering at one end will always strike the boundary between the two glasses at an angle greater than the critical angle. It will therefore undergo a **series of total internal reflections** before emerging at the far end.

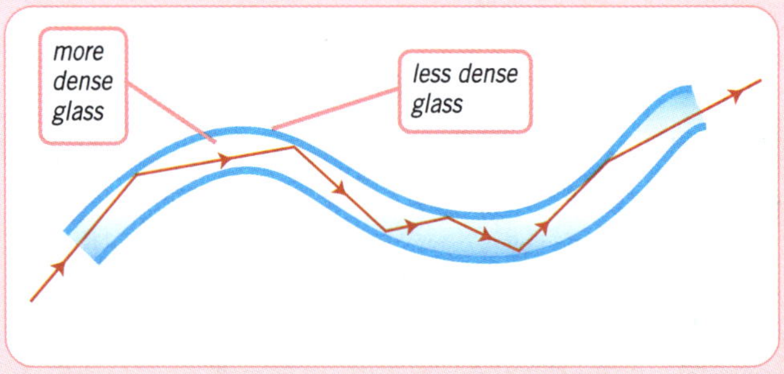

Advantages of using optical fibres

The fibres are cheaper than copper wires.

They are lighter.

They can carry more signals.

The signals they carry are more secure.

Communicating using analogue signals

As radio waves and microwaves travel from an emitter towards a receiver, there may be some **loss in signal strength**. To ensure a strong signal arrives at the receiver, it may be **amplified** several times at **repeater stations**.

Analogue signals vary continuously. When they are amplified at repeater stations, any **distortions** (**noise**) which has been added to the wave during its journey will also be **amplified**. If the noise is considerable, the final signal received may be very different from the original and therefore difficult to understand.

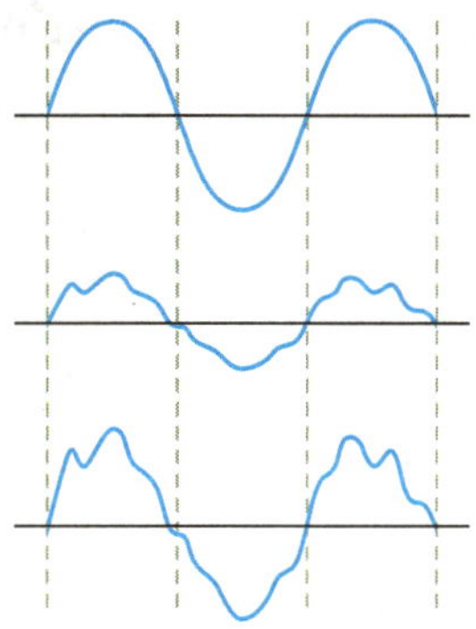

Analogue

Communicating using digital signals

Digital signals have only two values – 1 and 0. An analogue signal can be converted into a digital signal, i.e. its continuously changing shape can be described by a **code consisting of just 1s and 0s**. This code can then be transmitted. When the weakened signal arrives at a repeater station it is easy to recognise, even with lots of noise, those parts of the signal which should be a 1 and those that should be a 0. These are processed and amplified, producing a **perfect copy of the original**. At the receiver the digital code is converted back into the analogue signal, but without any noise distortion, i.e. the signal is very clear.

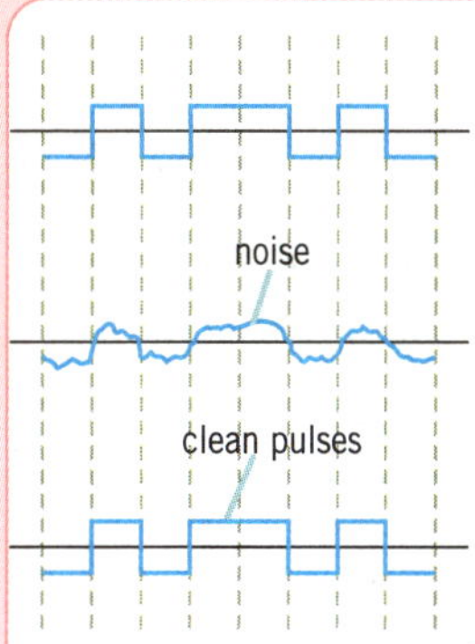

Digital

A second advantage of using digital signals is that they are already in a form which can be processed by computers.

KEY TERMS

- repeater station
- analogue signal
- noise
- digital signal
- refraction
- critical angle
- total internal reflection
- optical fibre

QUICK TEST

1. Why is light unable to escape through the sides of an optical fibre?
2. Name two different types of waves which might carry a signal along an optical fibre.
3. Give three reasons why optical fibres are replacing copper wires in telecommunications networks.

Nuclear radiations

The nuclei of some atoms are unstable. As a result they give out radiation all the time in order to become more stable. **These substances are said to be *radioactive*. There are three types of radiation which might be emitted. These are called *alpha, beta and gamma* radiation.**

These nuclear radiations can be very useful. They can also be very dangerous. It is therefore important that we understand their properties.

It is the nuclei of atoms that emit different types of radiation

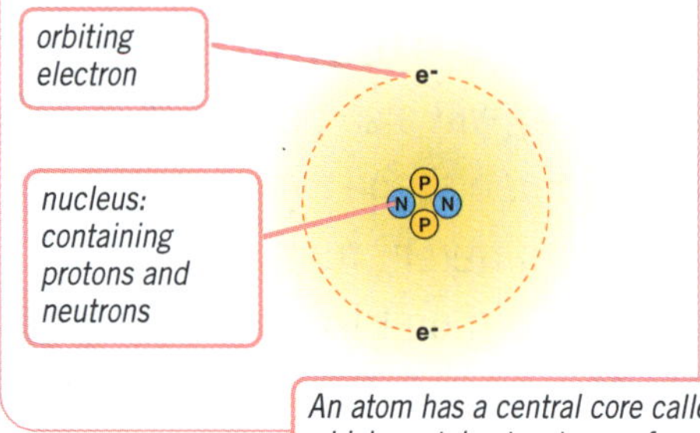

An atom has a central core called a nucleus which contains two types of particles called protons and neutrons. Very small particles called electrons orbit the nucleus

Alpha radiation (α)

Alpha particles are **slow moving helium nuclei**, i.e. they consist of **two protons and two neutrons**. They are **big and heavy** and so have **poor penetration** (just a few centimetres in air). They collide with lots of atoms **knocking some of their electrons off** and **creating ions**. They are **very good ionisers**.

An ion is an atom which has become charged by either losing or gaining electrons.

They are **positively charged** and so can be **deflected by electric and magnetic fields**.

How the actions of ions produce alpha particles

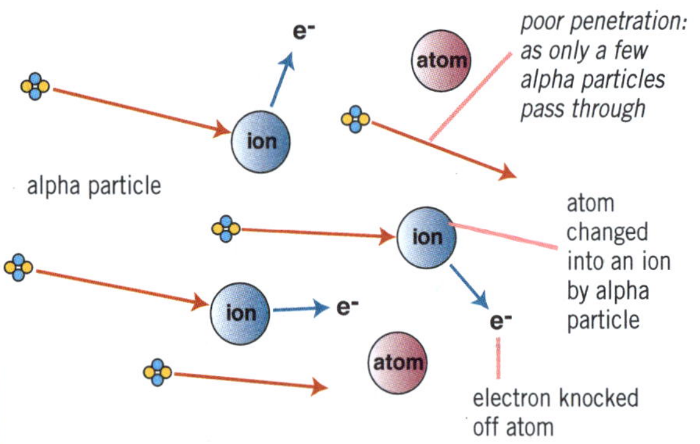

Beta radiation (β)

These are **fast moving electrons**.

They are small and therefore have **quite good penetrating powers** (up to about a metre in air).

They do collide with atoms and produce ions, but not as many as the alpha particles.

They are **negatively charged** and so can be **deflected by electric and magnetic fields**.

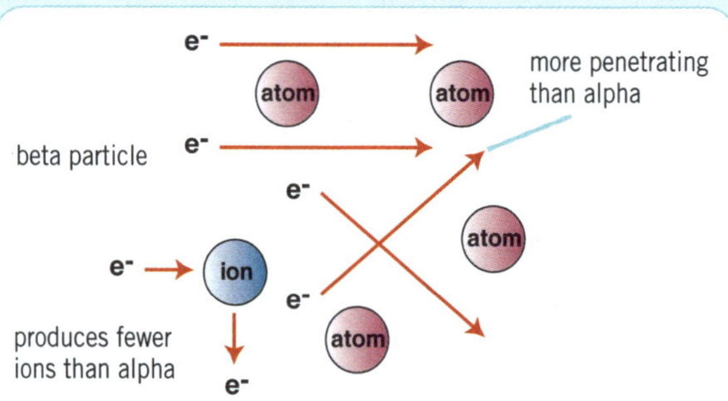

Gamma rays (γ)

These are **short wavelength electromagnetic waves**, similar to X-rays.

They **travel at the speed of light** and are **very penetrating** (can travel almost unlimited distances through air).

They don't hit many atoms as they travel through a material and so are **very poor ionisers**.

Gamma radiation **carries no charge** and so is **unaffected by magnetic and electric fields**.

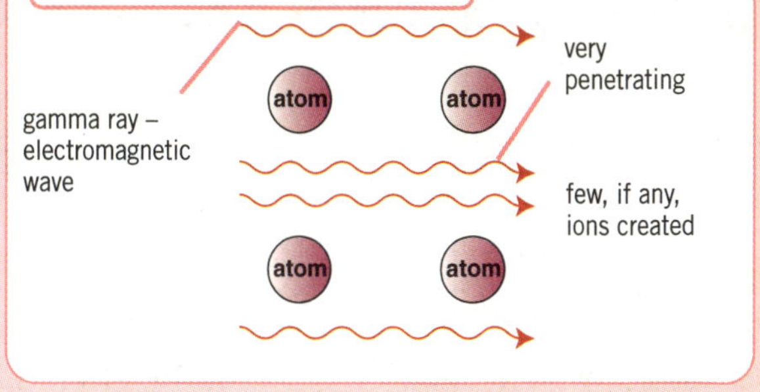

Comparison of the properties of alpha, beta and gamma radiation

Radiation	α	β	γ
Mass	4	negligible (1/2000)	0
Charge	+2	–1	0
Relative ionising power	100 000	1000	1
Approximate penetrating power in air	1–5 cm	10-80 cm	almost unlimited

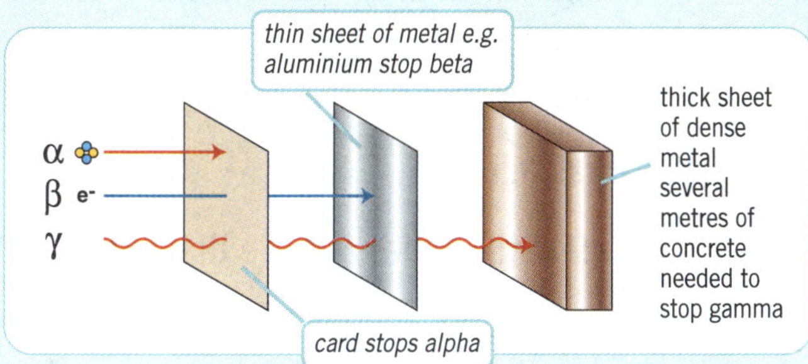

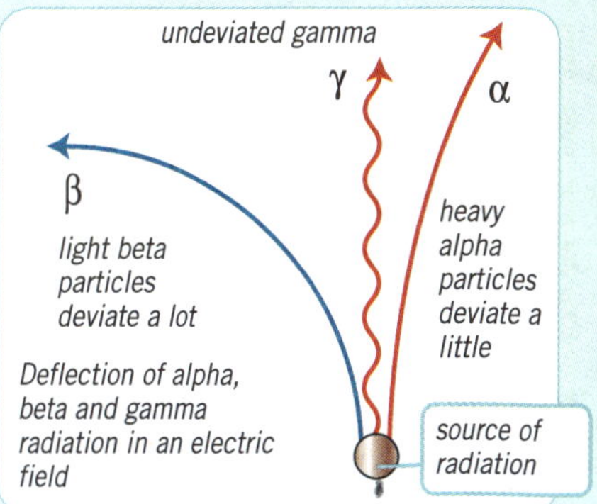

Deflection of alpha, beta and gamma radiation in an electric field

KEY TERMS

Make sure you understand these terms before moving on!

- unstable nucleus
- radioactive ion
- ioniser
- deflection
- penetrating power

QUICK TEST

1. Why do some nuclei give out radiation?
2. Why is it important that we understand the properties of alpha, beta and gamma radiation?
3. Which type of radiation:
   a) is most penetrating
   b) is the best ioniser
   c) is negatively charged
   d) is a fast moving electron
   e) is an electromagnetic wave?

Radioactivity and half life

There are radioactive substances all around us.

Some of them are manmade and used in hospitals, nuclear power stations and even in the home.

Sources of radioactivity

Most of the radioactive substances around us are naturally occurring. They are in the ground, in the food we eat, they are even in the air we breathe. Some radiation reaches us from space. The radiation produced by these sources is called **background radiation**.

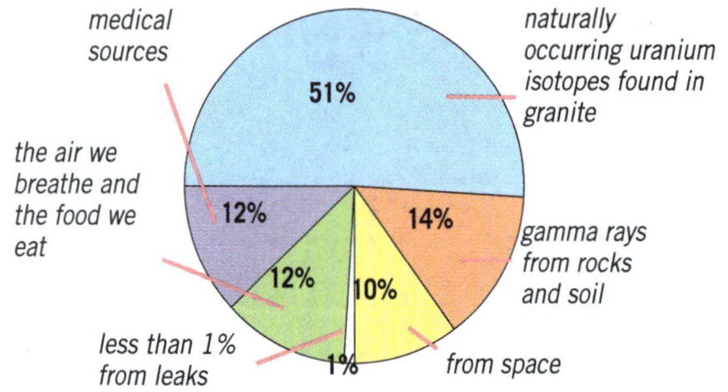

Sources of background radiation

Exposure to radiation

Absorption of any of the three types of radiation by living cells is potentially dangerous.

It may cause **cell damage** and lead to illnesses such as **cancer**. Higher levels of exposure to these radiations may **kill living cells**. It is therefore important that measures are taken to **reduce our exposure to nuclear radiation**.

Those at most risk, e.g. workers in the nuclear industry, radiographers etc., wear **radiation badges**. These contain photographic film which when developed show the **degree of exposure** to radiation for that worker.

Other ways in which exposure to radiation can be reduced are:

1 wearing protective clothing

Film badge dosimeter for monitoring exposure to radiation

2 handling radioactive materials at a distance, e.g. using tongs

3 limiting exposure time.

Nuclear radiation

Exposure from sources outside the body

- In these situations alpha radiation is the least dangerous as it is the least penetrating and unlikely to pass through the skin.
- Beta and gamma radiations are more dangerous because they are more penetrating. They may pass through the skin and cause cell damage inside the body.

Exposure from sources inside the body

- In these situations, alpha is the most dangerous radiation as it is most strongly absorbed by living cells and therefore causes most damage.
- Beta and gamma radiations are still dangerous, but less so than alpha as they are less likely to be absorbed by living cells.

How long will the radioactivity last?

As time goes by, the **number of unstable nuclei** in a sample **decreases**. We describe this decrease using the idea of a **half life**.

The half life of a radioactive material is the average time for the number of un-decayed nuclei in a sample of material to halve.

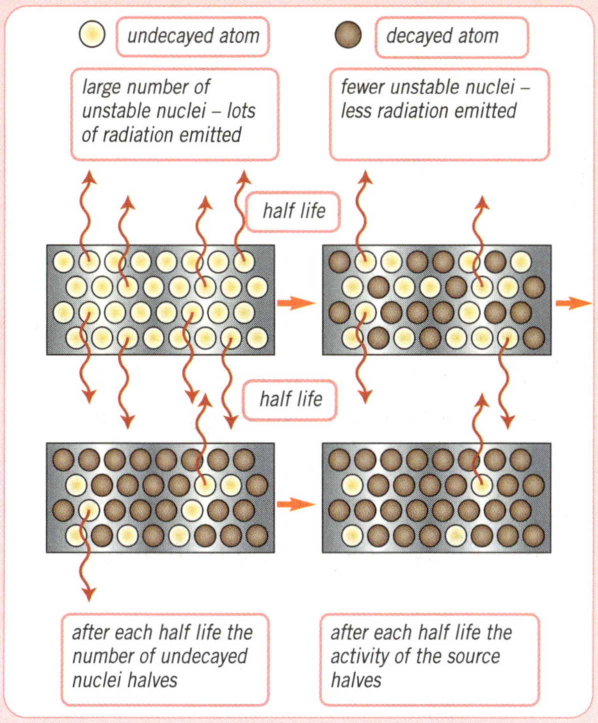

Different radioactive materials have different half lives. Here are some examples.

Isotope	Half life
Uranium-238	4500 million years
Radium-226	1620 years
Strontium-90	28 days

If we know the half life of a radioactive material we can calculate/estimate how the radiation it emits will decrease with time. This can be important when considering a radioisotope for a particular purpose. For example, any radioisotope which is introduced into the body should have quite a short half life so that the overall dose it delivers does not cause damage to living cells.

Example

A radioisotope emits 960 particles in minute. If the half life of the isotope is 20 minutes, calculate how many particles are being emitted each minute after a) one hour and b) one hour forty minutes.

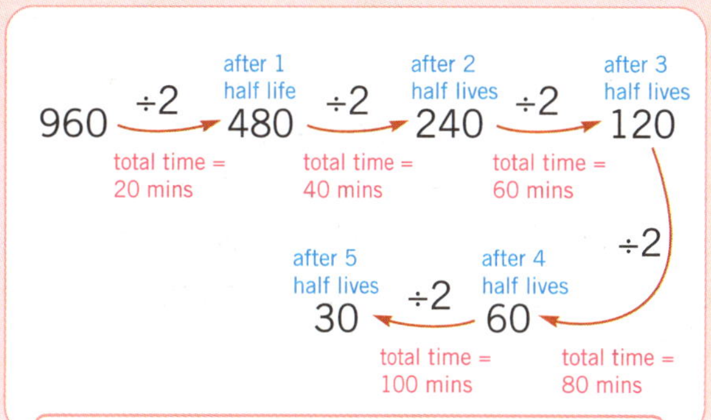

Answers

a) The activity of the source after one hour is 120 counts per minute

b) The activity of the source after one hour forty minutes (100 mins) is 30 counts per minute

QUICK TEST

1. Name three sources of radioactivity which contribute to background radiation.
2. Give one example of the kind of workers whose exposure to radiation must be carefully monitored.
3. Which type of radiation is most damaging when emitted from a source which is inside the body?
4. The count rate of a radioisotope drops from 600 counts per minute to 150 counts per minute in 6 days. Calculate its half life.
5. Which two properties of a radioisotope will need to be considered before choosing it for a particular use?

KEY TERMS

Make sure you understand these terms before moving on!

- background radiation
- radiation badges
- radioactive decay
- activity
- half life

Uses of radioactivity

We use radioactive materials in industry, in hospitals and even in our homes.

Quality control

Sheet material such as paper needs to be produced with a **constant thickness**. This can be monitored using the emissions from a radioactive source.

In this situation, a beta emitting source with a long half life such as strontium-90 is placed above the paper. A **beta detector** is placed directly beneath it.

If the paper becomes thinner more radiation reaches the detector and the control system decreases the pressure between the rollers.

If the paper becomes thicker less radiation is detected and the pressure on the rollers is increased.

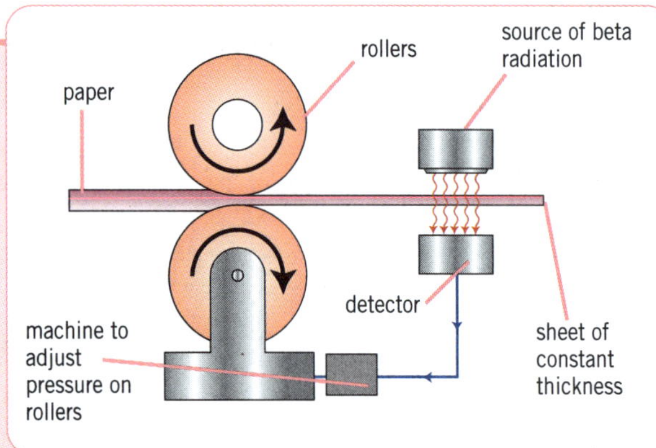

Continuous monitoring like this guarantees that the thickness/quality of the paper is correct. This arrangement can also be used to monitor the quality of **sheet metal**, but now we would have to find a gamma emitting source with a long half life to replace the strontium-90.

Radioactive tracers

Radioisotopes can be used to monitor the flow of **liquids and gases in pipes**.

If the pipe is underground, a gamma emitting radioisotope is added to the fluid flowing through it. This material is called a **tracer**.

If there is a **leak** in the pipe, a **higher concentration** of gamma radiation will be detected.

Using a radioisotope in this manner **avoids the need to dig up whole sections** of roads and piping in order to find the leak.

Tracers can also be used to check the progress of fluids such as blood and digested food through the body. For example, sodium 24 is a radioisotope that can be introduced into the body to check for **internal bleeding**.

Radiotherapy 1

Some forms of cancer can be removed by surgery. Others, like brain tumours, because of their position, may require a different solution, e.g. **radiotherapy**.

- A narrow beam of radiation is directed at the **tumour** from different positions.

Radiotherapy 2

- A **high dose of radiation** needed to kill the cancerous cells only occurs within the tumour.
- In other places, the dose is not large enough to cause cell damage.

Radiotherapy, as used on cancer cells

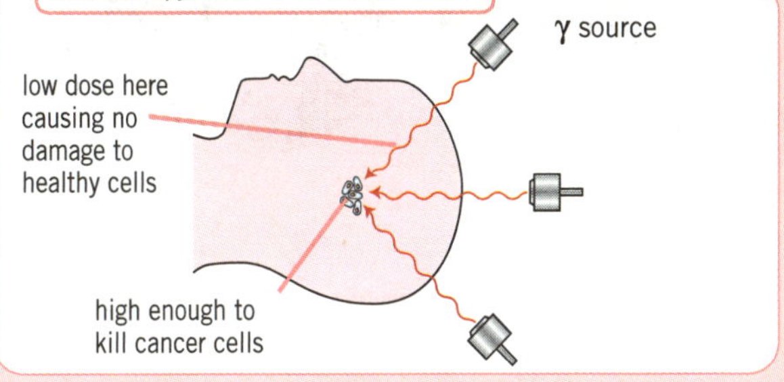

Smoke detectors

Some **smoke detectors**, like the one shown below, contain a small amount of americium-241. This is an **alpha emitter**. The alpha particles emitted collide with air molecules within the smoke detector **creating ions**. This in turn creates a **very small current**. If smoke enters the detector this **current stops or decreases**. It is this change in current which **triggers the alarm**.

One big advantage of this type of smoke detector is that when the battery is towards the end of its life, this too causes the current to fall and the alarm to sound, indicating that the battery needs replacing.

KEY TERMS

Make sure you understand these terms before moving on!

- quality control
- tracer
- radiotherapy
- sterilisation
- smoke detector
- creating ions

Sterilisation

Food rots because of the presence and growth of bacteria. Cooling and freezing slows down the growth of the bacteria but does not prevent it.

If food is exposed to gamma radiation before being frozen, the bacteria are killed and the food keeps for much longer. This process is called **sterilisation**.

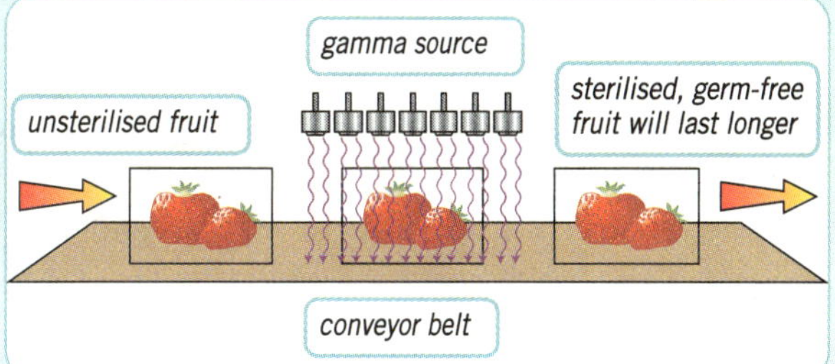

Surgical instruments used to be sterilised by putting them in boiling water. Nowadays, these instruments are sterilised by exposing them to gamma radiation.

QUICK TEST

1. What kind of radiation should a source emit if it is to be used for monitoring the thickness of a) card and b) sheets of steel?
2. What is the name given to a radioisotope which is injected into a fluid so that its flow can be monitored?
3. Why should a source which emits alpha radiation not be used to check the flow of blood through a body?
4. What is the treatment of cancer with radiation called?
5. Which type of radiation is used to sterilise surgical instruments?
6. What causes a current to flow in a smoke detector?
7. Why must the radioisotope used in a smoke detector not have a short half life?

Our universe

- **Did our universe have a beginning or did it always exist?**
- **Will our universe have an end or will it continue to exist for ever?**

Scientists and philosophers have been trying to answer these questions for a long time. We now have two clues which may help us provide an answer.

Red shift

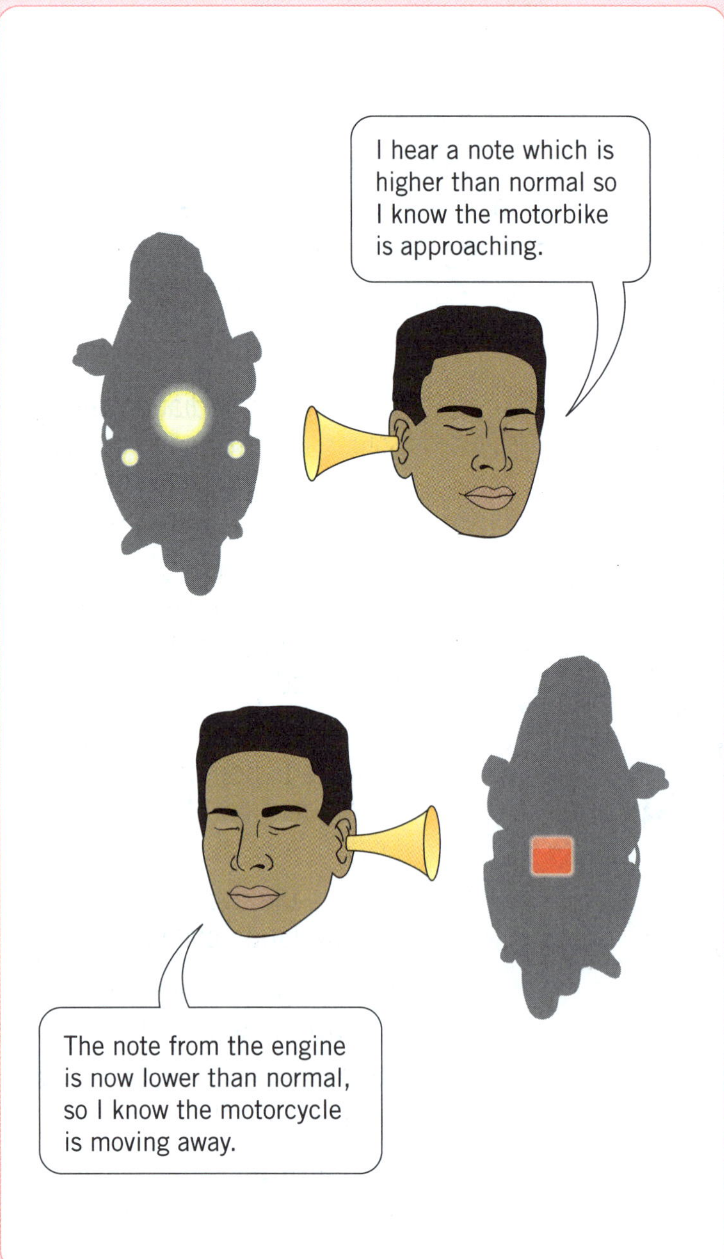

The **change in frequency** heard by the man allows him to identify which **way the motorcycle is moving** even though his eyes are shut.

Astronomers have seen similar changes when they look at the light from distant stars and galaxies. **The frequency of the light seems to be lower and moved towards the red part of the spectrum.** This is called **red shift**. With light from a very distant **galaxy**, the shift is **even greater**.

These **observations** tell us that all **galaxies are moving away** from us and the **further a galaxy is** from us the **faster it is moving away**.

This is precisely the **pattern of movements** we observe after an **explosion** and it therefore suggests that at one time in the past, all the matter in the universe was **in one place**. It was then scattered outwards by a huge explosion scientists call the **Big Bang**. The universe **is therefore expanding**.

Cosmic background radiation

When an explosion takes place, energy is released often in the form of heat and kinetic energy. Gradually the hotter objects will lose some of their energy to the surroundings causing it to become slightly warmer.

Scientists in the 1960s detected energy in the form of **background microwaves** in all parts of the Universe. They believe that this radiation is the remains of the energy released during the Big Bang.

Cosmic radiation from the Big Bang

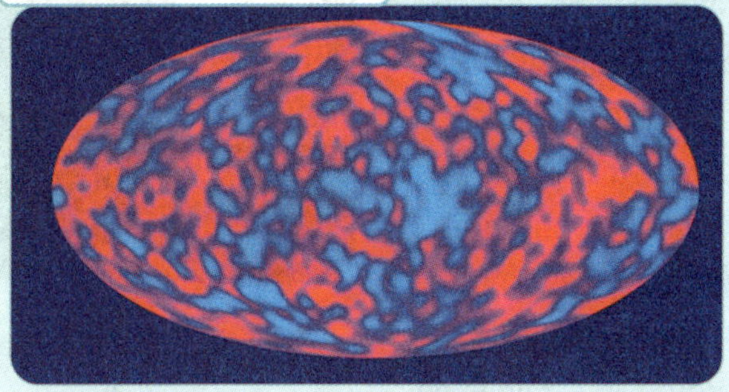

Scientists are now asking the question, 'Will this expansion continue indefinitely or will gravity gradually slow it down and then perhaps reverse the process, pulling all matter back to one place (**The Big Crunch**)?'

Perhaps then there may then be another explosion and the whole process will begin again (**The Oscillating Model of the Universe**). The total amount of matter in the Universe will determine its future. Whilst trying to measure how much matter there is in the Universe, scientists have discovered a new phenomenon called **dark matter** and it may be its presence that decides our fate.

Try to remember that two key observations suggest how our universe began – red shift and left over background energy from the explosion.

A dying star

KEY TERMS

Make sure you understand these terms before moving on!

- galaxy
- red shift
- Big Bang
- The Big Crunch

QUICK TEST

1. What happens to the frequency of the noise made by a motorcycle as it approaches and then passes an observer?
2. How does light appear if it is emitted by an object that is moving away from us very quickly?
3. What is this phenomenon called?
4. How does the red shift from a distant galaxy compare with that from a very distant galaxy? What conclusions can you draw from this?
5. How was matter in the universe distributed in the beginning, according to the Big Bang theory?
6. Describe two possible futures for our Universe.

Exploring space

Apart from the Earth and the Moon, humans have not visited any of the other bodies in the universe. Nevertheless, we have lots of information about them. Much of this has come from observations made by *telescopes*.

Telescopes

There are two main types of optical telescope. These are **refracting telescopes** which use **lenses** to gather the light and create images and **reflecting telescopes** which use **curved mirrors**.

Most observatories use reflecting telescopes because a) it is easier to produce accurately shaped mirrors than lenses and b) they do not colour the image as some refracting telescopes do.

Large optical telescopes, similar to the one shown, are often built on mountain tops.

Here the images we see suffer less **distortions** from the **Earth's atmosphere** than those at sea level. Also there is less 'light pollution'. Another way to avoid these distortions is to mount **telescopes on satellites** which orbit the Earth high above its atmosphere. A good example of this is the **Hubble Telescope** which was launched in 1990. It has seen **further into space** than any previous telescope.

The Hubble Telescope orbiting the Earth. It is able to see further into space and obtain clearer images than any earthbound telescope

Probes

Telescopes have also been sent into space on probes. Often these telescopes can send back images from view points which are just not possible from Earth. Also because they are closer to a body they can make far more detailed observations.

The probe Deep Space 1 was launched in 1998 to fly close to a large asteroid called Braille and study its surface

Making observations

Until the 20th Century, we learned about our universe by studying visible light from astronomical objects. Many astronomical objects emit radio waves, so astronomers also use **radio telescopes** which use large dishes to collect and focus these signals. Once they have been processed and analysed by computers, images can be created.

Many objects in space do not emit enough visible light to be visible when using an optical telescope. They may, however, emit enough radio waves to be visible using a radio telescope similar this one

A major advantage of using **radio telescopes** is that radio waves are **unaffected by sunlight, cloud or rain**. Also, in order to gather more information it is possible to link a large number of small dishes.

Astronomers also use telescopes which gather information from space using other parts of the **electromagnetic spectrum**. These include infrared telescopes, microwave telescopes, ultraviolet telescopes, X-ray telescopes and gamma ray telescopes. Each of the images created by these different telescopes adds to our understanding of the universe.

The photograph above right, taken with the Hubble Telescope, shows the importance of observing the universe using different parts of the electromagnetic spectrum. The star in the middle of the photograph is in the centre of our galaxy. It cannot be seen using visible light as it is obscured by clouds of interstellar dust, but using an infrared telescope, it is clearly visible.

Although there may be advantages in using different parts of the electromagnetic spectrum to make observations there are disadvantages too. **Gamma rays, X-rays, ultraviolet** and **some infrared** are **dramatically affected by the Earth's atmosphere**. So telescopes which use these waves must always be sited high above the ground or in space.

KEY TERMS

- refracting telescope
- reflecting telescope
- probe
- radio telescope

QUICK TEST

1. Describe the main difference between a refracting telescope and a reflecting telescope.
2. Why do most observatories use reflecting telescopes?
3. Give two reasons why some telescopes are sited on top of mountains?
4. Name four other parts of the electromagnetic spectrum which could be used to 'observe' space apart from visible light.
5. Name a telescope which is sited in space.

Practice questions

Use the questions to test your progress. Check your answers on page 112.

1. Name a device which transforms electrical energy into a) heat energy and b) kinetic or movement energy.

2. Name three fossil fuels. Why are fossil fuels called non-renewable sources of energy? Name a fuel which is renewable.

3. 500 J of electrical energy is transferred by a traditional light bulb into 25 J of light energy and 475 J of heat. Calculate the efficiency of the bulb.

4. The diagram on the right shows a hydroelectric power station.

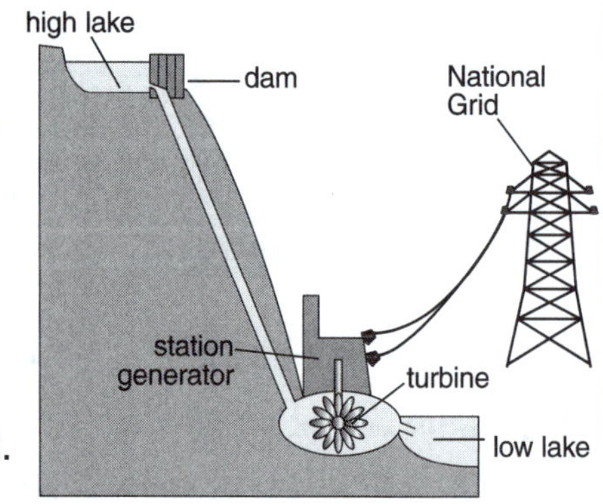

   a) What kind of energy does the water possess in the top lake?

   b) What kind of energy does the water possess as it enters the turbine?

   c) Explain how surplus energy could be stored until it is needed.

   d) Calculate the efficiency of a turbine which transfers 800 J of energy into 600 J of electrical energy.

5. Give two advantages and two disadvantages of generating electricity using nuclear power stations.

6. What is a thermogram? Give one use for a thermogram.

7. Calculate the electrical energy used in units when a 2 kW fire is turned on for 3 hours. Calculate the cost of this energy if the cost of one unit is 11p.

8. Calculate the payback time for each of the following methods of insulating your home using the information in the table below

Type of insulation	Cost	Annual saving
draft excluders	£50	£25
double glazing	£1200	£60
cavity wall insulation	£750	£75
insulating the loft	£150	£50

9. Two hoses containing water lie unused on a lawn on a sunny summer day. One hose is black the other yellow. Which pipe contains the warmest water and why?

10. A vibrating object produces 25 complete waves each second. What is the frequency of the sound it produces?

....

11. The diagram below shows the electromagnetic spectrum.

A	Microwaves	Infrared	Visible light	Ultraviolet	X-rays	B

a) Name the wave groups that would appear at positions A and B. ....
b) Name three properties which are common to all members of the electromagnetic spectrum.
c) Name two differences between the groups A and B..
d) Name two groups that could be used for cooking..
e) Name three groups that could be used for communicating. ....
f) Name two groups that could cause cancer...
g) Name one group used for seeing bones inside the body...

12. Calculate the speed of a sound wave which has a frequency of 170Hz and a wavelength of 2 m.

....

13. What three things may happen to a piece of living tissue which absorbs radiation?

....

14. Which type of radiation is causing concern because of the increase in usage of mobile phones?

....

15. Describe the structure of an optical fibre. What happens to a ray of light which enters a fibre?

....

16. Give two advantages of using digital signals rather than analogue signals.

....

17. Name the three particles that are found inside an atom. Which two of these particles carry charges?

....

18. Which of the three different types of radioactivity:
a) is not affected by a magnetic field ....
b) carries a negative charge ....
c) creates lots of ions as it travels through matter ....
d) travels at the speed of light in a vacuum? ....

19. Name three medical uses for radioisotopes.

....

20. Why is a source of alpha radiation outside the body unlikely to cause damage to vital organs inside the body?

....

21. A radioisotope has a half life of one day. How long would you have to wait until approximately $\frac{3}{4}$ of the nuclei have decayed?

....

22. What piece of information suggests that all the stars and galaxies in the universe are moving away from each other at high speeds? Which theory of the beginning of the universe does this information support?

....

23. Name three different types of telescope.

....

Answers

Biology

Page 5 The nervous system

1. Skin, tongue, eyes, ears, nose
2. Central nervous system
3. The brain and spinal cord
4. Sensory, relay and motor neurone
5. Sensory neurone
6. Motor neurone
7. Relay neurone
8. True
9. They protect us from harm
10. Reflex actions are automatic: voluntary actions you have to think about

Page 7 Hormones and the menstrual cycle

1. In the bloodstream
2. Lack of progesterone
3. Ovaries
4. Ovaries
5. FSH
6. Luteinising hormone/LH and follicle stimulating hormone/FSH
7. Development of an egg and release of oestrogen
8. Progesterone and oestrogen
9. Release of an egg
10. In vitro fertilisation

Page 9 A balanced diet

1. Energy
2. Starch and glucose
3. Starch carbohydrate
4. Fats
5. For insulation, store of energy and for making cell membranes
6. It helps repair or replace damaged cells
7. It helps food move smoothly through your system
8. Glucose
9. Vitamins and minerals
10. Cholesterol

Page 11 Nutrition and health

1. Increased blood cholesterol, which can lead to heart disease
2. Polyunsaturated fats
3. 6 g
4. 0.1 g
5. A high metabolic rate
6. In the liver
7. Heart disease, arthritis, diabetes, high blood pressure
8. Exercise lowers metabolic rate

Page 13 Causes of disease

1. Virus, bacteria and fungi
2. Pathogens or germs
3. Mosquitoes carry malaria
4. They reproduce inside living cells and kill them
5. Athlete's foot and ringworm
6. An organism that transports a diseases from person to person e.g. mosquito
7. Skin, digestive, reproductive and respiratory systems and vectors (any three)
8. Food poisoning, tuberculosis, cholera

Page 15 Defence against disease

1. It's a barrier and produces an antiseptic oil
2. It traps dust and germs
3. Sterilising, disinfectants, antiseptics and good hygiene
4. Phagocytes and lymphocytes
5. They engulf them
6. Antitoxins and antibodies
7. Destroy toxins
8. Attach to antigens and clump germs together for the phagocytes to engulf
9. Hairs that line the respiratory system
10. They contain foreign antigens on their surface

Page 17 Treatment of disease

1. Measles, mumps and rubella
2. Dr Semmelweiss
3. Penicillin
4. They mutate
5. Antibiotics only kill bacteria not viruses
6. Dead or harmless forms of the disease
7. Where neither the doctor nor the patient knows whether they are receiving the drug being tested
8. A dummy drug not containing the active ingredient being tested and will not have any affect on the patient
9. Because it caused birth defects in babies born to mothers taking the drug
10. Overuse leads to the bacteria becoming resistant

Page 19 Drugs

1. Brain, liver and nervous system
2. Class C
3. Tar, nicotine and carbon monoxide
4. Emphysema, bronchitis, lung cancer and heart diseases
5. Cirrhosis

Page 21 Adaptation and competition

1. Where an organism lives
2. The living things in a habitat
3. Animals or plants
4. Food, water and space
5. Light, space, water and nutrients
6. The number of predators will also increase at first
7. Because of the predator/prey cycle
8. White (camouflage), thick (insulation)
9. Enables it to lose heat to its surroundings
10. Only the best-adapted organism will survive

Page 23 Genes and chromosomes

1. Chromosomes
2. Proteins and enzymes
3. Sections of DNA that code for a particular characteristic
4. On the chromosomes
5. If they occur in reproductive cells
6. 46, nucleus
7. 2
8. Sperms and eggs
9. Asexual reproduction
10. Sexual reproduction and the environment

Page 25 Genetic engineering

1. A plasmid
2. Genetically modified
3. Using enzymes
4. They could develop resistance to herbicides or insecticides
5. Diabetes
6. They could be grown in cold countries throughout the year
7. The pancreas
8. Making insulin or human growth hormone
9. They may mutate into harmful bacteria

Page 27 Selective breeding

1. Breeding animals and plants together to produce the best offspring
2. Genetically identical individuals
3. Embryo transfer
4. Taking cuttings and tissue culture
5. Characteristics that may become useful later are bred out

Page 29 Evolution

1. 3 billion years ago
2. Charles Darwin
3. Environmental change, competition, disease and predators
4. The best adapted
5. Natural selection/survival of the fittest
6. Galapagos Islands off the coast of South America
7. A group of individuals that can breed together to produce fertile offspring
8. He saw that they all showed variation
9. There were more offspring produced than could survive
10. Evolution is a gradual process

Page 31 Evidence for evolution

1. The ground changed from marshy land to hard ground
2. The dark form, camouflaged against predators
3. Oxygen, moisture and warmth
4. They are unable to adapt
5. The remains of dead organisms that have not decayed and who lived millions of years ago
6. Yes because that is absence of warmth
7. Mutation caused by pollution from factories
8. By destroying habitats hunting or pollution
9. Near the surface with older fossils further down
10. Natural selection

Page 33 Environmental damage

1. Improved health care, medicine and agriculture
2. Problems in food chains
3. They are washed in by rain
4. Eutrophication
5. Building, farming, dumping rubbish and quarrying
6. Cutting down of trees and forests
7. Soil erosion, less rainfall and the destruction of habitats and increases the amount of carbon dioxide in the air

Page 35 How can we help?

1. Introduce quotas
2. Replant the woodland
3. Biological control
4. Land that is not used to grow crops and allows wildlife to remain
5. Breed in captivity and give them legal protection
6. Use catalytic converters, unleaded fuel, conduct research into more efficient engines or alternative transport systems
7. It would reduce the need for the use of fossil fuels to heat our homes
8. Manure

Page 36 Answers to practice questions

1. Microbes that cause disease
2. A sleeping pill
3. Using the best bull sperm and the best cow eggs, fertilising them and implanting them into surrogate cows
4. Artificial selection is when humans decide which animals breed together, natural selection is when nature decides
5. A chemical on the surface of germs that identifies it as foreign
6. It deprives the foetus of oxygen and leads to a low birth weight
7. Nowhere it's extinct!
8. Energy sources that do not harm the environment by causing pollution
9. A rise in blood cholesterol leading to increase risk of heart disease
10. Central Nervous System consists of brain, spinal cord and nerve cells
11. Relay, sensory and motor
12. Atherosclerosis, heart disease or high blood pressure
13. Asexual
14. Virus
15. Viruses
16. An organism that transports a pathogen from one organism to another e.g. a mosquito
17. Phagocytes and lymphocytes
18. Natural immunity is when the body can remember a disease and produce antibodies to fight it before any symptoms develop
19. The body maintaining a constant internal environment
20. 140 years ago
21. More crops can be grown in a smaller area of land which reduces the need to use more of the countryside
22. FSH, LH, oestrogen and progesterone
23. Bacteria
24. No, because measles is a virus, penicillin can only kill bacteria
25. Charles Darwin
26. Lamarck
27. Antibiotics
28. Changes in the environment
29. Organic farming
30. Inside the nucleus of your cells (except red blood cells)

Chemistry

Page 39 Atoms and elements
1. The nucleus
2. Elements are made of just one type of atom
3. By sharing electrons or by giving and taking electrons
4. O
5. Sodium
6. Chomium
7. Two hydrogen atoms and one oxygen atom

Page 41 Limestone
1. Calcium carbonate
2. Sedimentary
3. Igneous
4. Neutralise acidity in lakes and soils
5. Zinc carbonate → zinc oxide + carbon dioxide
6. Magnesium carbonate → magnesium oxide + carbon dioxide
7. Roasting clay and limestone
8. Heating limestone, sand and soda
9. Sodium carbonate, carbon dioxide and water
10. Sodium hydrogen carbonate → sodium carbonate + carbon dioxide + water

Page 43 Fuels
1. Coal, oil and natural gas
2. Mixture
3. Hydrogen and carbon
4. Runny, easy to ignite and have low boiling points
5. Short ones
6. At the top
7. They are more useful
8. Something that speeds up the rate of reaction but is not itself used up
9. Alkenes
10. A group of compounds with a similar number of carbon atoms

Page 45 Organic families
1. Four
2. 'Saturated' no double bonds; 'hydrocarbons' contain hydrogen and carbon atoms only
3. Methane
4. 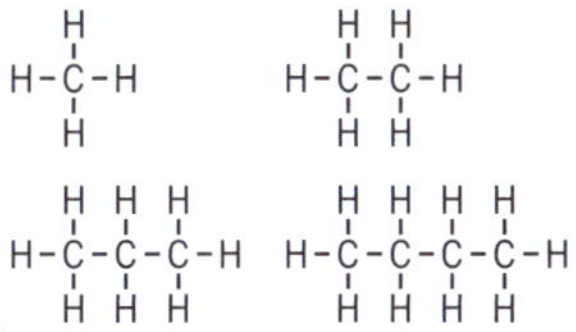
5. 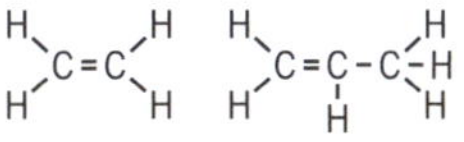
6. Alkenes
7. Alkenes decolourise bromine water while alkanes do not react
8. C_nH_{2n+2}
9. Alcohols
10. C_2H_5OH

Page 47 Vegetable oils
1. Fruits, seeds and nuts
2. Seeds
3. Vitamins A and D
4. Fats can reach much higher temperatures than water
5. Fried
6. Saturated
7. Lots of C=C bonds

Page 49 Plastics
1. 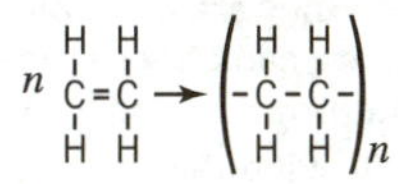
2. 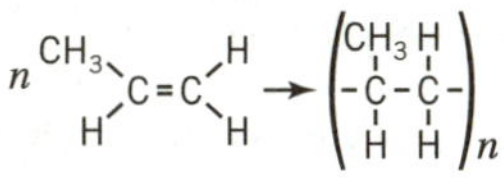
3. Addition polymerisation
4. Monomer
5. Chloroethene
6. Tetrafluoroethene
7. Special wound dressings
8. Polythene

Page 51 Ethanol
1. C_2H_5OH
2. Drinks, solvents and as a fuel
3. They could become blind or even die
4. Yeast
5. A type of sugar
6. It becomes denatured
7. Carbon dioxide
8. ethene + water/steam → ethanol

Page 53 Evolution of the atmosphere
1. 20%
2. Nitrogen
3. Carbon dioxide, water vapour and noble gases
4. Carbon dioxide, steam, ammonia and methane
5. Carbon dioxide
6. Removed carbon dioxide and produced oxygen
7. Became locked up in sedimentary rocks and fossil fuels
8. Filters out harmful UV rays
9. New, more complex life forms could develop
10. Burning fossil fuels

Page 55 Pollution of the atmosphere
1. Sulphur dioxide
2. Coal
3. If less electricity is required, fewer fossil fuels will need to be burnt
4. It will have a yellow colour
5. Carbon monoxide
6. Smoke particles
7. A reduction in the amount of sunlight that reaches the Earth's surface, which may even affect weather patterns
8. Carbon dioxide

Page 57 Pollution of the environment
1. Bauxite
2. Rainforests
3. Recycle aluminium
4. The quarries can scar the landscape
5. New jobs and brings money into the area
6. They can cause noise, congestion and damage the roads
7. Landfill sites
8. Non-biodegradable
9. Hydrogen chloride
10. Biodegradable ones

Page 59 Evidence for plate tectonics
1. Crust
2. Solid
3. Silicon, oxygen and aluminium
4. Iron and nickel
5. A few centimetres per year
6. Crust and upper mantle

Page 61 Consequences of plate tectonics
1. Past each other, towards each other or away from each other
2. When plates move past each other
3. There are too many factors involved
4. California, USA
5. Oceanic
6. Liquid rock
7. The oceanic plate melts
8. Because plates are moving past each other
9. West coast of South America
10. Changed

Page 63 Extraction of iron
1. Gold
2. Heat with carbon
3. Electrolysis
4. Haematite
5. Iron ore, coke and limestone
6. Oxygen from hot air
7. Carbon monoxide
8. More dense
9. It is heavy for its size
10. Slag

Page 65 Iron and steel
1. Making steel
2. Water and oxygen
3. Stops water and oxygen reaching the iron
4. Magnesium or zinc
5. Hard, strong, does not rust, but is brittle
6. Carbon

Page 67 Aluminium
1. Bauxite
2. It is soft and has a low density
3. An alloy
4. It is protected by a layer of aluminium oxide
5. Al_2O_3
6. Electrolysis
7. Oxide ions
8. Aluminium ions

Page 69 Titanium and copper
1. Alloy it with other metals
2. Titanium quickly reacts with oxygen to form a layer of titanium oxide, which stops any further reactions
3. To make replacement joints
4. Rutile
5. Titanium dioxide
6. Electrolysis
7. Alloys
8. The layers of copper atoms can slide over each other
9. Brass and bronze

Page 71 Transition metals
1. Free electrons
2. Middle section
3. High melting point, high density, shiny, tough, hard wearing, form coloured compounds and are good catalysts
4. Bridges, buildings, ships, cars and trains
5. The Haber process
6. Coins

Page 73 The noble gases
1. They have a full outer shell of electrons
2. It increases
3. 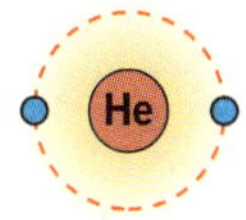

4. 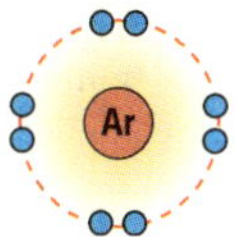

5. Individual atoms
6. Balloons and airships
7. It is less dense than air and it is not flammable
8. Electrical discharge tubes
9. Filament light bulbs
10. Lasers

Page 74 Answers to practice questions

1 a) Limestone/marble/chalk
  b) calcium oxide or carbon dioxide
  c) calcium hydroxide or slaked lime or lime water
  d) Glass

2. a) CH_4
  b) Ethane
  c) C_2H_4
  d) Propene

3. a) Fractional distillation
  b) More flammable
  c) Cracking

4. b)

5. a) Alloy
  b) Carbon

6. In the titanium alloy the layers of atoms cannot pass easily over each other

7. c), a), d), b)

8. a) Aluminium
  b) Aluminium
  c) Iron
  d) Gold

Physics

Page 77 Energy

1. Any 5 of: Heat, light, sound, electricity, chemical, gravitational potential, elastic potential, nuclear
2. Electric fire, loudspeaker, electric motor, etc.
3. Electrical energy into heat and light. Electrical energy into sound. Electrical energy into kinetic energy
4. Electric hairdryer
5. It is there for our use at the flick of a switch
6. a) Television
   b) Electric Lawn mower or hedge trimmer
   c) Transmitting electrical energy from the power stations to your home i.e. the National Grid
7. Because our energy sources are being used up. Their use is causing changes to our climate

Page 79 Efficiency

1. Chemical energy is transferred into light and heat energy. The transfer to heat energy is wasting energy.
2. Some electrical energy may be transferred to heat energy.
3. To reduce our energy demand so that sources will last longer and try to prevent environmental problems e.g. changes to climate
4. 90%
5. 70%
6. $33\frac{1}{3}$%

Page 81 Generating electricity

1. Coal, oil and gas
2. Uranium or plutonium
3. Cannot be replaced
4. There are no polluting gases released and the rate at which the fossil fuels are used is reduced
5. Expensive decommissioning, long term storage of nuclear waste material, possibility of leaks into the atmosphere of radioactive materials and the risk of a nuclear explosion

Page 83 Renewable sources of energy

1. Hydroelectricity, tidal, wave
2. Wind and waves
3. Wind and biomass
4. Geothermal and tidal
5. Wind and hydroelectric

Page 85 Heat transfer – conduction

1. Allows heat to flow through it
2. Metal, saucepan
3. Does not allow heat through it
4. Plastic, tablemat
5. Two panes of glass with air in between
6. Fibreglass in loft, double glazing, draft excluders carpets and underlay, cavity wall insulation

Page 87 Heat transfer – convection

1. Too much energy lost up the chimney
2. To prevent heat loss by convection
3. 

Air above the fire is warmed, expands and rises.

Cooler, fresh air enters the second shaft to replace the stale air.

Page 89 Heat transfer – radiation

1. Electromagnetic radiation or infrared waves
2. Because conduction and convection require particles only radiation can travel through a vacuum
3. Absorbed or reflected
4. Dark and rough
5. Light coloured and smooth
6. A photograph taken using the radiation emitted by an object and whose colours show the temperatures of different objects
7. So that they reflect the radiation and so are cooler

Page 91 Electrical power

1. a) 9 units
   b) 1 unit
   c) 3 units
   d) 2 units
   e) 1 unit

Page 93 Waves

1. Energy
2. 25 waves produced by source each second
3. a) Light waves and b) Sound waves
4. 15 m/s
5. Travel through vacuum, transverse
6. Wavelength and frequency

Page 95 The electromagnetic spectrum

1. Radio, microwave, visible
2. Infrared, microwaves
3. Ultraviolet, X-ray and gamma
4. Gamma
5. Visible light and infrared
6. Radioactive material
7. Microwaves can pass more easily through the Earth's atmosphere
8. There is the possibility that the X-rays may damage the foetus

Page 97 Analogue and digital signals

1. It strikes the sides at angles greater than the critical angle and so is totally internally reflected
2. Infrared and visible light
3. Cheaper, lighter, carry more signals, more secure

Page 99 Nuclear radiations

1. Because they are unstable
2. So that we can choose the most appropriate radiation for a particular use
3. a) Gamma b) Alpha c) Beta d) Beta e) Gamma

Page 101 Radioactivity and half life

1. Rocks, e.g. granite, medical sources, from space, the air
2. Radiographer, nuclear power worker
3. Alpha
4. 3 days
5. The type of radiation it emits and its half life

Page 103 Uses of radioactivity

1. a) beta and b) gamma
2. Tracer
3. Cell damage due to alpha radiation
4. Radiotherapy
5. Gamma
6. The creation of ions by the alpha emitter
7. The alarm would sound as the source activity decreases

Page 105 Our universe

1. There is a change from high frequency to lower frequency
2. It too appears to have a lower frequency
3. Red shift
4. The red shift from the very distant galaxy is greater than that of the nearer galaxy. This suggests that the further an object is from Earth the faster it is moving away from us
5. All in one place
6. It continues to expand. It stops expanding and contracts (Big Crunch). It may then explode and start to expand again (The Oscillating Universe)

Page 107 Exploring space

1. Refracting telescopes use lenses to collect light and create images. Reflecting telescopes use mirrors
2. Easier to manufacture a precise mirror, also avoids artificial colouring
3. To avoid distortions caused by the Earth's atmosphere and avoid light pollution
4. Radio waves, microwaves, ultraviolet, infrared, X-rays and gamma rays
5. Hubble Telescope

Page 108 Answers to practice questions

1. a) electric fire
   b) electric motor
2. a) coal, oil and gas
   b) once they have been used they cannot be replaced
   c) wood
3. 5%.
4. a) gravitational potential energy
   b) kinetic energy
   c) Water is stored in the top lake until electrical energy is needed
   d) 75%
5. Cost of producing electricity is low and there are no polluting gases. But building and decommission is very costly and waste material will need to be stored securely for a very long time
6. A picture which shows different temperatures as different colours. Used to find places where heat is escaping from a building
7. 6 units, 66 p
8. 2 years, 20 years, 10 years and 3 years
9. The black hose because it will absorb most of the radiation from the Sun, the yellow pipe will reflect most
10. 25 Hz
11. a) A is radio waves and B is gamma waves
    b) They can all be reflected, refracted and undergo diffraction. They all travel at the same speed in a vacuum
    c) gamma waves have shorter wavelengths and larger frequencies
    d) microwaves and infrared waves
    e) microwaves, radio waves and visible light
    f) ultraviolet waves and X-rays
    g) X-rays
12. 340 m/s
13. The tissue may be warmed, its cells may be damaged and become cancerous or the cells may be killed
14. Microwaves
15. More dense glass core with an outer coating of less dense glass. Undergoes a series of total internal reflections
16. Cleaner signal is received, can be handled by computer also replicates original more easily
17. Protons, neutrons and electrons. Protons and electrons
18. a) gamma
    b) beta
    c) alpha
    d) gamma
19. Radiotherapy, sterilisation and radioactive tracers (bloodstream)
20. Unable to pass through the skin
21. Two days
22. Red shift, Big Bang theory. Microwave background radiation
23. Reflecting, refracting and radio

Martin Partners • Adhoc Architects • Alberto Campo Baeza Arquitecto • Antoine Predock Architects • Architectures Jean Nouvel • ARM.RPVHT Pty Ltd • Atelier D'Architecture Franck Hammoutene • Atelier Hitoshi Abe • Axel Schultes Architekten • Azman Owens Architects • Baumschlager & Eberle • Behnisch, Behnisch & Partner • Bernard Tschumi Architects • Bo … Bucholz McEvoy • Centerbrook Architects • Cesar Pelli & Associates • Claudio Silvestrin Architects • Daly, Ge … Design Office • Dominique Perrault Architecte • Droog Design • Edouard François et Associés • (EEA) Er … Eric Owen Moss Architects • Fentress Bradburn • Foster & Partners • Gehry Partners • Gluckman Mayner Ar … Overdiek und Partner • Jakob + Macfarlane • Jarmund/Vigsnæs AS • Juhani Katainen Architects • Kisho Kurokaw … Pedersen Fox Associates • Koning Eizenberg Architecture • Kreykenbohm Architekten • Kuth/Ranieri Architecture • L … Daly Architects • Line and Space, LLC • Meili Peter • MGT Architects • Michael Hopkins & Partners • Morphosis … Calatrava • Ms Catherine Slessor • Murphy/Jahn • Patel Taylor • Perkins Eastman Architects PC • Perkins & Will • P … Renzo Piano Building Workshop • Rick Joy Architect • sauerbruch hutton architekten • Sean Godsell Architects • SH Architects • SHoP/Sharples … Pasquarelli • Sidnam Petrone Gartner Architects • Stein Halvorsen • Steven Ehrlich Architects • Studio Granda • TEN Arquitectos • The Cox Group • UN Studio van Berkel and Bos • Viiva Arkkitehtuuri • Williamson Pounders Architects • Yabu Pushelberg • 1100 Architect • AC Martin Partners • Adhoc Architects • Alberto Campo Baeza Arquitecto • Antoine Predock Architects • Architectures Jean Nouvel • ARM.RPVHT Pty Ltd • Atelier D'Architecture Franck Hammoutene • Atelier Hitoshi Abe • Axel Schultes Architekten • Azman Owens Architects • Baumschlager & Eberle • Behnisch, Behnisch & Partner • Bernard Tschumi Architects • Bohlin Cywinski Jackson • Bolles+Wilson • Bucholz McEvoy • Centerbrook Architects • Cesar Pelli & Associates • Claudio Silvestrin Architects • Daly, Genik Architects • Denton Corker Marshall • Design Office • Dominique Perrault Architecte • Droog Design • Edouard François et Associés • (EEA) Erick Van Egeraat Associated Architects • Eric Owen Moss Architects • Fentress Bradburn • Foster & Partners • Gehry Partners • Gluckman Mayner Architects • DEO London • Ingenhoven Overdiek und Partner • Jakob + Macfarlane • Jarmund/Vigsnæs AS • Juhani Katainen Architects • Kisho Kurokawa architect & associates • Kohn Pedersen Fox Associates • Koning Eizenberg Architecture • Kreykenbohm Architekten • Kuth/Ranieri Architecture • Leers Weinzapfel Associates • Leo A Daly Architects • Line and Space, LLC • Meili Peter • MGT Architects • Michael Hopkins & Partners • Morphosis • Mr Patrick Berger • Mr Santiago Calatrava • Ms Catherine Slessor • Murphy/Jahn • Patel Taylor • Perkins Eastman Architects PC • Perkins & Will • Polshek Partnership • Pugh + Scarpa • Renzo Piano Building Workshop • Rick Joy Architect • sauerbruch hutton architekten • Sean Godsell Architects • SH Architects • SHoP/Sharples Holden Pasquarelli • Sidnam Petrone Gartner Architects • Stein Halvorsen • Steven Ehrlich Architects • Studio Granda • TEN Arquitectos • The Cox Group • UN Studio van Berkel and Bos • Viiva Arkkitehtuuri • Williamson Pounders Architects • Yabu Pushelberg • 1100 Architect • AC Martin Partners • Adhoc Architects • Alberto Campo Baeza Arquitecto • Antoine Predock Architects • Architectures Jean Nouvel • ARM.RPVHT Pty Ltd • Atelier D'Architecture Franck Hammoutene • Atelier Hitoshi Abe • Axel Schultes Architekten • Azman Owens Architects • Baumschlager & Eberle • Behnisch, Behnisch & Partner • Bernard Tschumi Architects • Bohlin Cywinski Jackson • Bolles+Wilson • Bucholz McEvoy • Centerbrook Architects • Cesar Pelli & Associates • Claudio Silvestrin Architects • Daly, Genik Architects • Denton Corker Marshall • Design Office • Dominique Perrault Architecte • Droog Design • Edouard François et Associés • (EEA) Erick Van Egeraat Associated Architects • Eric Owen Moss Architects • Fentress Bradburn • Foster & Partners • Gehry Partners • Gluckman Mayner Architects • DEO London • Ingenhoven Overdiek und Partner • Jakob + Macfarlane • Jarmund/Vigsnæs AS • Juhani Katainen Architects • Kisho Kurokawa architect & associates • Kohn Pedersen Fox Associates • Koning Eizenberg Architecture • Kreykenbohm Architekten • Kuth/Ranieri Architecture • Leers Weinzapfel Associates • Leo A Daly Architects • Line and Space, LLC • Meili Peter • MGT Architects • Michael Hopkins & Partners • Morphosis • Mr Patrick Berger • Mr Santiago Calatrava • Ms Catherine Slessor • Murphy/Jahn • Patel Taylor • Perkins Eastman Architects PC • Perkins & Will • Polshek Partnership • Pugh + Scarpa • Renzo Piano Building Workshop • Rick Joy Architect • sauerbruch hutton architekten • Sean Godsell Architects • SH Architects • SHoP/Sharples Holden Pasquarelli • Sidnam Petrone Gartner Architects • Stein Halvorsen • Steven Ehrlich Architects • Studio Granda • TEN Arquitectos • The Cox Group • UN Studio van Berkel and Bos • Viiva Arkkitehtuuri • Williamson Pounders Architects • Yabu Pushelberg • 1100 Architect • AC Martin Partners • Adhoc Architects • Alberto Campo Baeza Arquitecto • Antoine Predock Architects • Architectures Jean Nouvel • ARM.RPVHT Pty Ltd • Atelier D'Architecture Franck Hammoutene • Atelier Hitoshi Abe • Axel Schultes Architekten • Azman Owens Architects • Baumschlager & Eberle • Behnisch, Behnisch & Partner • Bernard Tschumi Architects • Bohlin Cywinski Jackson • Bolles+Wilson • Bucholz McEvoy • Centerbrook Architects • Cesar Pelli & Associates • Claudio Silvestrin Architects • Daly, Genik Architects • Denton Corker Marshall • Design Office • Dominique Perrault Architecte • Droog Design • Edouard François et Associés • (EEA) Erick Van Egeraat Associated Architects • Eric Owen Moss Architects • Fentress Bradburn • Foster & Partners • Gehry Partners • Gluckman Mayner Architects • DEO London • Ingenhoven Overdiek und Partner • Jakob + Macfarlane • Jarmund/Vigsnæs AS • Juhani Katainen Architects • Kisho Kurokawa architect & associates • Kohn Pedersen Fox Associates • Koning Eizenberg Architecture • Kreykenbohm Architekten • Kuth/Ranieri Architecture • Leers Weinzapfel Associates • Leo A Daly Architects • Line and Space, LLC • Meili Peter • MGT Architects • Michael Hopkins & Partners • Morphosis • Mr Patrick Berger • Mr Santiago Calatrava • Ms Catherine Slessor • Murphy/Jahn • Patel Taylor • Perkins Eastman Architects PC • Perkins & Will • Polshek Partnership • Pugh + Scarpa • Renzo Piano Building Workshop • Rick Joy Architect • sauerbruch hutton architekten • Sean Godsell Architects • SH Architects • SHoP/Sharples Holden Pasquarelli • Sidnam Petrone Gartner Architects • Stein Halvorsen • Steven Ehrlich Architects • Studio Granda • TEN Arquitectos • The Cox Group • UN Studio van Berkel and Bos • Viiva Arkkitehtuuri • Williamson Pounders Architects • Yabu Pushelberg • 1100 Architect • AC Martin Partners • Adhoc Architects • Alberto Campo Baeza Arquitecto • Antoine Predock Architects • Architectures Jean Nouvel • ARM.RPVHT Pty Ltd • Atelier D'Architecture Franck Hammoutene • Atelier Hitoshi Abe • Axel Schultes Architekten • Azman Owens Architects • Baumschlager & Eberle • Behnisch, Behnisch & Partner • Bernard Tschumi Architects • Bohlin Cywinski Jackson • Bolles+Wilson • Bucholz McEvoy • Centerbrook Architects • Cesar Pelli & Associates • Claudio Silvestrin Architects • Daly, Genik Architects • Denton Corker Marshall • Design Office • Dominique Perrault Architecte • Droog Design • Edouard François et Associés • (EEA) Erick Van Egeraat Associated Architects • Eric Owen Moss Architects • Fentress Bradburn • Foster & Partners • Gehry Partners • Gluckman Mayner Architects • DEO London • Ingenhoven Overdiek und Partner • Jakob + Macfarlane • Jarmund/Vigsnæs AS • Juhani Katainen Architects • Kisho Kurokawa architect & associates • Kohn Pedersen Fox Associates • Koning Eizenberg Architecture • Kreykenbohm Architekten • Kuth/Ranieri Architecture • Leers Weinzapfel Associates • Leo A Daly Architects • Line and Space, LLC • Meili Peter • MGT Architects • Michael Hopkins & Partners • Morphosis • Mr Patrick Berger • Mr Santiago Calatrava • Ms Catherine Slessor • Murphy/Jahn • Patel Taylor • Perkins Eastman Architects PC • Perkins & Will • Polshek Partnership • Pugh + Scarpa • Renzo Piano Building Workshop • Rick Joy Architect • sauerbruch hutton architekten • Sean Godsell Architects • SH Architects • SHoP/Sharples Holden Pasquarelli • Sidnam Petrone Gartner Architects • Stein Halvorsen • Steven Ehrlich Architects • Studio Granda • TEN Arquitectos • The Cox Group • UN Studio van Berkel and Bos • Viiva Arkkitehtuuri • Williamson Pounders Architects • Yabu Pushelberg • 1100 Architect

international architecture

yearbook 8 | 02

Published in Australia in 2002 by
The Images Publishing Group Pty Ltd
ACN 059 734 431
6 Bastow Place, Mulgrave, Victoria 3170, Australia
Telephone (61 3) 9561 5544 Facsimile (61 3) 9561 4860
E-mail: books@images.com.au
Website: www.imagespublishinggroup.com

The Images Publishing Group Reference Number: 490

ISSN Set No: 1 875498 27 3
ISBN Volume 8: 1 87690 743 6

Designed by The Graphic Image Studio Pty Ltd,
Mulgrave, Australia
Film separations by Pageset Pty Ltd, Melbourne, Australia
Printed in Hong Kong by the Paramount Printing Company Limited

images Publishing

IMAGES has included on its website a page for special notices in relation to this and our other publications. It includes updates in relation to the information printed in our books. Please visit this site: www.imagespublishinggroup.com

international architecture

yearbook 8 | 02

Contents

Introduction

Catherine Slessor

In many ways and on many levels, architecture can act as a powerful force for transformation. From ambitious set piece projects to more modest interventions, architecture can give form to previously unresolved spaces, bring new life to neglected neighbourhoods and put cities on the world stage. Despite the ravages of war, economic slowdown and environmental crises, the capacity of architecture to act as a force for transformation continues to underscore the procurement and production of the best sorts of buildings around the world. Culture can be an especially effective engine of regeneration; the presence of the Guggenheim in Bilbao, for instance, heroically recast a languishing, provincial Spanish city. Sport has a similar capacity to act as an impetus for wider socio-economic development; the staging of the 1992 Olympics in Barcelona kick-started the city's remarkable rebirth, a process that still continues through an ongoing array of new parks and urban redevelopment projects. Sydney did not need to be revived to quite the same degree as Barcelona, but the city's highly professional and widely admired hosting of the 2000 Olympics was one of the year's global architectural highlights. The staging of the games generated an impressive new crop of sports buildings largely concentrated on a site at Homebush Bay, to the west of the city centre. Originally an industrial site, it was variously used as a brickworks, naval arsenal and rubbish dump. Masterplanned by Bligh Voller Nield, the site was cleaned up and redeveloped as a major metropolitan park and nature reserve, with the Olympic complex forming a permanent urban core. Like beads on a string, the new sports facilities are linked by a ceremonial, axial boulevard. Standout buildings included the mammoth Stadium Australia (a latter-day Colosseum designed by HOK + Lobb in collaboration with Bligh Voller Nield), Lawrence Nield's cone-shaped tennis stadium, Stutchbury & Pape's beautifully simple archery pavilion and the elegant, elongated caterpillar of Homebush Bay station (designed by Ken Maher of Hassell) that connects the site with central Sydney. (Nield's masterplan encouraged the use of public transport.) The theme of the so-called Green Games was to 'reduce, reuse and recycle' and the Homebush complex proved a robust embodiment of these principles.

To some extent, this was Australia's *annus mirabilis*. A successful Olympic building programme was accompanied by the completion of several museums, including the National Museum of Australia in Canberra, and Renzo Piano's huge office and apartment tower in Sydney, a conspicuous addition to the city's skyline. Built to celebrate 100 years of the federation of colonial Australian states, the National Museum of Australia by Ashton Raggatt McDougall houses a collection of national treasures in a collage-like accretion of volumes.

Away from the main architectural centres of Sydney and Melbourne, the work of Brisbane-based architects such as Brit Andresen, Peter O'Gorman and Donovan Hill attracted wider recognition. Described by critic and visiting professor Tom Heneghan as 'Matchstick Mannerism', Brisbane architects celebrate honesty, craft and lyricism and conceive of architecture primarily as a way of co-habiting with nature. Typically, buildings are framed by slender yet immensely durable hardwood members and clad in thin wooden slats that dissolve harsh sunlight in a sensuous play of shadows. In terms of material use and poetic handling of light, some reciprocity can be detected with traditional Japanese architecture.

Japan itself continues to generate an extraordinary diversity of buildings, but any evaluation of its present condition must explore the wider economic and social factors that govern the production of architecture. The economic crisis that arose in Japan at the start of the 1990s (the collapse of the so-called 'bubble economy') marked a significant turning point. Commercial commissions virtually dried up and public agencies such as the government and local prefectures became the main patrons of architecture. Ambitious public buildings programmes—covering everything from regional arts centres to police boxes—were put into place across Japan and the results of this are now coming to fruition. In some cases, an unlimited budget and a free hand allowed some architects to pursue an agenda that ignored the public's interests, but many projects avoided these pitfalls and have begun to incorporate community ideas, historical consciousness and regional culture.

More recently, there are clear signs that Japanese designers are abandoning technological or formal spectacle in favour of a re-examination and re-evaluation of their own traditions. The careful use of materials and details often harks back to historical forms and techniques of the past. Such approaches mark a distinct retreat from the frenetic styling that characterised architecture in the era of the bubble economy. Architects such as Kengo Kuma, Tadao Ando and Itsuko Hasegawa reinvigorate traditional forms and materials with sobriety and clarity, while at the other end of the scale, there is a delirious, funky energy to the work of emerging younger architects. Practices such as Hitoshi Abe, Tezuka Architects and Klein Dytham straddle a fluid cross section of architecture, urbanism, interiors, furniture and product design, deftly sifting and abstracting elements of Japanese popular culture. Yet while the country's economic slowdown is likely to curtail the scope of unfettered experimentation, it seems clear that Japanese architecture will continue to be as paradoxical and provocative as the culture in which it is conceived.

The notion of sport as a catalyst for wider architectural and social agendas underscored national preparations to host the 2002 World Cup. Both Japan and Korea have undertaken major programmes of stadium building and the jointly hosted event is intended to foster better relations between two historic antagonists. Among the Japanese projects, Hitoshi Abe's sports stadium in Sendai, a regional capital north of Tokyo, showed a young architect brilliantly responding to the opportunity to work on a large scale. His powerfully articulated composition of two curved roof planes recalls Kenzo Tange's Yoyogi Stadium (built for the 1964 Tokyo Olympics) and combines formal dynamism with a powerful sense of drama and occasion. Sendai has undergone something of a minor architectural renaissance, with Toyo Ito's extraordinary Mediatheque forming a popular new centre for culture and education.

China's successful bid to host the 2008 Olympics in Beijing is also envisaged as acting as a stimulus for long term development and change. An area in Bejing's Ya Yun Cun district has been earmarked for development as the Olympic centre, to be overseen by a combination of local Chinese and US designers. Elsewhere in China, booming development in the southern cities of Guangzhou and Shenzehn continued apace, reflecting the country's relentlessly buoyant economic growth.

However China's race to modernise has raised many issues, including the question of sustainable development, which is emerging as one of the most crucial factors to impact on planning and architecture world wide. For centuries, building has been seen largely as a way of living apart from the environment and dominating nature. It has turned out to be a hollow supremacy, but the current attitude of ecological despondency has motivated many professionals and academics to re-evaluate the fundamental premises that underpin how buildings and infrastructure are designed and produced. Beneath technical efforts to reconstitute the built environment lies the elusive but critically important concept of sustainable development. Across a wide range of disciplines, including architecture, conjecturing a built environment that mimics and complements rather than conflicts with nature is emerging as a vital goal of current theory and practice.

Architects clearly have roles and responsibilities in the context of ecological propriety, but tend not to be granted a great deal of latitude for reflection as they are swept along in the 'time is money'-dominated processes of building procurement and production. Moreover, it is rare to find a client interested in investing valuable time and money in responsive, sustainable architecture, even though it can yield demonstrable economic, social and cultural benefits. Yet it is clear that architects can lead by example, by suggesting ecologically responsive paradigms, that in turn can influence other agencies involved in determining the character of the environment, such as clients, planners, politicians and the public.

This hybrid approach explores notions of appropriate rather than high technology, to create buildings that are not only harmoniously integrated with the landscape, but are also climatically responsive, the soul and substance of an emerging ecological propriety.

In Europe, Germany and Scandinavia have led the way in evolving environmental policy and this is reflected in buildings that embody stringent codes relating to energy use, selection of materials, waste disposal and recycling. Individual architects such as Thomas Herzog, Günter Behnisch and Peter Hübner continue to mine a rich vein of ecological consciousness at both a macro level in buildings and on a micro level in the exploration of the potential of existing and new materials and technologies. In the UK, where the cultural landscape continues to be transformed by the resources from the country's National Lottery, green agendas have been explored by a succession of High Tech architects, including Norman Foster and Nicholas Grimshaw, in a synthesis that has been dubbed 'Eco Tech'. Located in a disused clay quarry in Cornwall, Grimshaw's innovative and extremely popular Eden Project aims to demonstrate the riches of global bio-diversity and potential for sustainable development. A series of giant glass biomes recreating examples of the world's ecologies are melded into a fluidly amorphous bubble that appears to evolve organically from the rock face of the quarry.

As a begetter not only of buildings but also of urban form, architecture cannot retreat from the city, and the quality of life in urban centres is an ongoing and increasingly important pre-occupation of architects and planners. The relationship of public life to public space is dynamic and reciprocal and made up of many strands. The task of architects and urban designers is to weave these diverse elements into a sustainable, integrated fabric that takes account of the spatial, social and technical systems that constitute the private and public life of the city. 'New urban architecture is not about appearances but about substance, about a holistic interaction of aesthetics, politics and finance', notes British architectural commentator Kenneth Powell.

Many European cities, such as Berlin, Rotterdam and Valencia, are the focus of ambitious programmes of urban regeneration and development in response to growth and change. Berlin's elevation to German capital has generated a host of new government complexes, diplomatic facilities and commercial buildings, reflecting its renewed political and economic importance. Notable new embassies include James Stirling and Michael Wilford's British embassy, Diener and Diener's stark cube attached to the existing Swiss embassy and the Nordic embassies compound, in which individual buildings by various Scandinavian architects are enclosed by a sinuous perimeter wall made of copper slats. In the commercial sector, Frank O. Gehry's ING Bank headquarters in Pariser Platz is a model of sobriety on the outside, but a huge glass vaulted courtyard at the centre of the building contains a meeting space in the form of a giant contorted fish. One of Berlin's largest government projects is Axel Schultes' new Chancellery building, a monumental complex of offices and apartments.

In Rotterdam, a run-down dock area in the south of the city, the Kop van Zuid, is currently being revived by new buildings, such as Bolles + Wilson's Luxor Theatre and housing by assorted high profile Dutch architects, in tandem with the repair and conversion of existing warehouses and industrial structures. In Valencia, Santiago Calatrava has designed a new cultural quarter on the site of a dried-up riverbed. The boldly formal plan brings a sense of vision to a neglected area and Calatrava's flamboyant, organically inspired structures rear up against the sky like the bleached bones of some long dead behemoth.

This year has been defined by many images of architecture as a backdrop to human events and endeavours, but perhaps the most memorable image, for all the wrong reasons, was a tableau of cataclysmic devastation. The notion that the twin towers of the World Trade Center could be destroyed in a terrorist attack was simply too implausible to contemplate, except in the most melodramatic and far-fetched of film scenarios. Built in the early 1970s, Minoru Yamasaki's audaciously soaring towers were familiar beacons in the Manhattan landscape. Mainly a forum for business, they also attracted tourists, diners, shoppers and New Yorkers marking high days and holidays, a reminder of architecture's power to transform the physical fabric of cities and give texture to lives.

Only days before September 11th, a Frankfurt-based conference on the design of tall buildings reverberated with the optimistic energy of architects, engineers and developers all united in the unstinting quest to build still higher. The 500-metre-high Shanghai World Financial Centre by Kohn Pedersen Fox is currently under construction, and the South Dearborn tower proposed for Chicago by Skidmore Owings & Merrill is due to become the world's tallest structure at 609 metres high. Now new uncertainties prevail, but tall buildings are still seen as a logical response to increased densities and the soaring cost of land in urban areas. By 2015, some 28 cities will have populations of more than 10 million inhabitants and a further 10 cities more than 20 million inhabitants. Future designs for tall structures will have to address issues such as mixed-use programmes of development, structural innovation and sustainability.

Beyond the events of last September, American architecture exhibited an increasing vigour and diversity. Major projects, such as Frank O. Gehry's Experience Music project in Seattle, demonstrated the power of technology to generate dramatic new forms, taking its cues from polychromatic dissected guitar parts. James Polshek's Rose Centre for Earth and Space was a spectacular addition to the American Museum of Natural History in New York. Overseas designers are also making their mark; Dutch architect Rem Koolhaas completed a new Guggenheim outpost in Las Vegas and Renzo Piano has been commissioned to design a new Manhattan headquarters for the New York Times. Away from the rarefied milieu of international superstars, the work of Samuel Mockbee and his Rural Studio in America's deep South brought dignity to the lives of marginalised and impoverished local communities, affirming architecture's capacity to heal and transform.

In an age of increased cultural and social homogenisation, the issue of regionalism has assumed a renewed and timely importance. At the end of 2001, the latest projects were premiated in the Aga Khan Awards for architecture, a triennial cycle of awards honouring projects across the Muslim world, from Morocco to the Philippines. Buildings are examined following three years of use and are assessed for functional and social performance, giving the programme unrivalled depth and continuity. This year's awards encompassed a broad social and economic spectrum, from a college by Barefoot Architects set up to train India's rural poor, to a tourist hotel in Malaysia by Kerry Hill Architects that re-interprets traditional forms with great sensitivity on a fragile rainforest site.

The best of these buildings seem able to draw upon indigenous wisdom, but without resorting to pastiche, penetrating beyond the superficial features of regional style to explore a more resonant architecture rooted in responses to landscape and climate. In its quest for re-invention, recent architecture has often found itself chasing ephemeral novelty rather than engaging with tangible realities. Invention generated as a result of abstract models is often vulnerable to irrelevance and misdirection. Investigation of the local, and an increased awareness of humankind's relationship with the planet, are vital steps in the rehumanisation of architecture.

Catherine Slessor is the award-winning Managing Editor of *The Architectural Review* and co-ordinating editor of this publication.

Corporate

25th Street Studio

Santa Monica, California, USA

Koning Eizenberg Architecture

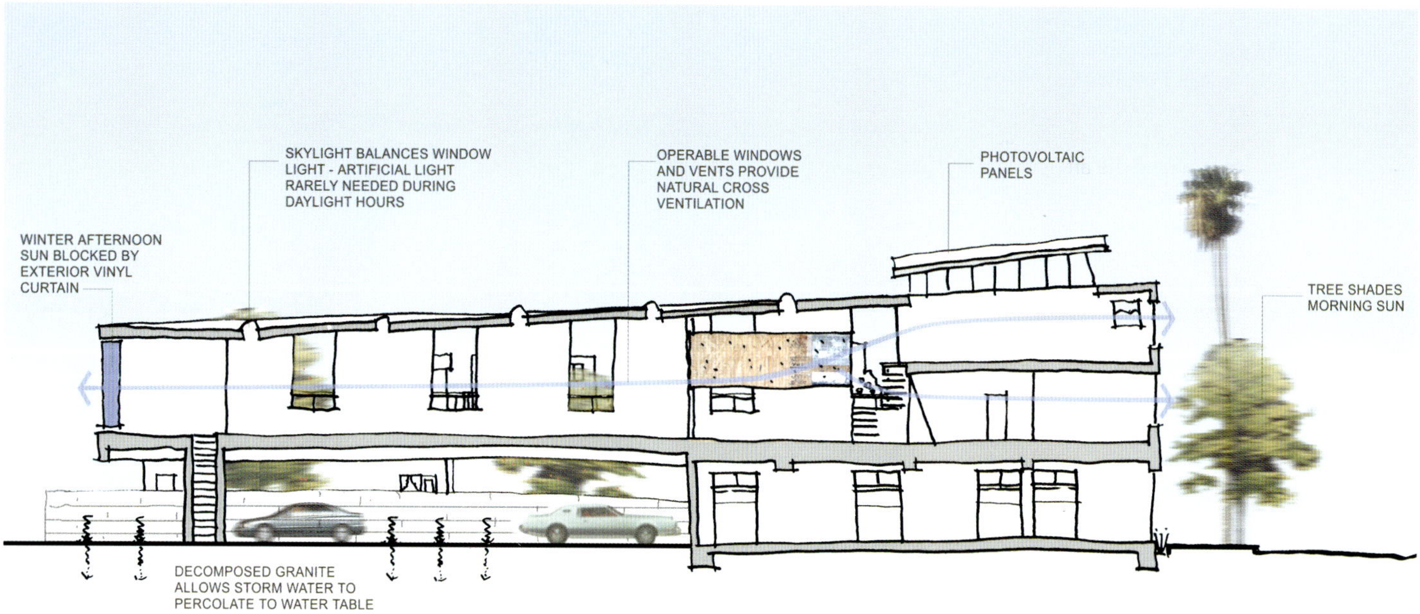

top North section

above North-east view

right Entry elevation

photography Benny Chan

The project is located in Santa Monica, California, and serves as both architecture studio and demonstration project for simple, environmentally friendly principles. It is not a building of meticulous details but of experimental intentions within a limited budget. The building sits on a site at the edge of a commercial zone, with multiple family housing to the north.

The building is on three levels. Ground floor commercial space is leased and the upper floor and mezzanine is used by the architect. The upper floors are entirely naturally daylit for the vast majority of daytime hours. Solar tube skylights balance the light from windows. Exterior passive shading is provided to the west by a big blue curtain that is drawn across in the winter in the late afternoon.

An improvised trombe wall to the south will vent, when finally complete, to better insulate the building in the summer and draw in warmth in the winter. Operable windows and cross ventilation minimise air conditioning use. Cheap materials, like painted pegboard, are used to shade windows and HDF sheeting provides a resource-efficient choice for the floor as does metal siding for the exterior walls. Responsible storm water disposal is also addressed. A plastic grid reinforced decomposed granite parking surface allows water to percolate back to the water table rather than to the storm water system and subsequently into Santa Monica Bay.

completion	January 2000
client	Hank Koning and Julie Eizenberg
area	678 square metres/7,300 square feet
structure	Standard wood and steel construction
materials	Steel, timber, MDF, corrugated steel, Hardi fibre cement board
cost	US$584,000
awards	2000 AIA California Saving by Design Energy Efficiency Award
top	Blue curtain as shading device photography Quito Banogon
middle	Third floor mezzanine looking north-east photography Benny Chan
bottom	Interior entry/reception photography Benny Chan

Aurora Place
Sydney, New South Wales, Australia
Renzo Piano Building Workshop Architects
in collaboration with Lend Lease Design Group Ltd and Group GSA Pty Ltd (Sydney)

Unlike contemporary podium-based buildings which separate and obscure the identity of the tower from the street, the shape of the Aurora Place Towers is immediately evident from the ground. The architectural composition of the two buildings was conceived to obtain a microcosm of 'urbanity' in the middle, a sense of compression between the curved façades, opening onto the street with a small piazza.

Covered by a spider web-like canopy, the piazza between the two towers is destined to become a meeting place. This hovering horizontal place of low iron glass shelters the piazza, cafés, retail areas and lobby entry from both the wind and rain. The same granite of the piazza extends into the office tower lobby. Here, terracotta tiled walls radiate a feeling of warmth and provide a backdrop to a series of large-scale public artworks.

The geometry of both buildings is straightforward, based on a simple faceted cylindrical geometry, which maximises repetition in the glazing panels in most areas. In the office tower, the shape of the southern part of the east façade changes on every floor, thus making the façade sweep out dramatically. This flaring form, part of a cone, has been generated by the use of diminishing radii at each floor, from the top down.

The significant advantage of this twisting form is that it not only produces increased floor areas in the top of the office building where space is more valuable, but also increases the size of the public piazza.

The extensions of the façade beyond the enclosure of the building are called 'fins' and 'sails'. The glass façades are gently curving and continuous from street level to the top (sail) and to the extremities in plan (fins). Trimmed like sails on a yacht, the fins and sails serve to mitigate the effects of wind, sun and rain on the façade and on the ground plane. The oblique cut at the top was determined by a 'light angle' to prevent unduly overshadowing of the Botanical Gardens.

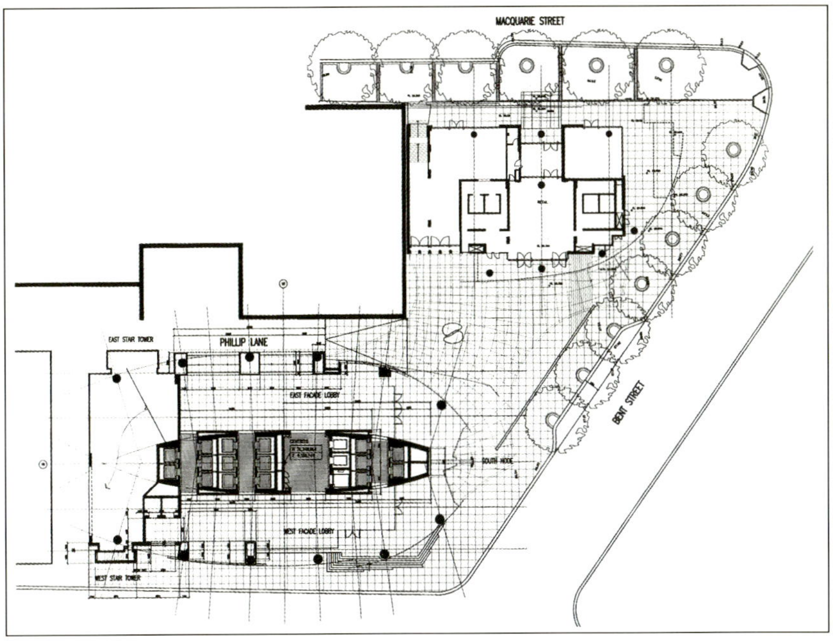

completion	2000
client	Lend Lease Development
area	49,500 square metres/532,818 square feet
structure	Steel, concrete
materials	Glass
cost	AUD$650 million
opposite	General view from harbour photography John Gollings
top	Site plan
bottom	Entrance of residential building photography Martin van der Wal

right Office building lobby
photography John Gollings
below Office building elevator lobby
photography Martin van der Wal
opposite right 'The Wing'
photography Olaf De Nooyer
far right South elevation
bottom right View of glass-covered square with Kan Yasuda marble sculpture
photography John Gollings

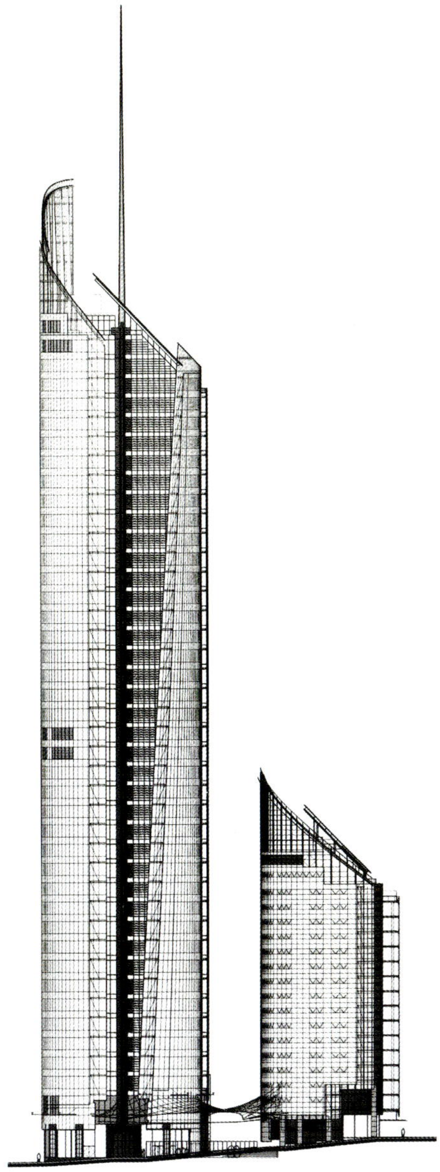

DG Bank Building
Berlin, Germany
Gehry Partners

The DG Bank Building is a mixed-use building comprising a commercial component housing the Berlin headquarters of the DG Bank, and a residential component consisting of 39 apartments. The commercial component is oriented towards Pariser Platz and the Brandenburg Gate, and the residential is oriented towards Behrenstrasse.

Each façade is clad in buff-coloured limestone that matches the Brandenburg Gate. The Pariser Platz façade features a series of simple punched openings and deeply recessed window bays, allowing the building to blend naturally into the unique urban fabric, which is the setting of the Brandenburg Gate.

A glass canopy covers the main entry to the building from Pariser Platz. A high-volume foyer immediately inside the main entry offers a view into the building's large interior atrium, which features a curving glass ceiling and a curving glass floor.

A wood-clad arcade leads to the office elevator lobbies, which are located on either side of the atrium. Office spaces are organised around the atrium, and are oriented inwards to take advantage of the natural light that floods through the ceiling.

The building's primary conference hall is located within a highly sculptural shell in the centre of the glass floor of the atrium. Clad in stainless steel on the exterior and wood on the interior, the hall appears to float in the fluid depth of the space.

A second, smaller interior atrium serves the residential component of the project. This atrium allows natural light to enter both sides of each apartment. A reflecting pool at the bottom of the atrium adds a dynamic quality to the light, best seen from the glass elevators that service the residential area. The apartments vary in size, from studios to maisonettes, occupying the top two floors.

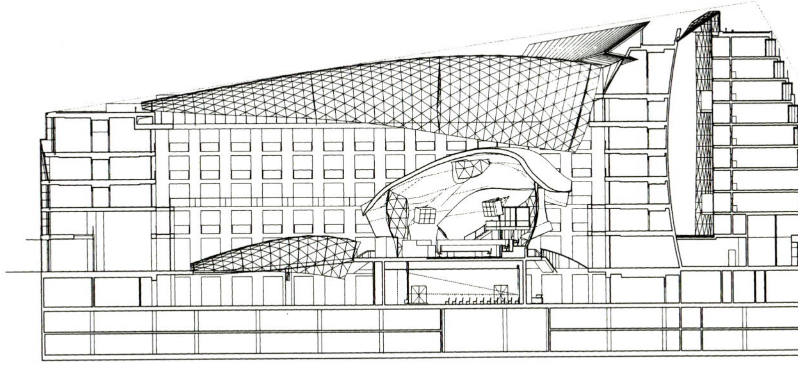

completion	May 2001
client	DG Immobilien Management GMBH, Hines Grundstucksentwicklung GMBH
area	20,000 square metres/215,280 square feet
structure	Concrete frame
materials	Stone, glass, stainless steel, Douglas fir
opposite	Interior view of ground floor
top	Section A
middle	Curved steel and glass lattice of barrel-vaulted roof over atrium
bottom	Staff cafeteria

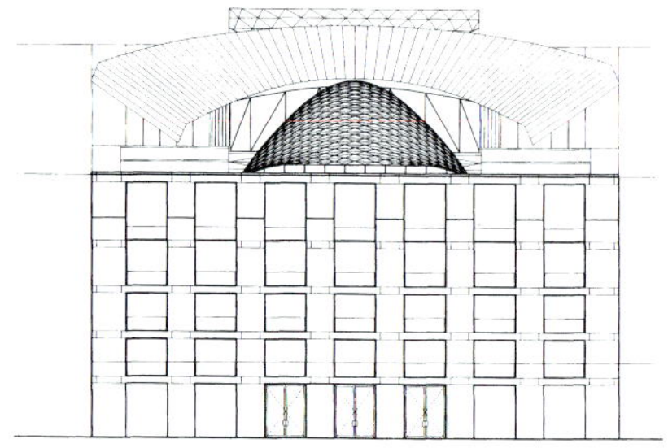

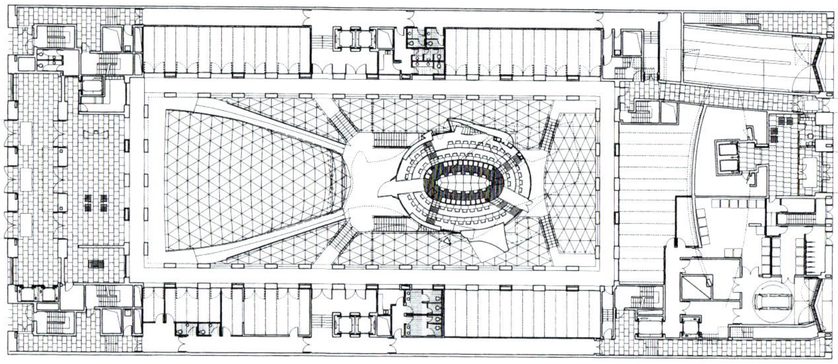

top right	North and south exterior elevations
right	Ground floor plan
bottom left	Façade of apartment block
bottom right	Main atrium
opposite	Conference chamber interior
photography	Roland Halbe

Gannett/USA Today Corporate Headquarters
McLean, Virginia, USA
Kohn Pedersen Fox Associates PC

The project consists of a new headquarters for Gannett and USA Today on a 12-hectare (30-acre) site outside of Washington DC. This represents a corporate move from an urban high-rise work environment to a suburban location, providing potential for site amenities, and the ability to design a more flexible space integrating new technology in a more productive work environment.

There are three basic functional program elements: common spaces are distributed at the entry level of the complex; flexible, high-ceiling newsroom and production spaces are on podium levels two and three; and typical office spaces are located above in linear towers, designed with flexibility for departmental change, and oriented on the site to maximise views. The narrow tower footprints allow maximum natural light for all occupants.

The design orients the community space and the complex as a whole towards the pond, allowing the southern orientation to maximise sunlight into the exterior courtyard and adjacent terraces. Site development incorporates employee amenities: health club, jogging trails, cafeteria and client dining with terraces overlooking the natural setting. Landscaping is used to reinforce the site features and as a buffer to noise along the adjacent highways.

The low-rise configuration of the complex respects zoning constraints, special requirements and view angles, while the sloping rooflines create a distinctive and visible profile from the adjacent highways.

The headquarters is designed to maintain operations at all times, around the clock, through redundant power and global satellite communications systems.

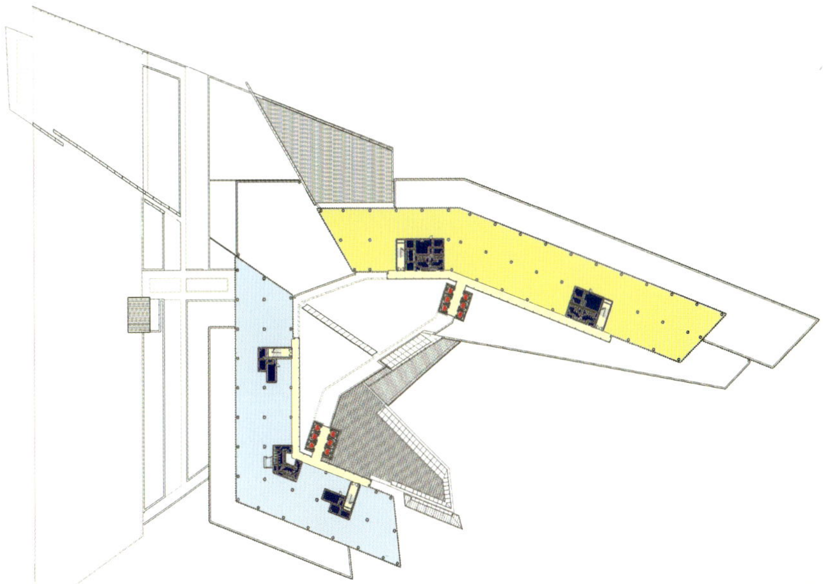

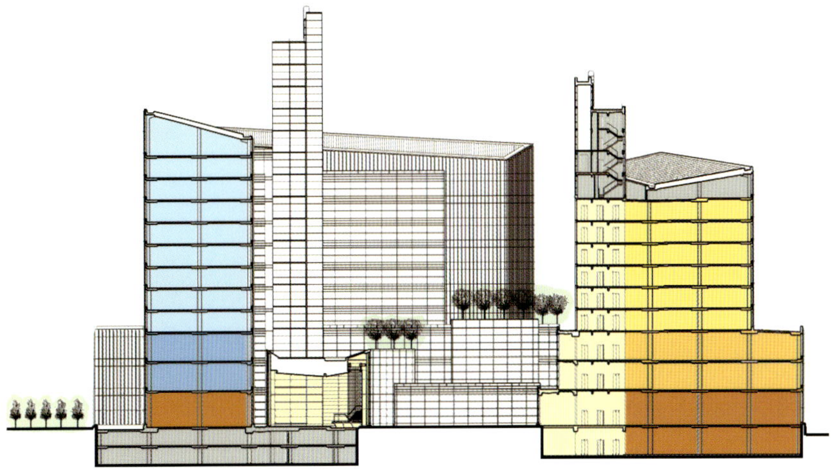

completion	October 2001
client	Gannett Company, Inc. and USA TODAY
developer	Hines
area	76,180 square metres/820,000 square feet
structure	Concrete
materials	Reflective glass, clear low-e glass, quarried stone base, standing seam metal roof
opposite	Articulated elevator towers act as beacons
top	Typical office floor plan
middle	Section
bottom	Glassy elevator towers, lobby and major circulation line animate courtyard
photography	Michael Dersin

GSW Headquarters

Berlin, Germany
sauerbruch hutton architects

This design forms the extension to an office tower, which was one of the first projects to be built during the reconstruction of Berlin in the 1950s.
The design endeavours to combine the 'as found' fragments of the city into a three-dimensional composition through which the existing building is able to be integrated into its context. The idea of conglomerate growth is not only accepted but also put forward as a model for urban development.
The new ensemble responds as much to the baroque logic of the street plan as it does to the rules of 19th-century urbanism. It also absorbs the object-like quality of the tower and registers the confrontational space which had developed between the high-rise buildings on either side of the Berlin Wall. In this combination of the disparate spatial configurations of consecutive generations, the new high-rise slab is the element associated with the present and the future.
The design of the high-rise slab is generated by a concern for the workplace in the city, and by a commitment to an architecture that is economical with the (built and natural) resources of the environment. This building not only offers an exemplary working environment in its passive control of energy consumption, but at the same time redefines an architecture in which the value of sensuous space is reassessed.

completion	January 2000
client	Gemeinnützige Siedlungs und Wohnungsbau, Gesellschaft Berlin mbH
area	47,873 square metres/515,305 square feet
structure	Concrete, steel
materials	Glass and aluminium façade, terracotta tiles with graphite coloured glazing, corrugated metal panels, fibre-cement panels, exposed concrete, glass, wood (American cherry, beech), stone (granite, basaltina, colombina)
cost	£58 million
awards	2001 Deutscher Fassadenpreis 2001 Shortlist, Five best buildings in Northern Europe, World Architecture Award 2000 High Commendation ar+d award 2000 Stirling Prize Shortlist, Royal Institute of British Architects 2000 BDA Berlin, Architekturpreis
opposite	Façade from east photography Bitter + Bredt
right	View from west photography Annette Kisling

top left View from east
photography Annette Kisling
middle left Detail west façade
photography Annette Kisling
bottom left View towards west façade
photography Annette Kisling
top right Section through atrium
middle right Third floor plan
bottom right Entrance hall
photography Bitter + Bredt
opposite top Conference room
photography Annette Kisling
opposite bottom Entrance from west
photography Bitter + Bredt

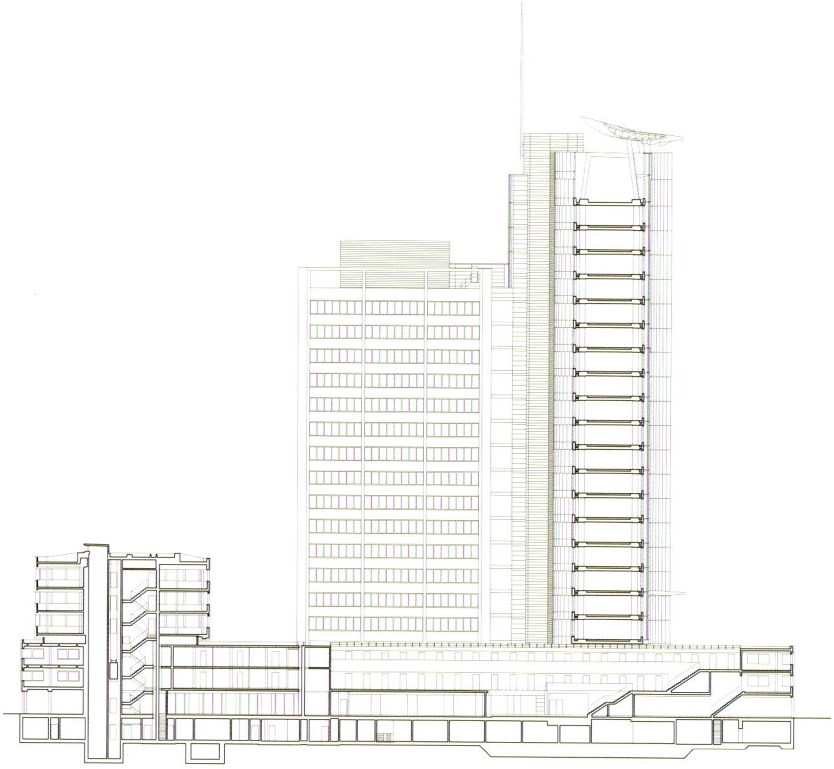

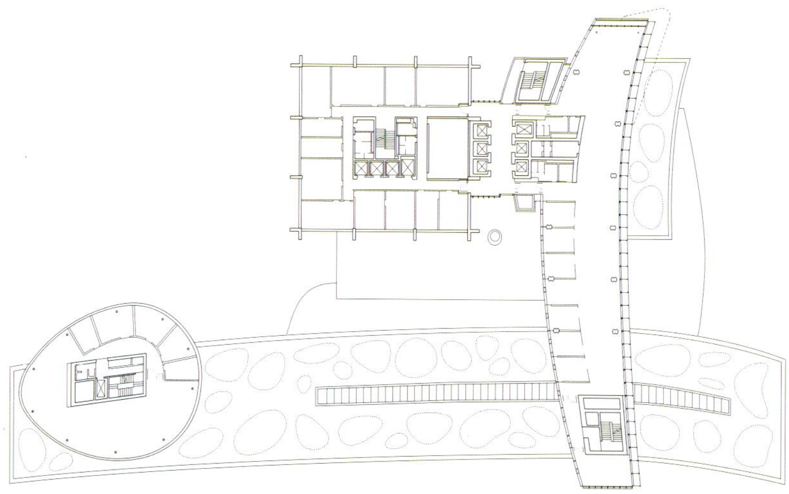

IBM Center for e-Business Innovation

Chicago, Illinois, USA

Design Office/Imaginary Forces

The IBM Center for e-Business Innovation was conceived from a holistic approach that represents a convergence of architecture, immersive media and 'smart' technology. Everything from network architecture to physical architecture is scaleable and upgradeable.

The interior space is 'open' in every sense of the word, creating an ambience of accessibility and approachability. Walls are not permanent, partitions do not create rigid segregation; instead they elegantly slide and rotate into place for situations that require more or less privacy.

The primary collaborative tool for bringing participants together with IBM-topic specialists is the 'interactive' conference table. This prototype for the traditional conference table offers participants the opportunity to interact and manipulate digital projections that appear on its surface while seated in a configuration that encourages non-hierarchical and collaborative dialogue.

Other features designed for the centre include voice recognition, touch screens and new media technologies, which make for an information-rich and interactive environment that responds to individual guests. 'Smart' technology is programmed and integrated into the space and allows IBM and the individual guest to develop and maintain a connection with each other before, during and after the briefing centre experience.

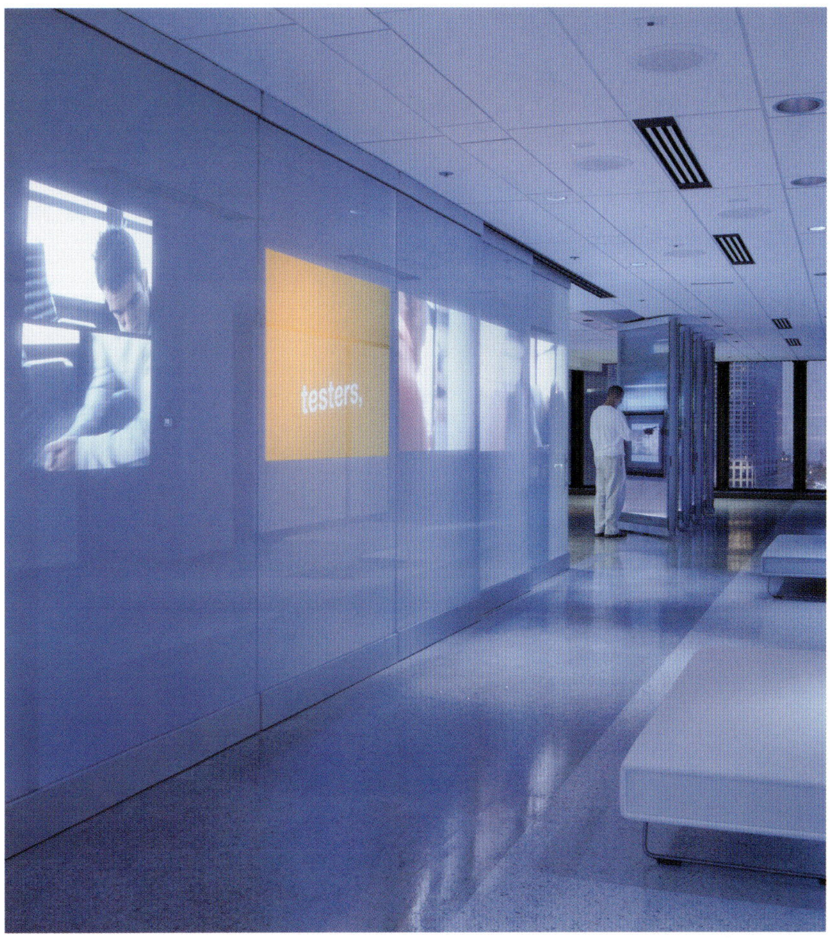

completion December 2000
client IBM
area 985 square metres/10,602 square feet
structure Existing steel structure high-rise
materials Custom epoxy terrazzo flooring, fibreglass wall panels, Perspex wall panels, metal wall panels, tempered clear glass, cast resin cabinetry
opposite top View of reception area with kiosks
opposite bottom Pivoting walls open up briefing room
top Detail of interactive conference table
bottom Gallery wall with media projections
photography Benny Chan

Main Administration Building Stadtsparkasse Düsseldorf
Germany
Ingenhoven Overdiek Kahlen und Partner

Stadtsparkasse Düsseldorf was re-opened in December 2000 after a three-year planning and building phase. It is located at Berliner Allee, one of the important north–south connections in inner-city Düsseldorf.

The competition for the redesign was won with a plan including both remodelling and expansion, concentrating on enhancing integration into the urban environment and communication by the preservation of the essential building structure. A glass parabola matches the height of the neighbouring buildings, and provides a clear, transparent bank landscape. The installation of 'One Hundred Heads' by Beat Streuli on the glass with transparent foils makes it complete – the façade becomes a medium, especially at night. The redefinition of the communications of the building gives it openness and transparency. This includes the complete removal of the entire closed wall and façade element of the complex. The result is a veritable glass building in which the street is part of the building, and from which the manifold life within the building is separated only by the transparent glass.

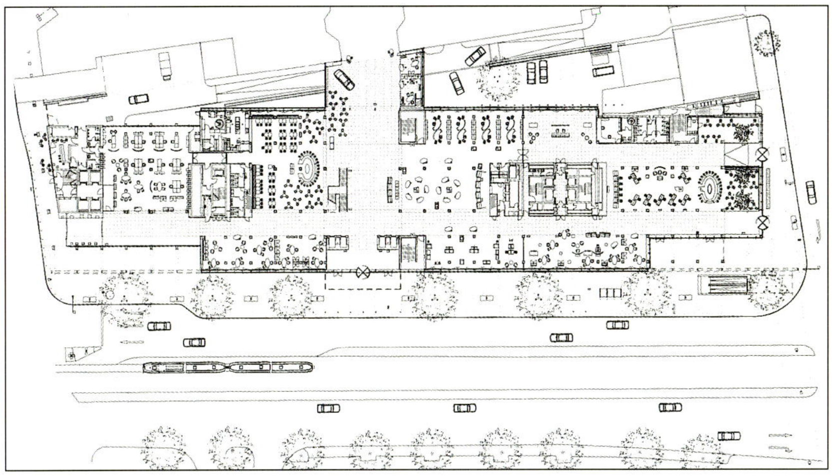

completion	December 2000
client	Stadtsparkasse Düsseldorf
area	35,021 square metres/376,966 square feet
materials	Steel, concrete, glass
opposite	Berliner Allee façade
top	Basement plan
right	Café

top	Elevator
bottom	Berliner Allee façade
opposite	Façade detail
photography	H.G. Esch

NMR Laboratories
Utrecht, The Netherlands
UN Studio van Berkel and Bos

The small pavilion-like NMR (Neutron Magnetic Resonance) laboratory is situated on the 'De Uithof' university campus in Utrecht. The organisation of the building is reflected in its surfaces, and the unusual research technique and the molecular structures that are uncovered in the laboratory have strongly influenced the architecture.
The two-storey laboratory contains eight spectrometers (high frequency magnets), eight consoles and other ancillary equipment, as well as public and office spaces. Each magnet has both specific behaviour and requirements, creating magnetic fields of different sizes and sensitivity. The performance of other equipment present within a variable radius of the magnets affects their performance. The equipment is sensitive to movement, types of structure, installation and climate. The magnetic field corresponds with the frequency of the magnet. The design had to ensure that the individual force fields were not disturbed.
As a result, the radiating powers of the magnets constitute the virtual core of the projects, and modify the organisation of the building. They provide permutations for the structure and surface of the building, dictate the materials that can be used, the disposition of the program and the equipment, and the possible routing systems. A second important structural principle is the column-free spatial organisation, which enables the efficient use of the small centre. The combination of these two central principles results in a multidirectional surface condition in which the walls flip over and meet each other to generate a situation in which all ends meet.

completion	2001
client	University of Utrecht
area	21,000 square metres/226,044 square feet
materials	Concrete, glass
cost	2.2 million EURO
opposite	Front façade
top	East corner
bottom	East façade

top East façade
bottom West façade
opposite Ramp
photography Christian Richters

Sony Centre
Berlin, Germany
Murphy/Jahn

In the reconstruction of Berlin, the Sony Centre stands for a new technical vision and order. It is not a building, but a part of the city. Surrounding the centre are the traditional urban streets and spaces. Inside is a new type of covered urban forum, for a changing cultural and social interaction. The spatial dynamics and variety are contrasted by a minimal and technological attitude. Light, both natural and artificial, is the essence of the design. The Sony Centre is luminous, not illuminated. The façades and roof act as a fabric that moderates the natural and artificial light – they become a screen. With its characteristics of transparency, permeability to light, reflection and refraction, there is a constant change of images and effects during day and night, affecting not only the appearance but also maximising the coming and minimising the resources.
Through Sony's sponsorship the vision of public space in the city becomes the centre's primary urban characteristic. The centre is a group of buildings for the new age of entertainment. There is a serious effort for tailoring architecture to the stimulating contemporary confusion of private and public space. The Sony Centre is a *kulturforum* for the millennium, where the serious business of entertainment is portrayed as the real challenge to the high art of classical music, theatre and painting.

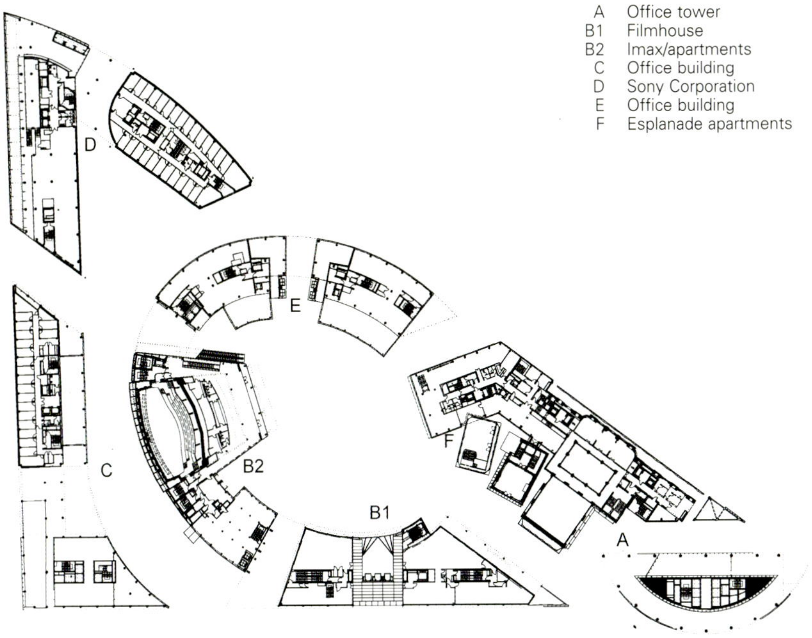

completion	January 2000
client	Sony with TishmanSpeyer Properties and Kajima
area	26,444 square metres/284,643 square feet
materials	Steel, glass, fabric
opposite	Sony headquarters
top	Floor plan
right	Entry gate to forum space

top Elevation
bottom left Overall view of Sony forum
bottom middle Glass skygarden
bottom right Wintergarden
opposite Night view of forum
photography Engelhardt/Sellin, H G Esch, John Linden & Sven Fiebig

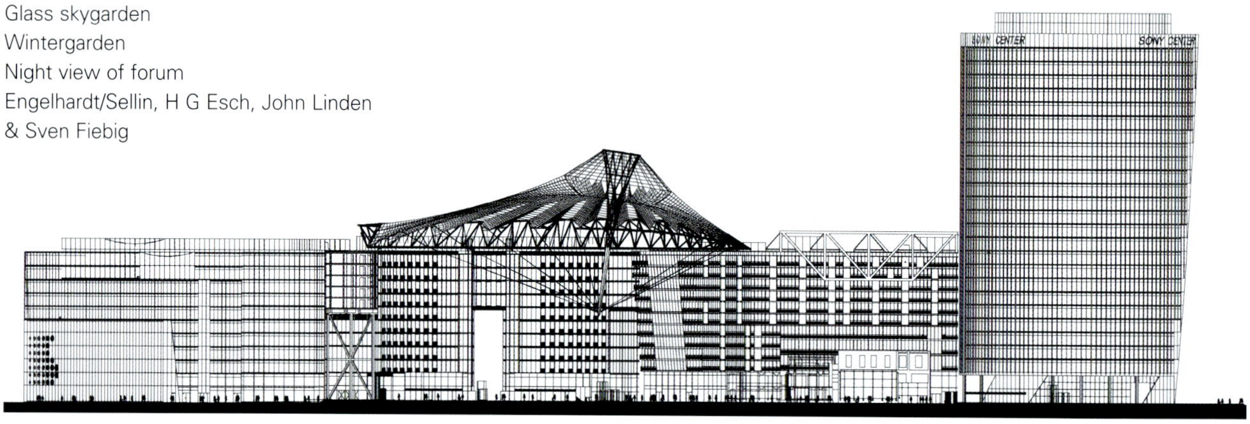

Volksbank Borken
Borken, Germany
Bolles+Wilson

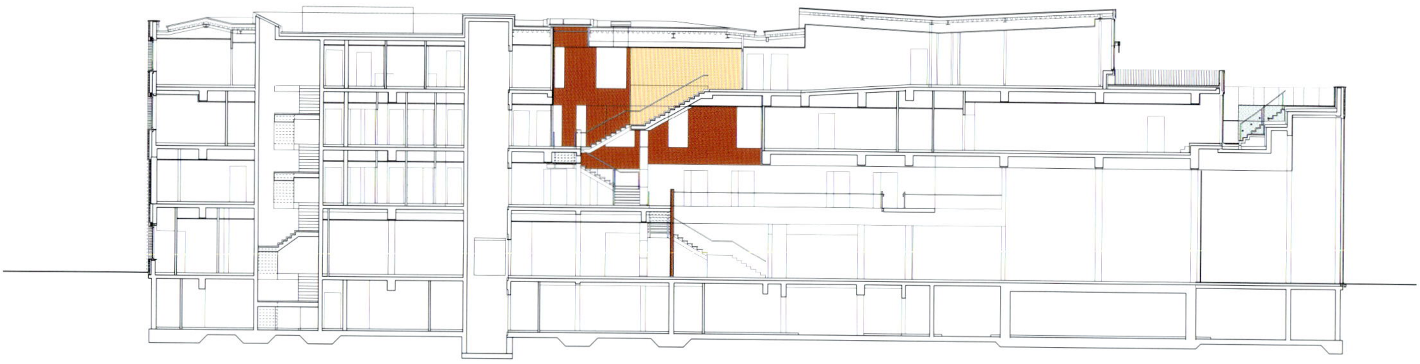

Virtual banking has caused a major restructuring not only in everyday exchange but also in the configuration of the bank itself. The Volksbank Borken translates this change of function and image into architectural form. The contradictory requirements of openness and discretion are here synthesised as an 'umbrella of discretion'. The bank opens to the street front, as a generous, dramatic-scaled and totally glassed bank hall. Within the bank the ceiling of this hall steps down from three-to-one floor height.

Above is a brick volume, with the 'discrete' rooms of the traditional bank (e.g. conference, directors). These also step down to stand finally at the back elevation on the ground. These two pieces dovetail together to form a precise cubic building – an 'umbrella of discretion' over a zone of openness and transparency.

The simple overall form anchors the surrounding context of supermarkets, small houses and traffic roundabout. The post-digital bank is within walking distance of the town centre, but also, in the age of mobility, is equally accessible to car-driving customers. The solid upper volume is in a warm and lively turf-fired brick; the glass façades form vertical stripes – stretch lines between roof and earth.

Most money transactions in the new bank are automated. The dramatic front ATM-hall is open 24 hours a day and divided by a 6-metre-high (64-foot) sliding wall from the bank hall itself. Roving bank personnel chat with customers at standing tables in the central hall, or withdraw to the glass cubicles at the rear. Deeper into the bank hall where the ceiling steps down, a new vertical vista opens up. The central staircase with wood panels and daylight from above leads landscape-like to upper floors, rooftop café and schooling rooms. This stair is illuminated by an internally lit glass column – both structural and ephemeral like money itself. A second illuminated column marks the entrance and plays an iconic role locating the bank in the City of Borken.

completion	2000
client	Borkener Volksbank
area	700 square metres/7,535 square feet
structure	Reinforced concrete
materials	Turf-fired brick
cost	7.5 million EURO
opposite top	Section
opposite	View into bank hall
top	North elevation
bottom	Entrance area

opposite	ATM hall
below left	Bank hall
below right	Main stairs to offices
photography	Christian Richters

Educational

Bucksbaum Center for the Arts

Grinnell, Iowa, USA

Cesar Pelli & Associates

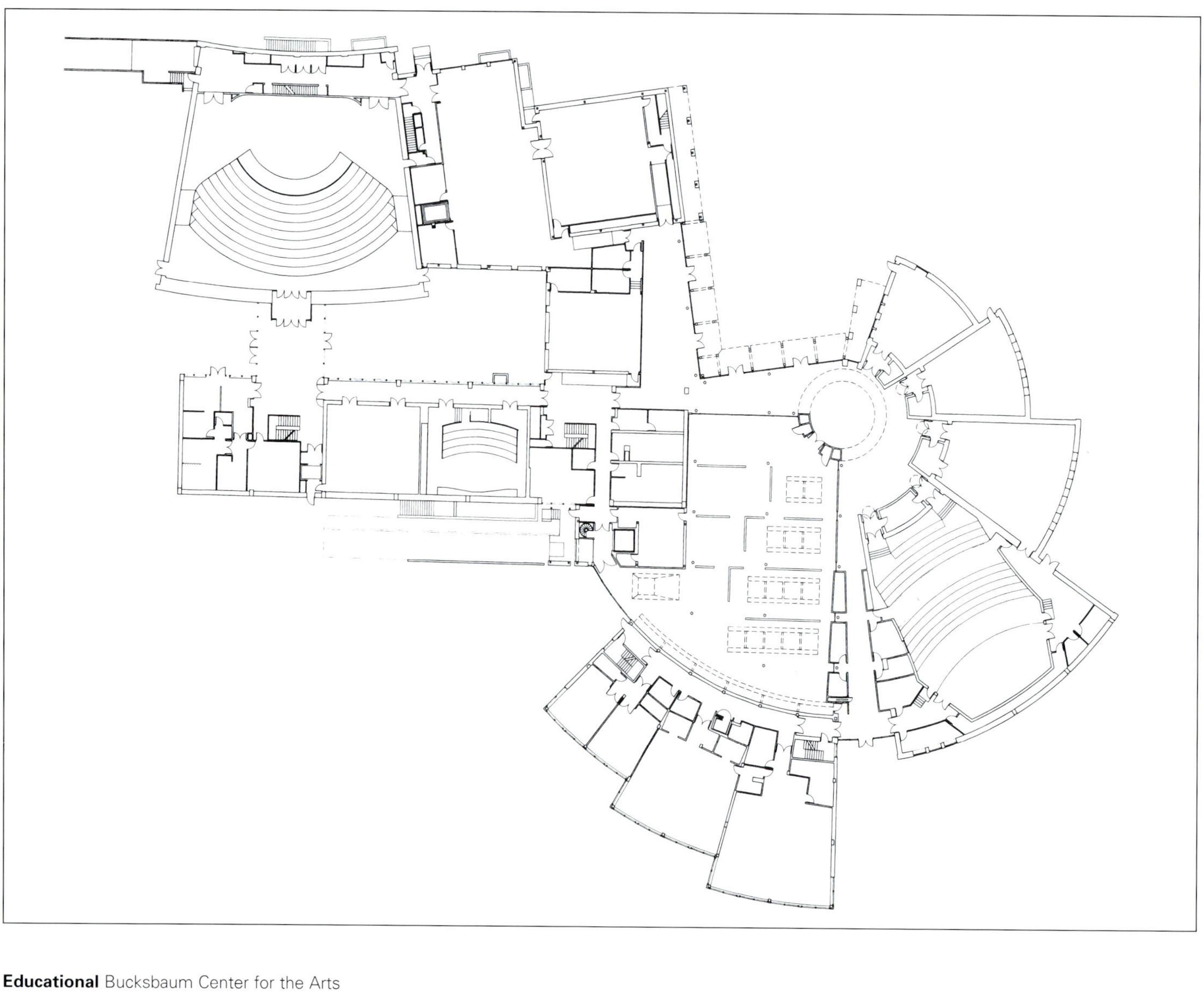

The Bucksbaum Center for the Arts combines teaching facilities with performance spaces for music, art and theatre/dance to serve both the college curriculum and the town of Grinnell. The building program called for instruction, rehearsal and performance spaces as well as an exhibition gallery.

The site for the building, which is on the south edge of the campus, faces one of the residential neighbourhoods of Grinnell. The building placement on the site was established and designed to create a presence of the arts on campus. The Fine Arts building faces Route 6, which is the main approach to campus, and completes the centre campus quadrangle at the south end.

The design of the Bucksbaum Center for the Arts acts as a bridge from the campus to the town by reaching out in both directions. The organisation of the building reflects integration of fine arts in a liberal arts college setting. Specifically, the entry courtyard creates a place for meeting, student and faculty interaction and performance. The new interior lobby collects the primary performance/public spaces including the gallery, recital hall and studio theatre.

Each public performance/display space received special attention to important design criteria. The gallery works with controlled environmental and lighting systems to protect and conserve the collection while also providing a wonderful space to inhabit. The music and theatre spaces are acoustically and technically sophisticated to ensure exciting spaces for users and participants.

completion	2000
client	Grinnell College
area	12,077 square metres/129,997 square feet
structure	Art wing: cast-in-place concrete; Black box theatre: steel frame; Music wing: concrete reinforced masonry with long span steel trusses
materials	Brick veneer
cost	US$22 million
opposite left	Art studios and recital hall
opposite right	Art studios
opposite	First floor plan
top	Entrance lobby and rotunda
middle	Gallery
bottom	Recital hall
photography	Timothy Hursley

Diamond Ranch High School

Pomona, California, USA

Morphosis

top left View of classrooms from field

top right View of school from parking lot

bottom left View of courtyard

bottom right View of courtyard

The school is built on a steeply sloped site, which was considered 'unbuildable' and donated to Pomona Unified School District. A natural landscape of Riparian oaks and native grasses surround the site.

The first goal was the desire to take advantage of the site's natural beauty by integrating the play fields and buildings into the surrounding hillside. The second goal was to create a dynamic built environment to foster maximum social interaction between students, teachers, administration and the community. This facilitates a flexible teaching environment with a solid foundation core curriculum for grades 9–10, and numerous specific program majors for grades 11–12.

The siting of the project took advantage of a natural bowl for the playing field and primary football field, embedding them in the sloped earth at the south of the site to create an economically efficient hillside seating area. The school is organised around separate groups of four classrooms each. This arrangement fosters team teaching and creates a more intimate environment, where students are moving between classes in a smaller cluster. Landscaped outdoor teaching areas at each cluster act as courtyards between buildings. From the parking court at the side of the gymnasium, the landscape/building events of the school weave together with a pedestrian street that unites the entire complex – a physical manifestation of the school's sense of community by encouraging student/teacher interaction. One of the major focal points of the scheme is a monumental stairway that allows movement from the main school areas to the roof terrace and football field above, while creating a student amphitheatre. The focus here was to integrate and take advantage of the site's topography, creating a dual usage of landscape as structure.

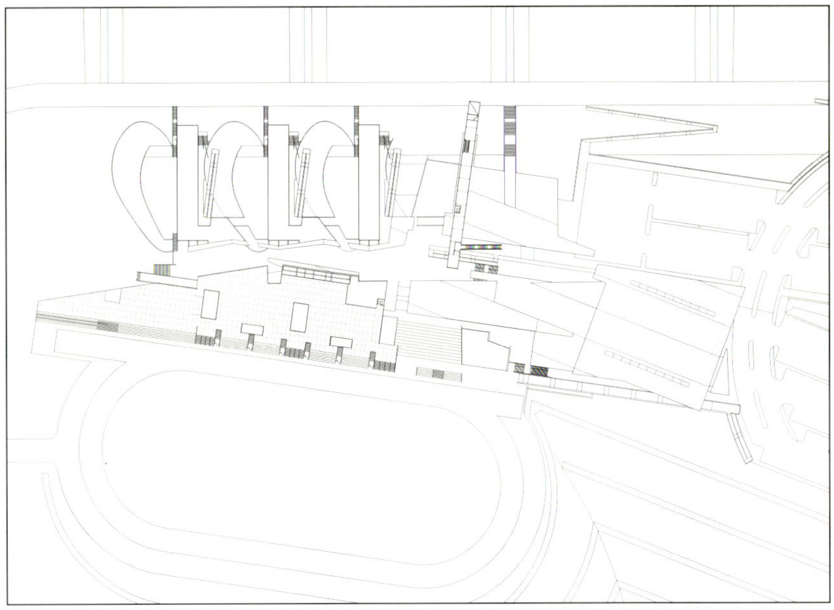

completion	January 2000
client	Pomona Unified School District
area	13,935 square metres/149,996 square feet
materials	Corrugated metal, steel, concrete
cost	$US20 million
awards	2001 CC AIA Award 2001 Los Angeles Business Council – Kaufman Broad Award 2001 Los Angeles AIA Honor Award 2000 Los Angeles AIA Honor Award 1997 Progressive Architecture Award 1995 AIA with the National School Board Association
top	Roof plan
middle	View of courtyard from platform
bottom	Library exterior
photography	Brandon Welling

Faculty of Economics and Business, University of Murcia

Murcia, Spain

Adhoc msl (Enrique Carbonell and Salvador Moreno)

top left South façade
photography Duccio Malagamba

top middle South-west view
photography Duccio Malagamba

top right East façade
photography Duccio Malagamba

bottom North-west corner
photography Juan de la Cruz Megias

The Faculty of Economics and Business is a complex of services for students and teachers, with four parallel linear blocks, which are small faculties themselves. The differences among the four blocks come from different uses – reception, administration, bar, restaurant, lecture hall, library, classrooms and auditorium.
To articulate these blocks, a line and point are used. The line is a street as a thoroughfare linking the other buildings of the campus. The point is a square, an inner courtyard, under the classrooms, containing the bar and restaurant. Wide corridors link every point of the faculty, so all the spaces for the inhabitants of the complex are as important as the classrooms themselves. The east-facing façade shows four aluminium towers with a custom-designed glass curtain wall showing the bands of classrooms and offices, acquiring at night the random composition of what is illuminated and what is not. The south façade contains corridors, protected from the sun by brise-soleils made of perforated metal. To the west, the concrete wall has a metal ventilated cellosy, previewing the interrelationship inside the building.

completion	February 2000
client	University of Murcia
area	26,000 square metres/279,864 square feet
structure	Concrete
materials	Concrete, galvanised steel, glass
cost	US$7.2 million
awards	XI Premios de Arquitectura de la Región de Murcia
top left	Detail entering courtyard photography Duccio Malagamba
top right	Main entrance photography Duccio Malagamba
middle	Inner street photography Duccio Malagamba
bottom	Auditorium photography Juan de la Cruz Megias

Gateway Center, University of Minnesota
Minneapolis, Minnesota, USA
Antoine Predock Architect

The new University of Minnesota Gateway Center – a ceremonial gathering place – occupies a major entrance to the campus. The design for the centre invites visitors to the campus through the embodiment of Minnesota images, ambiguously evoking a rock face or the iconic huddle of the Minnesota farmstead. The large glass, granite and wood memorial hall is adjacent to a sloping copper structure nestled against the regulating office block at the north.

Seen both as the casual and formal heart of the building, Memorial Hall is an irregular polyhedron of colliding granite planes and glazed fissures which allow sunlight into this large open gathering space. Abstracting the granite strata of Minnesota, the hall rises out of the ground as an 'upheaval', binding the building to the place. Once inside the space of the hall, one is confronted by the interweaving programmatic spaces with balcony and stair projections.

Sheathed in the same copper as the exterior, each floor level is expressed on the internal wall in solid and void relationships, while the facets of the main hall are clad in gapped hemlock planks. The salvaged 55-foot-high 'Memorial Arch' from the razed stadium formerly occupying the site was mandated as part of the building. It is 'hung' like a painting from one of the interior tilted polyhedral facets. The arch becomes a literal gateway to the past, serving as entry to the Heritage Gallery of the program.

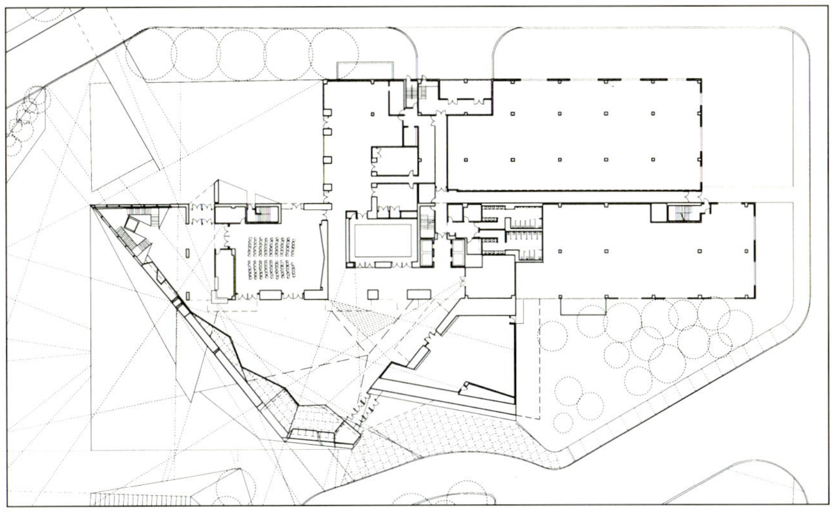

completion	2000
client	University of Minnesota Alumni Association, University of Minnesota Foundation, University of Minnesota Medical Foundation
area	21,367 square metres/230,000 square feet
structure	Steel frame
materials	Copper, granite, glass
cost	US$27 million
awards	2001 Grand Gold Award, Consulting Engineers Council of Minnesota, 34th Annual Engineering Excellence Awards 2000 Honor Award, AIA New Mexico
opposite	Interior view of Memorial Hall
top	First floor plan
middle	McNamara Alumni Center in morning light
bottom	Main entry looking west
photography	Timothy Hursley

Ichthus College

Rotterdam, The Netherlands

(EEA) Erick van Egeraat associated architects

The new Ichthus College at the Kop van Zuid refers to the adjacent harbour in urban scale as well as in typology of the late 19th- and early 20th-century industrial architecture. The ground floor conforms to the planned continuation of the adjacent building arcades. More specific and public spaces are placed on the first three floors, with the classrooms situated on the upper six floors.

An atrium space along the south façade develops over the full height of the building, creating the heart of the college. The materials are predominantly cobalt blue screen-processed glass and clear glass – an expression of the open character, the maximal flexibility and remarkable views.

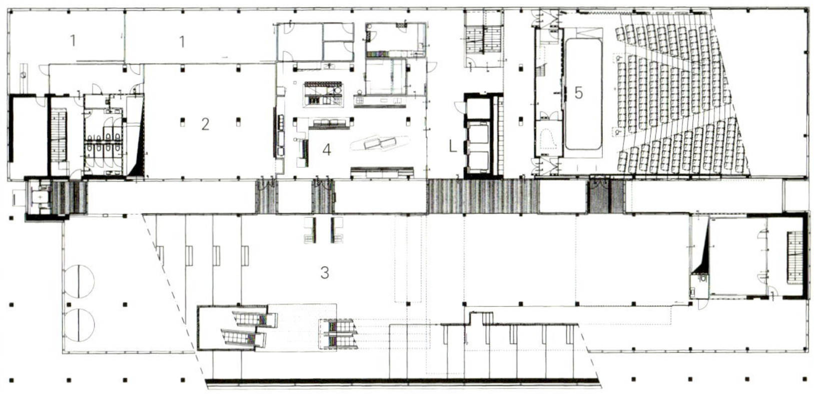

1 Meeting room
2 Staff cafeteria
3 Restaurant
4 Kitchen and buffet
5 Auditorium
L Elevator

completion	June 2000
client	Ichthus Hogeschool Rotterdam
area	20,000 square metres/215,280 square feet
structure	Steel skeleton, concrete floors
materials	Glass façades, aluminium frames, wooden bridges
cost	45 million NLG
opposite	South façade
top	First floor plan
above	South-west corner façade
right	Atrium/Cafeteria

top Longitudinal section AA
bottom Atrium
opposite Detail of view bridges
photography Christian Richters

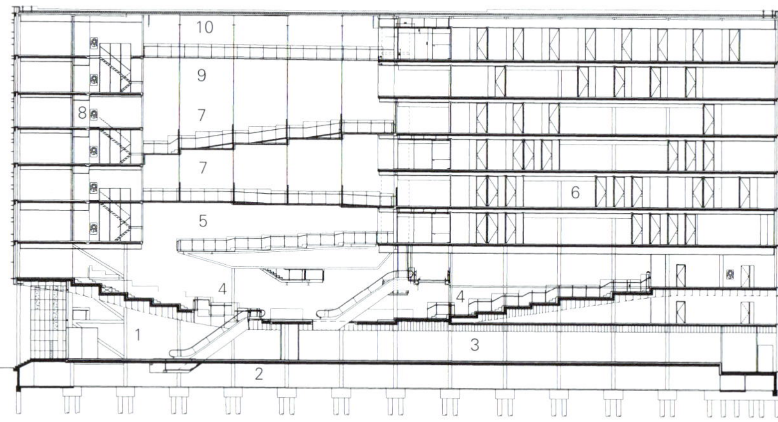

1 Entrance hall
2 Parking garage
3 Shops
4 Stepped floor restaurant
5 Study area
6 Offices and flexible work spaces
7 Suspended study area
8 Administration tower
9 Atrium
10 Suspended bridge

Jubilee Campus, University of Nottingham
Nottingham, England, UK
Michael Hopkins and Partners

The University's Jubilee Campus turned a former bicycle factory site into an innovative 'green' academic park for around 3,000 students, in a balance of communal, functional and operational priorities disseminating both environmental awareness and the viability of practical, affordable and sustainable industrial regeneration.

The competition-winning design created a lake along the site, which is the centrepiece of the new campus park. Three faculties, Learning Resource Centre, Central Teaching Facility and student residential halls with 750 beds enjoy lush planting and relaxing views. The principal faculty buildings are arranged along a lakeside promenade leading to the university playing fields.

The faculty buildings fronting the lake face in a westerly direction, taking advantage of the prevailing wind. Cool air is picked up from the lake surface and channelled through low level glazed louvres into the atrium/link spaces between the building blocks and out through high level glazed louvres at the opposite end, meaning that the planted atrium spaces are naturally ventilated.

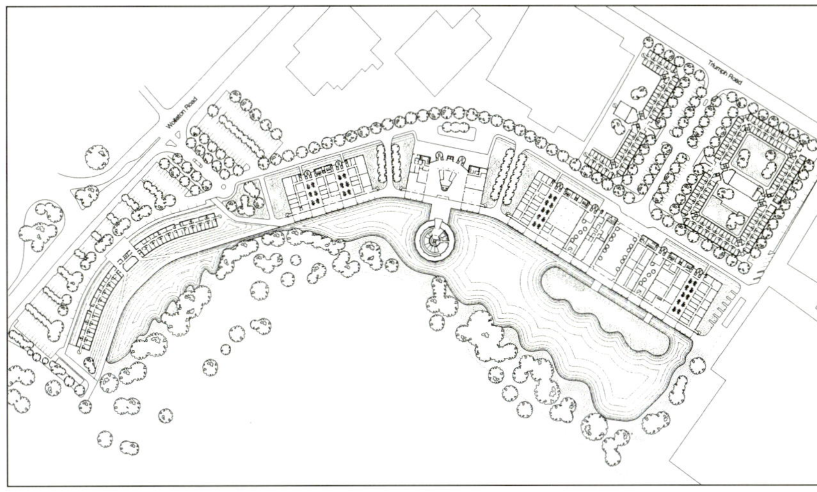

completion	1999
client	University of Nottingham
area	15,000 square metres/440,000 square feet
materials	Timber, glass, steel, concrete, brick, aluminium
cost	£24 million
awards	2001 Royal Institute of British Architects (RIBA) Award 2001 Aluminium Imagination Award – commended 2000 Hot Dip Galvanising 2000 British Construction Industry 2000 Lord Mayor's Special Award
opposite	Learning Resource Centre on its lake isle photography Martine Hamilton-Knight
top	Site plan
right	Tracking wind vane on faculty building photography Ian Lawson

top	Faculty buildings stand alongside lake
middle	Cross section of Learning Resource Centre and Central Teaching Facility
bottom	Three lecture theatres are enclosed in a concrete form
opposite	Atrium in School of Education
photography	Martine Hamilton-Knight

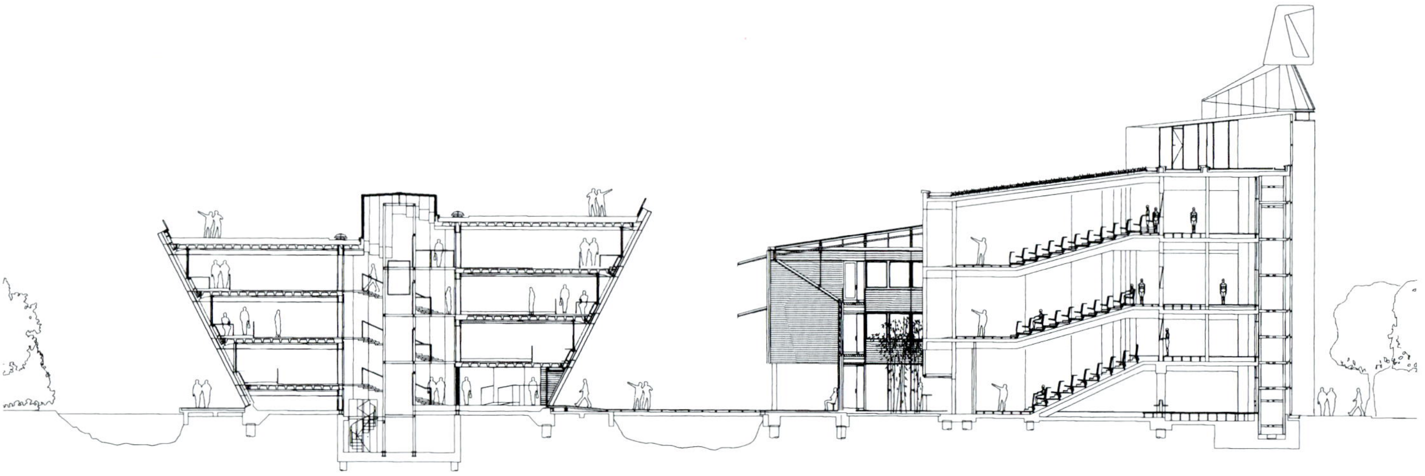

McDonnell Paediatric and Biomedical Research Building, Washington University

St Louis, Missouri, USA

Perkins & Will

Local affiliate architect: Polk Stanley Yeary Architects

This new research facility is located in the midst of a dense medical school campus, which includes Washington University School of Medicine and four prominent hospitals affiliated with the school. The new facility connects to an adjacent animal facility, currently being constructed, at every level. Connections provide direct circulation patterns between research and adjacent clinical services located at St Louis Children's Hospital.

One of the main goals of the research buildings was to foster interaction and create break spaces (lounges) for the researchers. To encourage interaction among researchers between floors an open, connecting stair was created between two floors and repeated four times throughout the building. The open stair is next to a break space on each floor and creates dynamic interaction and visually exciting spaces for the researchers.

The project construction was fast-tracked in order to accommodate the earliest move-in date for staff. The laboratory facility incorporates state-of-the-art technology and design to match the school's leading edge research. A repetitive laboratory plan was used to allow for maximum flexibility among the tenants and future research practices.

completion	February 2001
client	Washington University, School of Medicine
area	21,088 square metres/227,000 square feet
structure	Steel, concrete
materials	Brick masonry, glass, steel, maple panelling, slate
cost	US$55.5 million
awards	2001 Most Distinguished Building Award, AIA
opposite left	Exterior view of curved façade
opposite right	Ground level lobby area
top	Interior view of study lounge
bottom	Laboratory area
photography	Nick Merrick

The Scientia, University of NSW
Sydney, New South Wales, Australia
MGT Architects

The Scientia creates a ceremonial centre and symbolic heart for the post-war campus of Australia's largest university UNSW.

The building comprises three parts of different formal and material character: the sandstone podium, metal boxes and timber foyer trees.

A sandstone podium anchors the building, reinterpreting the natural sandstone of the hill on which the building stands. Woven through the stonework are precast concrete profiles that form continuous courses, with the presence of the sandstone granularly diminished to reveal the precast as louvres over openings, and terminating the podium in the form of balustrades. The podium is split at the line of the axial mall to create an open pedestrian passage though the building and into a new public square.

Two fine metal boxes enclosing the main rooms are raised on top of the podium either side of the central open passage. These volumes are clad in aluminium panels with continuous louvres to the east and west giving a translucency to the form, and filtering sunlight into the interiors. The interior of these volumes is characterised by the use of warm timber finishes and a

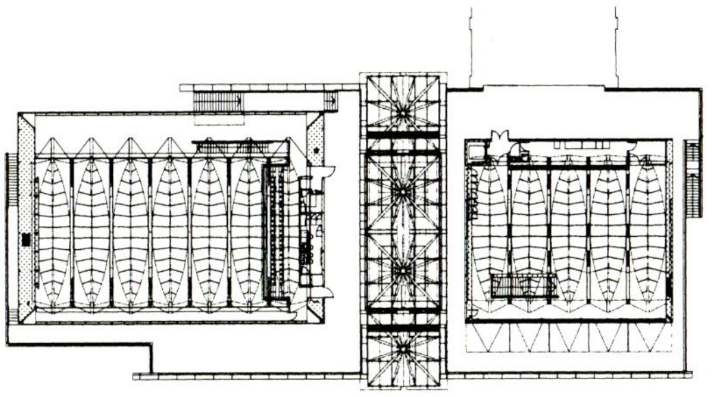

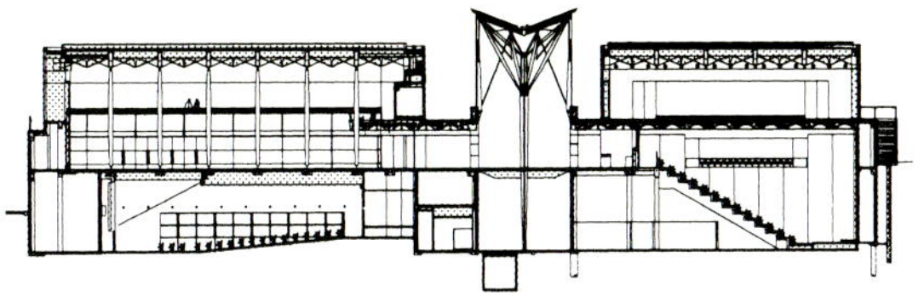

completion 2000
client University of New South Wales
area 4,500 square metres/48,438 square feet
materials Stone, precast, metal, timber, glass
cost AUD$30 million
awards 2001 Award for Excellence in Concrete Design, The Concrete Institute of Australia
2001 Kevin Cavanagh Medal for Excellence in Concrete, The Concrete Institute of Australia
2000 Sir Zelman Cowen Award, Royal Australian Institute of Architects (RAIA)
2000 Sir John Sulman Award for Architectural Excellence, RAIA
2000 Citation of Merit, Medium Structures, Lightweight Structures Association of Australia Design Awards
2000 National New Commercial Building Award for Construction Excellence, NSW Master Builders Association
2000 Outstanding Construction Award Educational Building $5M Plus category, NSW Master Builders Association
2000 Overall Winner for Construction Excellence, NSW Master Builders Association
2000 The Lloyd Rees Award for Excellence in Civic Design RAIA

opposite top Sketch
opposite bottom Western façade is dramatically illuminated to illustrate principal components of building
top Ceiling plan and section
bottom Glazed foyer supported on tree-like composite structures of timber and steel provides an iconic expression

below	Night view of Scientia provides a dramatic expression, welcoming staff, visitors and the wider community
right	Entry from foyer illustrating juxtaposition and palette of materials – stone, timber, concrete, steel and glass
bottom left	Controlled introduction of natural light into Ceremonial Hall
bottom right	Richly detailed interior absorbs afternoon sunlight
photography	John Gollings, Brett Boardman

ribbon-like ceiling of cast plaster supported by 12 columns of turned laminated Oregon. Standing between the two volumes in the central slot of the podium is the timber tree-like structure of the foyer. These tall open forms raised to the sky form the central focus for the building, the axial mall and campus as a whole. The forms of these structures, in steel, glass, turned laminated Jarrah and metal louvres, give a gentle form of enclosure, and break the sunlight not unlike the shelter of a natural tree canopy.

Swiss School of Engineering for the Wood Industry

Biel, Switzerland

Meili, Peter Architects with Zeno Vogel

The Swiss School of Engineering for the Wood Industry is situated between the residential areas on the outskirts of the city of Bienne and the industrial zones flanking the southern slopes of the Jura. The existing buildings consist mostly of one-storey production halls and storage sheds which, with their open layout, low-pitched roofs and close rapport with the surrounding landscape are typical of school buildings of the post-war period in Switzerland. The extension of the school called for a project that would exploit the full potential of the site while preserving as much as possible of the existing conditions. The design utilises structures that are fundamentally different in the way they relate to the outer and inner organisation of the ensemble. An extension to the production and processing halls on the southern part of the site wraps snugly around the existing buildings, responding to the low-lying character of the one-storey woodworking halls. In contrast, the new teaching building is a four-storey wooden structure that stands in harsh proximity to the halls and towers above the low-pitched roofs. Its proportions and dimensions verge on the dissonant, creating a tension with the low-rise buildings. To the north, the building extends to the street, almost touching the foothills of the Jura, highlighting the topographical situation. The teaching building consists of a series of wooden boxes with large skeleton frames. Because of the extensive spans, which are possible in wood-frame construction, it was possible to design the building in such a way that the modular structure corresponds to that of the classroom units and their partitioning. The structural beams are assembled in a grid-like planar system.

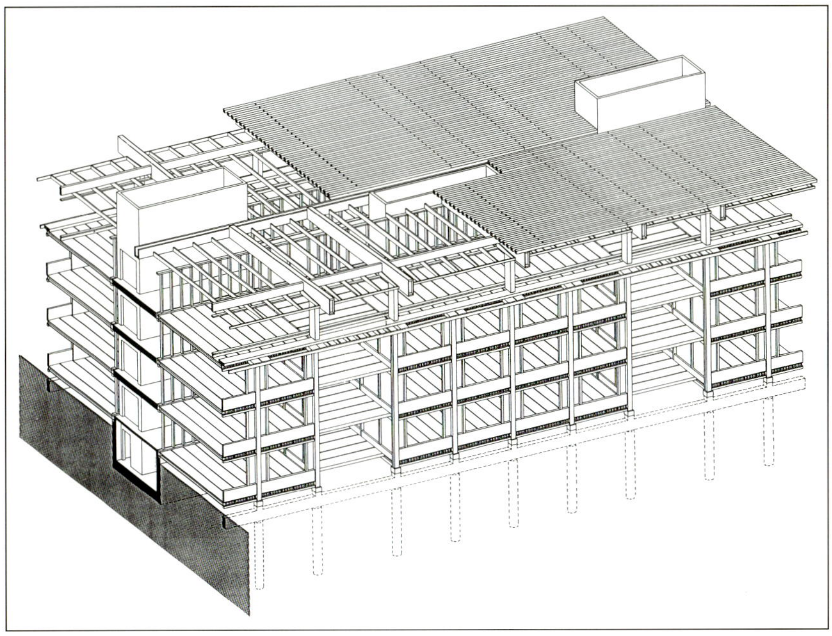

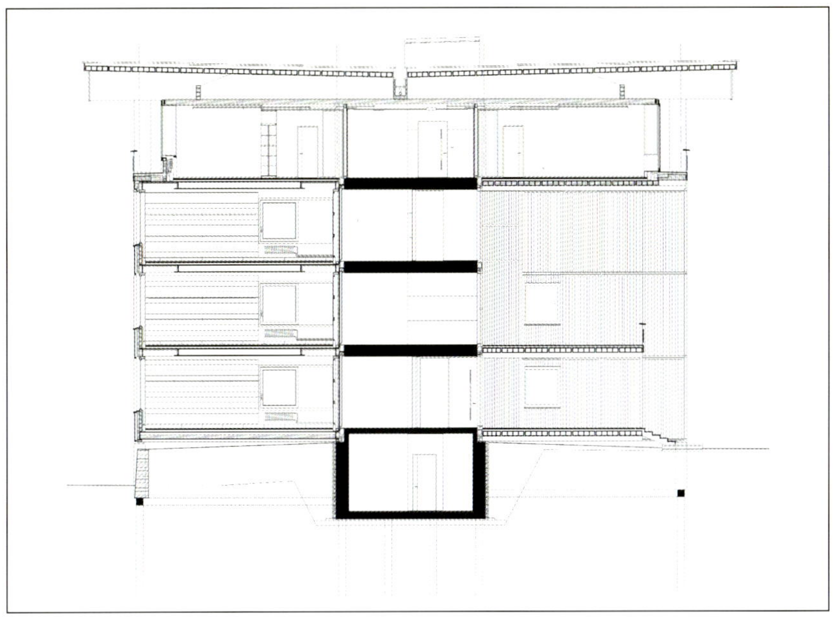

completion	1999
client	Kanton Bern
collaborators	Andreas Schmidt, Thomas Schnabel
art	Jean Pfaff
structural engineer	Jürg Conzett
area	9,000 square metres/96,876 square feet
structure	Concrete/Wood skeleton
materials	Windows: oak, pine, aluminium; exterior cladding: oak, aluminium; interior cladding: pine, alder, nickel-faced steel plates
cost	CHF 27 million
awards	Prix Lignum, ATU-Prix
opposite left	View from courtyard of classrooms and balconies
opposite right	View from main entrance
top	Isometric drawing of structure
middle	Cross section through classroom, central corridor and balcony
bottom	View from north

opposite View into central concrete core from classroom
below Lecture hall
photography Georg Aerni Fotograf

Over-sized apertures on the façade echo the underlying skeleton, which serves both as casing for the large windows and, through the balustrades, as supports for the ceiling below. The ceilings are composed of unclad, hollow, glued timber beams, which are laid edge to edge to form an uninterrupted surface for the floor above. The outdoor terraces span between the classroom boxes in such a way that the orthogonal change in the load-bearing direction is visible from both inside and outside.

The materials and structures were chosen for their resilience and functionality. Inside the building a monolithic central circulation zone made out of pre-stressed concrete conforms to the relevant fireproofing and load-bearing requirements. Prefabricated components of wood and wood-based materials, used on each side of the concrete core and over it, permitted speedy construction and roofing of the building. Although they provided an opportunity to test certain industrial wood-fabrication processes, the components are above all an essential part of the spatial concept of the design, in which the rigid box constitutes the basic element. The classroom volumes are treated as individual units, integrated with a structure that is composed throughout of open and closed spaces. These are aligned in such a way that light can penetrate the interior through the open spaces. The fine lines on the wooden surface of the façade elements alternating with views into the depths of the building result in a chiaroscuro effect.

University of Lapland, Extension

Rovaniemi, Finland

Juhani Katainen Architects

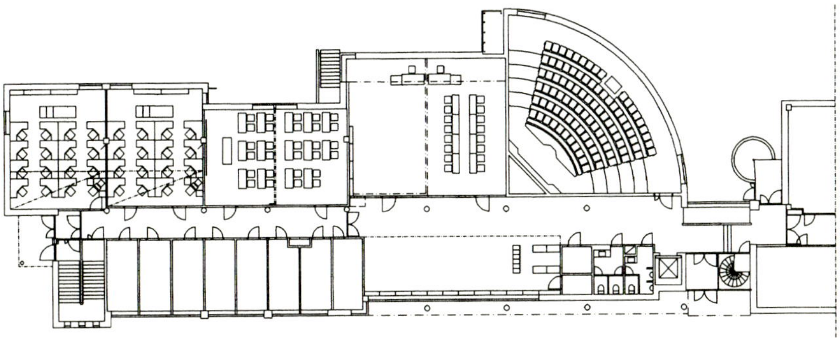

The characteristic features of the new building – the architectural concept, small scaling and materials – are closely connected to the old structures and the site. These choices were seen to be an advantage to the site and to strengthen the original concept as a whole. They play a very important role in the development process of the university, reflecting it in a closeness to the natural way of building.

completion	2000
client	Senaatti-kiinteistöt Oy, University of Lapland
area	1,975 square metres/21,259 square feet
structure	Post and beam construction, concrete slabs
materials	Brick, metal sheeting, steel, glass
opposite	Lobby
top right	Ground floor plan
top left	Elevation to courtyard
middle right	This auditorium can be connected to lobby to increase space
bottom left	Stair area is emphasised with handrail made of steel and wood
bottom right	Great auditorium
photography	Hannu Koivisto, Juhani Katainen Architects

Institutional

Arnold Bernhard Library, Quinnipiac University

Hamden, Connecticut, USA

Centerbrook Architects and Planners

This project undertook the renovation and expansion of a thoroughly inadequate library built in 1969 for a then young New England college. The front of the old building was remodelled to make its spire a beacon of radiating light and to provide a stepped proscenium at the spire's base for socialising and frequent ceremonies and concerts.

The rear of the building was largely demolished and replaced with a larger addition now open to a wooded glade and the panorama of stream and mountain beyond. Inside, the old structure was reduced from three floors to two, merged with each other via a skylit rotunda and open balconies. There is a variety of ambiences ranging from the lively cyber café to the secluded team study rooms cantilevered out into the treetops.

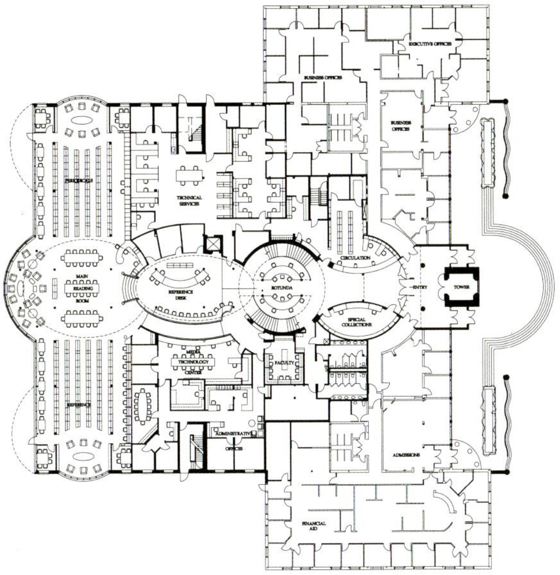

completion	September 2000
client	Quinnipiac University
area	5,574 square metres/60,000 square feet
structure	Structural steel frame, masonry wall construction, light-gauge and structural steel roofs
materials	Brick, asphalt shingles, EPDM, glass and aluminium curtain wall
awards	2001 *American School & University* Architectural Portfolio 2001 Honorable Mention Award, *Renaissance/Remodeling*
opposite top	Before renovation
opposite bottom	Remodelled front of existing building
above	On-line computer stations beneath rotunda bridge
top	First floor plan
middle	New addition at rear
bottom	Rotunda
photography	Jeff Goldberg/Esto

Coastal Traffic Centre
Kvitsøy, Norway
Jarmund/Vigsnæs AS Architects MNAL

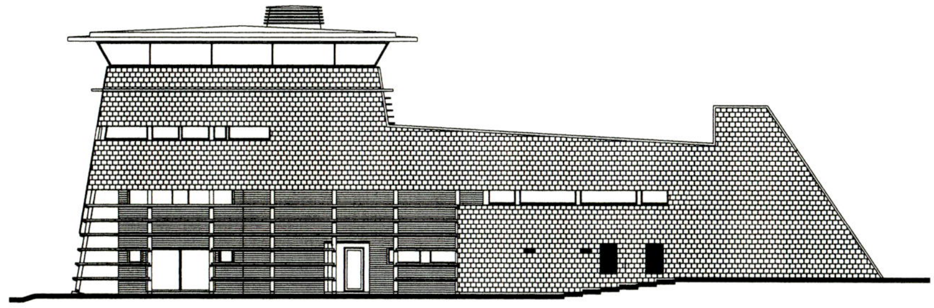

This design is a competition-winning scheme for the new pilot station at Kvitsøy on the west coast of Norway. Rather than building next to the old building, the architects decided to build on top of it, minimising construction and strengthening the profile of the pilot station as a beacon for sailors. The existing structure forms the core of the new building, with the new construction built around it; its surface broken in places to expose the inner structure. The angled walls of the entire building are clad in a unifying coat to mirror the pitched roofs of the surrounding village, which reflects the ever-changing conditions of light and moisture from the sea.

completion	September 2000
client	Statsbygg/Directorate of Public Construction and Property
area	928 square metres/9,989 square feet
cost	US$1.6 million
opposite top	Existing coastguard station has been enveloped by new building
opposite bottom	Walls are cut away to reveal inner workings of building
above	Orange stairway
top	East elevation
middle	Sloping slate-clad walls allude to pitched roofs of village below
bottom	Corridor
photography	Nils Petter Dale

Donald W. Reynolds Center on Aging, University of Arkansas
Little Rock, Arkansas, USA
Perkins Eastman Architects PC

The Donald W. Reynolds Center on Aging represents one of the first facilities in the United States to create an interdisciplinary home for gerontology programs in patient services, clinical research, basic science research, public policy and education. Reliance on state-of-the-art technology to connect the new centre of the University of Arkansas with other educational sites around the world and a clear mission to bring researchers, educators, students and patients together guided the design of this award-winning facility.

Two complementary components, a north volume serving research and education and a south volume serving patients and visitors, are bisected by a linear spine or atrium. These spaces offer the community of users a richly varied environment with contemporary, durable furnishings in attractive, airy and well-lit spaces. This combination of physical and technological features has positioned the Center on Aging to play a major role in shaping the next generation of treatments and caregivers for older adults. Commented Dr David A. Lipschitz, director of the Center on Aging and chairman of the Geriatrics Department, 'It's a truly remarkable facility'.

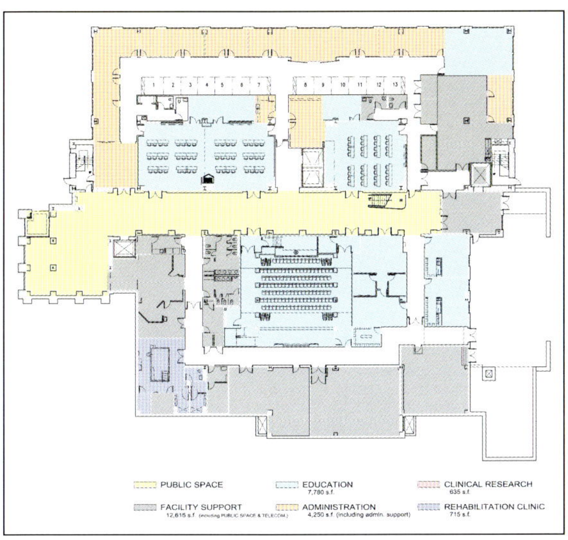

completion	January 2000
client	University of Arkansas Medical Sciences
area	8,918 square metres/96,000 square feet
structure	Steel, concrete
materials	Brick masonry, glass, steel, maple panelling, green and grey slate
cost	US$16.8 million
awards	Honor Citation, AIA, Gulf States Region
opposite	North exterior
above	Ground floor plan
top	Lobby
bottom	Atrium
photography	Timothy Hursley

Federal Chancellery

Berlin, Germany

Axel Schultes Architekten

The Chancellery forms part of a chain of federal institutions, 'ribbon' in form and 'thread' by function, adopted as a framework plan for redevelopment following an international competition in 1993. The linchpin of this urban design is the Civic Forum, though not yet implemented, which lies at the heart of the Inner Spreebogen and is intended to create a spatial and politico-programmatic link between the large-scale buildings isolated to each side of it. The architectural composition of the Chancellery takes as its sole point of reference this seat of sovereigns, this citizen's locus – which is yet to become one.

The Chancellery fulfils its 'compulsory programme' by means of two five-storey office tracts between the Forum and the River Spree. The comb-like structure, arranged around winter gardens for easy internal communication and lavish daylighting, accommodates 450 staff.

Up to the first 'urban edge' – the eaves, height of the offices – the executive building performs duties of a general nature: clustering access from the north and protocol entrances, with expansive foyers on levels 0 and 1 to embrace the international conference hall (for 150 people) and the government press and information rooms. Levels 3 and 4, inscribed within a 'great wave' above the foyers, absorb central services – emergency standby centre, crisis management, archives and the banqueting kitchens.

A clear incision equal in height to the roof edge over the offices marks the base of the chief executive tier. The 'sky lobby', the heart of each floor, is the communication centre linking essential Chancellery spaces.

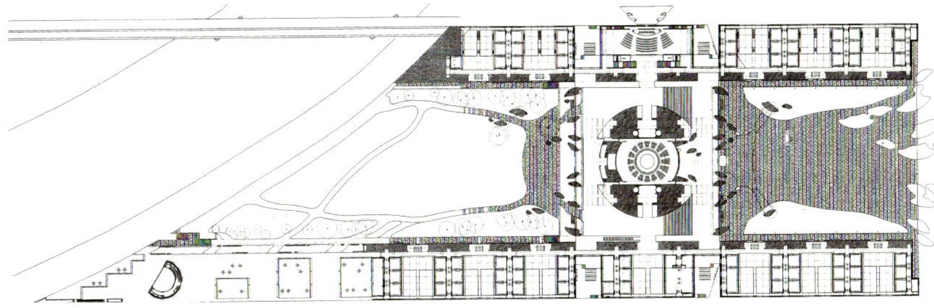

completion	2001
client	Bundesrepublik Deutschland
area	64,413 square metres/693,341 square feet
structure	Reinforced concrete, concrete
materials	Glass, serpentine
cost	465 million DM
opposite	Courtyard façade photography Werner Huthmacher
top	First floor plan
middle	Detail of garden façade photography Charlotte Frank
bottom	Detail of courtyard façade photography Charlotte Frank

right View of south wintergarden
photography Werner Huthmacher

far right Foyer
photography Werner Huthmacher

below View of north wintergarden
photography Stefam Müller

below right Sky lobby
photography Werner Huthmacher

CVF

Fingal County Hall
Dublin, Ireland
Bucholz | McEvoy Architects
in association with BDP Dublin Ltd

The county of Dublin was reorganised in 1992, creating four new governmental areas, one of which is Fingal County.
The program consists of a council chamber, a civic space in which the public meets and conducts business with county officials and office accommodation for the 450 employees of the council, divided into 10 departments.
The site is a town park in the centre of Swords, an 11th-century village, which has become a suburb of Dublin. Sited in the park, the new County Hall links together elements of Swords through the creation of a public space. The building is an open and transparent expression of local government reflecting the three roles of a county hall: as the centre of local democracy; providing services to the community; and providing an environment in which to work.
The internal public space is organised along a curved spine to which are attached three shallow plan office wings, interspersed with courtyard gardens or outdoor 'atria'. The arc is conceived as a 'vertical main street', the meeting point of the public and the council. On the lower levels of the atrium are the public counters, waiting areas, interview areas and the Council Chamber with public galleries, while on the upper levels are the communal areas serving the office spaces, including meeting rooms and service cores.
Fingal County Hall is an entirely naturally ventilated building; the primary building components – the structure and façade – have been carefully 'tuned-in' to the environment. The offices are laid out along the polar axis, using shallow depth blocks, allowing the movement of the sun and wind to affect the natural lighting and cross-ventilation of the office space.

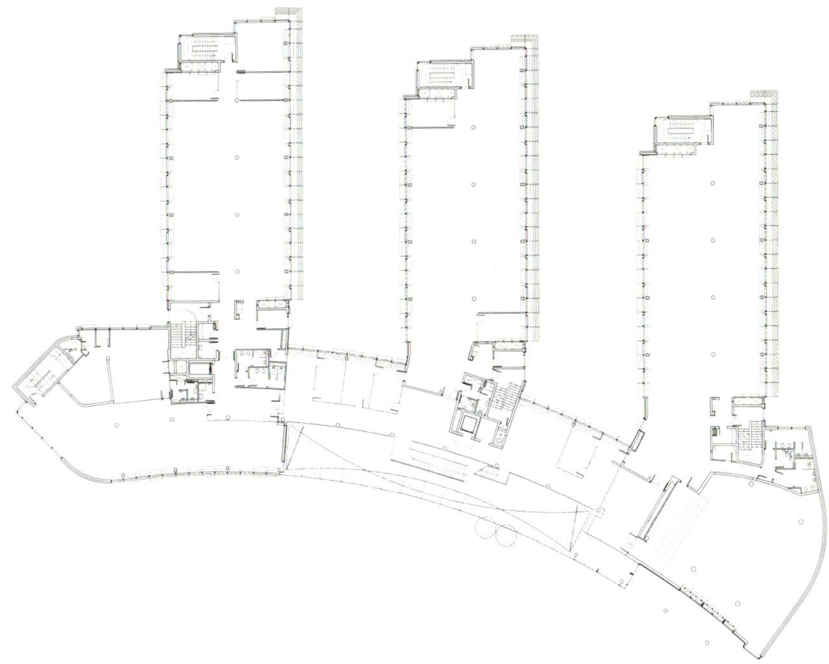

completion	September 2000
client	Fingal County Council
area	11,244 square metres/121,030 square feet
structure	Concrete
materials	Concrete, glass, terracotta tiles, profiled metal cladding, polished render, aluminium rainscreen
cost	£14 million
awards	2001 Royal Institute of the Architects of Ireland (RIAI) Award
opposite	West elevation looking south
top	First floor plan
bottom	View from inside atrium/public space

top	East elevation
middle left	Junction of office wings and curved spine
bottom left	Council Chamber looking west
bottom right	Office façade; typical bay viewed from outside
opposite	Outdoor atria between office wings
photography	Michael Moran

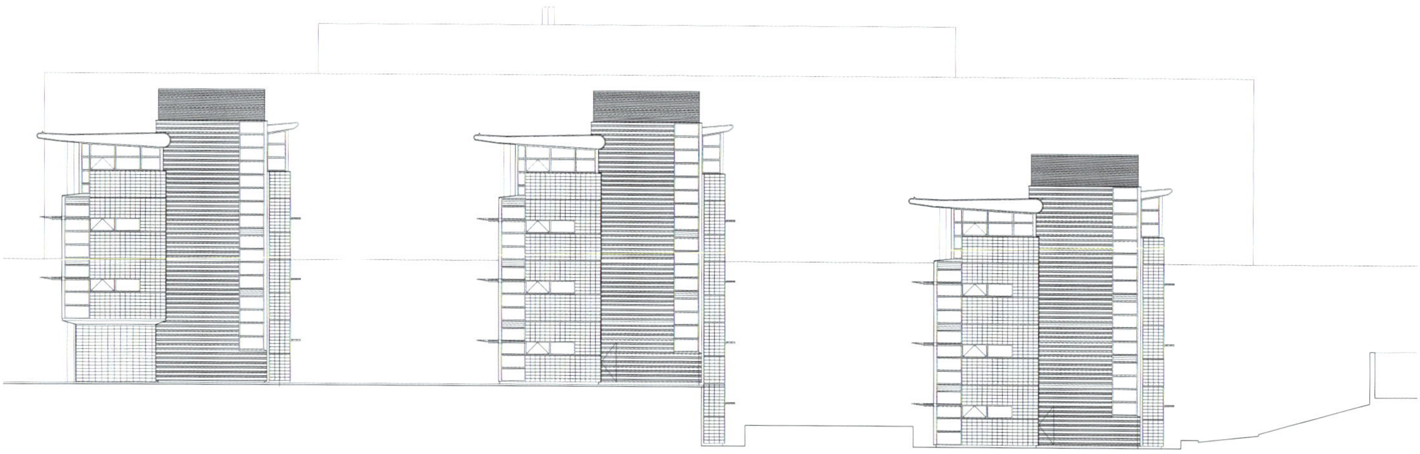

Finnish Embassy

Berlin, Germany

Viiva Arkkitehtuuri (Rauno Lehtinen, Pekka Mäki & Toni Peltola)

The Finnish Embassy in Berlin has been built in a joint embassy centre of the Nordic countries. The site is located in the heart of the reunified Berlin on the southern side of Tiergarten Park. The Nordic Embassy complex is a clear and independent entity of which the most important part is a 15-metre-high copper band wall. The copper band surrounds the five embassy buildings and it gathers them around the inner plaza.

The Finnish Embassy is light, transparent and vivid. It stands in contrast to the copper wall, which is opaque, dense and mineral. The building is a combination of simplicity and clarity, which creates both Finnish national identity and prominent and timeless surroundings for the activities of the embassy.

The transparent glass façades of the building are covered with slats of larch wood. This wooden latticework acts as a venetian blind. It protects the interior and filters the incoming light. Direct views are provided by opening parts of the lattice. The variety of different positions of the slats gives animation to the façade during the day, with the basic form regained as the slats are closed for the night.

The interior is dominated by a sequence of spaces that traverse the building. It starts from the entrance and goes through a central hall and ends in a small external courtyard. The copper wall behind the courtyard has an opening out to the surrounding townscape. The circulating aluminium stair and the birch-covered conference room, which is suspended above the skylit central hall, contribute to the complexity of these spaces.

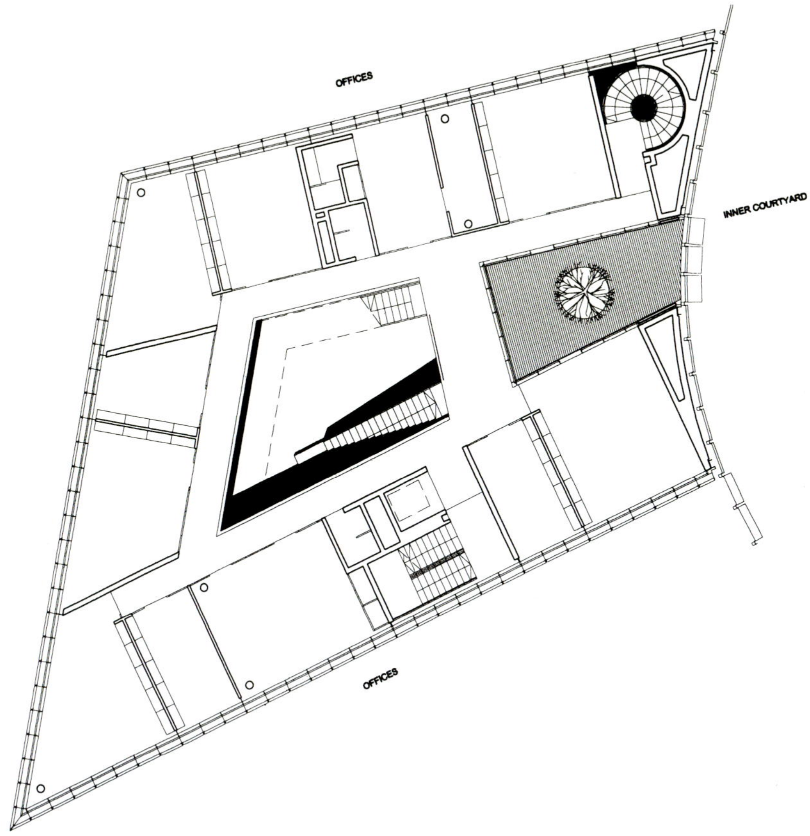

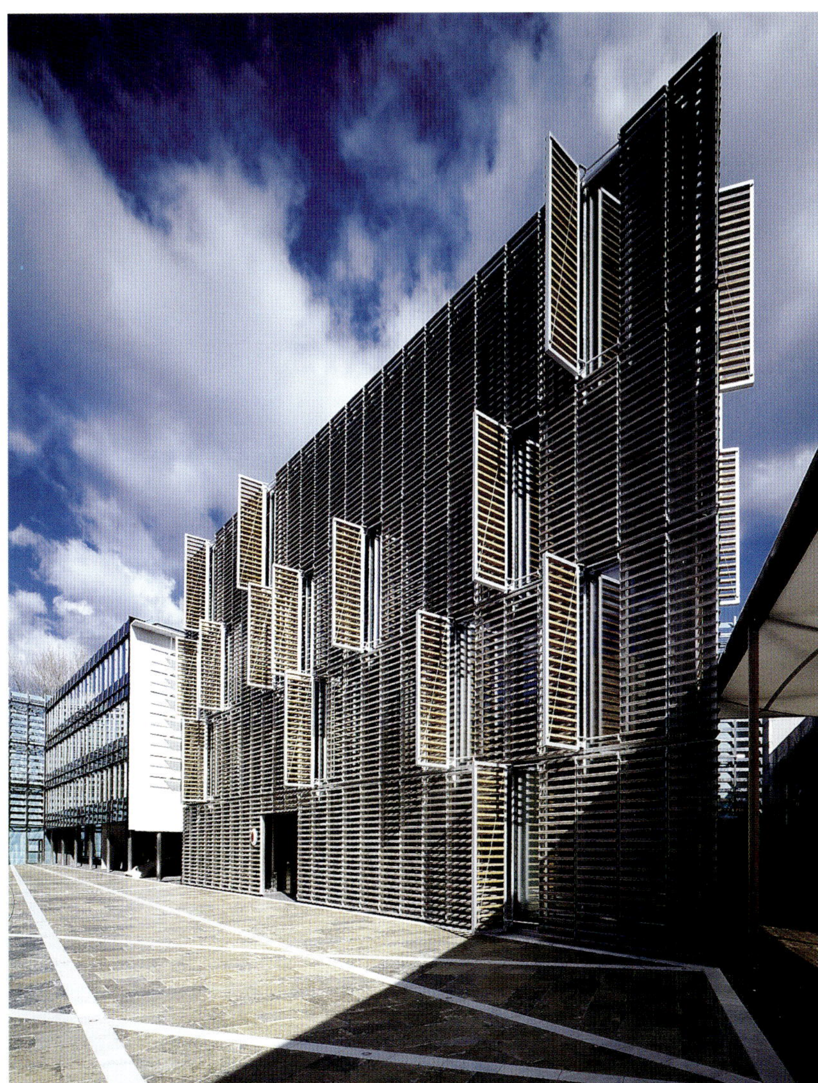

completion	September 1999
client	Ministry for Foreign Affairs, Finland
area	1,860 square metres/20,021 square feet
structure	Cast-in-site concrete
materials	Larch, birch, concrete, steel, glass, aluminium
awards	2001 Best Overall Building, Arup World Architecture Awards 2000 Highly Commended, ar+d Award 2000 Finalist, Blueprint Architecture Awards
opposite	Façade illuminated from inside
top	Second floor plan
bottom	Façades are covered with wood lamellas that open

left	Aluminium stairs surround entrance hall
right	Wooden conference room
opposite	Entrance hall extends towards exterior with a courtyard
photography	Jussi Tiainen

Juliette K. & Leonard S. Rakow Research Library, Corning Museum of Glass

Corning, New York, USA

Bohlin Cywinski Jackson

The Corning Museum of Glass' Rakow Library is the world's pre-eminent repository for information on the history and technology of glass. Its new facility was designed as a secure, environmentally stable, permanent and expandable setting for an irreplaceable collection.

After evaluating various campus sites, the library was located within the shell of a vacant office building. Renovation of this building took the form of a radical reconstruction, including significant reinforcement of the steel structure to permit future installation of compact shelving, and cutting new openings in the second floor to link upper and lower levels in a linear atrium. All building systems were replaced to meet the demanding temperature, humidity and air quality tolerances of the building's new use.

The design celebrates glass, thematically relating the library building to its subject matter, and to the museum's nearby glass centre. Extraordinary glass detailing characterises the 'building within a building', which houses the collection, as well as special features such as glass-floored stairs and bridges. The south-facing reading areas enjoy a river view through a glass sunscreen, or brise soleil. This screen serves as a large 'environmental sculpture' and thus transforms the character of the former office building. Its ceramic-frit and acid-etched linear patterns interact with seasonal sun angles to maximise visual transparency while excluding direct sunlight from the library's interior.

The design candidly expresses the fact that the library is an adapted reuse of an earlier structure. In contrast to the meticulous detailing of new work, much of the original building remains exposed and unadorned, such as the original roof joists and deck of the second floor ceiling. The exterior was modified only minimally, serving as background against which the glass brise soleil offers a strong counterpoint.

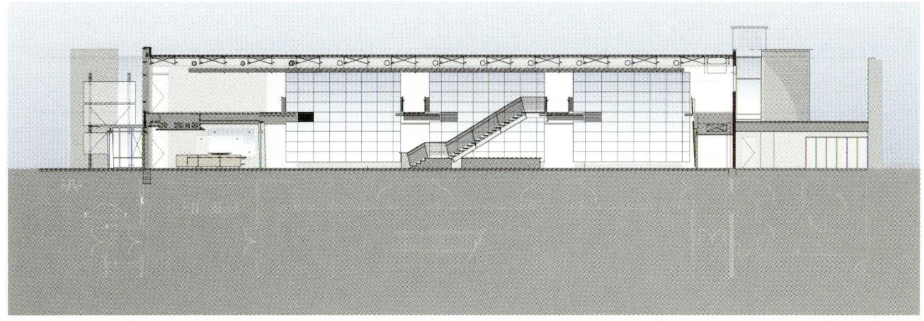

completion	July 2000
client	Corning Incorporated
area	5,574 square metres/59,998 square feet
structure	Steel
materials	Glass, brick, wood
cost	US$5.7 million
awards	2001 Excellence in Design Award, AIA New York State 2000 Silver Medal for Design, AIA Pittsburgh 2000 Certificate of Merit for Detailing, AIA Pittsburgh
opposite	South façade photography Matt Wargo
top	Stair section
middle	Library photography Matt Wargo
bottom	Stair photography Karl Bacus, AIA

Law Courts
Nantes, France
Architectures Jean Nouvel

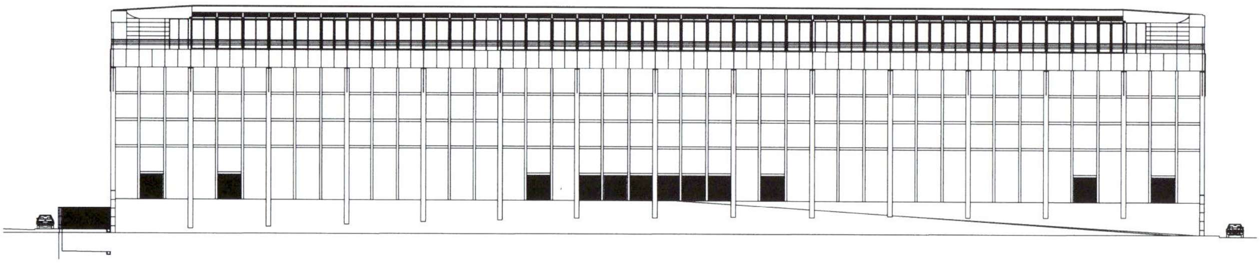

This building is a reflection of the role of power in the justice system, using both criteria and symbols. That symbol of power is represented in official architecture. The project is realistically defined as a 'fair' architecture applied to the façade and in the interior details. The architectural composition is based on 'fairness', 'equality', 'dignity' and 'character'.

completion	June 2000
client	Ministère de la Justice
area	20,000 square metres/215,280 square feet
structure	Metal structure
materials	Steel, glass
cost	FF230 million
opposite top	Elevation of north façade
opposite bottom	North façade
above top	Upper level patio
above bottom	Court lobby
top	South façade
bottom	Detail of court lobby
photography	Philippe Ruault

Lied Library, University of Nevada Las Vegas
Las Vegas, Nevada, USA
LEO A DALY

The Lied Library at the University of Nevada Las Vegas houses a collection of two million books, scholastic resources and 2,500 reader stations, all available to students and the public 100 hours each week. The brief called for a centre of knowledge and learning for the next 50 years. The resulting five-storey building responds with a hi-tech environment housing both a traditional print-centred library and digital library technology.

The striking steel-framed structure is clad in split-face concrete block, zinc alloy panels and a tension-supported low-e insulated glass curtain wall system. Rounded and angular forms are enhanced by exposed steel roof trusses.

Interior spaces centre on a dramatic five-storey 'living room'. A glass-enclosed three-level volume housing reading rooms protrudes into the inspiring central atrium space. A separate three-level wedge-shaped component opens to the south-east corner of the atrium and houses a 100-seat extended hours study/coffee shop, administration suite, boardroom and honours suite.

A central information commons located on the ground floor offers immediate access to 96 interactive computer stations, which are surrounded by collaborative study booths and small classrooms to provide Internet access and serve research needs. Vertical transportation between levels is provided by elevators, escalators and an open sculptural stairway that links all levels.

A technological focal point of the library is its energy-saving robotic automated storage and retrieval system that accommodates 1.2 million volumes. Book-to-counter delivery time is five minutes. This system is complemented by a shelved library collection spread throughout the library.

completion	January 2001
client	State of Nevada Public Works Board and University of Nevada
area	28,955 square metres/302,000 square feet
structure	Steel moment frame
materials	Split-concrete block, zinc alloy cladding, tension-supported low-e glass curtain wall system
cost	US$41.5 million
awards	2001 American Schools & Universities, Louis I. Kahn Award 1997 Honor Award for Unbuilt Projects, Nevada Chapter, AIA
opposite top	Main entry, south-east elevation
opposite bottom	Main entry, east elevation
top	South-east elevation
middle	Main entry, south-west elevation
bottom	North elevation

top North-south section
middle left Administrative boardroom
middle right Level three glass-enclosed reading room
bottom left Automated storage and retrieval system
bottom right Main atrium looking east
opposite Main atrium and glass-enclosed reading area
photography Paul J. Brokering

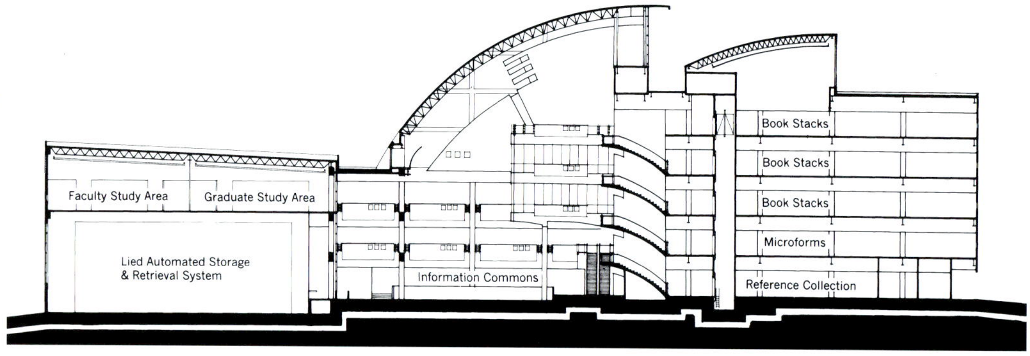

Portcullis House

Westminster, London, UK

Michael Hopkins and Partners

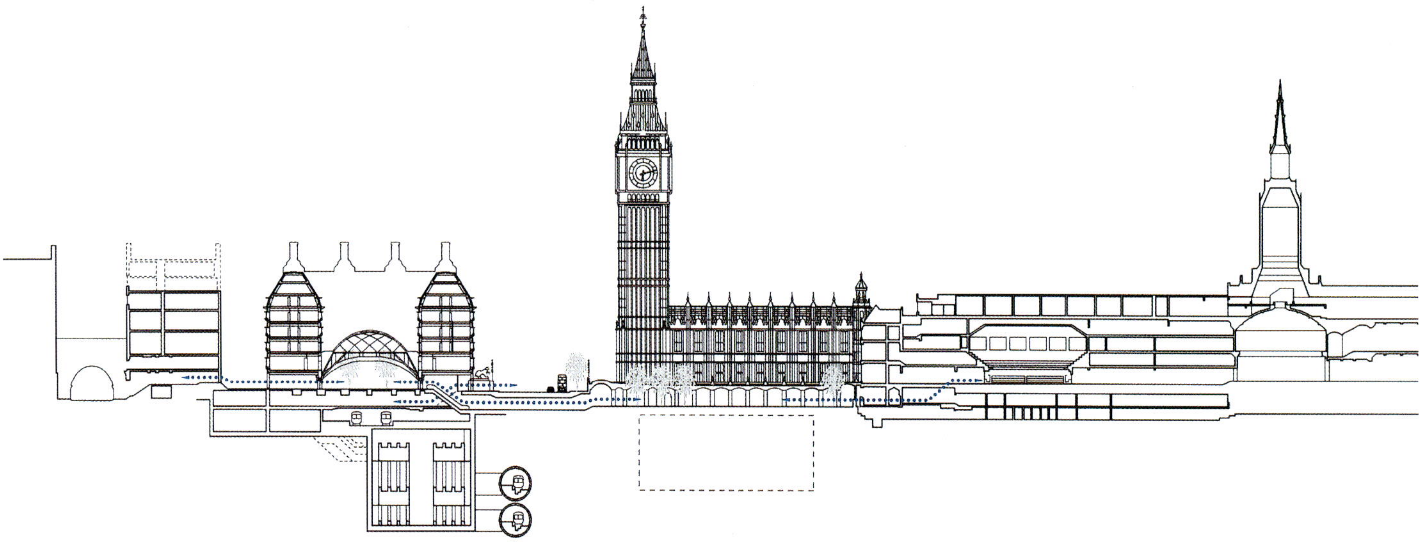

The need for a Jubilee Line interchange at Westminster led to a holistic review of the site. Michael Hopkins and Partners conceived a complete solution with a new parliamentary building above the new underground station. A transfer structure spanning over existing diagonally configured tracks was incorporated into the building above as huge arches, releasing space below for a new ticket hall. Six massive columns supporting these arches are integrated with the station structure, creating a vast underground cavern for escalators.

The building form was derived from the generic form of the courtyards of the Palace of Westminster. The rectangular courtyard form of the building provides maximum external frontage and natural light to the individual offices for parliamentary members and their staff on the upper floors. The building has seven floors of accommodation arranged around the courtyard.

The central courtyard space is surrounded by facilities for members and staff including restaurants, e-library, vote office, post office and coffee shop. At first-floor level there are new select committee rooms, conference rooms and catering areas. From second-floor level to fifth-floor level there are individual rooms for members and their staff, and in the roof there are plant rooms and six further rooms for members.

Support facilities such as kitchens, catering, staff accommodation, stationery stores and plant rooms are located in the lower ground and basement storeys in the north-west corner. Core areas containing bathrooms and lavatories have been positioned in the corners of the building near the lifts and stairs.

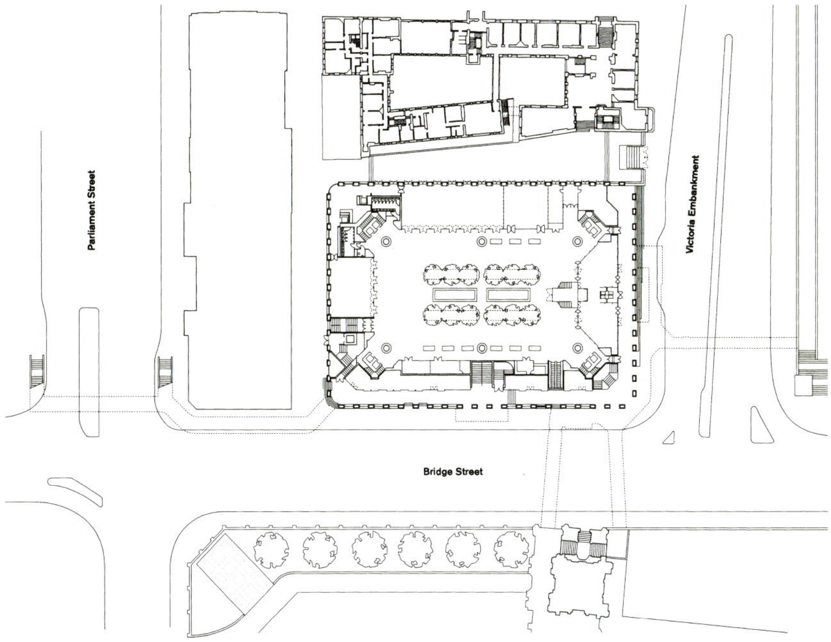

completion	2000
client	Parliamentary Works Directorate
area	20,000 square metres/215,280 square feet
materials	Stone, concrete, bronze
cost	£162.5 million
awards	2001 Institute of Structural Engineers David Alsop Award
	2001 Royal Institute of British Architects (RIBA) Award
opposite top	Site section
opposite bottom	View across River Thames
top	Street level floor plan
bottom	Offices overlook glass courtyard roof

top Energy section of office
middle Courtyard timber-framed roof
bottom left Typical member's office
bottom right Energy section
opposite Courtyard is social focus
photography Richard Davies

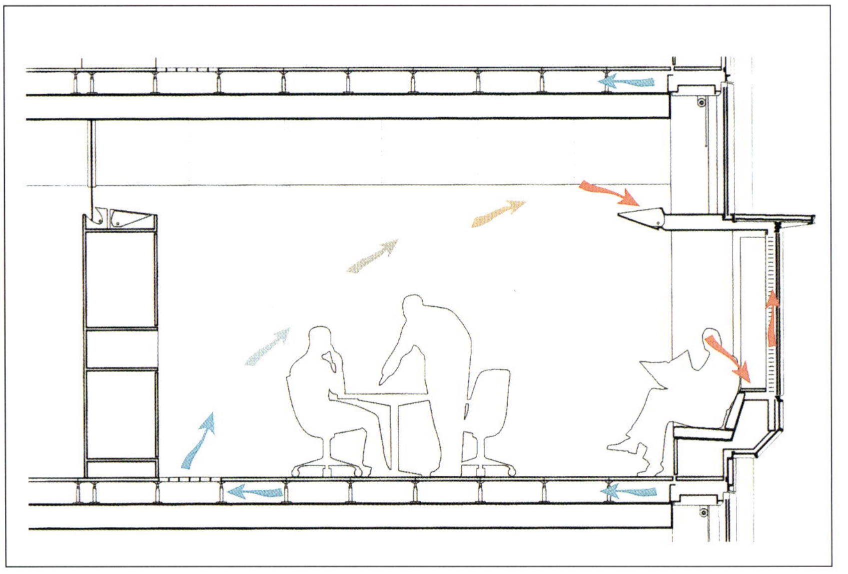

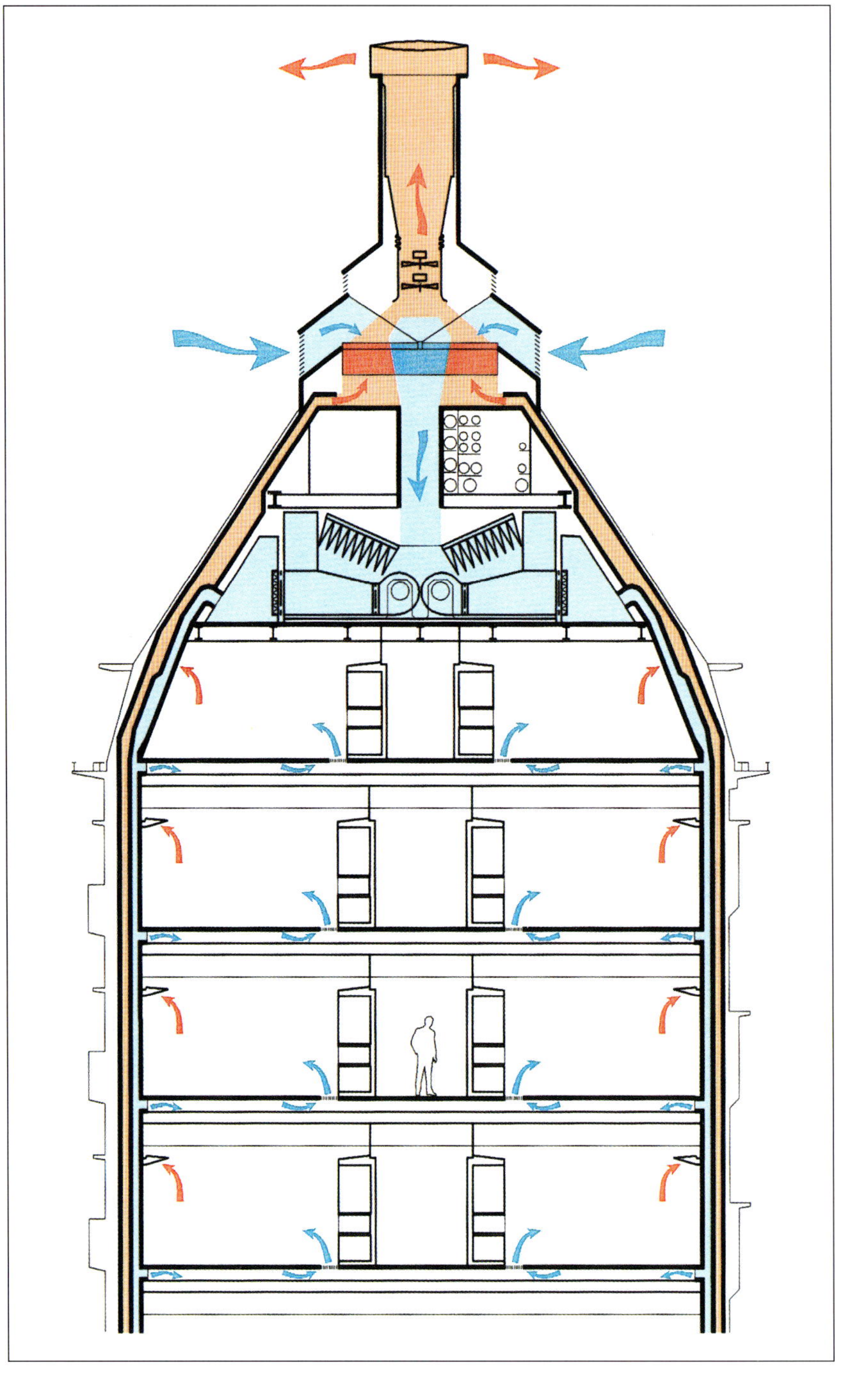

Sametinget (The Sami Parliament)
Karasjok, Norway
Stein Halvorsen as sivilarkitekter MNAL
in co-operation with Christian Sundby

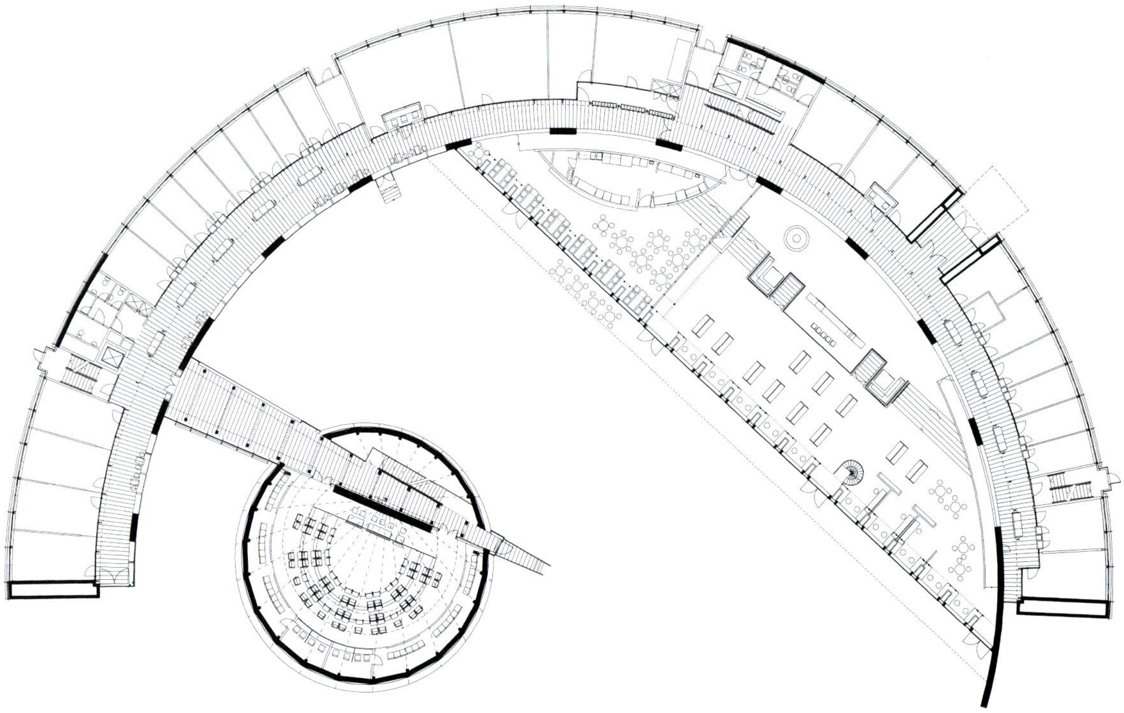

The precise geometry of the building lends to its dignity. A half circle embraces a cone-shaped assembly hall and a beautiful south-facing atrium with a view of Karasjok. It was imperative to let the house stand free in natural landscape with heather and moss, rather than in a cultivated landscape. Open and vast plains prompted the thematic use of the reindeer fencing.

The tilted outer wall encloses the building functions and gathers people. It rises straight from the heather and the airy covering gives the impression of a wrapping of skin or cloth.

The Wander Hall is the most important space as it binds the different functions together. It has visibility to the outdoor atrium. This circular space and the other open interiors form an open stage from which each interior is visible, making the house a colourful and pulsating place in contrast to the enormous plains outside.

The assembly hall is exposed as an independent volume. Glass underneath the high ceiling brings a characteristic light to the hall and lends atmosphere to either the midnight sun or pitch dark with the northern lights flickering above. A small reading lamp at each representative table defines intimate spaces inside this voluminous room.

The library is terraced, forming a space in between the Wander Hall and the atrium. Entering the library, the enormous room opens, the books fill the walls, and the assembly hall can be seen through the large glass openings to the south.

The exterior and interiors of the building are executed in warm materials – Siberian larch outside and untreated pine inside. The fast and beautiful ageing process of larch is demonstrated creating a silver-grey patina that makes the house slide into both landscape and history.

completion	July 2000
client	Statsbygg – The Directorate of Public Construction and Property
area	5,300 square metres/57,049 square feet
structure	Concrete, steel, laminated timber
materials	Siberian larch wood, steel, untreated pine
cost	88.240.000 NOK (Norwegian kronor)
awards	2001 Statens Byggeskikkspris – Norwegian State Prize for Architecture
opposite top	Ground floor plan
opposite bottom	Main building embraces south-east facing court and assembly hall
top	Sametinget seen in its context
bottom	Assembly hall

opposite Library
top East-west section through assembly hall
bottom Assembly hall
photography Jaro Hollan

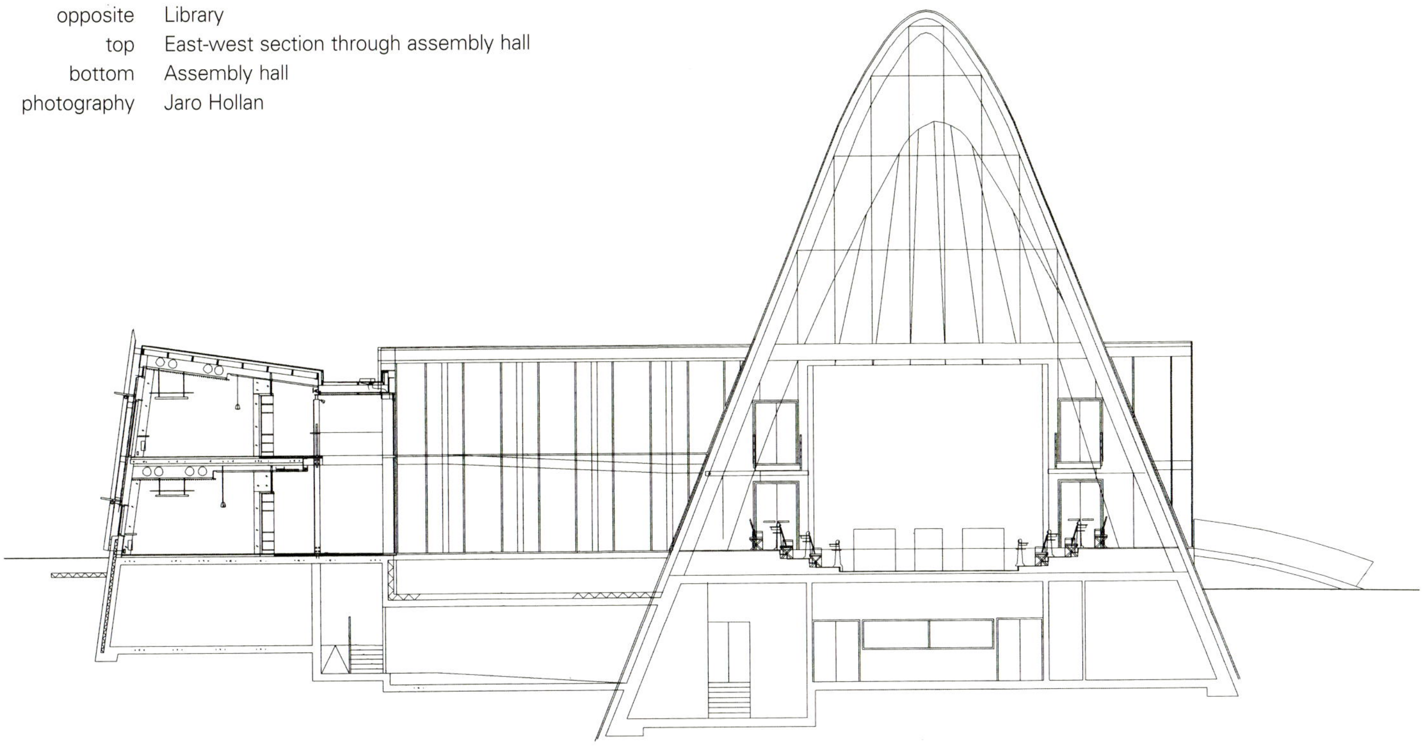

Public

City of Arts and Sciences, Science Museum and Planetarium
Valencia, Spain
Santiago Calatrava

In an attempt to maintain the city of Valencia's cultural standing the government of Valencia wished to establish a museum of national importance. The site chosen for this large complex is located on the southern banks of the dried-up bed of the River Turia, midway between the old city and the coastal district of Nazaret. This challenging and audacious architectural ensemble brings new focus to an incoherent and under-developed area, while linking and providing a marker for the outer areas of the city.

The two principle buildings are organised around a raised promenade along the defining, longitudinal axis of the site, and offering views out towards the sea. This walkway, an integral part of the overall landscaping, serves as an ordering element: gardens extend to either side and, as a reminder of the site's fluvial past, shallow reflecting pools embrace the planetarium, covering the roof of the library, cinemas, several auditoria and restaurants beneath. Further strips of water mark the northern boundary of the science museum.

The science museum is contained in a large linear volume. The sunken garden extends beneath the walkway to optically connect the museum to two levels of car parking, while a new motor bridge, crossing the river bed to the north-east, is arranged to pass over a shopping mall on the south-east corner.

The science museum is a spatial tour de force. Like the grand and traditional pavilions of the great exhibitions of the past, a longitudinal building has been created from the modular development of transversal sections that repeat along the whole length of the site. The white supporting concrete framework of the south-facing façade is filled with glass; the north façade is a glass and steel screen that forms a continuous curtain along the full length of the building.

The globe of the planetarium – which also houses the Omnimax theatre – is roofed over by an elliptical shell structure. In a subsequent version, longitudinal sections of this shell can open to the sky. In a further development, this globe is placed within an elliptical pod and cradled like the pupil of an eye.

completion	Science Museum: 2000; Planetarium: 1998
client	Government of Valencia
area	Science Museum: 41,530 square metres/447,029 square feet; Planetarium: 7,100 square metres/76,424 square feet
materials	Concrete, glass, steel, granite
opposite	Exterior of Science Museum
top	Exterior of Planetarium
bottom	Main street inside Science Museum
photography	Palladium Photodesign

Concert Hall and Exhibition Complex (Zenith)

Rouen, France

Bernard Tschumi Architects

The concert hall belongs to the popular, multipurpose 'Zenith' series, first developed in France by the Ministry of Culture in the 1980s. It accommodates musical events, sports spectaculars, political conventions and theatrical events. Additional seating allows the hall to serve an audience of up to 8,500 people. The 107-metre (350-foot) diameter transforms the typology of the classic concert hall through a slight asymmetry in the seating, lending spontaneity to the atmosphere of pop music as well as permitting the theatre to be reconfigured into three smaller volumes. Fireproof seats designed out of transparent, ergonomically moulded plastic turn the hall into a shimmering, vitreous spectacle.
Acoustical concerns led to a double envelope surrounding the concert hall.
The inner skin, made of concrete stepped seating, is doubled by the exterior, a broken torus formed of insulated corrugated metal. The entry lobby is located between the two skins, where multi-levelled walkways formed of brushed concrete result in a Piranesian promenade through space. The 15 entrances to the concert hall permitted through this arrangement allow the concert hall to be evacuated easily within 10 minutes after performances. A permanent, independent kiosk located in the public plaza outside provides continuous sales.
The structural system of the roof allows both an economically long span for the concert hall and long-distance visibility, due to three masts that are illuminated on concert evenings. Tension cables hold the middle of the spans, permitting a lighter truss system.
The glass and steel exhibition hall permits a number of organisation schemes, accommodating conventions for large public crowds or trade fairs for limited professional groups. The hall is conceived as a simple structure with a vaulted ceiling designed to maximise the flexibility of the spaces below.

completion 2001
client District of Rouen
area 20,438 square metres/220,000 square feet
structure Metal, concrete
materials Masonry, metal/glass curtain wall, concrete, steel, metal doors
cost US$35 million
awards 2001, Excellence in Design, AIA New York State Design Award
1999, Citation, AIA New York City Chapter Design Awards
opposite Exterior view of concert hall with exhibition space to left
photography Robert Cesar/Archipress
top Interior view of concert hall with transparent plastic seating
photography Peter Mauss/ESTO
bottom Exterior view of entrance
photography Peter Mauss/ESTO

The Great Court, British Museum

London, UK

Foster and Partners

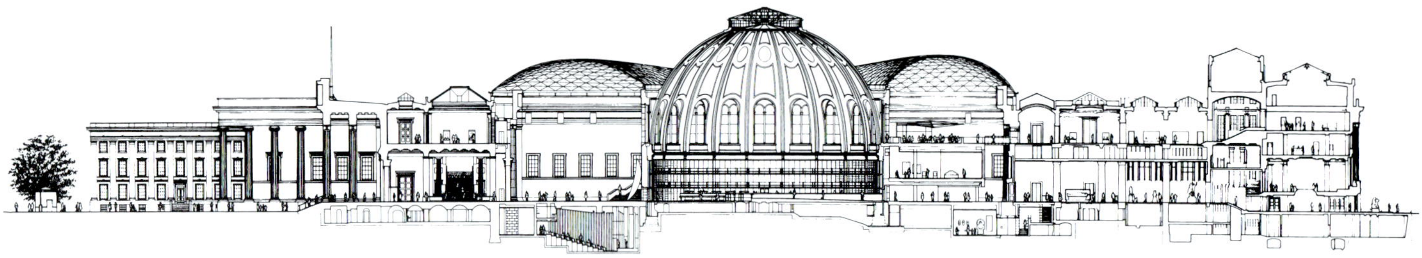

The British Museum's Great Court is one of London's long-lost spaces; before its rediscovery the Museum was like a city without a park. The Great Court is a new visitor hub for the museum and a new civic space for London. As a cultural square, it lies on the pedestrian route from the British Library, in the north, to Covent Garden, in the south. The Great Court is a contemporary architectural intervention that acknowledges the past without reverting to pastiche.

Originally an open garden, the courtyard was lost to the pubic with the advent of the Round Reading Room and its associated book stacks. Over the years this caused a critical level of congestion throughout the building as popularity of the British Museum increased. The departure of the British Library to St Pancras created the opportunity to recapture this magnificent space and enhance facilities for the millions who visit the museum each year.

Covering an area equivalent to the football pitch at Wembley, the Great Court is the largest enclosed public space in Europe. Its glazed canopy is a fusion of state-of-the-art engineering and economy of form. Its unique triangulated geometry is designed to span the irregular gap between the Reading Room dome and the restored 19th-century courtyard façades. The lattice steel shell forms both the primary structure and framing for the glass, which is designed to reduce solar gain.

The court is entered from the museum's principal level, through its great Ionic portico. Two staircases encircle the drum of the Reading Room, leading to the upper-level galleries and two mezzanine levels, which provide a temporary exhibition gallery and restaurants. Beneath the floor of the court are galleries for the African Collection of Ethnography, an education centre, and facilities for visiting school children.

To complement the Great Court, the museum's forecourt has been freed from cars and restored to form a new public space. Both are open to the public from early in the morning to late at night, creating a major public amenity for London.

completion December 2000
client British Museum
area 19,000 square metres/204,516 square feet
materials Concrete, glass, steel, stone, gold leaf
cost £100 million
awards 2001 'Special Award' with Buro Happold, Institute of Civil Engineers
2001 Special Recognition, DuPont Benedictus Awards
opposite top Long section through building and Great Court
opposite bottom Exterior view of glazed roof at night
top General view of Great Court from south end
bottom Interior view of Great Court
photography Nigel Young/Foster and Partners

Incheon International Airport Passenger Terminal

Incheon Island, Republic of South Korea

Fentress Bradburn Architects

Incheon International Airport has only been open since March 2001, but its location – within three-and-a-half hours flying time of 40 cities with populations over one million – is quickly transforming it into a regional Asian hub. The airport is located on a artificial land bridge between two islands in the Yellow Sea, 50 kilometres west of the city centre of Seoul, South Korea.
Organised around a Great Hall, the terminal features 46 connected wide-body gates, a number that will grow at full build-out to 174 gates.
Fentress Bradburn Architects, in association with Korean Architects Collaborative International (KACI), was awarded the commission to design the passenger terminal by unanimous decision in an international design competition in 1992.
Rejecting the cold, homogenised, high-tech feel of so many modern airports, the architects worked to create a feeling of warmth and welcome at Incheon. These gestures include the embracing arc of the terminal, the use of natural materials such as wood and granite, the contextual reference of the masts and cable system of the roof, which emulate the large anchored ships in nearby Incheon Harbour, and the extensive skylights that flood the interior with enough light to nurture traditional gardens indoors.

But the architects' primary guide was the rich heritage of the country's culture. The gentle roof arc of ancient Korean temples is seen in the terminal's sweeping rooflines. Structural colonnades bring a rhythm and pattern to the space reminiscent of Korean palace columns, which pay homage to the harmony between heaven and earth. Floor patterns subtly cue passengers in navigating the airport, just as the lines of ancient Korean structures helped direct royal processions.

completion	January 2001
client	Korea Airport Construction Authority
area	551,632 square metres/ 5.9 million square feet
structure	Concrete, steel
materials	Precast concrete exterior wall panels, exterior granite columns, painted tubular structural steel, green insulated glass, aluminium exterior panels, point-fixed glazing system, single-ply membrane roofing, stainless steel ticket counters, granite, wood
cost	US$1.1 billion
opposite	Wood, trees and standing pool warm the atmosphere of Great Hall at heart of terminal photography Architecture Culture Magazine
top	Trees growing up from gardens in level below enliven curbside entrances photography Jeff Goldberg/Esto
middle	Wedge-shaped granite column and grid-like shading devices evoke traditional Asian building motifs photography Nick Merrick, Hedrich-Blessing
bottom	Waveform of lamps by standing pool in Great Hall emulates gentle curve of terminal's roofline photography Architecture Culture Magazine

Melbourne Museum
Melbourne, Victoria, Australia
Denton Corker Marshall

The new Melbourne Museum is sited in Carlton Gardens on the northern edge of Melbourne's central business district and immediately to the north of the Great Hall of the Royal Exhibition Building constructed in the 1880s.

The museum plan uses a campus mode – an arrangement of varied elements grouped together beneath a formal volumetric framework that constitutes a reference to the formality of the site and even evokes a sense of the Hoddle Grid – a Melbourne icon.

The enveloping grid framework is a significant element of the design. Its formal qualities allow the complex and varied elements within the 'campus' to read as individual components; separate elements, say, the Research Centre, the Imax or the Aboriginal Centre, have greater individuality than would be possible or appropriate without the ordering frame – as in a less campus-like, singular, monumental built form.

The scheme physically separates the new museum from the Great Hall by an Events Plaza – a pedestrian concourse aligned on an east-west axis. Beneath this is an underground car park. The campus design integrates the buildings of the complex and the gardens and establishes a visually interdependent whole, maintaining the formal order of the Carlton Gardens precinct with its strong axes.

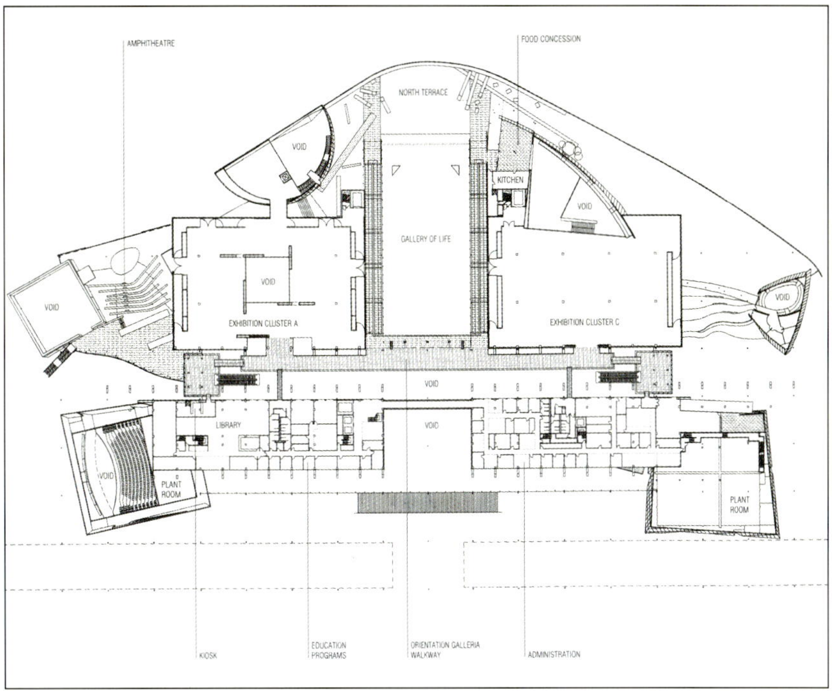

completion	October 2000
client	Victorian Government
area	75,000 square metres/807,300 square feet
structure	Steel grid, reinforced concrete with various lightweight materials
materials	Steel, concrete, glass, aluminium, fibre cement sheet, 'Cor-ten' steel
cost	AUD$250 million
awards	2001 Project of the Year, Victorian Architecture Medal, Royal Australian Institute of Architects 2001 William Wardell Award (Institutional–New), Victorian Chapter, Royal Australian Institute of Architects
opposite	View from Carlton Gardens to north
top	Level four floor plan
middle	Main entry
bottom	Museum approach from Nicholson Street

top Main foyer
right Lower west foyer
bottom Playground courtyard
photography John Gollings

Museum fatigue is a principal planning concern, and the public space is made simple and orthogonal – visitors can easily chart their own routes through the complex and always return to two parallel boulevards and understand where they are. Within the external grid, the IMAX cinema and Touring Exhibition Hall are expressed as dynamic, tumbling metal-clad boxes breaking out of the framework. The Children's Museum and Aboriginal Cultural Centre, smaller in scale, are also expressed as eccentric forms lodged within the grid.

The structural grid and the symmetrical order of the front elevation give way at the back, facing Carlton Gardens, to an irregular sculptural composition of forms that is held in tension by the dramatic cantilevered blade, on central axis with the Royal Exhibition Building, recalling the generative order of the complex at the point of maximum formal fragmentation.

Museum of Fantasy, Buchheim Collection

Bernried, Germany

Behnisch, Behnisch & Partner

Lothar-Günther Buchheim, best known as the author of 'Das Boot', the story of a World War II submarine and its crew, has collected art all his life. Along with an important collection of expressionist paintings and graphics, he has filled two villas in his hometown with curiosities ranging from nutcrackers and Thai shadow puppets to paperweights and carousel horses. The museum is meant to bring the collection under one roof and make it accessible to the public.

The museum's setting in the landscape, its orientation and also its intrinsic order has lent itself to a design that stretches towards the lake like a thread or spine along which the various building elements are located. In this way they can freely develop according to their function, order and shape.

From almost every interior space the visitor is able to view and enter the remarkable landscape. Fluid transitions lead from one part of the museum to another. Shorter and longer round tours can be chosen via the two-storey 'spine' and also via the return route through the park. The building elements remain lean. The trees, lake or individual situations, as well as the play of light and shadow, provide the appropriate setting for the exhibition objects.

Central to the overall concept and part of its composition is the 'Buchheim Total' area. This part of the museum, which is dedicated to Lothar-Günther Buchheim himself, includes the collections of the expressionists and Buchheim's curiosities, and should be seen as part of this 'life in art'. The casual, but evocative juxtaposition of 'high' and 'low' art is a major feature of the museum.

completion	2001
area	6,450 square metres/69,428 square feet
structure	Concrete
materials	Wood, steel, glass, plaster
cost	38 million DM
opposite top	Elevation
opposite left	Contextual relation
opposite right	Entrance
top	Internal gallery
middle	View into courtyard
bottom	Exhibition space
photography	Christian Kandzia

National Museum of Australia
Canberra, ACT, Australia
Ashton Raggatt McDougall
with Robert Peck von Hartel Trethowan

The intention for the National Museum of Australia was to make a place in both visible and invisible space. At first it was imagined as a kind of platonic triangle like an ideal knot, a cloud, a bodily epistemology, and then as if projected to the ground, like a shadow and a promise made visible.

The architects like to think that the story of Australia is not one but many tangled together – not an authorised version but a puzzling confluence, not merely the resolution of difference but its whole-hearted embrace.

The intention was to make a place vividly local, rooted in Walter Burley Griffin's garden city and rooted in the local country, but also it was hoped to make something projective, to make a sign of the Australian longing.

Instead of any singular entity, it was envisaged as a series of intensely adjacent structures, like puzzle pieces, as if each tests plausibility, becomes an evocative typology, belongs to another language, encouraging the idea of reading and hope in an exegesis of promise.

A great open space at the centre of the museum is the Garden of Australian Dreams like the field of a sporting stadium or a new cultural arena and a palimpsest of times.

The hall is the cast of a vast self-intersecting knot, itself a precise tangle along the way, which is perhaps only properly fulfilled by the throng of its occupation. The canopy/loop is a visible sliver, a physical approximation of an otherwise invisible thread now continuously changing direction.

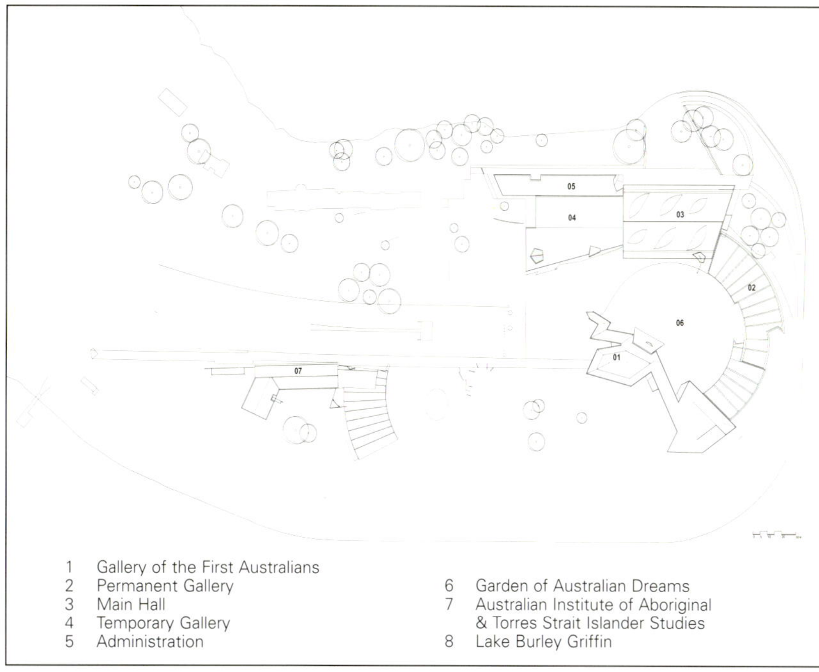

completion	March 2001
client	Department of Communication, Information Technology and the Arts
landscape architect	Room 4.1.3
area	20,000 square metres/215,280 square feet
structure	Steel structure, reinforced concrete floors
materials	Aluminium cladding, precast concrete panelling
cost	AUD$155 million
opposite	Acton Peninsula on Lake Burley Griffin opposite the Parliament House
top	Site plan
middle top	Night view across lake
middle base	Gallery of the First Australians at night
bottom	Water feature in Garden of Australian Dreams

top — Looking into Garden of Australian Dreams and Great Hall beyond

middle — Entry cave by Boolean subtraction and canopy

bottom — Aerial view – Great Hall on left, Aboriginal Gallery on right, around the Garden of Australian Dreams

top — Great Hall ceiling
middle — Central space of Gallery of the First Australians
bottom — Great Hall interior – cast of a vast self-intersecting knot
photography — John Gollings

The National Wine Centre

Adelaide, South Australia, Australia

Cox Grieve

an association of The Cox Group & Grieve Gillett

The National Wine Centre is conceived as the flagship of Australia's burgeoning wine industry, acting simultaneously as a cultural and education centre, and as a major tourist attraction. The centre will inform visitors of every aspect of the wine industry, including wine-growing, winemaking and new technologies being developed. It will contain an interactive exhibition, a comprehensive range of wine-tasting and educational facilities, restaurant, offices of Australian wine industry organisations and a functional space for events.

The semi-circular planning is devised to continually associate interiors with landscape, while encouraging visitors to experience each component of the centre in a sequential manner.

The building forms are partly inspired by segments of wine barrels and partly by the skeletal nature of winter vines. The layout of the building components preserves significant trees on the site, with the new plantings radially oriented to focus views into the gardens. The building materials have been chosen to evoke both the traditional nature of the wine industry, timber and rammed earth, as well as aluminium and steel suggestive of the modern, scientific approach that has helped establish Australia's reputation in the wine industry.

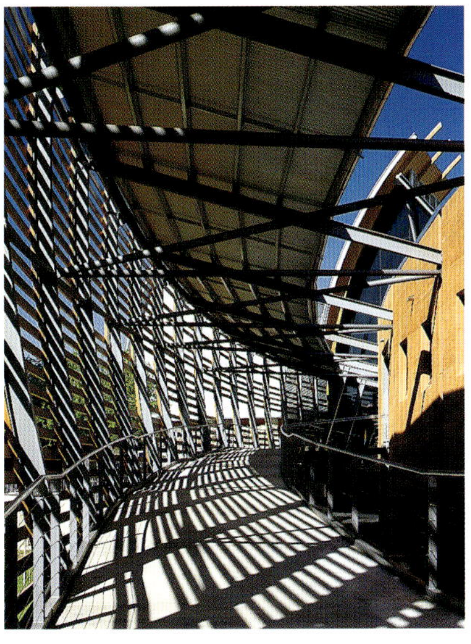

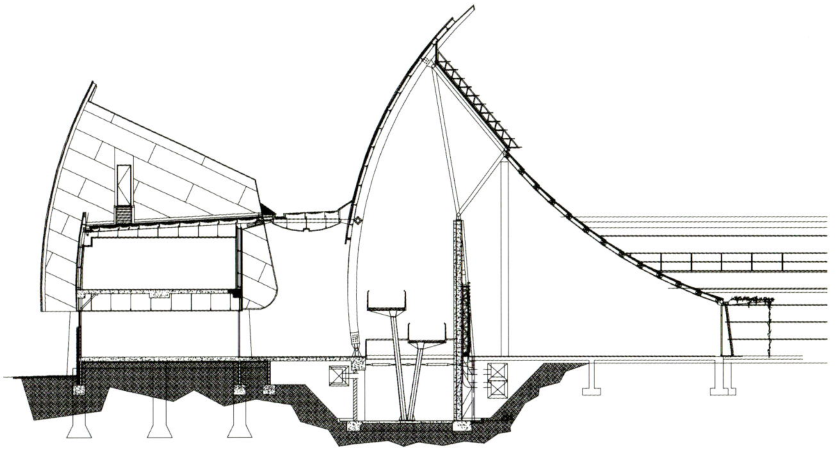

completion	August 2001
client	The National Wine Centre
area	6,000 square metres/64,584 square feet
materials	Concrete floor slabs, concrete, steel and timber framing, pise (rammed earth), metal cladding and blockwork wall construction, steel and zinc roof cladding
cost	AUD$25 million
opposite top	View from north of restaurant and tasting gallery
opposite bottom	View from east of entry ramp
above	Entry ramp internal view
top	Section
bottom	Entry ramp external view

below Ground floor plan
right Concourse from east entry
bottom Busby Hall
opposite Cellar
photography Trevor Fox

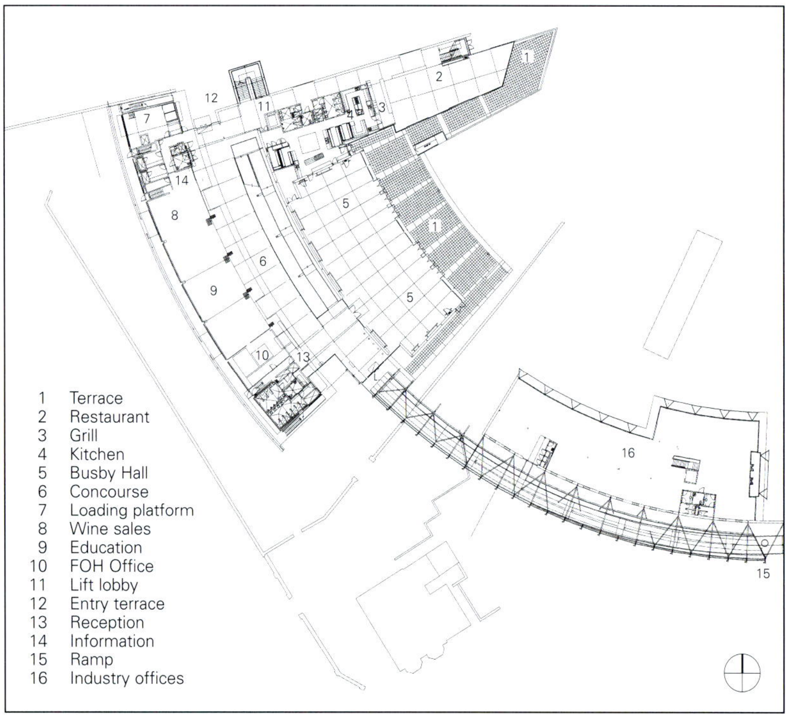

Pope John Paul II Cultural Center
Washington DC, USA
LEO A DALY

The Pope John Paul II Cultural Center, located in Washington DC, houses exhibits from the Vatican, interactive exhibits exploring faith and culture, and the Intercultural Forum, an interfaith think-tank. This important new building has been heralded as 'an architectural landmark of a high order – an at-time demonstration of architecture's power to move the soul'. The team of architects, engineers and interior designers worked closely with Cardinal Maida, Archbishop of Detroit and advisor to the Pope, for over eight years on the architectural design of the centre. The goal of this collaboration was to create a contemporary, signature building that integrates art, architecture and state-of-the-art technology while also expressing the more traditional vocabulary found in Catholic architecture. It is designed as an open and welcoming structure, visually representative of its mission to encourage visitors to actively explore their experiences of faith and culture.

Set back from the road and approached along an allee of red maple trees, the building's imposing, partially transparent linear form is built of limestone, granite, copper and sandblasted glass. Access to the exhibit floors is achieved through a series of gently sloping translucent-sided walkways that give visitors a glimpse of the activities within the building. Important architectural elements in its design include the reflecting pool, which serves as an architectural counterpoint and as a place of contemplation; the copper-clad wing roof that hovers over the building, surround by a 190.5 centimetre (75-inch) off-centre cross; and the cylindrical volume, housing an airy, double-height entry rotunda. The rotunda also symbolically connects the interactive exhibit and museum levels with the Intercultural Form, a centre of research and teaching for scholars through endowed chairs of Faith and Culture, housed on the third floor.

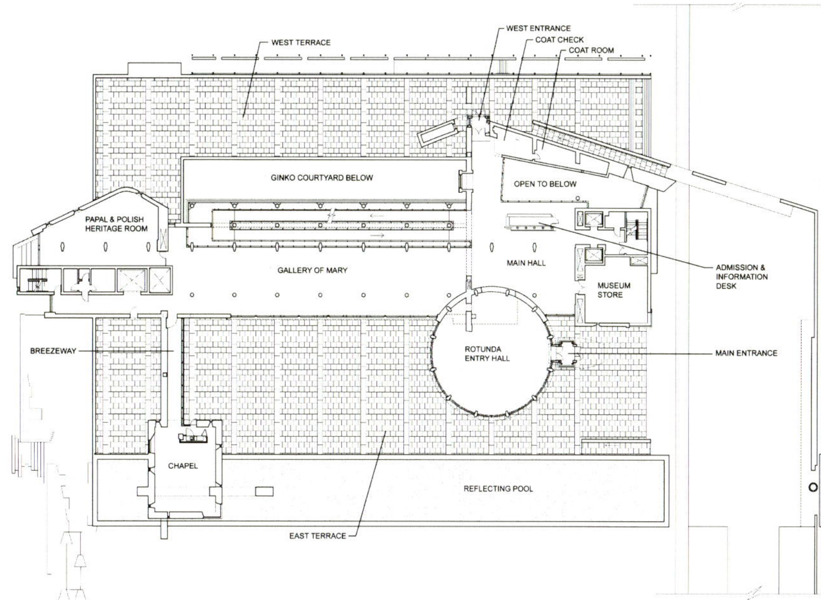

completion March 2001
client Pope John Paul II Cultural Foundation
area 8,965 square metres/96,500 square feet
structure Reinforced concrete
materials Granite, limestone, metal, glass, concrete, copper, aluminium
awards 2001 Award for Excellence in Architecture, Virginia Society of the AIA
2000 Award for Excellence in Architecture, Virginia Society of the AIA
1999 Award for Excellence, Conceptual Design, Northern Virginia Chapter, AIA
opposite View of south elevation
top Entry level plan
middle Front of building viewed from Harewood Road
bottom Ginko courtyard re-emphasises connection to site

below	Gallery of Mary; exhibit designed by ESI
right	Chapel features windows at ceiling and floor
bottom left	Entry rotunda with ecclesiastical calendar inlaid in floor
bottom right	West entrance skylight emphasises connection with outside world
opposite	Intercultural Forum on third floor; Scholar's conference room
photography	Maxwell MacKenzie

Reykjavik Art Museum

Reykjavik, Iceland

Studio Granda

The new art museum occupies two floors of the south wing and three floors of the north wing of a concrete warehouse built around an open court between 1933–9. The main pier in Reykjavik occupied the site at the turn of the century – Iceland's umbilical cord to the world. This link is reawakened in the art museum.

Externally the building is predominantly painted 'Fishery Protection Vessel' grey with the museum demarcated in white.

A concrete canopy marks the entrance and new windows either contain hermetically sealed doors or allow glimpses into the south gallery. Internally the canopy reflects light into the double-height lobby, which is one of a series of spaces, lined with hot rolled steel sheets and black walnut floors, which collectively form the 'pier link'.

Flanking the lobby is the raw concrete museum shop and reception with white and walnut furnishings. Cloakrooms are contained within a crystalline glass box.

Bisected by the pier, the court is split into a large external exhibition space and a small multipurpose room, each with white concrete floors. Two steel doors allow the pier to open to the court and two pairs of folding steel doors offer an array of openings to the room. A skylight box illuminates the pier and at night its glow fills the court.

The pier is terminated on the north façade by two huge glass panes on the ground and first floors. These openings serve the library and café respectively.

The six galleries share a common pallet of concrete and white, however placement, form and scale give each one a distinctive character. Daylight is generally admitted indirectly to the galleries, and sliding or folding plates allow total blackout when necessary. Delivery, workshop and storage are all located on the ground floor.

Administration and the architectural archive are located on the second floor next to an external sky gallery on the roof of the multipurpose space.

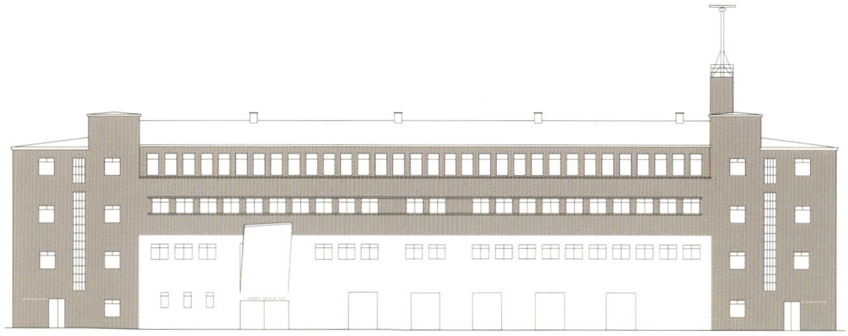

completion	April 2000
client	City of Reykjavik
area	3,710 square metres/39,934 square feet
structure	Concrete
materials	Concrete, American black walnut, hot rolled steel, tempered glass, cement render, gypsum
cost	US$5 million
opposite	View from multipurpose room with court doors open
top	South elevation
middle	Doors to court open
bottom	Double-height entrance lobby with steel-clad columns
photography	Kristján Pétur Gudnason & Christopher Lund

Tang Teaching Museum and Art Gallery
Saratoga Springs, New York, USA
Antoine Predock Architect

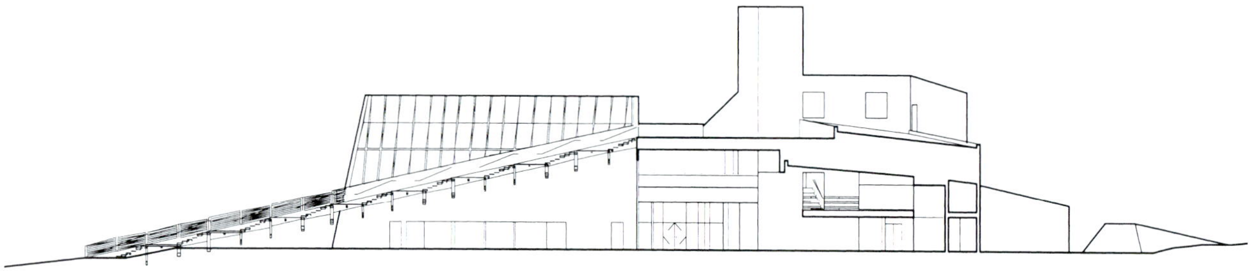

An earthbound stair rises from geologic origins of water shed and limestone caves and culminates in 'one ivory tower', engaging earth and sky, beginning the journey of encounter. The building, sited in a circle of White Pines, radiates armatures or wings organised about a stone-clad tower. The resulting geometry of the building reinforces campus circulation patterns and creates a link to an existing pond.

Constructed primarily of white concrete masonry the building is morphologically connected to the limestone bedrock of the site, which is carefully exposed at selected areas. A steel stair leads from the pond to an observation deck and engages the stainless steel mass of the Temporary Exhibition Gallery.

The 2,787-square-metre (30,000-square-foot) building includes classrooms, administrative and curatorial offices, and spaces for the display of permanent collections and temporary exhibitions. Generous back-of-house spaces facilitate the handling, preparation and archiving of art; while a 204-square-metre (2,200 square-foot) interdisciplinary space provides a broadcast-capable lecture hall with the flexibility to accommodate a reception or a fully catered banquet. The Teaching Museum and Art Gallery was funded by private donations to the college.

completion	2000
client	Skidmore College
area	2,787 square metres/30,000 square feet
structure	Masonry bearing wall with localised structural steel supporting beam and composite floor and roof framing
materials	Exterior: stainless steel, CMU and glass block; interior: ground-faced masonry unit, sheet rock, polished dyed concrete floors, stainless steel
cost	US$7.5 million
awards	2000, Merit Award, AIA New Mexico
opposite top	Section
opposite bottom	Looking west through circle of trees
top	Detail of stair to upper terrace
middle	Looking south towards main entry
bottom	Gallery inside stainless steel volume
photography	Timothy Hursley

Recreational

Arcthe.hotel

Ottawa, Ontario, Canada
Yabu Pushelberg

top left Reception
middle View to mezzanine lounge
top right Stairwell detail
bottom left Bedroom
bottom right Bathroom

Arcthe.hotel is one of Canada's first design-driven hotels. The hotel has been repositioned as a travel respite that caters to the upwardly mobile with its high sense of design and unprecedented comfort. Predicated on the European model which privileges comfort over style, the design impetus stems from the desire to create a hotel that has character and longevity. Intimacy is central and an undercurrent of understated luxury combined with a familiarity that takes root in earlier, liveable materials and fixtures.

As a low-cost two–three star hotel with low ceilings, the interior was created to visually change the portions of the hotel in both height and depth. The front of the building, refaced in French limestone, has been dressed to counteract the dreariness of the street by opening up the lobby through a large expanse of glass, while the lobby itself is both intimate and small with private seating areas for a variety of activities.

An upper lobby continues the theme and is the antithesis of the 'grand hotel' lobby as it has been designed to serve a multipurpose function with a designated lounge/library where patrons can enjoy quiet time for reading, personal work, continental breakfast, client meetings or cocktails.

The key to achieving the overall aesthetic was that the hotel was to be driven by the qualities of the patron's lifestyle, and so while the hotel incorporates an art-driven objective with particular interest in art of the Canadian landscape, it too embraces a separate aesthetic with supreme comfort being the purveying motif.

Custom-made furniture and fixtures were created as an extension of the overall design statement to underscore and unify the interior look for a sense of flow and completed architecture. Pieces include such elements as free-standing light fixtures, concierge/reception desk, library tables, chairs and sofas. The corridor is softly lit with deep-toned, dark, rich coloration, as are the elevator cabs for added intimacy.

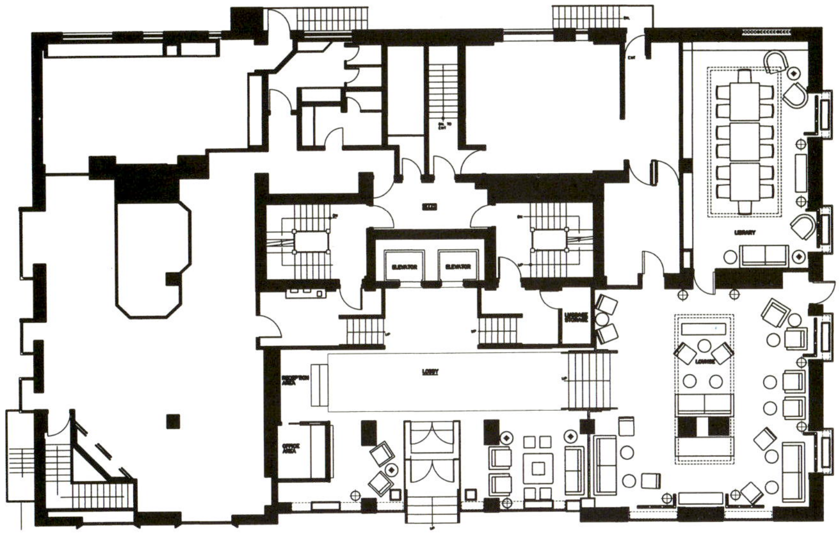

completion	September 2000
client	Westmont Hospitality Group
area	661 square metres/7,111 square feet
materials	Limestone, concrete, metal, glazing, carpet
cost	CAN$5 million
awards	2000 Award of Merit, National Post/Design Exchange, Design Effectiveness Awards
top	Ground floor plan
middle	Lounge/lobby
bottom	Library/Casual meeting place
photography	Evan Dion

Hotel Habita

Mexico City, Mexico

TEN Arquitectos

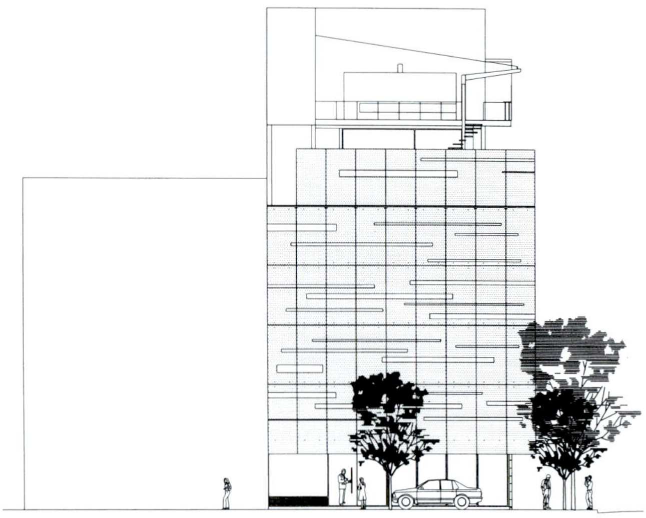

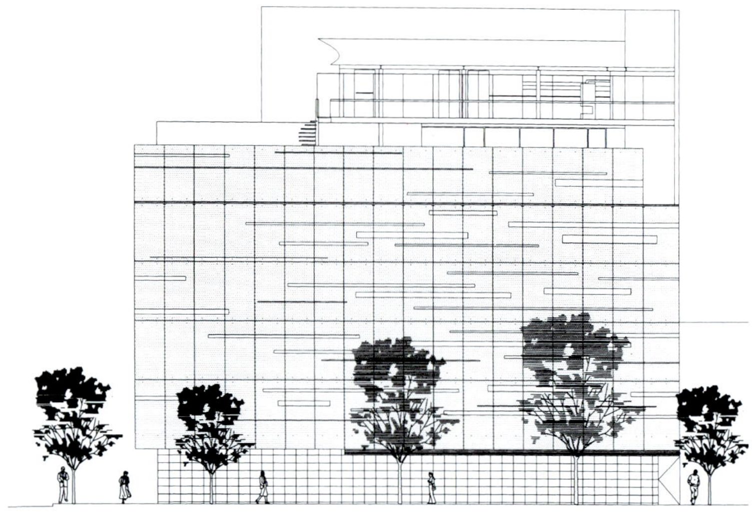

top left South façade
top right East façade
bottom Main façade during day
middle right Main façade at night
bottom right Façade (skin) detail

On a commercial street lined with high-end stores and office buildings, the firm was commissioned to convert a five-story 1950's apartment building into a 36 room boutique hotel. The old structure gains an entirely new identity with a new wrapper – a frosted glass box of mullionless rectangular glass panels floating several feet from the original façade. Sandwiched between the new and old façades are the original balconies and new corridors.
An interstitial space was created between the two skins, which works as a climatic and acoustic 'buffer', regulating the gain/loss of heat and shielding the private spaces of the hotel from the hectic urban environment of its surroundings.
From a distance, the clean new façade appears to be an expressionless mask, but this impression is undone at close range as the shadows of walkways and balconies become visible. Small, randomly distributed unfrosted lines and rectangles are the new façade's only adornment. These strategically tight transparent slots give each room controlled views to the city beyond, framing the desirable and screening out the unsightly. At night, the entire building appears as a lantern with a changing checkerboard pattern of illumination, varying with the occupancy of the rooms.
The new services and amenities – such as a swimming pool, gym, sauna, bar and restaurant – were added to the roof on two superimposed plans, which seem to be floating above the existing structure. The rooms themselves, looking outward to two planes of floor-to-ceiling glass (the inner transparent, the outer translucent), are imbued with natural light all day while maintaining complete privacy. The décor of the rooms mirrors the austerity of the outer enclosure. This minimalist aesthetic enlarges the experience of the otherwise compact rooms.

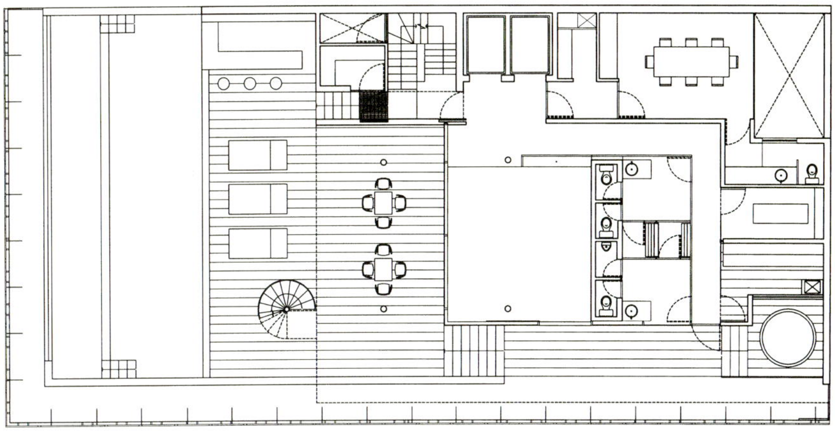

completion	2000
client	Carlos Couturier, Moises Micha, Jaime Micha, Rafael Micha
area	2,500 square metres/26,910 square feet
structure	Renovation of concrete and bearing wall structure
awards	Recognition Award, Open Competition, DuPont Benedictus Awards
top	Pool level plan
middle left	Reception desk; view from restaurant
middle right	Room looking to balcony
lower left	Terrace looking to swimming pool
lower right	Swimming pool at night
bottom	Restaurant; view from entrance
photography	Luis Gordoa

Loewenberg Visitor Center, Lichterman Nature Center
Memphis, Tennessee, USA
Williamson Pounders Architects

Formerly the suburban estate of a wealthy family, the 23-hectare (65-acre) site was donated to the city for use as a nature centre and is operated by the city's museum system. The original house, 1920s-era log building, served as the nature centre office and visitor centre until it was destroyed by fire in the 1990s. A master plan for the property was prepared describing four new structures along with parking, trails, boardwalks, teaching pavilions and an amphitheatre. The visitor centre is the first new building constructed on the site.

The visitor centre is located adjacent to the pond environment. From its stone entrance plaza, the facility appears to be more residential in scale. A prominent entry porch with steel, glass and timber detailing leads the visitor into a large wood and glass lobby and orientation room overlooking the water. Skylights and large expanses of glass put the visitor in immediate contact with nature.

Natural materials are expressed throughout the building. Wildlife exhibits fill the large orientation room and introduce the visitors to the three natural environments of the centre – the forest, meadow and pond. A covered stone terrace, adjacent to this orientation space, overlooks the pond and its boardwalk system. The visitor functions are located on the upper floor with views into the park, and with support spaces located on the lower floor with walkway access to the grounds.

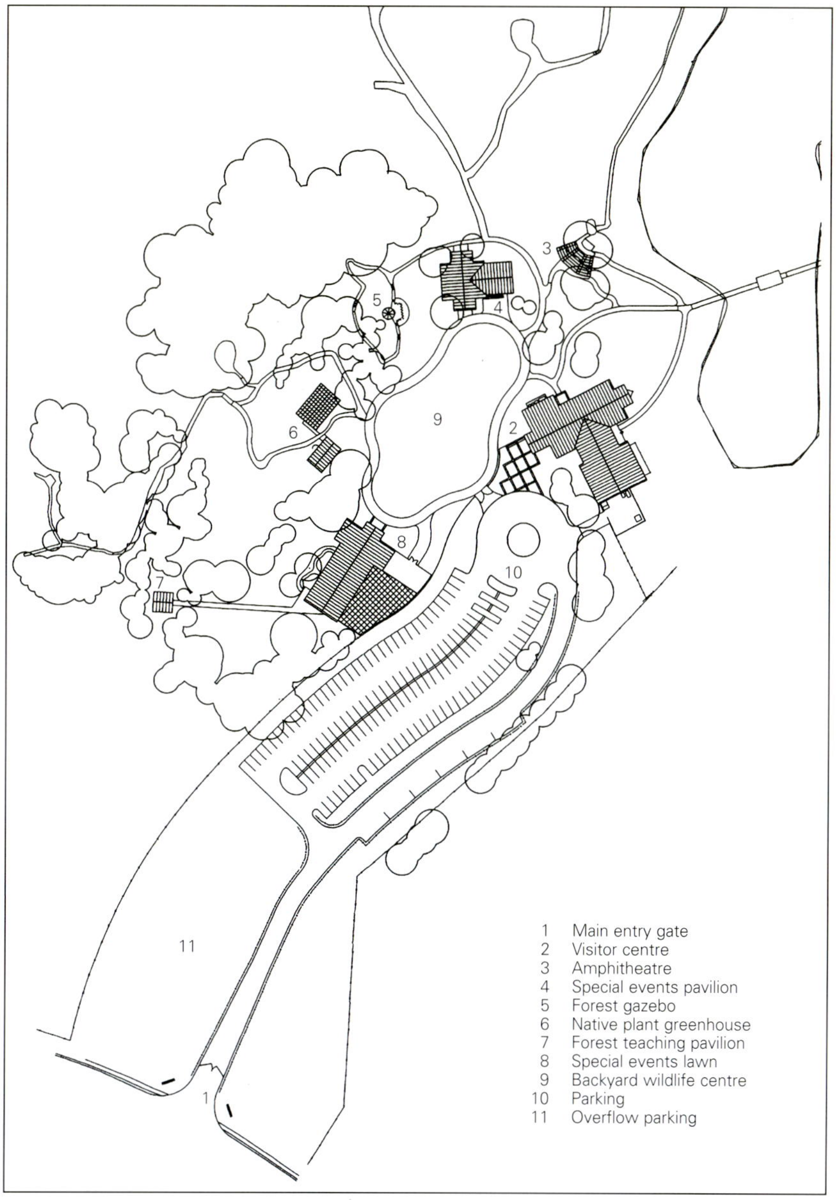

completion	2001
client	Pink Palace Family of Museums
area	1,486 square metres/16,000 square feet
materials	Steel, glass, timber
cost	US$3.2 million
awards	2001 Award of Excellence in Architecture, AIA, Tennessee
opposite	View of visitor centre and boardwalk across pond
top	Site plan
bottom	Exterior night view of orientation room

Human Impact
Seasons

opposite	View from exhibit area towards lobby and entrance
top left	Lower floor plan
bottom left	Main floor plan
top right	Building entrance featuring stone terrace and wall
bottom right	View from lobby into exhibit area
photography	Alan McCoy

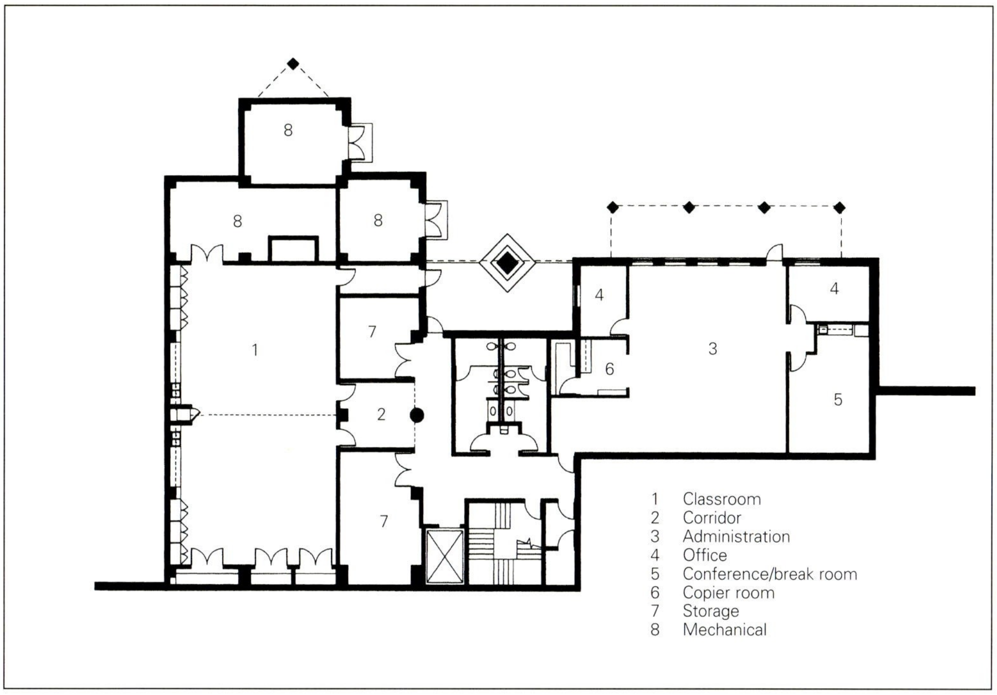

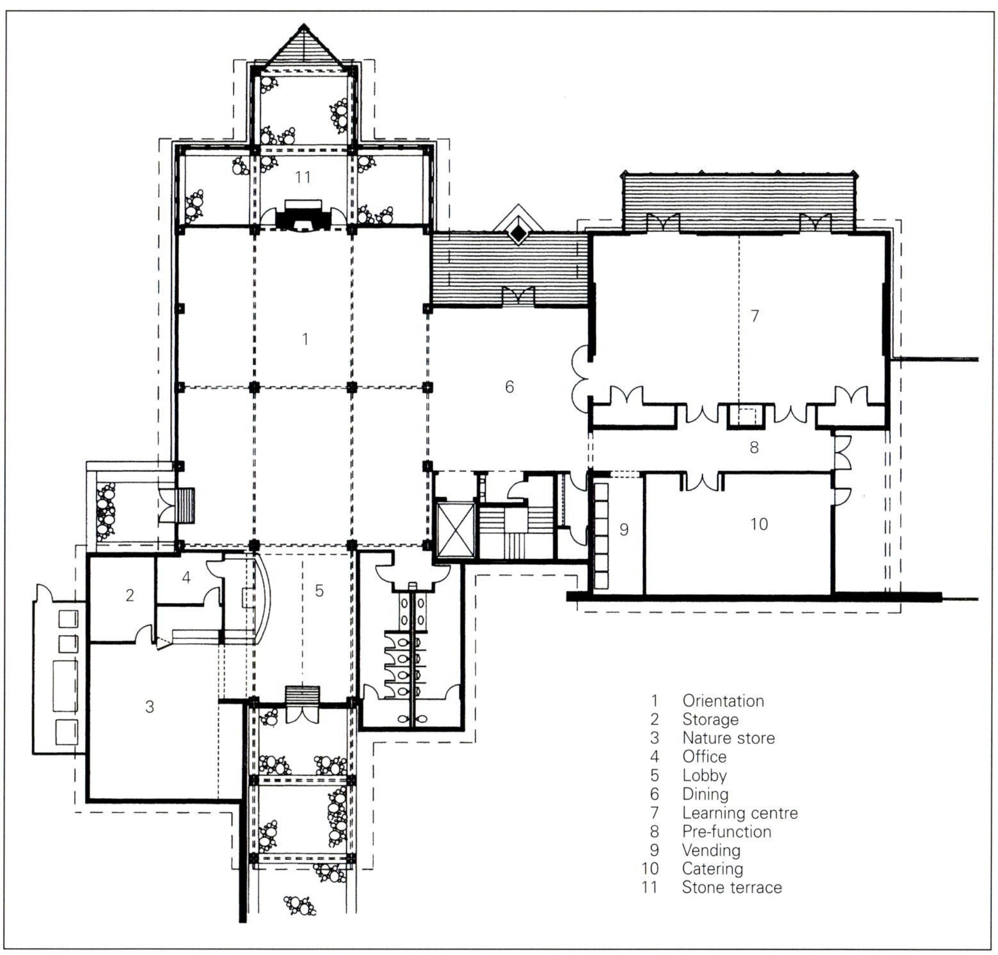

Luxor Theatre

Rotterdam, The Netherlands

Bolles+Wilson

The new Luxor faces both the Maas River and Rijn Harbour, a new actor on the urban stage. The Luxor thematicises its multiple orientation with a single wrapping façade. The ramp roof's foyer floor, an architectural promenade, spiralling the audience from ground floor entrance hall to the dramatic views of the south facing Rijnhaven foyer, sequential unfolding.
The Luxor houses an audience of 1,500. Enclosing wooden panels and acoustically transparent side screens produce the effect of a giant-scaled musical instrument – an `intimate room'. In addition, the audience sit in Bolles + Wilson-designed red and black `Kirk' chairs.
Crumpled reflecting clouds by the Rotterdam artist Joep van Lieshout modify the acoustics to the precise requirements of opera or electronically amplified musicals. The traditional symmetrical proscenium stage reflects the expectations of both audience and performers within the strong popular culture of musical and cabaret in The Netherlands.
Atmosphere Red, the traditional colour of the theatre, is thematicised on the external spiral façade, the inside of this wrapping is lined in red-orange wood panels. Arrival and intermission rituals are theatrically orchestrated in the spacious ascending foyers (their five bars.) Windows frame specific incidents as interruptions to this internal choreography.
The external red fibre-cement panels are overlapped with an exaggerated shadow line, like scaled-up curved planks of a wooden boat. This façade detail allows a vertical curvature in the west elevation and grading of light tones around horizontal curves.

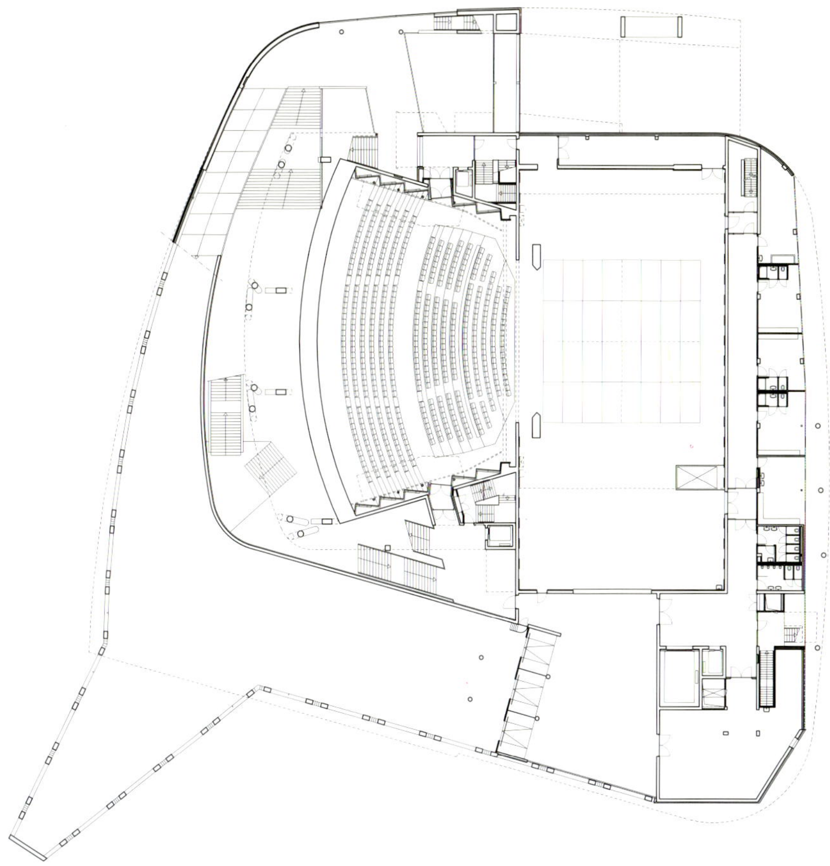

completion	2001
client	City of Rotterdam
area	16,800 square metres/180,835 square feet
structure	Reinforced concrete
materials	Fibre-cement panels, stone, aluminium metal sliding, marble composite tiles, Oregon pine, veneered panels, maple parquet flooring, acoustic gypsum board
cost	41 million EURO
awards	2001, Shortlisted Mies van der Rohe Prize
opposite	Entrance
top	Delivery level plan
bottom	Spiral façade

right Ramp
below South foyer
opposite Auditorium
photography Christian Richters

Mii amo Spa, Enchantment Resort
Sedona, Arizona, USA
Gluckman Mayner Architects

This 3,159-square-metre (34,000-square-foot) spa is comprised of a main building and six casitas, located at Enchantment Resort in Boynton Canyon, a narrow box canyon with 122-metre-high (400-foot) red rock walls.

Organised along a 52-metre-long (172-foot) horizontal circulation spine, a grand hallway is defined by a timber-framed roof and a terrazzo-ground concrete floor. A continuous skylight runs along its length on one side and opposite are five adobe brick towers rising up from the spine. The towers echo the masonry structures of Chaco Canyon and other ancient architectural sites of the south-west United States.

The main floor is dedicated to public spaces including indoor and outdoor pools, library, retail store, gym and café. Private treatment rooms and exercise areas are located on the upper floor. The towers house the heart of the spa experience – private massage rooms, health treatments and relaxation. Natural light and water are essential elements through the spa. Designed as simple white boxes and lit by corner windows and skylights, treatment rooms offer spectacular canyon views. The main entry walkway leads visitors along a stream that originates from the interior then feeds a garden of native vegetation at the main arrival area. The stream emerges from a round room within the spa – the Crystal Grotto. With its earthen floor, domed ceiling and oculus aimed at the sun on the summer solstice, the grotto is the symbolic heart of the building.

Six casitas are located amid an existing grove of cottonwood trees and house 16 guest rooms, featuring custom-tiled bathrooms, fireplace and private walled patios. The casitas are designed around interlocking landscaped courtyards maximising privacy and views.

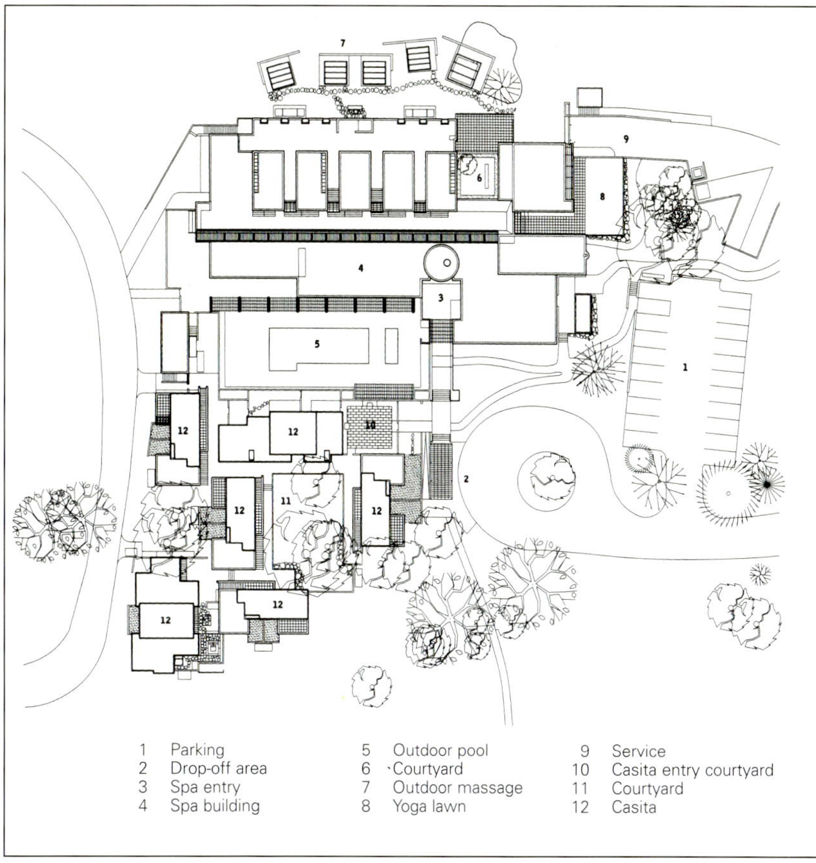

completion	January 2001
client	Sedona Resort Management
area	3,159 square metres/34,000 square feet
materials	Mexican fired adobe brick, stone, terrazzo-ground concrete, stucco, plaster, timber
cost	US$7.2 million
opposite	Exterior view at night
top	Site plan
bottom	Lobby

right	Dining area
middle right	Casita living area
far right	Casita plan
bottom	Main hall
bottom right	View of casita bedroom
photography	Harry Zernike

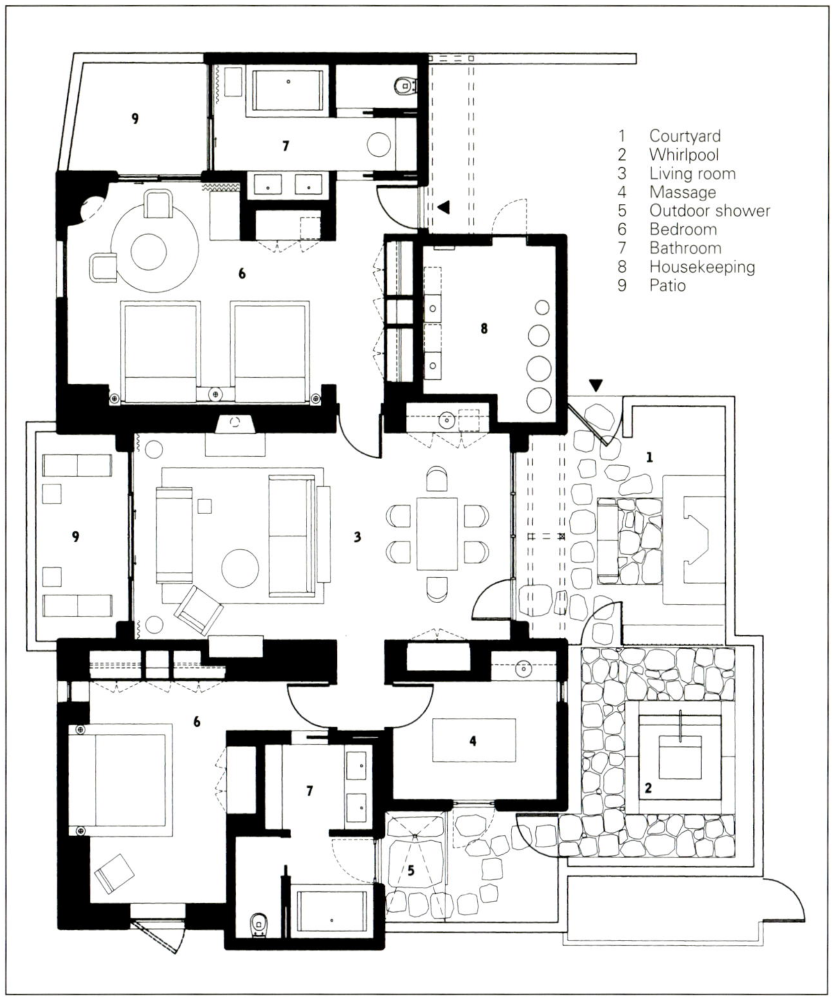

1 Courtyard
2 Whirlpool
3 Living room
4 Massage
5 Outdoor shower
6 Bedroom
7 Bathroom
8 Housekeeping
9 Patio

Mitchell Park

Greenport, New York, USA
SHoP/Sharples Holden Pasquarelli

This waterfront park was commissioned following placement in an international competition for waterfront revitalisation. Phase One was completed in June 2001, and Phase Two is currently in the construction documents phase, with an anticipated construction start date of spring 2002. The program required the design of a waterfront park, including a carousel house, dockmaster's house, harbour walk and central gathering place. The site was an open field in a village that was composed of dislocated and scattered municipal programs.

Immediate to the design was the influence of a set of distinct programmatic zones surrounding the park site. The commercial wharves located to the east, municipal and retail structures to the north, train station and ferry terminal to the west and a new marina to the south, define the programmatic zones or fields of influence surrounding the park site.

The vectors and flows produced by the fields of influence were analysed and a tactical mapping responding to the surrounding contextual forces was constructed providing a plan for the deployment of program on the park site. This methodology permitted programs drawn to the site to be tactically realigned, blended and focused to flow across the site, exploiting the paths of least resistance whilst acknowledging the temporal and cognitive conditions of place.

An ambient flow is further maintained through a monochromatic blending of materials including weathered hardwoods, steel, etched glass, lead-coated copper roofing and bluestone with a network of light planks set into the walk. The park can be seen as a state of flux that blends the events within a field into a comprehensive responsive whole.

completion	June 2001 (Phase One)
client	Village of Greenport
area	2 hectares/5 acres
cost	US$9 million
opposite	View of carousel house
top	Night view of shade arbour and harbour walk with lightplanks
bottom	Interior view of carousel house
photography	David Joseph

Miyagi Stadium
Rifu-cho, Miyagi, Japan
Atelier Hitoshi Abe
in association with Syouichi Haryu Architect

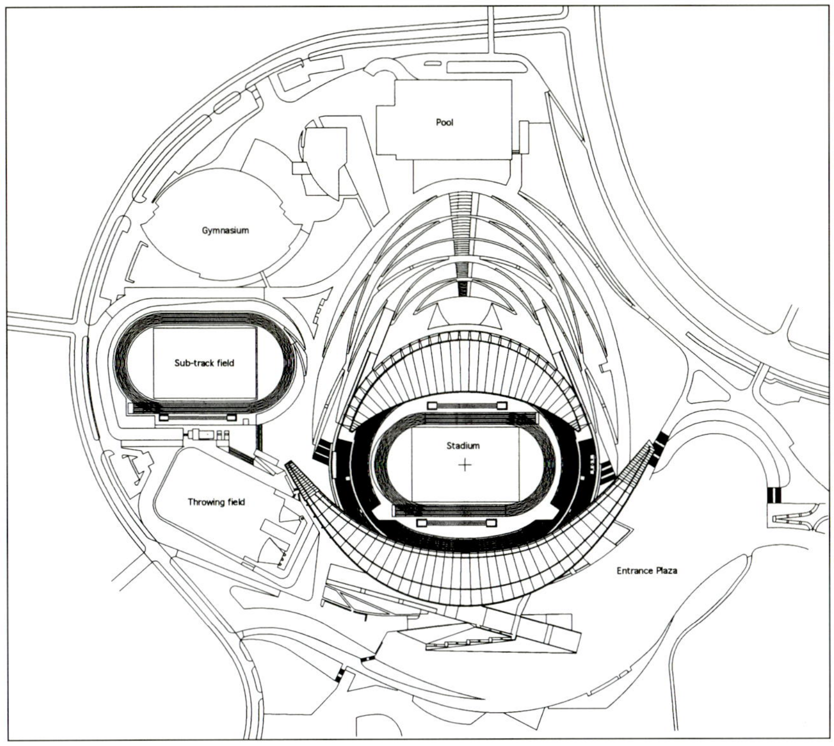

The stadium as a building type is ruled by the geometry of concentric circles derived from its basic requirement: to act as a place where people can focus on its centre. This geometrical character makes the stadium's configuration stable and creates a strong enclosure separating interior from exterior. In order to loosen this rigidity, the Miyagi Stadium combines two typologies: stadium and park. These two programs have been interwoven to create a multifaceted facility.

completion	March 2000
area	57,600 square metres/620,006 square feet
structure	Reinforced concrete with steel, reinforced concrete
materials	Concrete, aluminium
cost	¥14 billion
awards	2001, 42nd Building Contractors Society Award
opposite	View from north with surrounding landscape photography Eiji Kitada
top	Lit-up view of stadium photography Shunichi Atsumi
top right	Site plan
bottom	View of south abut photography Eiji Kitada

top	Third floor plan
middle	Sixth floor and roof plan
bottom	Backstand with audience
right	View of abut of backstand
photography	Eiji Kitada

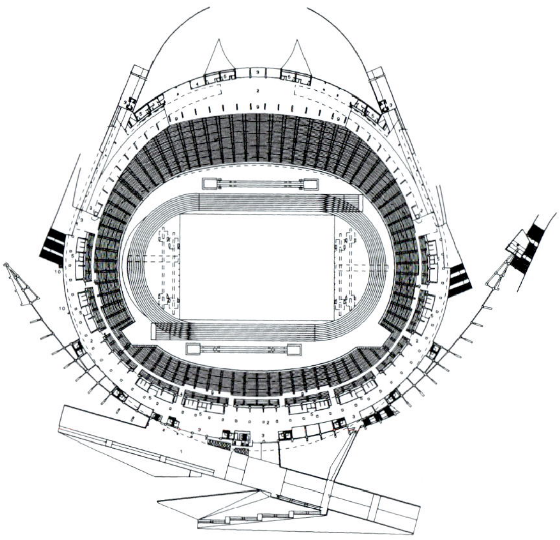

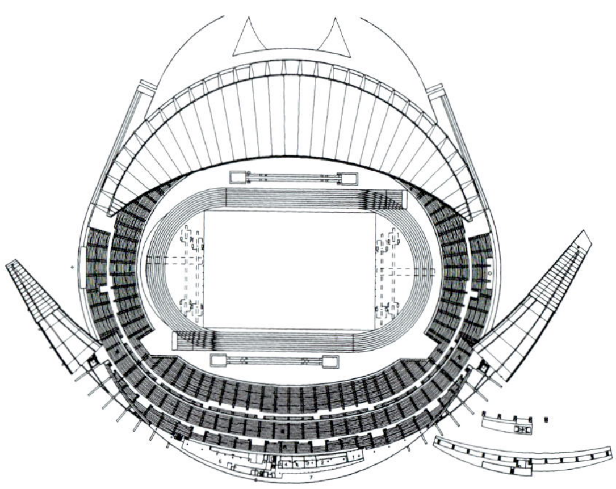

SC
12
SC
12

Mugar Center for the Performing Arts, Cambridge School of Weston

Weston, Massachusetts, USA

Leers Weinzapfel Associates

This new performing arts centre provides a versatile setting for the rehearsal and performance of music, drama and dance education in a campus environment. The centre includes a 250-seat experimental theatre that can flexibly accommodate audiences from 150 to 300, an intimate 75-person multi-use recital and dance hall space and a small 'black box' theatre. Music classrooms, practice rooms, costume shops, dressing areas, theatre control rooms and backstage workspaces are included with related faculty offices and support areas.

The idea of 'performance at every level' emerged in the development of program and is completed in the interior and exterior design. The design consists of three volumes, stepped back and downhill from the quad to minimise the building mass on the smaller scale campus. Forming the main entry on the quad is a daylit multilevel reception lobby. A grand stair cascades down through the building, following the natural slope of the land. With theatre and performance wings to either side, the linear reception lobby functions as a unifying element, providing access to the lower floors and spectacular views from each level of the landscape beyond.

The theatre's upper lobby forms a backdrop and access to an outdoor stage terrace and natural gathering space. The upper level also includes a spacious music recital and dance performance room, music practice rooms, a rehearsal lab and a music theory room. The music performance rehearsal and practice rooms overlook the trees and wetlands. The upper rear of the theatre is entered from this level while the stage level is accessed from the middle level. The middle level houses a costume room, lockers, a theatre office and the backstage. The lowest level includes a smaller 'black box' experimental theatre for more intimate performances and for teaching stagecraft and stage lighting.

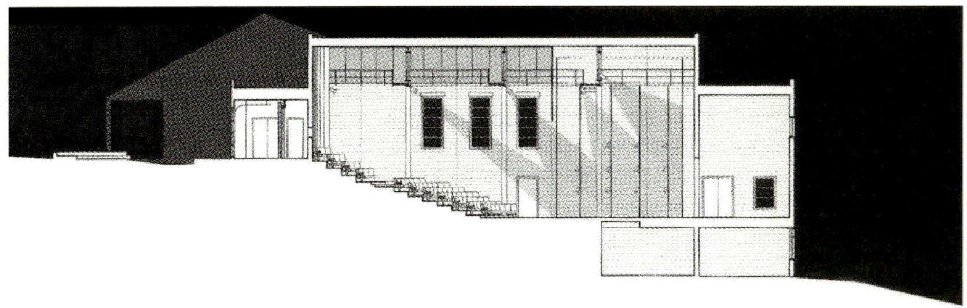

completion	2000
client	Cambridge School of Weston
area	1,655 square metres/17,814 square feet
structure	Steel frame
materials	Exterior: painted MDO plywood with battens; interior: exposed cellular deck ceiling, gypsum wallboard walls and polished pigmented concrete floors
cost	US$3.6 million
awards	2001 American Architecture Award 2000 AIA, New England Citation
opposite	Quad entry; evening
top	Theatre section
middle	Main theatre
bottom	Main lobby
photography	Chuck Choi

Oita Stadium

Oita City, Japan

Kisho Kurokawa architect & associates

The Oita Stadium has been chosen as an arena for the World Cup Games in 2002. The area of the site measures 255 hectares (630 acres). Following the third construction stage the site will feature additional facilities including: a general fitness centre, a training and lodging centre, a botanical pool, two multi-purpose athletic fields, two soccer and rugby training fields, a sub-training field, a softball field, a public baseball field, 11 tennis courts, a throwing event practice field, a gate-ball field and a large open field.

The main stadium also features an open track for events other than soccer or rugby matches. Moreover, aided by the retractable roof feature, the stadium can be used year-round for events such as concerts. To enhance the feeling of being part of the soccer arena, the spectator seating was placed right up to the edge of the field. This type of feature would normally be inconvenient for track events, but the problem was resolved with the inclusion of a retractable seating system. Through the gentle curves of the spherical design, the stadium is well matched with the surroundings in the background. The choice of a sphere is naturally an expression of abstract symbolism, but the shape actually enables the retractable portion to move along its surface. The use of ultra-modern teflon membrane panels with 25 percent light-permeability removes the need for artificial lighting during daylight hours.

completion	March 2001
client	Oita Prefecture
area	92,882 square metres/992,782 square feet
structure	Arch frame and triangular lattice skeleton frame, rigid frame including seismic-resistant walls
opposite top	General view from south-west
opposite bottom	Overall view from north-west
top	General view from south-west
middle	Foyer of main stand
bottom	Overall view of field
photography	Koji Kobayashi

Performing Arts Center, Flintridge Preparatory School
La Cañada-Flintridge, California, USA
AC Martin Partners, Inc.
Design partner: David C. Martin, FAIA

The Flintridge Preparatory School is comprised of multiple residential-scale classrooms, administrative, athletic and assembly buildings arranged on slightly more than 2.4 hectares (6 acres) of wooded landscape. Topographically, the site is divided into an upper and lower plateau by a steep slope that presents challenging circulation issues. The school has a proud tradition of high quality education and maintains strong programs in the performing arts, including theatre, choral and instrumental music.

The new Performing Arts Center is a two-level building covering a former tennis court on the lower campus. Located directly against the dividing slope between the upper and lower campus, the new facility is uniquely positioned to serve as a unifying landmark structure in the campus plan.

The new facility includes a black box theatre, dance studio, music rehearsal room, practice rooms, seminar rooms and associated dressing rooms, storage and other ancillary spaces. The primary design goal was to integrate the new facility into the campus through the use of simple scale, form, colour and materials of similar type to existing buildings on campus, while adhering to a strict budget.

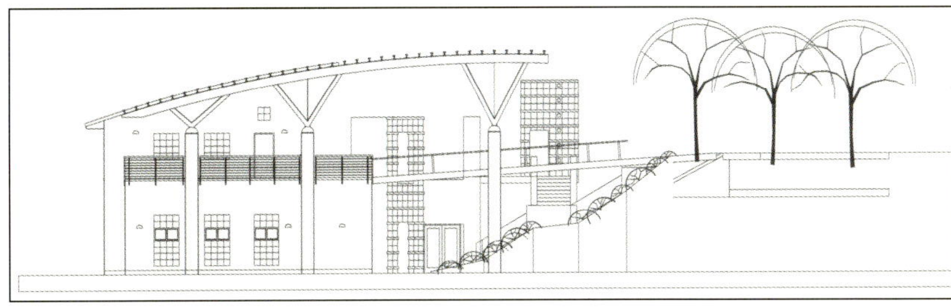

completion	October 2000
client	Flintridge Preparatory School
area	900 square metres/9,688 square feet
structure	Reinforced concrete, steel
materials	Concrete, steel
cost	US$5 million
awards	2001 AIA American Architecture Awards 2000 Design Award AIA San Fernando Chapter
opposite top	View of exterior from 'campus street'; oak trees inspired design for canopy and supports
opposite bottom	Performing arts building serves as new 'centre' for campus
top	South elevation
middle	Dance classroom
bottom	Stepped 'piazza' provides circulation, congregating area and small amphitheatre for outdoor performances
photography	John Edward Linden

Thames Barrier Park
Silvertown, London, UK
Patel Taylor Architects

Thames Barrier Park covers about 9 hectares (22 acres) on the north bank of the river. The site was formerly industrial, housing a chemical works, a dyeworks, and an armaments factory, amongst others. These industries declined leaving the site derelict and the soils and groundwater contaminated.

The strategy was to create a clear urban and park framework which envisaged contrasting spaces for different uses of the park. The park was considered from the general to the particular: from landscaping to urban design and building. The primary concern was to create a rich and inviting public space – a park that knits into its surroundings through a clear and logical urban strategy.

To give the park strong landscape significance, simple strategies were adopted which in turn will determine the future architectural composition of the area. The form of the housing development becomes integral to the park and a series of settings for housing and contrasting park activities suitable for use throughout the year have been established.

Responding to the specific heritage and artificial topography, these settings comprise the following areas for different activities: the Plateau; Green Dock; River Promenade; Peripheries; and Play areas.

In the wider urban context the design principle was to fully integrate the proposals with adjacent areas. This was proposed by physical and visual links from Pontoon Docks/Royal Docks to Thames Barrier and River.

completion	November 2000
client	London Development Agency (LDA)
area	9 hectares/22 acres
cost	£12.5 million
awards	2001 Royal Institute of British Architects Award 2000 Millennium Marque
opposite top	Overview
opposite bottom	Water plaza
above	Visitor pavilion
top	Site plan
bottom	Green dock
photography	Martin Charles

Residential

188 **Housing**
Baumschlager & Eberle

192 **Ian/Stolz Residence**
Kuth/Ranieri Architecture

186 **De Blas House**
Alberto Campo Baeza Architect
in collaboration with Raul Del Valle

194 **Private Residence**
Sidnam Petrone Gartner Architects

184 **Chateau Le Lez, the 'Sprouting' Building**
Edouard François & associés

198 **Tyler Residence**
Rick Joy Architect

180 **Canyon Residence**
Steven Ehrlich Architects

182 **Carter/Tucker House**
Sean Godsell

200 **Valley Centre**
Daly, Genik Architects

Canyon Residence

Los Angeles, California, USA

Steven Ehrlich Architects

A series of vertical masses of coloured burnished stucco form a structural ordering element that aligns in the north-south direction. These masses house elements that serve the adjacent spaces such as fireplaces, stair, mechanical core and storage. They cascade through the house responding to need while forming a kinetic rhythm of colour and form. Counterpointing these vertical planes is a series of cascading copper-clad horizontal canopies. They protect natural wood, glass windows and doors from rain and runoff and form a horizontal balance of floating planes that becomes part of the critical sculptural ordering system.

The ensemble of vertical coloured mass in conjunction with the copper horizontal planes, glass and painted stucco mass dances harmoniously as indoor space fuses into the natural environment.

The L-shaped parti embraces the grandeur of the sloping site adjacent to a creek. The house steps down following the site's slope and is never more than two stories at any location. An 18-foot-high living room area separates the two-story bedroom wing from the family-kitchen zone. The house strongly connects each indoor space to the verdant landscape beyond replete with native Californian trees around which the house has been designed. An amphitheatre of stairs and floating decks facilitates this connection

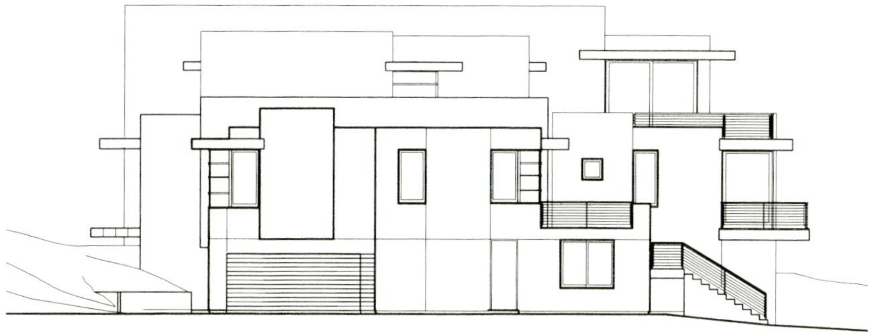

completion	2000
area	687 square metres/7,400 square feet
materials	Wood framing, plywood, steel, cement plaster, copper, Douglas fir, Brazilian cherry wood, stone, stucco, glass
awards	2000 LABC Design Award
opposite	Rear façade of house dances among existing Sycamore trees from backyard and infinity-edge pool
top	West elevation
middle	Front façade from street
bottom	Living room with deep recesses for art
photography	Tim Street-Porter

Carter/Tucker House

Breamlea, Victoria, Australia

Sean Godsell

A three-level, 12-metre by 6-metre (39-foot by 20-foot) box was embedded into the side of a sand dune. The house has three rooms. The lower ground floor is for guests and the single space can be divided by a sliding wall into two rooms if required. Similarly the single space on the middle level can also be divided to separate the owners' bedroom from a small sitting area. The top floor is for living and eating and takes advantage of views across a rural landscape. The top floor is also a daylight photographic studio.

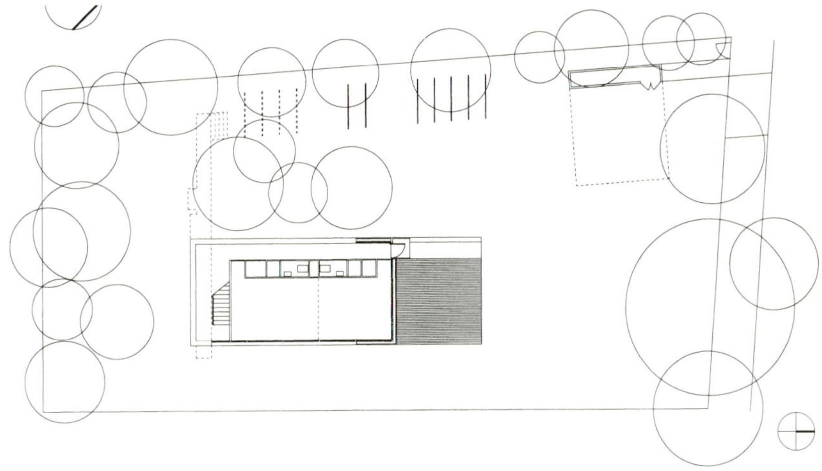

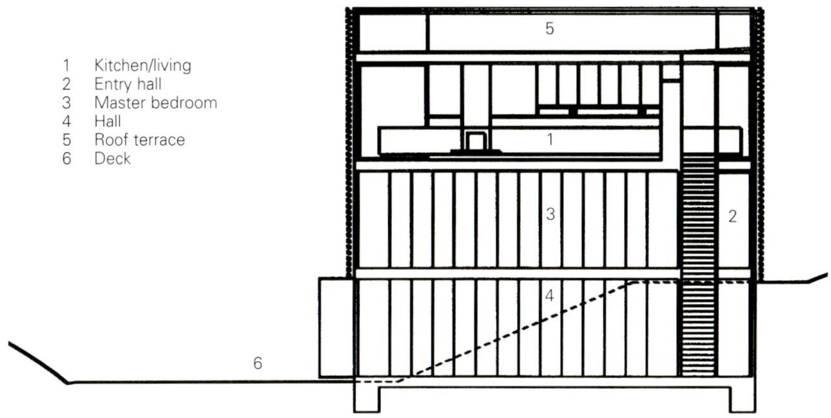

completion	2000
client	Earl Carter and Wanda Tucker
area	210 square metres/2,260 square feet
materials	Victorian ash, Western red cedar, steel
awards	2000, Award of Merit, RAIA
	2000, Robin Boyd Award Commendation, RAIA
	2000, Highly Commended, AR+D
	2000, Best Building in Region, World Architecture Awards
opposite page	
top left & right	View of north elevation
bottom left	West elevation detail
bottom right	East elevation detail
above top	View from south-west
above bottom	Screen detail
top	Site plan
middle	Section
middle left	Stairwell
middle right	Stair detail
bottom left	Meals area
bottom right	Kitchen
photography	Earl Carter

Château Le Lez, the 'Sprouting' Building

Montpellier, France

Edouard François & associés

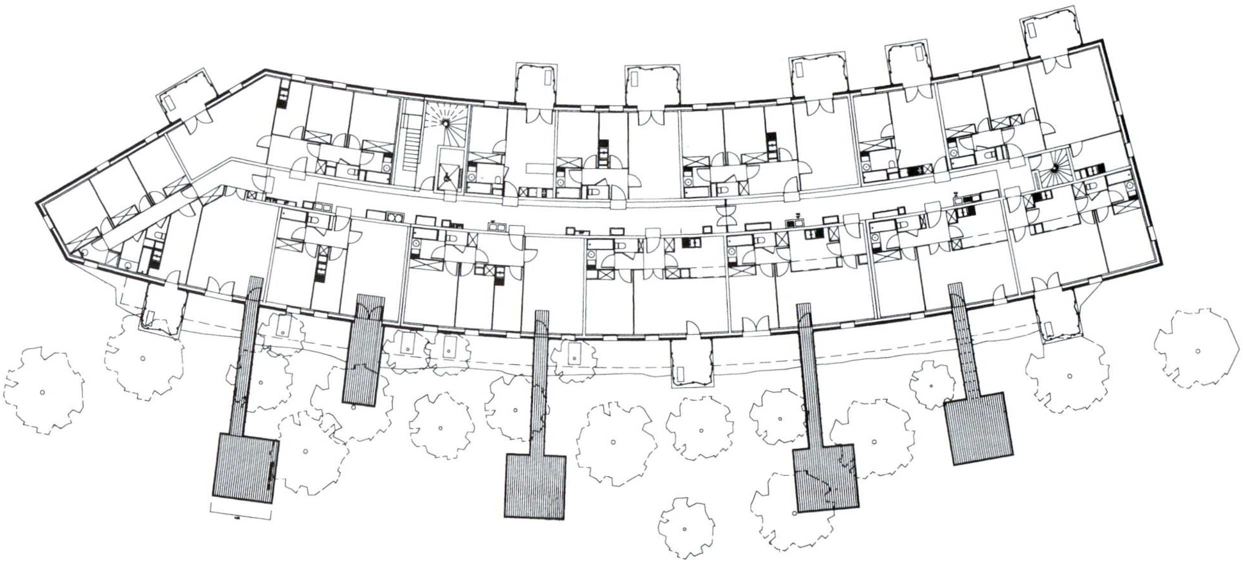

Attempting to invest in speculative housing with a measure of formal invention is generally a thankless enterprise. However, the design for this new apartment block uninhibitedly explores and celebrates materials and nature. The brief from the property development company was for 64 flats and 47 parking spaces on a tight budget. The architect's proposal followed a logical pattern based on making the most economical use of the site and exploiting techniques of prefabrication. For the most part the flats are single-orientated either to the east or west, and are entered from a central corridor. The curved block, inscribes a gentle arc in the landscape and gradually steps up from three to six stories, terminating in a prow at the south end.

The most radical aspect of the scheme is the treatment of the exterior as a massive rock face that will eventually bloom into a spectacular vertical garden. Moored on a solid stone base, the walls are formed from a series of prefabricated concrete panels, the external face of which is clad in a layer of steel wire cages, containing loosely compacted quarry stone. The panels were produced on site. Stainless steel wire cages were set within the steel formwork and studded with a double layer of frost-resistant stones. A layer of sand followed, then lava pebbles and seeds of rock plants contained in growth bags. The ends of the cages are set within a layer of concrete that forms the inner face of the panel. A watering system installed between the joints of the panels nourishes the emerging plants.

The elevations are also articulated by various types of balconies, some enclosed by rustic wooden fencing, others by timber panels. Larger enclosed cabin-style balconies are supported on steel tripods and connected to individual flats by narrow walkways.

completion	April 2000
client	Pragma, Michel Troncin
area	5,800 square metres/62,431 square feet
structure	Concrete
materials	Stainless steel gabions filled with dressed quarry stone, lava pebbles, felt strips, seed bags, small succulent plants, strutted to bearing concrete wall, quarry stone
cost	3.3 million EURO
awards	Official Project for French Millennium 2001 Nominated for 'Equerre d'Argtent' 2001 Nominated for Mies van der Rohe Award
opposite top	Second floor plan
opposite bottom	Overall view from south-east
top	Balcony on south end of building
bottom	Detail of east elevation with balconies and wood cabins
photography	Edouard François & associés

De Blas House
Sevilla de la Nueva, Madrid, Spain
Alberto Campo Baeza Architect
in collaboration with Raul Del Valle

This house has been placed at the crest of a north-facing hill with views to the mountains outside Madrid. It provides a settlement option for a plateau. A platform has been created from a concrete box, upon which a transparent glass box, with a delicate, white, light-steel roof placed on the concrete podium.

The poured-in-place concrete box at the base forms a cave that encases the traditional features of the house. The serviced rooms are to the front and the service spaces are to the rear.

One rises from within the house to the belvedere, which is a glass box placed on the platform. The cave below is a refuge. The space above is like an urn, and forms an area from which to contemplate the environment.

The entire project is confirmed by the precision of its dimensions. The concrete box is 9 metres by 27 metres. The metallic structure is 6 metres by 16 metres. The glass box is 4.5 metres by 9 metres and 2.26 metres high.

The house attempts to be a literal translation of tectonic and stereotomic questions: a tectonic piece set upon a stereotomic box. It is a distillation of what is essential in architecture; once again, 'more with less'.

completion	February 2000
client	Francisco de Blas
area	220 square metres/2,368 square feet
materials	Concrete, steel, glass
opposite	View of house to the north
top	North façade
middle	South façade at sunrise
bottom	South-west corner
photography	Hisao Suzuki

Housing
Innsbruck, Austria
Baumschlager & Eberle

This residential development is located at the west end of the Franz-Baumann-Weg and forms the border between the residential area and the agriculture zone in the west of Innsbruck. The 298 apartments of the complex are spread over six blocks of between five and seven storeys. The blocks are accessed via a system of paved paths and areas that have been designed by various artists and used as playgrounds for children. The areas are also kept free of cars. The blocks have direct access to an underground area with parking for 287 cars. A covered entrance area leads to the large stairways with overhead lighting from which the residential units are accessed. All openings to the outside are floor-to-ceiling French windows, which provide access to the terraces/balconies that run around the blocks. Copper shutters and satinated glass parapets are mounted in front of the balconies to provide both weather protection and privacy.
High urban density has optimised space between the buildings with the use of compact blocks with different height extensions. The landscape design relates to both the inside and the outside, and offers public space. A natural roof has been provided in the areas between the blocks by a kind of lime tree with widespread branches, which creates a contrast with the work of the artists. The relationship between the inside and the outside is changed continuously with the opening and closing of the balcony shutters, corresponding to the needs of the specific inhabitant.

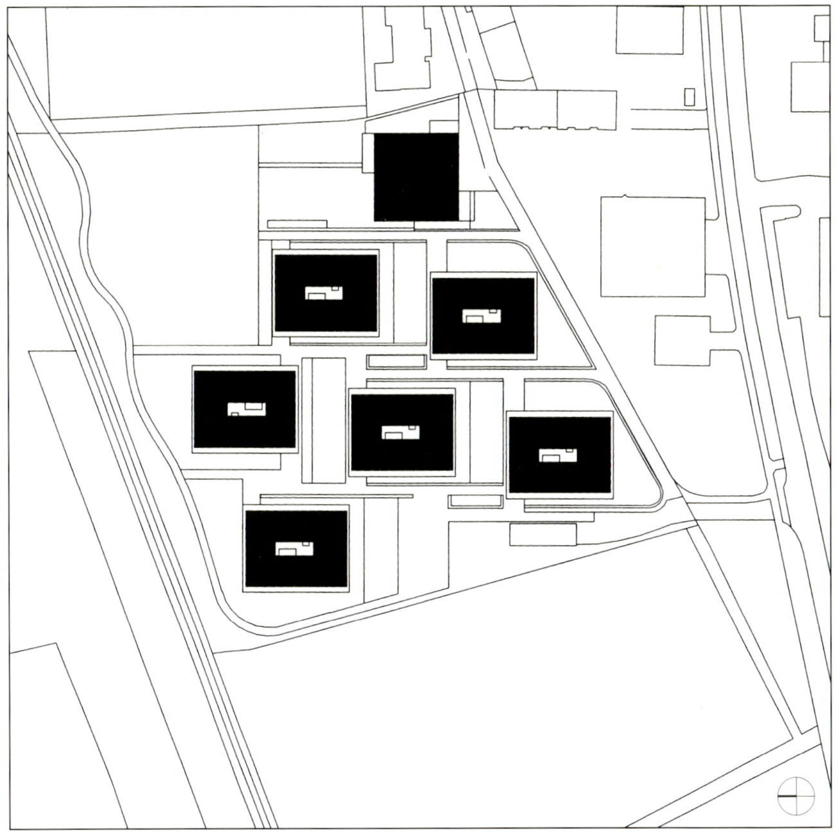

completion	May 2000
client	Neue Heimat Tirol
area	4,580 square metres/49,299 square feet
materials	Concrete, wood, plasterboard, glass, copper
cost	270 million ATS (Austrian Schillings)
awards	2001 Best Residential Building & Best Green Building, World Architecture Awards 2000 Bauherrenpreis 2000 Tiroler Niedrigenergiehauspreis
opposite	South façades and public space
top	Site plan
bottom	Night view of access path

below left Balconies run around the edge of each block, enclosed by shutters and glass balustrades
below right Ground floor plan
bottom Blocks are framed by alpine peaks; with external skin of copper-clad folding shutters

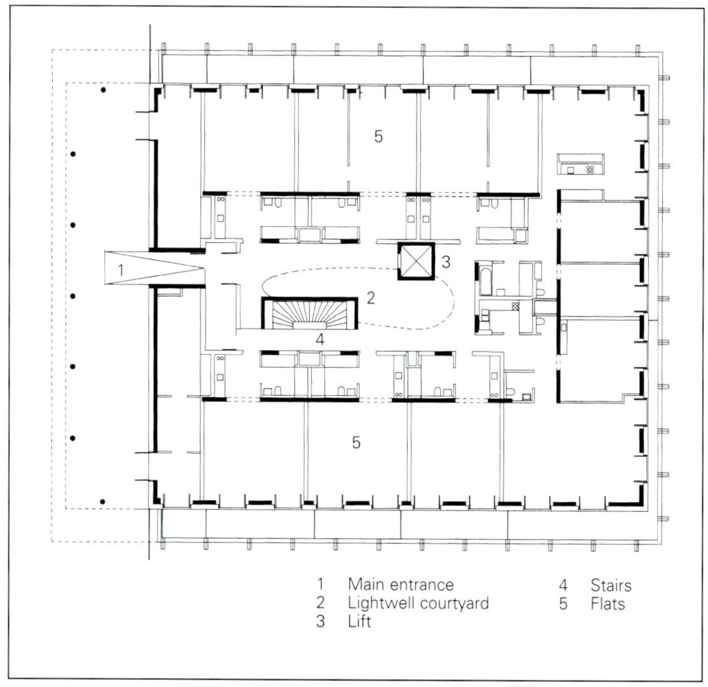

left Galleries give access to individual flats
below At the heart of each block is a lightwell
bottom Looking down towards lobby space
photography Eduard Hueber

Iann/Stolz Residence

San Francisco, California, USA
Kuth/Ranieri Architecture

The house is sited on a narrow alley that transforms from street to garden at the building's front door. The project falls between the grid of the city and the organic nature of a garden landscape. Vistas from the house include the Golden Gate Bridge and the hills of Marin beyond.

The plans at each floor are organised to remain as open as possible to the views, with the central living zones bracketed by support areas, such as stairs and bathrooms, to either side. Like the plan, the façade responds to the context through the transformation of typical typological elements specific to the Bay Area (i.e. bay window, front-facing garage door and street -side roof deck). These elements are folded into a synthetic assembly of clear-sealed mahogany panels and ledges.

The regimented order of the horizontal ledges is set in contrast to the inflection and modulation of the façade's planer surface; the interplay of these regular and indeterminate systems represents a fusing of the different orders of city, garden and building into a singular and integrated image.

Included in the project was a new laminated glass garden wall, strategically placed at the south side of the building where the main floor opens to an adjacent garden. The challenge was twofold – to provide privacy to the occupants and to reframe the landscape. Like the garden beyond, the wall is a volume filled with light and shade. In the daytime, the glass is animated by the dappled and changing light of the sun and in the evening it is illuminated by an internal lamping that infuses the exterior walls, patio and interior rooms with an iridescent sheen.

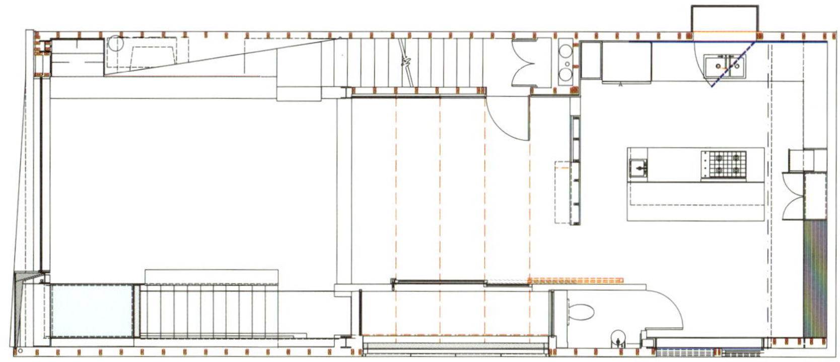

completion	January 2000
client	Adriane Iann and Christian Stolz
area	167 square metres/1,800 square feet
structure	Wood-frame construction with concrete retaining walls and steel moment frames
materials	Clear sealed marine-grade mahogany, blackened steel, stainless steel, bleached maple floors, hand-troweled stucco, limestone, laminated glass
awards	2001 Merit Award for Excellence in Single-Family Residential Design, AIA, California Council 2001 Design Distinction – Environments, I.D. Magazine Annual Design Review
opposite left	Oblique façade photography David Wakely
opposite right	Façade photography Cesar Rubio
top	First floor plan
middle	Dining room photography Cesar Rubio
bottom	View from deck at night photography Cesar Rubio

Private Residence

Harrison, New York, USA

Sidnam Petrone Gartner Architects

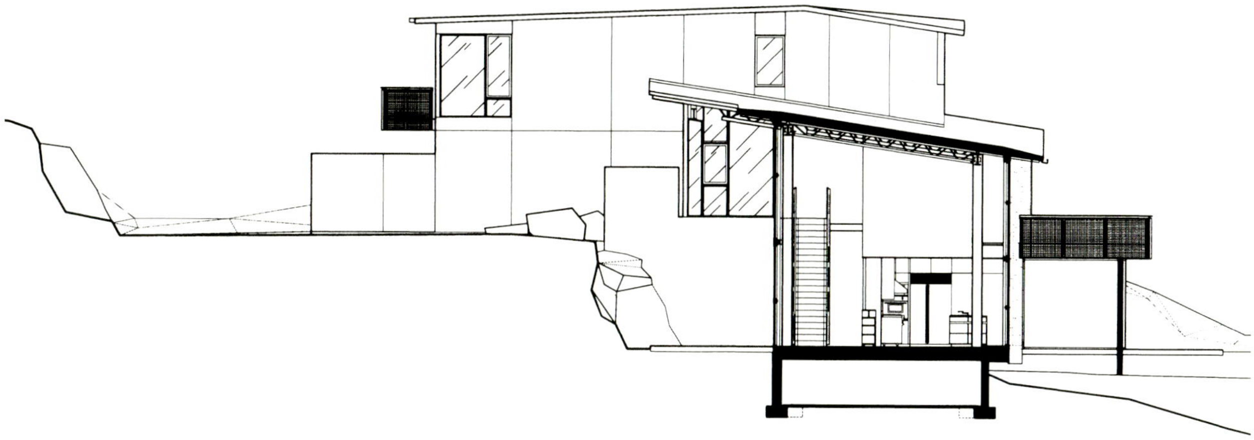

The 0.6-hectare (1.5-acre) site on which this residence is located is densely wooded and is enriched with rock outcroppings and dramatic topographical changes. To embrace these qualities and reflect them back onto the landscape is the primary goal of this design. Aided by the client's desired program adjacencies, the house nestles into a position where a double-height great room rests just beyond, and facing, the most prominent rock feature.

The steel structure of the great room is left exposed and allowed to penetrate beyond the envelope in order to heighten the distinction between natural and artificial. A sloped butterfly roof sheltering the entry, master bedroom, great room and kitchen enhances the transition from one level to the next, both programmatically and topographically. At the north end, a second volume, which locks into this roof, contains a garage, mud room and master bath at entry level, and guest bedrooms above. This mass is counterbalanced by the chimney on the south end, allowing the skin of the great room to stretch between while framing the view of the bluff beyond.

completion	September 2000
area	334 square metres/3,595 square feet
structure	Reinforced concrete, structural steel, open-web steel trusses, light wood framing
materials	Fibre-cement board, stucco, glass, wood, metal, steel, concrete
awards	2001 American Architecture Award, The Chicago Athenaeum 2000 Silver Medal, Award for Excellence in Architecture, AIA New Jersey
opposite	Exterior view
top	Section
bottom	Side of house

top	Kitchen
bottom	View to kitchen
opposite	Great room with view to garden
photography	Michael Moran

Tyler Residence
Arizona, USA
Rick Joy Architect

The site was chosen for its southern orientation towards panoramic views, isolated mountain ranges and expansive desert landscape. The building site is sloped approximately 10 per cent to the south and is covered with scrub, native mesquite trees, and low wild grasses.

A one-bedroom house, with garage, shop and two-bedroom guesthouse was requested by the client. A large linear courtyard is defined by two simple shed forms, which are arranged with orientation towards prime views. The courtyard provides relief from the overwhelmingly expansive setting while the two buildings frame a cropped view of Tumacacaori peak – the client's favourite.

The visitor arrives from above the house via gravel road, and is greeted by only the glazed ends of the above-grade portions of the master bedroom, shop and office, which at night will appear as abstract glowing forms hovering just above the ground.

Guests then descend into the courtyard by way of a stair wedged between the two retaining walls. This courtyard plays an important role in the entry experience with its large shade trees and water features. Planting arrangements and detailing in the courtyard will assert a very refined artificial character. Protruding steel box forms penetrate the building in carefully selected but apparently random locations to frame specific views. A negative edge pool located at the west end of the courtyard expends the experience to the view beyond.

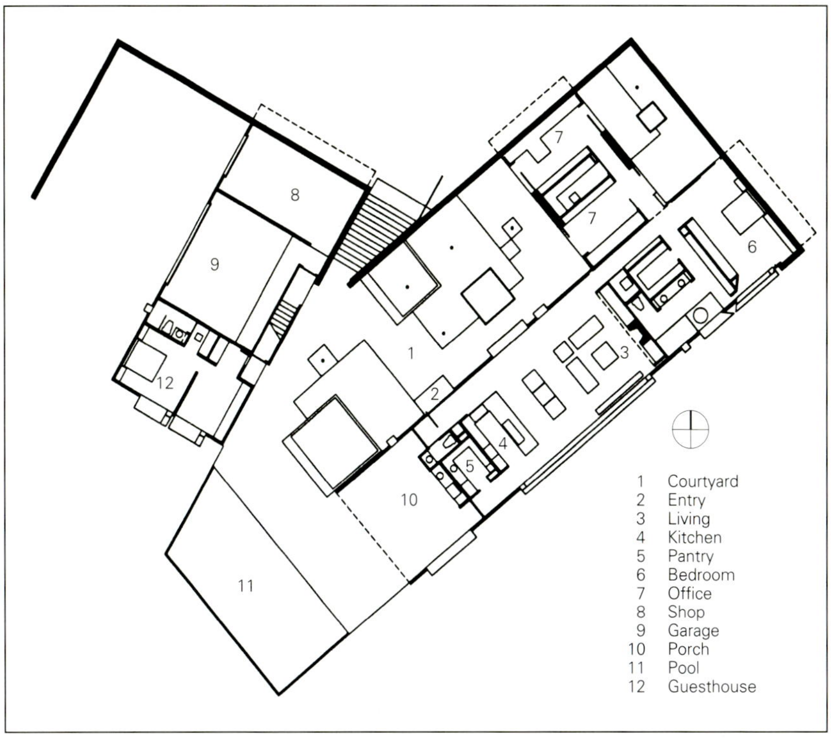

completion	2000
client	Warren and Rose Tyler
area	418 square metres/4,500 square feet
materials	Concrete, wood, steel, plaster, translucent glass, maple
awards	2001 Honor Award, AIA Arizona 2001 Record Houses
opposite	Main living space and courtyard open up over negative edge pool to distant mountain vistas
above	Descending stairs to courtyard below
top	Floor plan
right	Bedroom
photography	Bill Timmerman

Valley Centre

North San Diego County, California, USA
Daly, Genik Architects

top left	Pool
top right	Side view
bottom left	View at sunset
bottom right	Entry façade

Located at the edge of a citrus and avocado ranch the house replaces a ranch house, that burned to the ground in a wildfire in November 1996. The client, a retired chemical engineer, is a second generation citrus rancher.

The house is the client's primary residence, but was also intended to serve as a guest house for holiday and vacation visits from his three grown daughters and their families. There are two bedrooms in the house, with the other sleeping quarters located within alcoves off a glazed corridor that can be closed off by means of large sliding panels. These spaces can be used as study or play spaces when the house is less than fully occupied.

The client requested a house without interior stairs that was easy to maintain and economical to heat and cool. Sun shading was an important consideration and the mechanical systems of the house are zoned to allow one wing to be closed off from the rest of the house when it is uninhabited. In addition, the client requested that a fire-resistant construction system be employed for the house.

completion	2000
area	274 square metres/2,950 square feet
structure	Wood and steel frame, cantilevered concrete floors
materials	Corrugated concrete board, corrugated perforated metal screens
cost	US$330,400
awards	2001, AIA/Los Angeles Honor Award
above	Bedroom
top	Floor plan
middle	Dining room
bottom	Sitting room
photography	courtesy Daly, Genik Architects

Retail

208 **M-Pries Supermarket**
Dominique Perrault Architecte

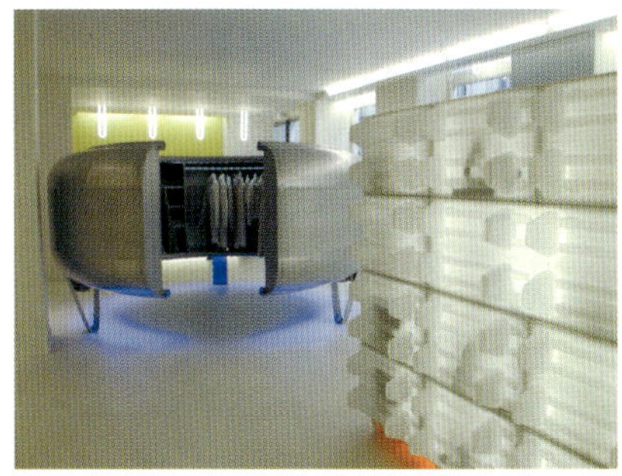

210 **Mandarina Duck Flagship Store**
Droog Design with NL Architects

204 **Alexander McQueen Flagship Store**
Azman Owens Architects

212 **MoMA Design Store, SoHo**
1100 Architect, PC

206 **Giorgio Armani Boutique**
Claudio Silvestrin architects

214 **Paul Smith, Palazzo Gallarati Scotti**
Sophie Hicks, SH Architects

Alexander McQueen Flagship Store
London, UK
Azman Owens Architects

At the outset of the design process, the flagship store for the British fashion designer Alexander McQueen would need to be beyond an ordinary outlet and would have to respond to the ever-changing collection of the McQueen House.
The original building at the front combines the entrance and shop front display. The shop window is left simple and adaptable and allows visibility to retail areas. The fully serviced glass box that links the different collections visually from the street provides a story backdrop for the evolving window display as well as simulating the catwalk shows of McQueen.
A narrow transition space has been created between the retail area and the entrance. An 8-metre-long aluminium display and pay counter is situated within this tunnel-like section, which connects the entrance to the rear. The wall opposite is punctured with internally lit display boxes, containing accessories. A wall of sandblasted panels screens off the women's changing rooms, which have partial glass floors lit from underneath. This glass wall continues to become a frontage for storerooms.
A steel 'framework' installation in the main shop area, comprising multimedia panels, facilitates a responsive shopping environment. The composition of the 'framework', which has bays of interchangeable moveable steel frames, can be continually redesigned, allowing collections to be represented seasonally, in response to the changing themes of the collections.
The use of timber in the men's section with a 10-metre-long shelf and timber and glass cabinets on a track, are a reference to the 'Saville Row' background of Alexander McQueen.

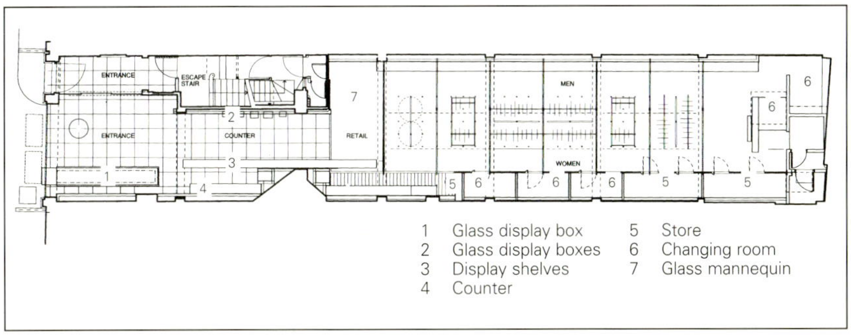

completion	October 1999
client	Alexander McQueen and Onward Kashiyama UK Ltd
area	200 square metres/2,153 square feet
structure	Existing building of timber and masonry
materials	Limestone tiles, polished concrete, aluminium, glass, timber
cost	£450,000
awards	2000 Second Position, Best Independent Store, FX International Design Awards
far left	Conduit Street façade with projecting glass display case
top left	Interior view showing partially cantilevered aluminium pay and display counter
bottom left	Interior view showing steel 'framework' system and hardwood display cases
top	Ground floor plan
middle	Interior view showing partially cantilevered aluminium pay and display counter
bottom	Interior view showing wall punctured with internally lit glass display boxes
photography	Keith Collie

Giorgio Armani Boutique
Milan, Italy
Claudio Silvestrin architects

Claudio Silvestrin has been asked to design all of the Giorgio Armani boutiques worldwide following his commission of the Giorgio Armani boutique in Vendôme, Paris. It is the first time that Armani has allowed an architect to put his name to one of his stores. The second store in the project to be completed is the Giorgio Armani boutique in Milan's via Sant Andrea.
The enormous flagship store in the heart of Milan's fashion district continues with the theme developed for the Place Vendôme. Silvestrin describes it as a style that transcends minimalism and instead strives for timeless elegance. One of the distinguishing features of the store is a dramatic 50-metre-long perspective view of the double-height space seen from outside the store through the window, or from the top of the stairs inside. The walls and floor are raw French limestone and the furniture, designed by Silvestrin, is Macassar ebony.

completion	September 2000
client	Giorgio Armani
area	1,000 square metres/10,764 square feet
structure	Existing structure
materials	Stone, glass, Macassar ebony, brass
opposite	Shop façade
above	Cash desk
top & bottom	Ladies wear shop floor
photography	courtesy Claudio Silvestrin architects

M-Pries Supermarket

Wattens, Austria

Dominique Perrault Architecte

top left Main façade at night
top right Entrance of supermarket
bottom left Inside entrance
bottom right Display

The architect was requested to design a supermarket for a prominent Austrian supermarket chain. The site is unique in two respects: firstly, it is opposite a crystal factory that attracts millions of tourists; and secondly, it is surrounded by fantastic mountainous scenery. The idea of the project was to position a crystal into a patch of nature, and thus show respect to the scenery, and create something magical to connect the building with the image of the town.

This crystal building, totally geometric, fulfils all the requirements of a supermarket. The patch of nature is its exact opposite, its forms are round and natural – birch trees and black pines, just like the ones found on the surrounding mountains. The natural light in the supermarket comes exclusively from this nature inset. This patch of nature makes up the main façade of the building – its characteristic.

The other façades, made of a white crystal glass, break the light and provide natural filtered light throughout the supermarket. They obscure all direct views from the outside to the inside while the views from the inside to the outside are very clear. The surrounding scenery is always present. It is a fascinating play of shadows and light, night and day, and full of effects. However, this building allows the normal operation of a profitable sale outlet despite being an enigmatic and sparkling image of a room of glass carved from a block.

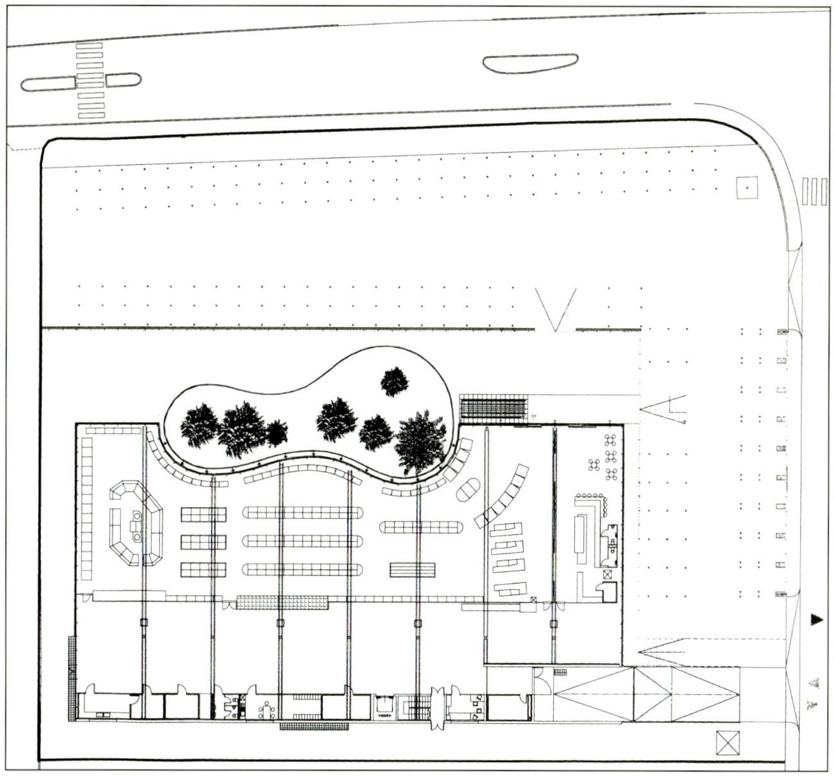

completion	December 2000
client	M-Pries
area	2,200 square metres/23,681 square feet
cost	26.6 million ÖS
top	Plan
middle	Nature in supermarket
bottom left	Detail of garden façade
bottom right	Detail of furniture
photography	Wett, GLP; André Morin

Mandarina Duck Flagship Store

Paris, France

Droog Design with NL Architects

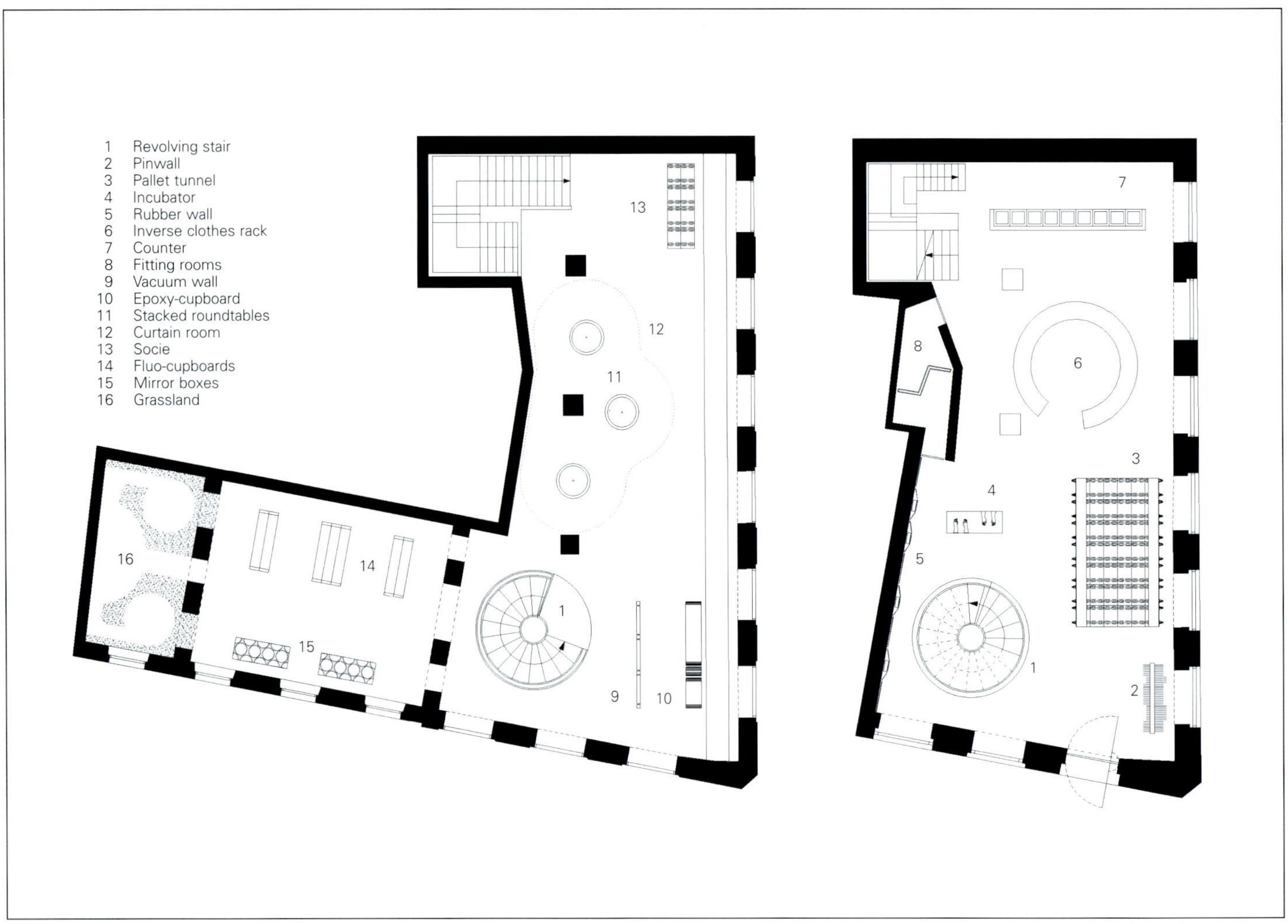

Mandarina Duck rather unexpectedly asked Droog Design to contribute to the identity of its Paris store. Droog was granted exceptional freedom. Together with NL Architects who already have a reputation for crossing professional boundaries, a store was created that features surprise. Droog allows the shopper to explore the simple but the unfamiliar. The space is adventurous, confronting shoppers with ideas that can be recreated in their minds. NL Architects came up with colourful and playful 'installations'. On the ground floor near the shop entrance is a trench, the walls on either side of which are displayed accessories. An enterable 3.6-metre (11.8-foot) diameter floating metal cocoon has been positioned at the rear of the shop. Coloured rubber bands span one of the walls and hold bags and purses.

The second floor is accessed via a motorised spiral staircase, which turns to deposit the shopper descending the stairs in a different place from that which they ascended. The second level features a curtain made from transparent fibres around an area where clothes hang. A vacuum wall is used, as is a pin wall that can enclose objects according to their size and shape.

Whispering sounds emanate from within the fitting rooms, which are large rooms behind a forest of glass fibres.

completion	October 2000
client	Mandarina Duck
area	300 square metres/3,229 square feet
materials	Aluminium, rubber, steel, glass, epoxy, copper
opposite left	Interior of ground floor
opposite right	Metal curtains and 'vacuum wall' designed by Stijn Roodnat
opposite	Ground floor plan and first floor plan
top	Ground floor with rotating staircase
bottom	Fittings rooms are a wild forest of glass fibres
photography	Erica Calvi

MoMA Design Store, SoHo
New York, USA
1100 Architect, PC

The MoMA Design Store is a conversion of two floors of an existing warehouse building into a commercial store for the growing popular retail arm of the museum. The modern design seeks to redefine the existing structure by exposing sections of the historic landmark building. The two-level store, consisting of a ground floor and a cellar floor, carries MoMA Design Store merchandise and includes a selection of furniture and a bookstore featuring an architecture and design book collection. The wide stairwell allows the customer a glimpse of the merchandise on the cellar floor below.

A translucent polyvinyl (Barrisol) membrane extends along the ceiling and far wall of the ground floor down to the wall of the cellar floor in a continuous curve. This membrane is lit from behind and illuminates the interior with a diffused glow, unifying the space above and below and transforming the store into an illuminated light box. The cast iron columns are enclosed with translucent glass to subtly exhibit the historic foundation. The stairwell leads to the cellar floor, where furniture and prints are displayed.

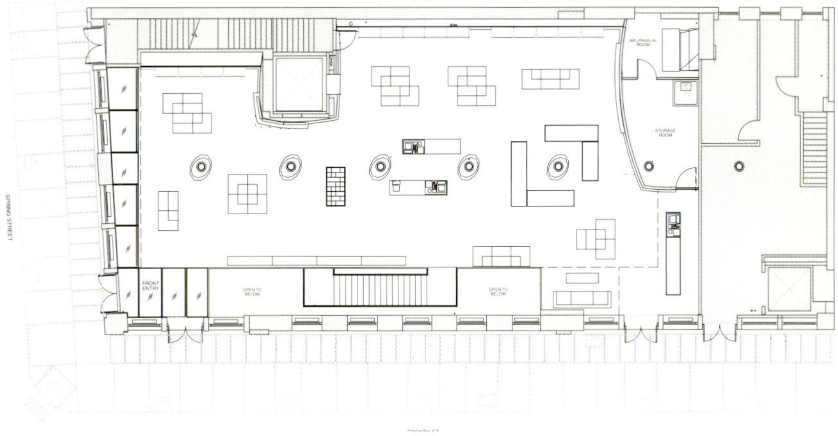

completion September 2001
client The Museum of Modern Art
area 815 square metres/8,773 square feet
structure Existing building of cast-iron, timber, masonry
materials Steel, concrete, polyvinyl (Barrisol), glass, Plexiglas, metal, plastic laminate
opposite Cellar floor
above Cellar floor bookstore
top Ground floor plan
bottom View of ground floor from entrance
photography Peter Aaron, Esto

Paul Smith, Palazzo Gallarati Scotti
Milan, Italy
Sophie Hicks, SH Architects

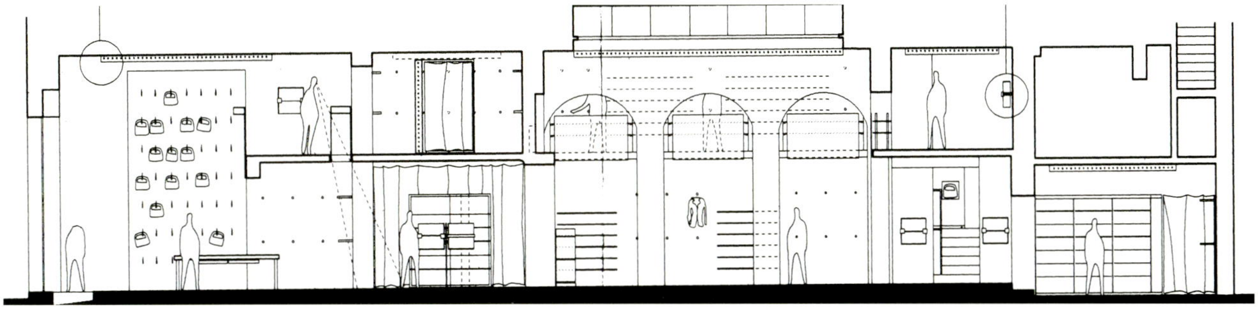

Paul Smith believes that each of his shops has an individual character and he rejects the current trend for worldwide shops laid out to a formula. This project, which combines British and Italian style, is set within a vast 18th-century palace facing onto the noisy streets of Milan. The collections are laid out in double-height rooms and part of a former courtyard. The visitor discovers intimate spaces as well as dramatic views from upper galleries.

completion March 2001
area 270 square metres/2,906 square feet
structure Original stone structure
materials Glass, steel
cost £500,000
opposite page top row
left Double-height space at entry
middle Workbench in rear of shop
right Ground floor showing double-height space
photography courtesy SH Architects
opposite page middle row
left Glass cabinet with underwear
middle Display table
right Detail of workbench
opposite page bottom row
left Mirror room
middle Mezzanine staircase
right Glass cabinet detail
photography Lee Funnell, Graphicphoto
above Longitudinal section
right View from street
photography Lee Funnell, Graphicphoto

Other

watercycle

Bergamot Artist Lofts
Santa Monica, California, USA
Pugh + Scarpa

The Bergamot Artist Lofts are located at Bergamot Station, an art centre comprised of a series of industrial buildings converted into 45 art galleries, including the recently opened Santa Monica Museum of Art. Located on a narrow site that was incorporated into the Bergamot Station Arts Center, the artist lofts, mixed-use program includes a ground level studio/gallery space with three artist live/work spaces above. The fundamental concern was determining how to maintain continuity and coherence with the character of the existing industrial warehouse buildings without compromising formal and material innovation. This project evolved as a carefully considered response to its context with the primary palette being the existing industrial materials at the site. Corrugated metal, steel and glass blend in with the surrounding context while cold-rolled steel and translucent lexan panels create moments of distinction in the details of the buildings that set it apart and help establish its idiosyncratic identity.
The ground floor of the building features commercial space organised around an open plan that allows maximum flexibility of use. A separate entrance leads to three loft units above. With a live-work studio environment in mind, these units feature spacious interiors that are awash in natural light. Polished concrete floors create a uniform field condition. Clean, pristine painted walls and an exposed steel truss and metal deck roof system create a modest yet refined background on which feature elements are constructed with spatial and textural complexity.

completion	January 2000
client	Bergamot Limited Partners, Inc., Wayne Blank
area	1,300 square metres/14,000 square feet
structure	Exposed steel frame, metal deck, light gauge steel framing
materials	Corrugated sheet metal, lexan, concrete block, cold-rolled steel, glass, gypsum board
cost	US$1.2 million
awards	2001 Westside Prize 2000 Design Award, AIA/Los Angeles
opposite top	View of interior photography Marvin Rand
opposite bottom	View of interior courtyard façade photography Benny Chan
top & bottom	View of interior photography Marvin Rand

Bilbao Airport

Bilbao, Spain

Santiago Calatrava

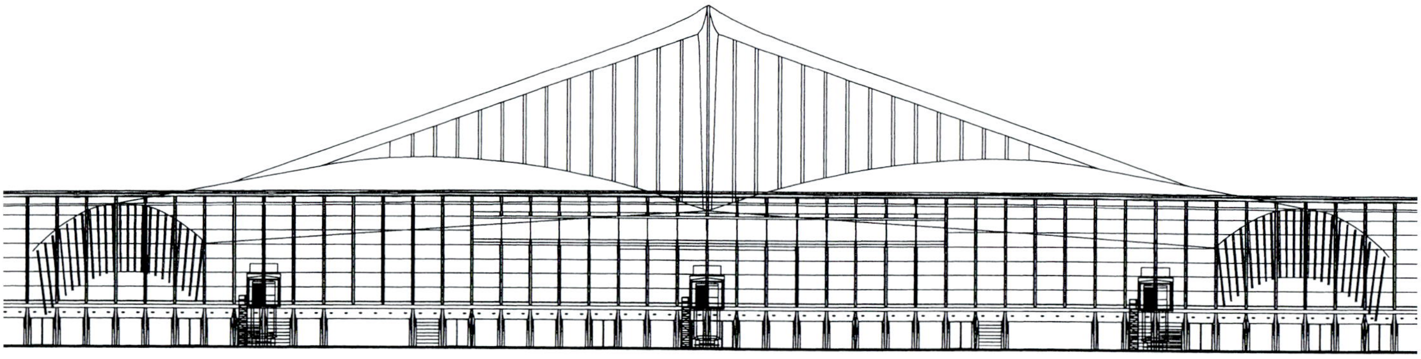

Approximately 10 kilometres to the north of the city and with a metro connection planned, the new airport is situated across the airfield from the old terminal, which had been built to cope with internal flights only. Within this new design, there is considerable potential for future expansion – two million passages per annum by the year 2000, and future expansion up to 10 million.

The organisational and architectural centre of the complex is the large glazed hall. The steel structure of the aerodynamic roof rises up towards the airfield to span the administrative areas and restaurants, as well as the waiting areas behind the canted glazed façades that overlook the apron and runways. The triangular plan of the hall echoes the natural flow of passengers towards the transverse linear walkway leading to the gates, while the generously curved, glazed entrance on the northern side allows full use of the 36-metre traffic drop-off area: the elevated, upper level of this vehicle access is for departures; the lower level is for arrivals.

The building is divided into three heights: the installation galleries, the arrival area and the area for passenger boarding and departures with direct access to the planes. The check-in area is the most important architectural element and, along with the control tower, provides the project's central image. It is a very large and high-ceilinged lobby with an innovative form and sufficient spans of glass.

The entire central axis is dedicated to transportation: the organisation of sales and information, and access to the boarding gates or connectors. The interior of the departure lobby is made of steel and glass enclosed by concrete bases.

The airport is connected by a 100-metre (328-foot) subterranean passageway to the four-storey parking garage (1,400 vehicles), which is partially recessed into a landscaped rise. The overall plan includes future expansion in the form of hotels and a recreational complex.

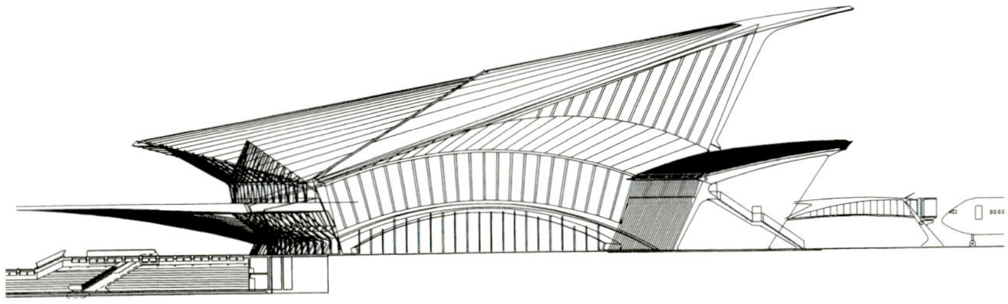

completion	2000
client	Aeropuertos Españoles y Navegación Aérea
area	74,430 square metres/801,164 square feet
materials	Concrete, glass, steel
opposite top	South elevation
opposite bottom	Main departure hall
top	Longitudinal section
middle	General view of airport
bottom	Access to arrival area
photography	Palladium Photodesign

Cantera
Wunstorf, Germany
Kreykenbohm Architekten

Cantera, located in a commercial park, combines a hotel with bistro and sauna. Eleven uniquely designed bedrooms and a conference room form the hotel, each design with a variety of colours, materials and furniture. The design is carried into the landscape with an outdoor sauna, garden areas and walkways composed of stone. Considerable transparency in the foyer and bistro areas merge the inside with the outdoor garden courtyard. Sandblasted and rough stone is used as 'anti-slip' material for the grounds and a massive granite stone forms the 'diving-basin' of the sauna. A two-storey foyer is brightened with light filtering in through a skylight which projects an ever-changing, dramatic play of light and shadow on the wall. The only column in the building is found here, constructed of recycled cast iron. A large stone porch marks the entrance of which the sidewalls and roof are cut from a large piece of stone imported from Spain.

completion	2000
client	Jörg Horstmann
area	1,200 square metres/12,917 square feet
materials	Brick, limestone, slate, marble, wood, bamboo
cost	3.5 million DM
opposite left	Two-storey foyer photography Jochen Stüber/Hamburg
opposite right	Upper floor with skylight photography Kreykenbohm Architekten
top	Night view photography Jochen Stüber/Hamburg
middle	Courtyard during winter photography Kreykenbohm Architekten
bottom	Room with combination of bamboo photography Jochen Stüber/Hamburg

Condé Nast Cafeteria
New York, New York, USA
Gehry Partners

The 260-seat Condé Nast Cafeteria provides employees with a convenient dining and meeting facility, including a main dining area, a servery and four private dining rooms.

The main dining area is organised to provide a variety of seating arrangements in an atmosphere that is both intimate and open. Custom-designed booths that accommodate four–six people each are distributed along the perimeter walls.

The perimeter walls, which are clad in perforated blue titanium panels that include an acoustic backing to insure acoustic absorption, undulate in response to the geometry and overall configuration of the booths. Additional booths are located on a raised seating platform, which is enclosed within curved glass panels in the centre of the main dining area. Free-standing tables and chairs, designed by the architect, will be distributed throughout the main dining area. The floor is ash-veneer plywood, and the ceiling is clad in perforated blue titanium panels that match the perimeter walls.

The servery, which is adjacent to the dining area, is a fully equipped facility that provides a selection of different hot and cold entrees. The servery's curvilinear angel hair finish stainless steel countertops, blue titanium walls and canopies, and ash veneer floor and ceiling complement the sculptural and aesthetic character of the main dining area.

The four private dining rooms are located on the same level as the main dining area and the servery, but they are distinct and separate spaces to be used for special lunch meetings and presentations. The walls, floors and ceilings of the private dining rooms are ash-veneer plywood. Curved glass panels articulate the east wall of each room, providing an even natural light illumination through clerestory windows.

completion	March 2000
client	Condé Nast Publications Inc.
area	1,003 square metres/10,800 square feet
structure	Existing structure
materials	Titanium panels, glass panels, ash-veneer plywood
opposite	Main dining room
top	Curved glass panels on left; booths on right
bottom	Walkway leading to raised dining platform

top Private dining room
bottom Handrail in main dining room
opposite Private dining room with frosted glass panels
photography Eduard Hueber, Arch Photo Inc.

Notre Dame de Pentecôte Church

Paris, France

Atelier D'Architecture Franck Hammoutene

top left View from north; above motorways at end of day photography O Wogensky

top right West façade and main entrance photography O Wogensky

bottom View from street of La Division Leclerc

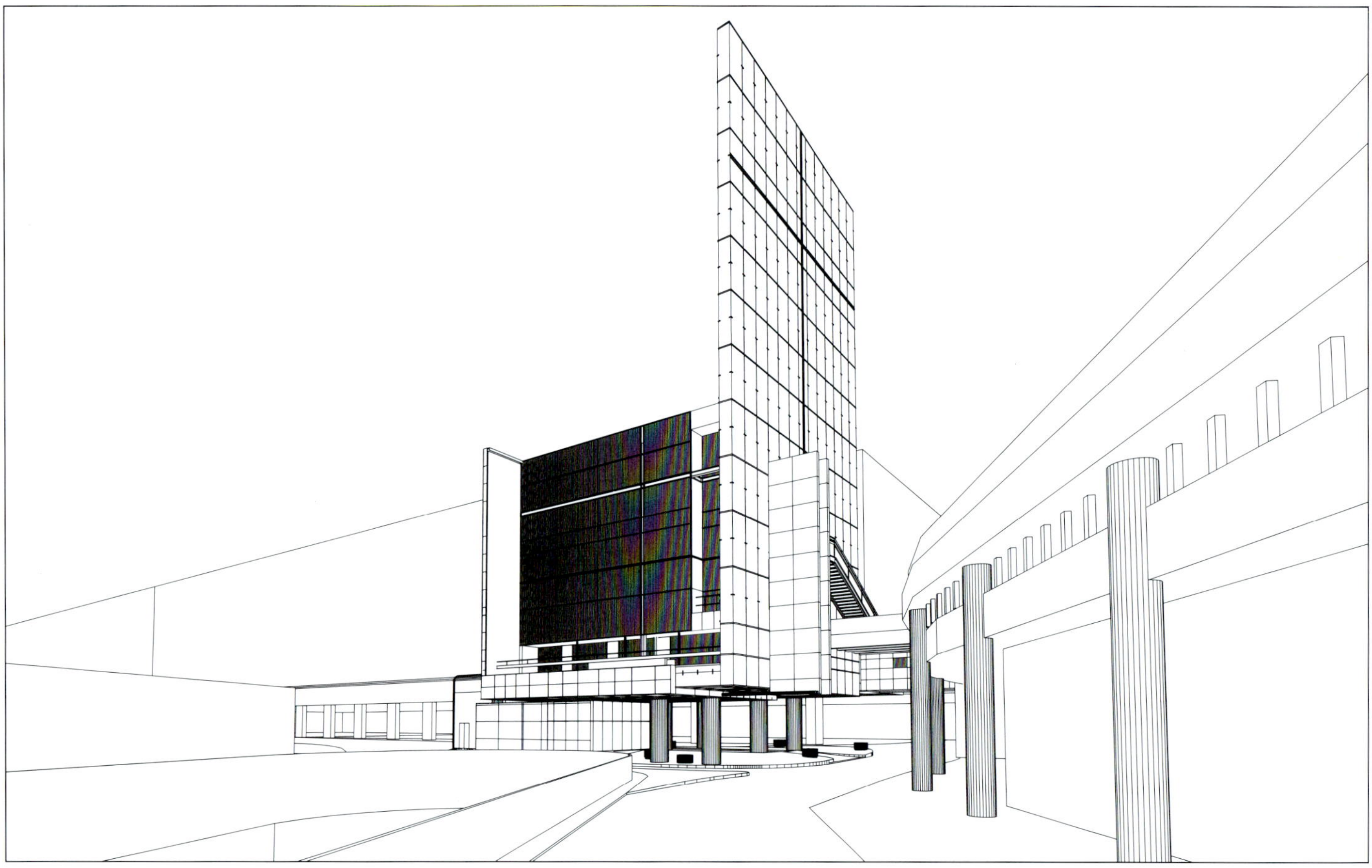

Notre Dame de Pentecôte is built above an empty space overlooking expressways: the building has exceptional visibility. The three sections of the project are organised vertically: an 'upper' hall on the top level, direct access from the square for receptions and meetings, and meeting rooms beneath the square but still above the empty space.

The outline is the result of a series of planes that protect with enclosure, define the interior space, generate variation in scale and openings and leads into the building, erasing the outside world. Two high, vertical, opal planes, one with a filigree cross, the other closing off the nave and concealing the expressway behind the altar, suggest, protect, order the outlook and filter the light.

Therefore the façade is a luminous mask, both a boundary and an invitation to enter a place primarily designed as a shelter (the porch, open and transparent for its full height), then to welcome (the hall and its low proportions, the shadow and distance with the surroundings) and finally leading up to the church and the confrontation with unattainable light. Before returning to the world, visitors view the Grande Arche above the span of the CNIT's vault.

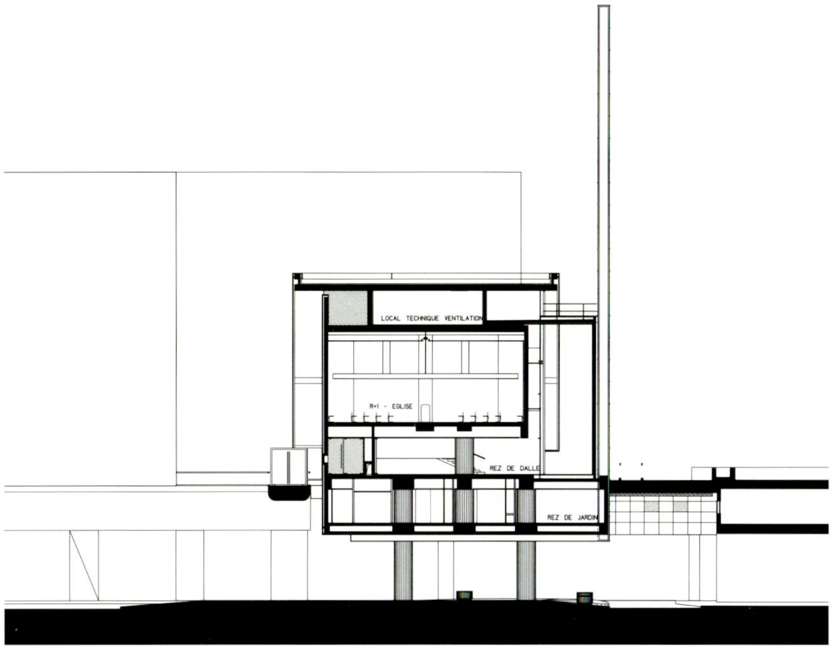

completion	December 2000
client	Les Chantiers du Cardinal
area	1,250 square metres/13,455 square feet
structure	Reinforced concrete, steel
materials	Concrete, aluminium, glass, steel, granite
cost	FF45 million
top	West elevation
middle left	West façade and main entrance photography Frenchie Cristogatin
middle right	North-west corner photography O Wogenscky
bottom	Interior view with altar and glass wall photography Frenchie Cristogatin

Restaurant, Pompidou Centre
Paris, France
Jakob + MacFarlane

The program brief was to create a restaurant on the sixth floor of the Centre Georges Pompidou. A space that would need to contain all the usual programmatic requirements of a restaurant, opening out onto an exterior terrace.

A series of volumes are slid beneath the floor surface or 'skin': kitchen, bar, coat check and private reception room, finding their eventual form and position through the usual negotiation process of design. This skin acts as a stretchable surface that eventually absorbs all the programmatic changes. The project then became finalised at some point, caught or frozen in a state of movement. This sense was something to capture, creating architecture that records the dynamic of program and actuality.

Another aspect of the response to this site and specifically the floor as developable form, was in appropriating the building grid of Pompidou, i.e., every structural and surface increment is divisible into an 80 x 80 grid at the smallest up to the primary structure of 12.80. This 'real' grid, was appropriated as the 'conceptual' one, which then becomes deformed by the volumes or pockets.

The furniture is designed in such a way that all pieces are aligned at 70 centimetres (27.5 inches) above the floor, in order to create a sea of furniture, making outside terrace join seamlessly with inside space.

completion	January 2000
client	SNC Costes
area	900 square metres/9,688 square feet
structure	Aluminium, monocoque
materials	Aluminium, rubber
cost	FF18 million
opposite left	Mouth of bar
opposite right	View to bathroom volume
top	View from terrace
middle	View from inside bar
bottom	Entry to kitchen
photography	Nicolas Borel, Archipress

Rose Center for Earth and Space

New York, New York, USA

Polshek Partnership Architects

A cubic volume, approximately 120 feet (36.5 metres) on a side, encloses a hollow sphere 87 feet (26.5 metres) in diameter. As the programmatic and iconic heart of the architectural concept, the sphere houses the Space Theater in the upper hemisphere and the Big Bang Theater in the lower hemisphere. Critical to the design concept are the sphere's apparent disengagement from the enclosing structure, the transparent curtain wall and the cantilevered spiral ramp encircling the sphere. The ramp, which is central to the scientific narrative about space and time, completes a circulation system connecting the upper and lower levels of the volumes and introduces an asymmetry that destabilises the otherwise Platonic composition.

Three pairs of hollow tapered steel columns, which engage at the equator, support the sphere. The seeming weightlessness of the sphere results from only one column's set being visible at any given point and from its apparent isolation from the other supporting columns.

The support system for the diaphanous wall, as for the roof, is a co-dependent system of tubular steel wall trusses braced by high-strength stainless steel tension trusses. The near-perfect optical clarity of the glass makes the wall so transparent that the surface plane appears seamless, defined only by its pattern of flush bolt heads and nearly invisible joint lines. The upper extension of the glass wall folds over the top and down at a 45-degree angle, transparently mediating its uppermost profile against the sky.

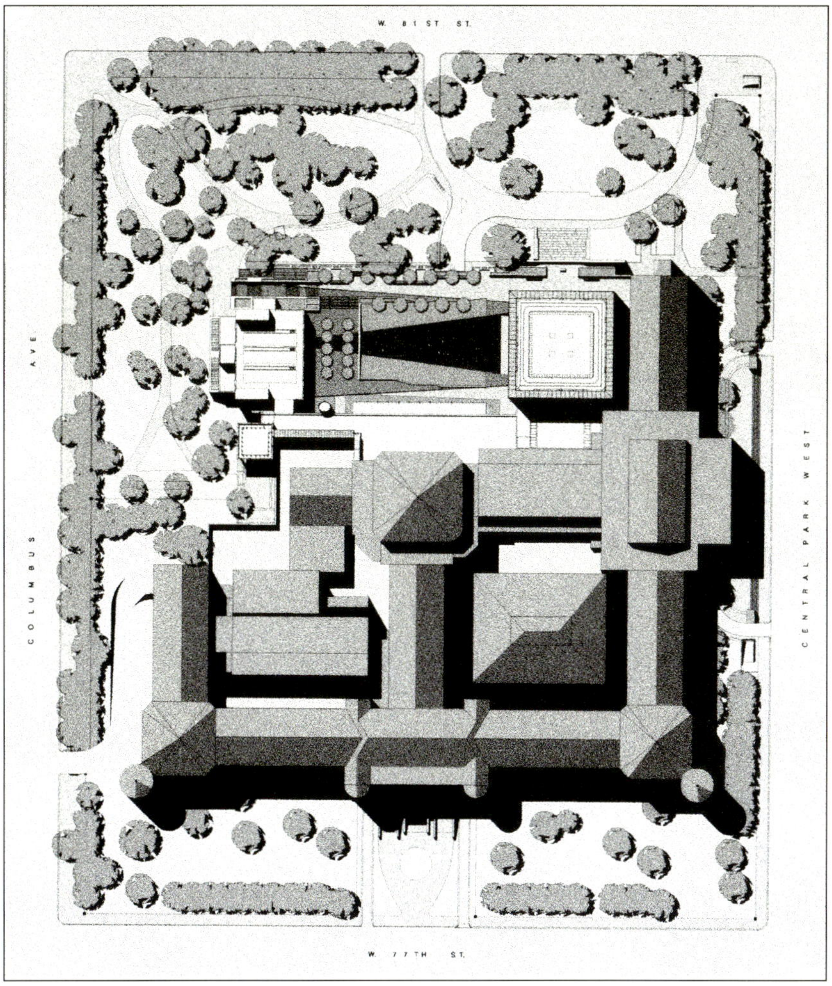

completion	January 2000
client	American Museum of Natural History
area	33,100 square metres/356,288 square feet
structure	Tubular steel wall trusses, stainless steel tension trusses, reinforced concrete
materials	Monolithic 'water white' glass, steel, concrete, granite, pre-patinated copper, terrazzo, brick
cost	US$210 million
awards	2001 AIA New York City Award for Architecture 2000 Business Week/Architectural Record Award, AIA/Business Week Magazine 2000 Best in Design, Time Magazine Best of 1999 Award, New York Construction News 2000 Bronze Plaque for Excellence in Design, The Municipal Art Society of New York 2000 NYACE Diamond Award for Engineering Excellence in Design, New York Association of Consulting Engineers 2000 Award for Design Excellence, New York Concrete Industry Board
opposite	View of east elevation across terrace
top	Site plan
bottom	View of timeline ramp with Hall of the Universe beyond

The enclosing cube is a symmetrical polygon with two glazed sides and two solid sides, which brace the overall structure. The multiplicity of circulation routes within the cubic volume creates a perceptual asymmetry. An apparent sense of weightlessness defines the formal perception of the 110-metre-long (360-foot), 2.4-metre-wide (8-foot) Helibrunn Cosmic Pathway, a timeline that helically wraps around the lower half of the sphere and is cantilevered from a 76-centimetre (30-inch) diameter steel torsion tube and spans 27 metres (90 feet) from each of its supporting columns. The linear spiralling geometry further reinforces the sense of the sphere's levitation.

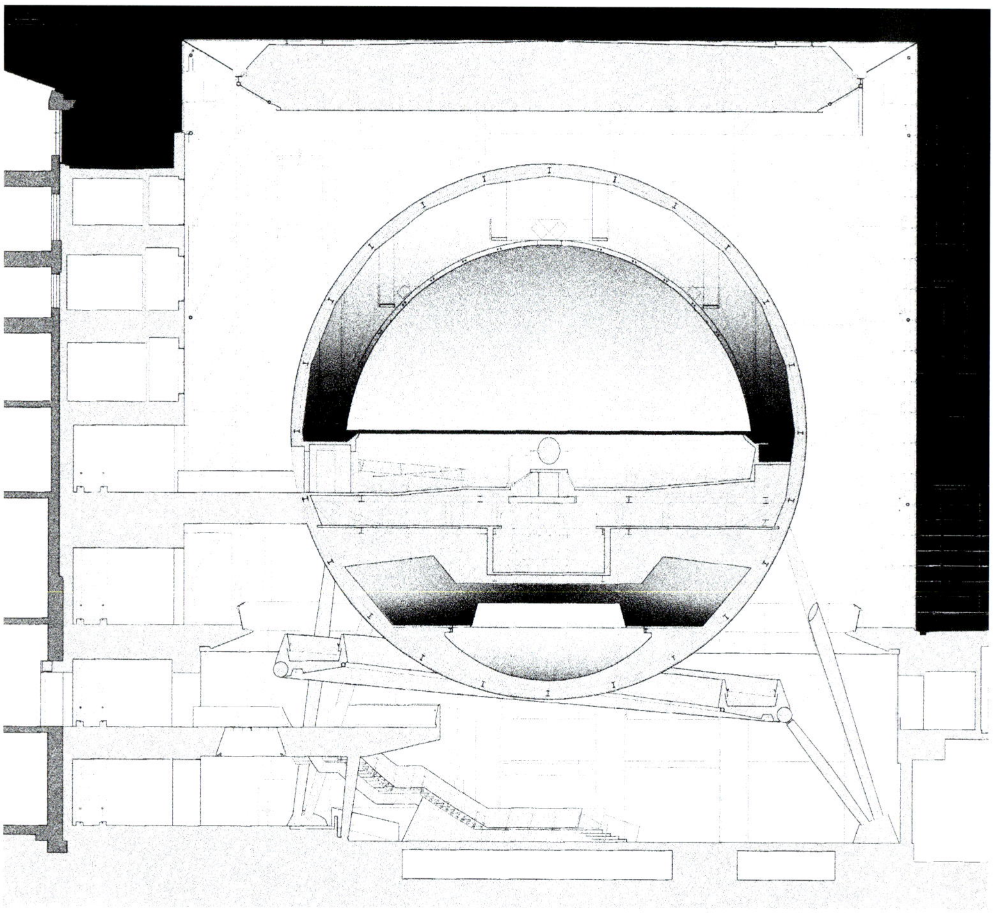

opposite	View of Hall of the Universe with sphere beyond
opposite middle	East-west section
opposite bottom	View of Hall of the Universe
right	Close-up of sphere at night; north facing
below	View of Space Theater
photography	Denis Finnin/AMNH

The Umbrella

Culver City, California, USA
Eric Owen Moss Architects

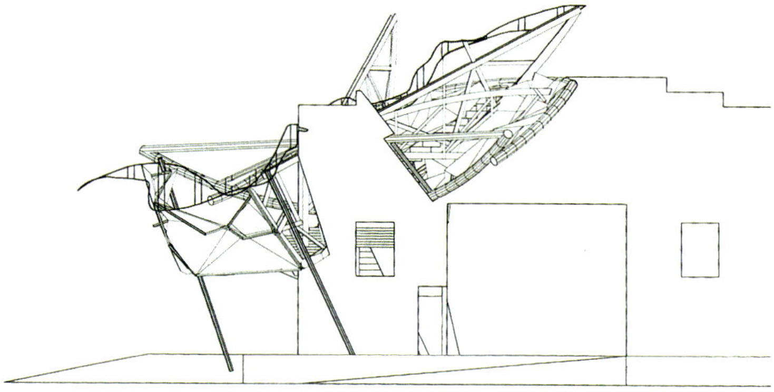

top Elevation
above View of performance platform
middle right View of Umbrella
bottom right View of performance platform

The Umbrella was originally designed as an outdoor performance balcony for the 'Green Umbrella', an experimental series put on by the Los Angels Philharmonic Orchestra. The fundamental design intention was to provide a venue for a small number of musicians (5–10) who would perform on the balcony for an audience seated below.

The Umbrella itself is a cascading series of laminated glass panels mounted on a steel structure over the open-air platform and stairs. The glass was arranged to both shelter the musicians and enhance them acoustically. The interior was designed to accommodate numerous different performance arrangements from multiple small venues to a 30–40-person orchestra. When the tenants change, the Umbrella continues to function as a bandstand for musicians or speechmakers as well as a lunchtime seating and roof deck/lounge area. The building is now the headquarters of a major Internet and graphic design company. Because of how the company functions, the interior programmatic requirements included a wide range of uses from open production areas, private offices, conference areas, exhibition areas and kitchens to the highly technical avid bays for film editing. Avid bays are typically small rooms with low ceilings. The three avid bays in the Umbrella are large open rooms with high ceilings that provide an enjoyable work environment, as well as providing a more versatile room for future uses.

Directly below the Umbrella on the interior is a large meeting and videoconference centre. The concrete shell of the Umbrella becomes the ceiling for this space. The exterior of the building is clad in cement board. Because of the program of the building, the majority of the building is introverted except for the glazing along the entrance ramp. Natural light is brought into the building through skylights. The surrounding area of the building is landscaped and designed to encourage informal meetings of people using the building.

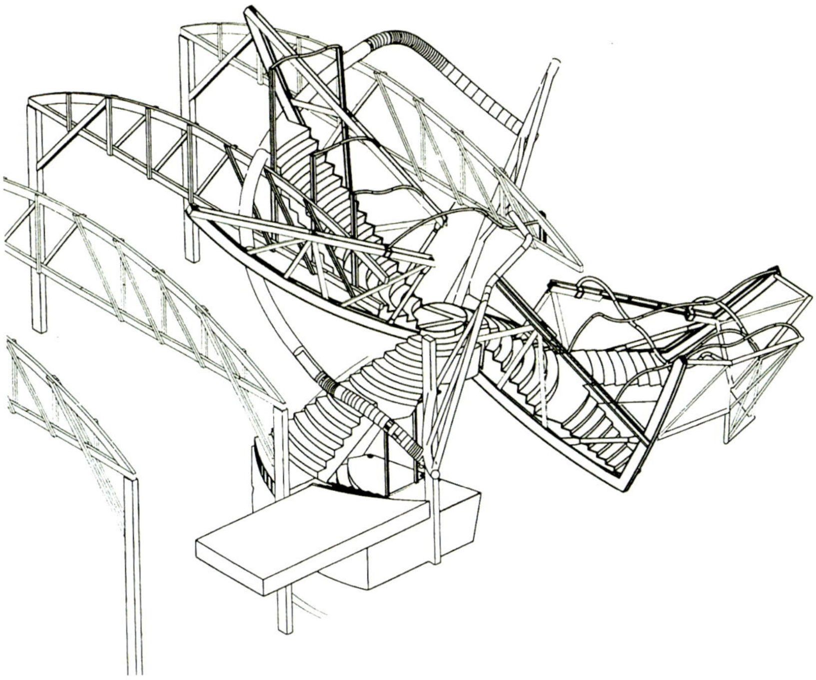

completion	January 2000
client	Frederick and Laurie Samitaur Smith
area	1,858 square metres/20,000 square feet
structure	Existing wood frame and truss warehouse with infill framing, rigid steel framing, steel reinforced concrete
materials	Glass, steel, wood, drywall, plaster, concrete
cost	US$1.9 million
awards	2001 Saflex Glass Design Award 2000 Los Angeles Urban Beautification Award 1999 Honor Award for Design, American Institute of Architects, Los Angeles
top	Section
middle	View of Umbrella
bottom	Side view
photography	Paul Groh

Watercycle Pavilion
Greenwich, London, UK
Sam Hecht/IDEO London

In June 1996, Thames Water started to conceive and plan a new watercycle system, based upon an 'in-building' recycling process. The site for this experiment was the Millennium Dome, which is designed to incorporate sophisticated water recycling technologies as part of its building infrastructure.

Very simply, when it rains, the Dome's roof acts as a giant collector that funnels the run-off to 12 hoppers, located where the Dome's roof touches the ground. The water is then passed through reedbeds and a treatment plant before being used to flush 900 toilets around the site. Water from the washbasins is similarly readied for reuse, and to ensure a constant source of water, a borehole has been drilled to bring up ground water.

The Watercycle Pavilion, a glass structure located along the living wall of the Dome, is activated and framed by the circulation of water on its horizontal and vertical surfaces. From under the shelter of the pavilion's glass roof, visitors see water, reclaimed from the pool surrounding it, sprayed onto the glass roof. The water cascades down the glass wall and returns to the pool, and then back onto the roof, in a continuous cycle. The architecture itself is used to describe the central concepts.

The pavilion is attached to the treatment plant and serves as a window onto its mechanical inner-workings. Elements of the recycling processes are displayed on a sequence of tall, mirrored, rotating panels that turn incrementally, to reveal the treatment plant. There is a message inscribed across the seven panels: 'Clouds make rain that falls on the roof, is collected, filtered, and cleaned for toilet flushing.' The rotation is orchestrated so that the mirrored panels reflect and reveal the viewers, the information, the Dome, and the inside of the treatment plant. Each panel momentarily pauses at 180 degrees, and is synchronised with glass display cases that move between transparent and translucent.

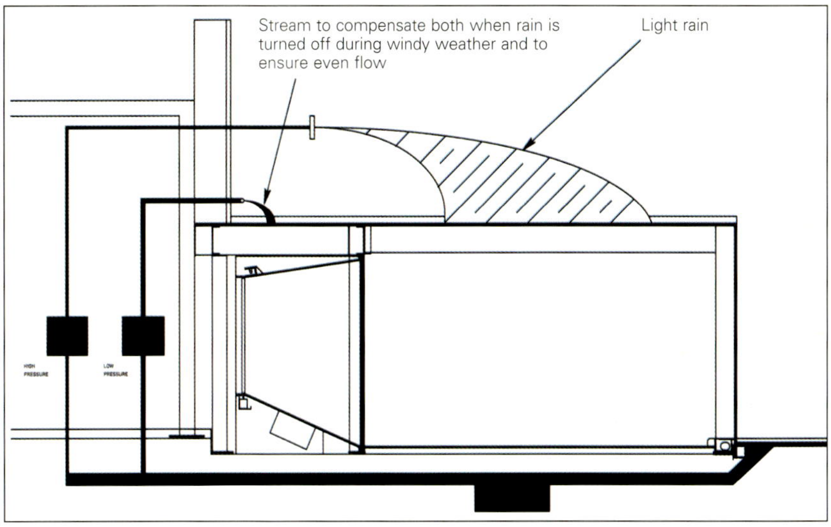

completion	January 2000
client	Thames Water
structure	Steel and glass beams, cladding with concrete slab
materials	Metal, glass, concrete
cost	US$375,000
awards	Design and Art Direction Environment Finalist Young Emerging Architect Award, Danish Design Institute
opposite	Completed pavilion with water surface wall
top	Cross wsection of water feature
middle	Front view of pavilion
bottom	Exhibition with rotating panels revealing working treatment plant
photography	Richard Davies

1100 Architect, PC

1100 Architect is the New York-based firm of David Piscuskas and Juergen Riehm. Since the practice was founded in 1983, their work has demonstrated a contemporary sensibility that is at once elegant, sophisticated and inviting. The skilful use and manipulation of light, and interesting use of materials for which 1100 is recognised, are continually at play in the varied projects undertaken by the firm. Within this fluent language, the architects forego pre-set conclusions in order to serve each project – whether free-standing construction, renovation or the development of raw environment – through its own process of discovery.

AC Martin Partners, Inc.

AC Martin Partners, Inc. (ACMP) is one of the oldest, continuously operating, family-owned architecture and engineering firms in the western United States. Founded in 1906 by Albert C. Martin, Sr. the firm has been guided by three generations of the Martin family, providing a continuity of management philosophy, goals and objectives.

In nearly a century of practice in Los Angeles, the firm has designed many landmark buildings. ACMP has been recognised nationally for a wide range of project types, having an extensive background spanning six decades in the design of facilities for higher education.

As a fully integrated architecture and engineering firm, ACMP has a long history of providing a thorough and complete design approach for its clients, many of whom are repeat customers. These clients are testimony that the AC Martin approach is an enduring one.

ACMP is headquartered in Los Angeles with offices in Irvine and Sacramento.

Adhoc msl

The Faculty of Economics and Business at the University of Murcia is the first joint project for Murcia-based architects Carlos Jurado + Juan Antonio Sánchez (Adhoc msl), Enrique Carbonell and Salvador Moreno. Carbonell worked with Rafael Moneo on the town hall, and on the headquarters for the bank Cajamurcia.

Adhoc msl will soon complete the offices of the Cervantes Institute in New York, an organisation founded by the Spanish government to promote its language and culture, and also the Court House at Cartagena

Alberto Campo Baeza

Alberto Campo Baeza was born in Cadiz (Spain) and completed his first degree in architecture in 1971. He was awarded his doctorate in 1982. In 1986 he became chair and professor of the School of Design at Madrid University.

He has built a select number of very precise buildings: Fene Town Hall 1980, S. Fermin Public School in Madrid 1985, Public Library in Orihuela 1992, Public School in Cadiz 1993 and Center BIT in Inca-Mallorca, and his very well-renowned houses in Turegano, De Blas and Gaspar, just to name a few.

He has won many prizes and awards and his work has been exhibited widely and published in most major architectural magazines in the world.

In 2001, he will complete the Cathedral Plaza and Office Building in Almeria. On 21 June, 2001 the Headquarters of the Caja General de Ahorros de Granada was inaugurated, following his win in the 1992 competition. Construction of the SM Editorial in Madrid, Spain has also commenced

Antoine Predock Architect

In his work, Antoine Predock Architect makes choices which come from the spirit and from an understanding of the actual world around him, both in terms of the present and the past. He responds to the forces of a place – to geology, culture, myth and ritual – and evokes these qualities in his buildings. In the studio, connections are explored between the earth and the sky, as in the Turtle Creek House which has a ramp that aims towards the sky, establishing a trajectory that one follows on ascent. The buildings in the desert often suggest an analogous landscape. The American Heritage Center in Wyoming is an abstraction of land forms in this area – an 'archival mountain' in the landscape, with a village, the art museum, at its base.

The built work, for almost three decades, expresses these initial physical and spiritual impulses. Antoine Predock Architect's practice includes projects throughout the United States, and in France, Spain, Morocco and Denmark. In the United States, projects include sites in Massachusetts, New York, Minneapolis, Florida, Texas, New Mexico, Arizona, Colorado, Nevada, Washington, California and Oregon. The work includes housing, museums, theatres, academic buildings, hotels, libraries and civic buildings. Antoine Predock is a Fellow of the American Institute of Architects and a Fellow of the American Academy in Rome.

Ashton Raggatt McDougall

with Robert Peck Robert Peck von Hartel Trethowan

Ashton Raggatt McDougall (ARM): is a leading design consultancy working in architecture, master planning and urban design. Founded by the three Directors in 1988, ARM receives both local and international recognition for their innovative design work. ARM has received over 25

Biographies

design awards in 11 years, including the top Victorian award twice. Projects include: RMIT University Storey Hall, the master planning of the Melbourne Docklands, St Kilda Town Hall and Library and Marion Cultural Centre.

Robert Peck von Hartel Trethowan: is a National Design practice specialising in architecture, planning and interior design with offices in Melbourne, Canberra and Sydney and a professional staff of over 75 personnel. The practice was founded in 1980. Work is undertaken in all areas of architectural practice including commercial buildings, residential, tourist and mixed developments, health care, interior fitouts, heritage work, urban design and conservation studies. The practice has been the recipient of many awards through its 21-year history.

Axel Schultes Architekten

Axel Schultes Architekten is a full-service firm operating primarily in Germany in architecture and public urban design. The firm's projects include museums, institutional and commercial projects.

The practice was founded by Axel Schultes (57) in Berlin in 1992, with longstanding colleagues Charlotte Frank (42) and Christoph Witt (51), after being in partnership with Bangert, Jansen, Scholz for 20 years.

These senior architects are surrounded by a group of about 15 younger people, with qualifications ranging from management of development processes via building techniques, to model making with special interior spatial skills. The firm is fully equipped with an all-round CAD network.

Azman Owens Architects

Azman Owens Architects, established in 1993, practice architecture and urban design. The firm undertakes a varied range of projects including residential, retail, restaurant schemes and commercial developments.

A portfolio of completed projects includes the refurbishment of many listed residential buildings, residential projects, offices and retail interiors for Canary Wharf Ltd, the fit-out of a production bakery in the borough of Market for Konditor & Cook Ltd, and a new flagship store for Alexander McQueen in London's West End.

A defined approach to architecture is founded in a desire to create simple, functional and crafted buildings. When working with existing buildings the practice places value on the historic integrity of the architecture and preserves original fabric of value whilst creating complementary modern interventions.

The practice offers a high standard of contemporary design that reflects the clients' needs and context which is delivered through efficient management, construction and cost control. The work of Azman Owens Architects has been the subject of extensive coverage in the national and professional press and has featured in a recent BBC documentary titled 'Modern Times – Minimal'.

Behnisch & Partner/Behnisch, Behnisch & Partner

Behnisch & Partner/Behnisch, Behnisch & Partner have planned and realised many different types of buildings in nearly 50 years of practice from Stuttgart, Germany including sports facilities (Olympic Games Stadium in Munich), public buildings (the former German Bundestag in Bonn), office and bank buildings, schools, museums, etc. The workforce of both offices varies between 90 and 110 people, depending on the current workload. In 1990 a branch office was opened in Los Angeles, California, to support the firm's overseas activities.

Since almost all projects have been won through architectural design competitions where only design skills decide, B&P/B,B&P consider themselves as an office that cannot afford to – and does not want to – simply repeat designs or deliver routine jobs. Instead, they try to develop, together with the client and the users, an appropriate solution for each task. Though manual drawing still plays an important role in the office and is part of their philosophy, state-of-the-art EDP tools are used as well.

Bernard Tschumi Architects

Bernard Tschumi Architects is an internationally based firm dedicated to the interface between contemporary conditions and architecture. It was established in Paris in 1982, and since 1988 its main offices have been in located in New York with the Paris office acting to co-ordinate European projects. Over its 18-year history, Bernard Tschumi Architects has been the recipient of numerous national and international honours, and has established a world reputation as a leading design firm known for its innovative solutions to, and long-range strategies for, the problems of both public and private communities.

Bernard Tschumi Architects undertakes mostly large-scale work, from cultural buildings to urban interventions, but its primary interest is in forward-looking projects that articulate the contours of the emerging century. Skilful and innovative responses to the challenges posed by renovation, additional and historical context are evident in the recent proposal for the expansion of the Museum of Modern Art, New York; in Le Fresnoy, a centre for advanced film, video and electronic production and display, housed in a remarkable entertainment complex dating from the 1920s; and in the imaginative interpretation of the 19th-century McKim Mead and White master plan, coupled with the demands for a lively centre for student life, that is exposed in the Alfred Lerner Hall. Bernard Tschumi's Parc de la Villette in Paris (1982–1995) is one of the most significant projects of the end of the 20th century.

Bohlin Cywinski Jackson

Bohlin Cywinski Jackson, founded in 1965, has offices in Wilkes-Barre, Pittsburgh, Philadelphia, Seattle and Berkeley. The firm's work is known for exceptional design, for its commitment to the particularity of place and user, and for an extraordinary aesthetic based on a quiet rigor which is both intellectual and intuitive. The firm's work ranges greatly in scale and circumstance. Its architecture is alive to the subtleties of place – man-made or natural, to the varied natures of people, to the sensibilities of individuals, to the character of institutions, and to the rich possibilities of materials and the means of construction. Bohlin Cywinski Jackson has received more than 190 regional, national and international awards for design. In 1994, the practice received the Architecture Firm Award from the American Institute of Architects. The firm's work is published regularly in professional journals worldwide.

Architekturbüro Bolles+Wilson

Founded 1980 in London Julia Bolles-Wilson and Peter Wilson transferred their practice to Germany in 1989. This move marked a shift from teaching and research at the Architectural Association to the realisation of a wide range of private, cultural and institutional projects in Japan, UK, Germany and the Netherlands.

The New City Library in Münster has become a yardstick not only in the architectural world, but also as one of their most successful libraries in Germany. Other works include the New Luxor Theatre in Rotterdam and two Blocks at the Domplatz in Magdeburg.

Bolles+Wilson not only design individual buildings but also landscape and urban planning, interiors and furniture design. They have won more than 20 First Prizes in architectural competitions and been short listed twice for the Mies van der Rohe Prize and for the Carlsberg Prize.

Bucholz | McEvoy Architects

Bucholz | McEvoy Architects was established in March of 1996 having won the international open competition for the new £13.6 million civic office building for Fingal County Council in Dublin, Republic of Ireland. Bucholz | McEvoy Architect's work includes Limerick County Council's new £13.5 million Headquarters in Dooradoyle, two Welcoming Pavilions in front of the

Government Buildings, Merrion Street, Dublin, Ireland, and German software company SAP's new £6.5 million headquarters in Ireland, among other projects.

Founded by Karen McEvoy, trained at University College, Dublin, and Merrit Bucholz, trained at Cornell University and Princeton in the United States, the practice provides architectural, space planning and urban design services. Published extensively, Bucholz | McEvoy has quickly established itself as an architectural practice capable of design excellence and quality at an international level.

Invention: the basis of any solution to a design

Bucholz | McEvoy critically reject style. Each project is a solution to a complex set of issues, an innovative approach to the requirements of the client held within the parameters of context.

Context is understood as a complex set of relationships between a place (physical context), a function (programmatic context), a society (cultural context) and certain limits (economic and technological contexts). Bucholz | McEvoy do not consider one context to be more important than another, instead they believe all to be working simultaneously together, exerting influence on any design.

Centerbrook Architects and Planners, LLC

Centerbrook is an architecture and planning firm established in 1975. Located in a renovated factory on the Falls River in the rural town of Centerbrook, Connecticut, it has five partners, one principal, 14 associates and an overall staff of 80.

The firm's approach is distinctly American – its work is eclectic and its methods democratic. Centerbrook has received 210 awards for design excellence, including seven national American Institute of Architects (AIA) Honor Awards for a wide variety of projects. These range from highly crafted private residences and furniture to evocative institutional complexes and fully implemented city plans. In 1998, Centerbrook was named recipient of the National AIA Firm Award, the highest honour the AIA can confer on a firm. Centerbrook has pioneered collaborative methods for innovative design. Interactive techniques are used to involve people in the programming and design of buildings, campuses and cities. This has resulted in 21 hours of Centerbrook-produced prime-time television as well as on-site offices, interactive workshops and other outreach techniques.

The firm's work has been the focus of 275 articles and books and is the subject of *The Enthusiasms of Centerbook*, written by the firm and published in 2001 by The Images Publishing Group; *Centerbrook*, Volume 2, by Andrea Oppenheimer Dean, AIA Press, 1997; and *Centerbrook: Reinventing American Architecture*, by Michael J. Crosbie, AIA Press, 1993.

Cesar Pelli & Associates

Established in 1977, Cesar Pelli & Associates is a full service architectural practice of some 80 persons. The firm has worked with corporate, government and private clients to design major public spaces, museums, airports, laboratories, performing arts centres, academic buildings, hotels, office and residential towers and mixed-use projects. The number of commissions the firm accepts is carefully limited to ensure a high degree of personal involvement by the principals.

The work of Cesar Pelli & Associates is not constrained by a personal style or a signature that would limit his architecture; instead, it tries to celebrate the unique characteristics of each project. With this approach, the firm has designed several exceptional buildings in the United States and abroad.

The AIA awarded Cesar Pelli & Associates its 1989 Firm Award in recognition of standard-setting work in architectural design and Cesar Pelli received the Gold Medal from the AIA in 1995.

Claudio Silvestrin

Born in 1954 Claudio Silvestrin was educated in Milan by AG Fronzoni and studied at the Architectural Association in London, where he still lives and practices. Claudio Silvestrin's integrity, clarity of mind, inventiveness and concern for details is reflected in his rigorous, minimal architecture; austere but not extreme, contemporary yet timeless, calming but not ascetic, strong but not intimidating, elegant but not ostentatious.

Claudio Silvestrin opened his practice in early 1989, gaining a reputation with art galleries and residential projects for art collectors and, most recently, his store design for Calvin Klein and Giorgio Armani. In association with Rolfe Judd, Claudio Silvestrin was one of the 13 finalists for the Tate Gallery Bankside Competition.

Claudio Silvestrin's distinctive architecture has attracted the attention of television, radio, newspapers and international architecture magazines. He has been a tutor at the Bartlett in London and has lectured extensively in the UK and Europe, as well as the Tate Gallery, RIBA and the Ecole Supérieure d'arts Visuels in Lausanne. He has recently won the competition for the new Fabbrica Arte Contemporanea in Turin in association with SB Tietz & Partners Engineers.

The Cox Group Pty Ltd

The Cox Group Pty Ltd was first established in Sydney as Philip Cox & Partners in 1967. Since that time the company has grown to a national practice with offices in Sydney, Perth, Brisbane, Melbourne and Canberra.

The Cox Group is a progressive and diversified architectural company covering the fields of public buildings, commercial and retail developments, tourism, sport and recreation, education, housing, health and conservation. In each field the firm offers services in planning, urban design, architecture and interior design.

The architecture produced is the result of both philosophical reflection and a response to the conditions affecting each particular commission – contextual, cultural, economic, political or environmental.

The company has developed a reputation for innovative and exciting design, with projects, both current and completed throughout Australia, South Africa, Italy, China, Indonesia, Thailand, Papua New Guinea and Singapore. The group's success is evidenced by the numerous national and international awards it has received since 1967.

Daly, Genik Architects

Kevin Daly received a Bachelor of Arts from the University of California Berkeley in 1980 and was the principal of Design Build Studio in Berkeley until 1985. After receiving a Master of Architecture from Rice University in 1985, he worked for Hodgetts & Fund and Frank O. Gehry where he was an associate from 1986–90.

Chris Genik received a Bachelor of Architecture degree from Carleton University in Ottawa, Canada in 1983. After receiving a Master of Architecture from Rice University in 1985, he was a partner and co-founder of Peter Waldman Studio in Dallas from 1985–89.

Daly Genik was formed in Los Angeles in 1989. Teaching has always been an important component of the practice with both principals having been on the faculty of SCI-Arc since 1989 and holding various visiting appointments. The firm has received numerous design awards including three from the Los Angeles AIA in 2000, a 1998 Arizona AIA and a PA citation in 1997 for the Topanga Residence.

Completed projects include the Camino Nuevo Charter Academy in Los Angeles (2000); Offices for Rioport in Santa Monica (2000); Valley Center Residence near San Diego (1999); Jefferson Canopies in Los Angeles (1998); Windmill Lane Productions in Los Angeles (1996); Arizona State University Campus Cafes in Tempe, Arizona (1998); Slot Box House in Santa Monica (1998); and an extension to the Mar Vista Residence in Mar Vista, California (1996).

The work of Daly, Genik has been exhibited internationally in London, Frankfurt and Sophia and published in various books including *ARCHITECTURE NOW* (Taschen: 2001), *Pacific Edge: Contemporary Architecture on the Pacific Rim* (Rizzoli: 1998) and *The New American House 2* (Whitney Library of Design: 1997).

Denton Corker Marshall Pty Ltd

Denton Corker Marshall Pty Ltd was founded in Melbourne, Australia in 1972, and also has offices in Hong Kong, Jakarta, Singapore, Ho Chi Minh City, London and Warsaw, with a total staff exceeding 160 worldwide. The practice – a well-established and highly regarded multidisciplinary firm – provides consulting services in architecture, landscape architecture, planning, exhibition and interior design and project management, to private individuals, companies, institutions and government bodies in Australia and overseas.

Denton Corker Marshall has earned a reputation for a high degree of design and planning skill and has been successful in a substantial number of design competitions, several of international importance. This recognition has led to the firm being commissioned by significant client groups and government bodies in each of the countries in which it operates.

Denton Corker Marshal is Australia's most awarded practice, as recognised by the Royal Australian Institute of Architects (RAIA) National Awards, and in 1996 John Denton, Bill Corker and Barrie Marshall jointly were made the RAIA Gold Medallists for that year, the highest honour the Institute bestows.

DESIGN OFFICE

DESIGN OFFICE, the partnership of George Yu and Jason King, is an architecture and creative design collaborative. Based in Los Angeles and Vancouver since 1992, DESIGN OFFICE represents an entirely new model for architectural and creative design practice. The partnership responds to the rapidly changing social and economic landscape with design solutions that encompass a variety of disciplines including environmental design, industrial design, new material research, science and fabrication, information technology, static and motion graphics, lighting and audio design to construct a completely holistic experience that both challenges and transcends the limits of exiting paradigms.

For DESIGN OFFICE, architecture is above all concerned with the creation of environments that are the physical embodiment of social relationships and values made manifest through the integration of space, material and technology. They attain this level of integration through collaboration and team building, drawing on an extensive, multidisciplinary network of strategic partners enabling them to offer a greater range of services, and to be as fluid and diverse as the clients they serve.

Dominique Perrault Architecte

Dominique Perrault Architecte was founded in 1981. That same year Dominique Perrault was prize winner in the Programme Architecture Nouvelle XII (PAN) national competition. His first built project, the Someloir factory in Châteaudun was awarded the Architecture et Maitre d'Ouvrage prize for quality in 1983. Between 1981 and 1983 he was also involved in urban regeneration projects as consultant architect-urbanist at the Atelier Parisien d'Urbanisme (APUR).

In 1989, Dominique Perrault won the international competition for the French National Library, which established his reputation and gave his office an international dimension. The challenge was taken up by the office and an efficient organisation was put in place. The building, completed in 1995, opened its doors to the public in December 1996, with furniture designed by Dominique Perrault.

In 1992, he won the international competition for the Olympic Velodrome and Swimming Hall in Berlin and an office was opened close to the site in order to run the project.

In 1993 the French National Award for Architecture was conferred upon him by the French Ministry of Infrastructures, Transport and Tourism. In 1997 Dominique Perrault was awarded the Mies van der Rohe Pavilion Award for European Architecture for the French Library project. Prestigious as it is, the project for the French National Library with which the name of the architect is today often associated, should not occult the density and the diversity of Dominique Perrault's work.

The firm's work has been widely published including: 1988/ESIEE; 1990/Hôtel Industriel Berlier; 1994/Monography; 1995/La Bibliotheque Nationale de France; 1996/Exhibition Catalogue for the AEDES Gallery in Berlin; 1996/Exhibition Catalogue Des Natures; and 1997/Furniture and Fabrics.

Droog Design

Droog Design was founded in 1993 by Gijs Bakker and Renny Ramakers in Amsterdam. Droog Design presents a mentality in which they initiate and develop experimental projects. Young designers, graphic designers, fashion designers and architects from all over the world are invited. Droog makes a contribution to the international debate about design through projects, exhibitions, workshops, paper presentations and publications. Droog Design is also commissioned by international firms and invites young designers to participate.

(EEA) Erick van Egeraat associated architects

(EEA) Erick van Egeraat associated architects is a European architectural office which stands for innovative and challenging architecture of high quality standards. Located in Rotterdam, London, Budapest and Prague, EEA is challenged by working with clients who dare to be different. Specific, appropriate, open-minded and creating a sensual and intuitive architecture are the keywords of EEA's direction in architecture, continuous research and any field beyond. Influenced by the cultural and historical context as well as by contemporary life, their aim is to develop architecture that responds to a known language with new emerging sensations in order to capture the life that is ahead of them; to develop architecture that reflects all characteristics of modern times, that benefits from fashion and design. Their aim is not to state but to relate; not to consider but to seduce, to continuously search to resolve the client's brief differently, not to irritate but to persuade and surprise.

Erick van Egeraat (1956, Amsterdam) studied architecture at the Technical University of Delft Department of Architecture, 1974–84. In 1983 he co-founded mecanoo architecten and was a partner in that office until 1995. In that year he established (EEA) Erick van Egeraat associated architects in Rotterdam and Budapest. In 1998 he extended his practice to London and in 1999 EEA Prague was opened. Today there are 90 permanent members of staff in these four offices.

Edouard Francois & associés

As architect of the recent 'Sprouting Building' or Château Le Lez, Edouard Francois & associés have become one of the leading firms of green architecture on the international scene. Their work focuses on matter, context, use, economy and ecology, following the pre-occupations of sustainable development.

Edouard François has been a consultant for the French Ministry of the Environment, and has been a teaching professor at the School of Landscape Design in Versailles and at the Architectural Association in London.

Currently François' European team of architects, urbanists, landscape designers, graphic designers and artists are working on projects in Belgium and Paris, where they are commencing the 'Flower Tower', a building bordering a park, completely veiled in white bamboo.

Their work is exhibited in the permanent collection of the Museum of Modern Art, Georges Pompidou Centre in Paris.

Eric Owen Moss

Eric Owen Moss opened his office in 1973 in Los Angeles. Moss was educated at Berkeley and Harvard. He has recently held professorial chairs at Yale, Harvard, and appointments in Copenhagen and Vienna, in addition to Sci-Arc, where he began teaching in 1973 and is currently on the Board of Directors.

His work has been recently exhibited in Duren, Germany; Barcelona, Spain; Mexico City, Mexico; Glasgow, Scotland; Copenhagen, Denmark; and he was one of the four American architects invited to represent the United States at the 1996 Venice Biennale. He is currently part of the '100 Years of Architecture' exhibit at the Museum of Contemporary Art in Los Angeles and 'Projects 2000' at the GA Gallery in Tokyo, Japan.

Current projects include work in St. Petersburg, Russia; Gothenburg, Sweden; London, England; Los Angeles, and Culver City. The latest completed buildings are 3535 Hayden Ave, the headquarters of an international motion picture design firm, and The Umbrella, a film production and performance facility. The Stealth, the headquarters for an international advertising firm, and The Beehive, a conference facility, are presently under construction. Upcoming projects include high-rise towers in Los Angeles, a mixed-use development in London, and residential projects in Hollywood and Calabasas.

Moss is the recipient of 41 design awards from Progressive Architecture and the American Institute of Architects. He is the winner of the 2001 Los Angeles AIA Gold Medal Award as well as the 1999 Award in Architecture from the American Academy of Arts and Letters. Moss is a fellow of the American Institute of Architects.

Fentress Bradburn Architects

Since its founding in 1980, Fentress Bradburn Architects has practised innovative, client-driven, technologically advanced architecture in locations throughout the world.

Fentress Bradburn's design approach ties a building to its region and context and puts the end user at the centre of the design. Versatility has been a hallmark of the firm's work in government facilities, airports, museums and convention centres, not only throughout the United States but also in Asia, the Middle East and Latin America. Among its current projects are the expansion of the Colorado Convention Center to 2.4 million square feet and, in association with HNTB, design of Invesco Field at Mile High, which opened in August 2001.

Among its 154 design honours, awards and citations, Fentress Bradburn counts 55 awards from the American Institute of Architects. The firm has also won 15 national and international design competitions, including airports in Seoul, Korea, and Doha, Qatar, and civic structures in Oakland, California, and Las Vegas, Nevada.

Foster and Partners

Foster and Partners is an international studio for architecture, planning and design led by Norman Foster and four partners – Spencer de Grey, David Nelson, Ken Shuttleworth and Graham Phillips.

The studio has established an international reputation with buildings such as the new German Parliament in the Reichstag, Berlin, The Great Court for the British Museum in London, Headquarters for HSBC in Hong Kong and London, Commerzbank Headquarters in Frankfurt, the Metro Bilbao, the Carré d'Art Nîmes, Sainsbury Centre for Visual Arts in Norwich and Research Centre Stanford University California. A wide range of supporting skills underpins the work of the practice, including model making, CAD and visualisation, with in-house visual, photographic and printing services.

Foster and Partners has received more than 230 awards and citations for design excellence, and won over 50 national and international design competitions. Norman Foster was Knighted in 1990, appointed by the Queen to the Order of Merit in 1997 and in 1999 was honoured with a Life Peerage, taking the title Lord Foster of Thames Bank. In 1999 he became the 21st Pritzker Architecture Prize Laureate. The practice has been awarded the Queen's Award for Export.

Gehry Partners

Gehry Partners is a full service firm with broad international experience in museum, theatre, performance, institutional, commercial and residential projects. Located in Santa Monica, California, the firm has a staff of over 130 people, which includes a group of senior architects who are highly qualified in project management and in the technical development of building systems and construction documents, as well as extensive model-making facilities and a model building staff capable of executing everything from scale architectural models to full size mock-ups. The firm employs a network of sophisticated computer aided design workstations in the development of projects and in the translation of design ideas into the technical documents and the information required for construction.

Gluckman Mayner Architects

Gluckman Mayner Architects is a New York-based firm committed to the articulation of space through the simplicity of structure, material and light. Established in 1977, Richard Gluckman Architects formed a partnership with David Mayner in 1998, to found what is now Gluckman Mayner Architects.

A career that began with the renovation of a townhouse on Manhattan's Upper East Side for Heiner Friedrich and Phillipa de Menil, founders of the Dia Art Foundation, led to the conversion of a warehouse for exhibition spaces for the Dia Center for the Arts. Subsequent commissions from The Whitney Museum of American Art, New York; the Andy Warhol Museum, Pennsylvania; the Georgia O'Keeffe Museum, New Mexico; and Mary Boone Gallery and Gagosian Gallery, New York, established a reputation for the firm as a leader in the design of art-oriented spaces.

Gluckman Mayner Architects has received national acclaim for its residential, commercial and institutional projects.

A monograph entitled, *'Space Framed: Richard Gluckman Architect'*, was published by Monacelli Press in 2000.

Grieve Gillett Pty Ltd

Grieve Gillett Pty Ltd (formerly Steve Grieve Architects Pty Ltd) is an innovative and diversified architectural, interior design and urban design firm. Since its establishment in the early 1980s the company has gained a reputation for its arts and cultural tourism projects.

With recent specialisation in heritage projects and lighting design, the company has completed a wide range of projects including buildings, interiors and urban design of a public and commercial nature, retail developments, education, housing and health in South Australia, Victoria, New South Wales and Northern Territory.

Grieve Gillett Pty Ltd aim to create buildings and places of excellence and innovation within economic, environmental, social and functional constraints. This is achieved through a high level of commitment, teamwork and problem solving which satisfies the requirements of the client and end user.

Atelier D'Architecture Franck Hammoutene

Franck Hammoutene, born in 1954, is an architect and urban planner. He has worked on a number of varied projects: institutional buildings and company head offices (Police Station in Bobigny, the Notre-Dame de Pentecôte Church, the ATYA Building, the Renault Workshop and the Gutenberg Library in Paris); urban development studies (Beirut, Cannes, Paris); educational buildings (IECB, University Campus in

Vélizy, Science Faculty in Tours); residential (Paris); design (Maison Blanche Restaurant in Paris), and museums (Museum of Music in Paris).

His projects are contextual, the result of a precise process of rationalisation during which the vocabulary is continually redefined, thereby ruling out habit and convention. His mark can be found in his close attention to detail, his taste for paradox and secrecy, his concern to stress hospitality and wellbeing, whatever the scale of the project.

His buildings, like his unconstructed projects (Canal +, Locstar, Palais de Tokyo), have won numerous awards and have been widely published and exhibited.

Atelier Hitoshi Abe

Atelier Hitoshi Abe was established in 1992 by winning a competition to design the Miyagi Stadium in Sendai, Japan. The Miyagi Stadium seats 50,000 people and is a venue for World Cup 2002. Hitoshi Abe has a worldwide reputation for sensitive design which has received global exposure, especially since 1999.

Located in Sendai, northern Japan, the firm has eight staff, and is constantly evolving, and developing its design process, using models, computer-aided design and simulations, and ongoing meetings with clients to develop new creations.

Sam Hecht/IDEO London

Sam Hecht, head of Industrial Design at IDEO, has been responsible for a number of building and transportation interiors, but it is his and IDEO's first venture into building architecture. Having previously produced some award-winning exhibition installations, Hecht's belief that the involvement of ideas is more powerful than mere representation, has now been carried through into architecture. He is currently working with OMA/Rem Koolhaus, developing the future stores of Prada.

Ingenhoven Overdiek und Partner

Düsseldorf is home to the main office of Ingenhoven Overdiek und Partner. Established as a joint firm of architects in 1992, it is headed by Christoph Ingenhoven and Jürgen Overdiek, who in co-operation with six project partners lead a team of 150 staff.

The main themes of the projects are office and administration buildings, commercial and insurance company headquarters, high-rise buildings in Germany and internationally, department stores and infrastructure projects (airports, railway stations), urban planning and landscape architecture, project development and general planning.

The aim in all the projects is to work closely with engineers and other specialist consultants throughout the whole of the design process. The make-up of a project is always judged according to criteria of efficiency, ecological consciousness, economy of resource usage and buildability. This results in an architecture characterised by the use of innovative technology that meets the needs of the people living and working in the buildings. In this way, the architects not only pay attention to aesthetic visions, but also reflect their responsibility for the environment.

Jarmund/Vigsnæs AS Architects MNAL

After years of teaching and independent practice Håkon Vigsnæs and Einar Jarmund founded the firm Jarmund/Vigsnæs AS Architects in 1995. Both graduated from the Oslo School of Architecture in the late 1980s. Håkon Vigsnæs spent one year at the Architectural Association in London under Peter Salter, while Einar Jarmund spent three years in Seattle, Washington, studying for a masters degree from the University of Washington, teaching and working. Both have been teaching at the Oslo School of Architecture with Professor Sverre Fehn, although not during the same period. The office has gradually increased in size from two people to today's staff of nine with eight architects. They have entered a series of competitions, both open and invited, for which they have often been awarded. The most important projects to date are:

Office building for The Norwegian Governor in Longyearbyen at Svalbard – a hybrid office/housing/tourist/information centre.

Coastal Traffic Centre at Kvitsøy – a building on the west coast of Norway dedicated to radar control of all large ships on the coast and the distribution of pilots.

The new Oslo School of Architecture – a result of winning first prize in an open architectural competition in 1998. Completion is schedule for the summer of 2001.

Extension of Regional College in Molde – a result of winning first prize in an invited competition in 1998. Completion is schedule for mid-2002.

In addition to these fairly large projects, they have a series of one family houses and vacation houses, both built and ready for commencement on site, including a summer house in Sineu, Mallorca, schedule for completion in summer 2001. These projects were the subject of an exhibition at The Norwegian Museum of Architecture in September 2000, entitled '14 houses – Jarmund/Vigsnæs'.

Jean Nouvel

Jean Nouvel has a strict code of principles and convictions which guide his architectural approach:

- architecture is not an autonomous discipline, it is the petrifaction of a civilization and expresses all of the latter's aspects;
- each project is specific: the geographical context, the social and cultural context, the economic context and the climate determine for each building a series of particular conditions which the architect must take into account;
- during the last century the Arts have burst out of all formal conditions – in architecture materiality and light have become more important than space and form.

Jean Nouvel has proved the relevance of his convictions through such projects as the Arab World Institute in Paris, the Opera of Lyon, the Conference Center in Tours, the Cartier Foundation in Paris, the Galeries Lafayette department store in Berlin, and the Lucerne Cultural & Conference Center. In his contrasted aesthetic, which owes much to industry, science and technology, to fine arts and visual arts, to cinema, television and video, Jean Nouvel's architecture continues a constant exploration.

Juhani Katainen Architects

Juhani Katainen Architects was founded in 1968. From the very first, the office concentrated on major public building design projects. Design work is based on an exact analysis of the users' needs, with the plans, construction costs, schedules and technical implementation tailored to fit those needs.

The office aims to produce high-quality professional design and architecture. It strives to recognise its responsibility towards the client and to optimise design concepts with regard to the life-span of the building. Working practices are based on an atmosphere of openness and co-operation, respecting the views of the client and colleagues.

Juhani Katainen has been a Professor of Architectural Design in the Department of Architecture at Tampere University of Technology since 1988. In 1995, the Ministry of Education appointed Professor Katainen Finland's representative on the EC Advisory Committee on Education and Training in the Field of Architecture.

The Finnish Association of Architects appointed him as their representative on the Council of European Architects, Standing Committee No. 2, 'Profession of Architecture' 1995–97 and Permanent Committee No. 1, Task Force Education & Research 1998–99.

He was appointed by the Finnish Association of Architects as a Vice-Presidence for the Architects' Council of Europe in 2001. Professor Katainen was also appointed as the president of the Finnish Association of Architects (SAFA) for the period 1996–98.

Kisho Kurokawa architect & associates

Kisho Kurokawa architect & associates (KKAA) executes each project with three basic characteristics: the first characteristic is the atelier-like creative atmosphere, with Kisho Kurokawa as the core architect; the second characteristic, an antitheses of the first, is the large-scale and efficient engineering-oriented atmosphere. These two elements are kept in good harmony by the talent of the architect Kisho Kurokawa, and the dedication of its staff.

The last characteristic is the introduction of in-house computers, or Computer Aided Design Systems (CAD System). Developing a sophisticated design system with high technology continuously updated, the multi-purpose adaptability of the architecture is encouraged and the rationalisation of the design itself is considered.

On the basis of the three elements mentioned above, the scope of services KKAA provides is unlimited, eliminating the borderline between the architecture and the city. Furthermore, KKAA provides general services to the construction management, and other services that are deemed necessary to fulfil the particular requests from a client. KKAA has syndicates all over the world, and provides international services actively.

With a total staff of 205 people, KKAA specialises in the following fields: architecture, government buildings, museums, theatres and cultural centres, educational buildings, retail development, hotels, recreational centres, sporting facilities, research institutes, hospitals, welfare facilities, religious buildings, airports, expo-pavilions, residences, urban planning, regional development, landscape and interior design, artwork and furniture. Recent clients include: the Republic of Kazakhstan; Japanese Ministry of Culture; Japanese Foreign Department; the Government of Malaysia; Van Gogh Museum, The Netherlands; Shenzhen City, China; Fukui Prefecture, Japan; Osaka Prefecture, Japan; Oita Prefecture, Japan; Toyota City, Japan; Kyocera Co., Ltd., Japan; and Fractal Design and Construction Company, Germany.

Kohn Pedersen Fox Associates, Architects and Planning Consultants

Kohn Pedersen Fox Associates offers full architecture, master planning, space planning, programming and building analysis services for a prestigious roster of international clients in both the public and private sectors. KPF's diverse portfolio includes mixed-use, corporate and institutional master plans; investment office buildings, retail development, entertainment complexes, sport stadiums/arenas and corporate headquarters; educational, institutional and health care facilities; hotels, resort and conference centres; residences; transportation facilities; and museums. Since its founding in 1976 by A. Eugene Kohn FAIA, RIBA, JIA, Williams Pedersen FAIA, FAAR and Sheldon Fox FAIA, KPF's practice has grown from three to over 350 people, with offices in New York, London and Tokyo and projects that span the globe. Among their many award-winning designs are 333 Wacker Drive, Chicago, Illinois; the World Bank Headquarters, Washington DC; Westendstrasse 1/DG Bank Headquarters, Frankfurt, Germany; and Samsung Plaza and Rodin Museum, Seoul, Korea. Recent projects include The Rothermere American Institute at Oxford University, The City University of New York/Baruch College and the Gannett/USA Today Headquarters in McLean, Virginia.

Koning Eizenberg Architecture

The Koning Eizenberg practice of 20 years has become well known for their design of small buildings for everyday living including affordable housing, community centres, recreation centres, schools, custom homes, hotels, stores and work places. Most were accomplished within a 25-mile radius of their studio in Santa Monica, California. Many of the buildings have won multiple awards and have been published in architectural and general interest publications in the United States and internationlly. The influence of Koning Eizenberg's approach to design can also be measured by the numerous invitations to speak at engagements and teaching appointments at Universities around the world.

Hank Koning and Julie Eizenberg have refocused the attention of their peers on the value and design potential of socially responsible projects by demonstrating architectural excellence in the design of many tight budget affordable housing projects and community buildings. In turn their ability to achieve design excellence without pretension in other buildings types grew from this groundbreaking work. Their buildings might best be described as brilliantly sensible. They are comfortable environments where suggestion rather than statement is used to engage the viewer or user of the buildings. In Koning Eizenberg's buildings one is encouraged to discover space and architecture for oneself guided by compositional cues, landscape strategies, spatial sequence and scale change. The result is innovative architecture with a rare kind of humanity.

Kreykenbohm Architekten

Kreykenbohm Architekten was established in 1997. It is a small architectural practice with a maximum of five staff. Professor Bernd and Susanne Kreykenbohm worked for renowned German firms V.Gerkan, Marg und Partners and Schweger + Partners prior to establishing their own practice. In addition to designing office buildings, hotels, schools and urban planning they have also participated successfully in architectural competitions. Situated in Hannover, Kreykenbohm Architekten also undertake lighting and exhibition design. Both partners teach architectural design in Hannover and Braunschweig, and provide their expert opinion and judgement in architectural competitions. In addition, they regularly organise architectural study tours of the USA, Netherlands and Switzerland for the Association of German Architects, student groups and other interested parties.

Kuth/Ranieri

The San Francisco-based architecture studio of Kuth/Ranieri has worked as a dynamic multidisciplinary office extending the scope of residential and commercial work to include interiors, furniture, custom systems and exhibition. The principals, Byron Kuth AIA and Elizabeth Ranieri AIA, are both teachers and builders; their design process is lodged at the convergence of the two disciplines.

Informed by an academic discourse that touches politics, psychology and pop culture; and tempered by a building industry that has become progressively standardised, the office looks for opportunities to inscribe the work with cultural and tectonic attitudes that anchor a project to its program, place and time. From feasibility studies and project management, to high level detailing of custom systems, the firm shapes work to each individual project, recognising the uniqueness of each client, site, program and budget.

Kuth/Ranieri has had their work displayed in commercial and university galleries in New York City, Boston, San Francisco and Houston. Their work has received Regional, State and National Honor Awards from the American Institute of Architects, *I.D. Magazine*, and the Architectural League of New York. The projects designed by Kuth/Ranieri have been featured in publications both in the United States and internationally.

Leers Weinzapfel Associates

Leers Weinzapfel Associates is a 35-person firm with an established national reputation for solving unusually complex building challenges with uncommon design distinction. In recent years, they have created a number of award-winning facilities including the Massachusetts Institute of Technology, the University of Pennsylvania and the General Services Administration.

Founded by Andrea P. Leers, FAIA and Jane Weinzapfel, FAIA, Leers Weinzapfel Associates is a pioneering and distinguished practice that combines a rigorous exploration of design ideas with pragmatic, thoughtful solutions to the realities of program, site, budget and schedule. The firm's designs reflect a consistent desire for simplicity and strength, order and harmony, integrity of construction and detail, with each building precisely suited to its use and firmly rooted in its particular community context.

LEO A DALY

LEO A DALY is an internationally renowned planning, architecture, engineering and interior design firm. Consistently ranked among the top 10 largest architecture/engineering firms and the top 10 interior design firms in the United States, the firm has nearly 900 professionals in offices world wide. The firm's diverse portfolio includes world-class projects in over 50 countries, and all 50 states of America.

Founded in 1915, by Leo A. Daly Sr., the firm rose to national prominence for pioneering the use of interdisciplinary project teams to ensure maximum efficiency and client satisfaction. Project types range from high-rise corporate offices to data and research centres; airline terminals to retail, recreational and hospitality facilities; elementary schools to universities; and healthcare clinics to full-scale medical centres.

Today, under the leadership of Leo A. Daly, III, FAIA, RIBA, RAIA, the firm continues its legacy of innovative leadership and commitment to design excellence by enhancing the built environment.

Meili, Peter Architekten

The architecture studio of Marcel Meili and Markus Peter was established in 1987. At first, most of the work consisted of projects and studies, several of them under the guise of competitions and consultations (major public works, office buildings, industrial plants and urban planning). With most of these projects being published by the architecture press, and since 1992, several of them were realised.

Among the most recent built works in Zurich are the Riff Raff Cinema, the new roof for the main railway station and the conversion of the Zypressenstrasse Factory into housing and office building. In the fall of 1999 the Swiss School for the Wood Industry was opened in Biel and the reinsurance company Swiss Re Centre for Global Dialogue opened in the fall of 2000. The firm as also participated in collaborations with architects such as Herzog & de Meuron, Diener & Diener, Consolascio & Betrix, Fickert & Knapkiewicz and Staufer & Hasler, among others. Architect Zeno Vogel became an associate of the studio in 1999. The studio is located in Zurich and currently employs 16 collaborators, 10 of which are architects and two are student interns.

Marcel Meili and Markus Peter are frequent collaborators of the architectural press and juries of national and international competitions. Marcel Meili is also Professor of Architecture at the 'Studio Basel' of ETH Zurich together with Roger Diener, Jacques Herzog and Pierre de Meuron.

MGT Architects

MGT Architects was established in Australia in 1980 upon winning the international design competition for the new Parliament House in the nation's capital, and has since successfully completed a wide range of projects throughout Australia and Southeast Asia.

MGT has a central focus on the development of a humane architecture creating rich places for people within urban, interior and landscape environments. Much of the firm's contemporary work explores and develops 'green' building technology and environmental sustainability as a conscious responsibility to society at large. The firm intentionally works at both large and small scale and, in addition to its core practices of architectural and interior design, regularly undertakes major consultancies for master planning, cultural planning, community consultation, and public art programs.

MGT places emphasis in its broad professional practice on the design of public projects, cultural facilities and government buildings, including a special expertise in the master planning and design of university projects, and high-density housing developments.

MGT's projects have received numerous design awards attesting to the commitment and excellence achieved within the firm's design teams.

Michael Hopkins and Partners

The goal at Michael Hopkins and Partners is to design innovative, cost-effective and beautiful buildings that enable clients to make the most of their site, programme and budget. The firm creates logical and clear designs starting from our clients' needs, using the principles of truth to materials and expression of structure, from which stems aesthetic quality, efficiency and the popular appeal of their building.

Since their establishment in 1976 they have pioneered a series of strategies including: fabric roofs, lightweight structures, energy-efficient design, weaving new structures into existing ones, and recycling brown land. Their contribution to architecture has been recognised in numerous design awards, the RIBA's Royal Gold Medal in 1995, and knighthood for Michael Hopkins.

In nearly 25 years the practice has expanded to develop the variety of skills needed to serve the diverse needs of their clients, becoming one of the largest architectural firms in the UK. Bill Taylor joined Michael and Patty Hopkins as a partner; there are five further directors and nine project directors, among a staff of over 100. Since 1984 the firm has worked in Marylebone, which has developed into an office campus with drawing studios, offices and a model shop.

Michael Hopkins and Partners believe that the best buildings come from close co-operation between architect, client and other members of the project team. Dialogue between everyone who has an interest in the project helps to establish appropriate parameters, which are a necessary spur to the design approach synthesising creative imagination with rational logic.

Morphosis

1n 1972 Thom Mayne founded the firm, Morphosis, to develop an architecture that would eschew the normal bounds of traditional forms and materials, and would go beyond the limiting dualism of modern and postmodern. Concretizing the ephemerality of feeling, he creates fusions that, as with the Diamond Ranch High School in Diamond Bar, California and the Hypo Alpe-Adria-Center in Klagenfurt, Austria, blur the demarcation between the ground and the building.

The synthesis of building and landscape in uniquely imaginative modes is manifest in projects such as the Centro Cultural y de Negocios JVC in Guadalajara and the Eugene Federal Courthouse. Morphosis has won 20 Progressive Architecture Awards and 39 American Institute of Architecture Awards.

Thom Mayne was educated at both the University of Southern California and Harvard and was a founder of the Southern California Institute of Architecture (SCI-Arc). He has taught at many universities in both the US and Europe, including Harvard, Yale, Columbia, Cornell, and The Bartlett and is currently a professor at UCLA. His work has been exhibited extensively throughout the world and is the subject of numerous books and other publications.

Murphy/Jahn

Murphy/Jahn is a unique architectural firm conceived to meet the challenges posed by the new millennium. Under the leadership of Helmut Jahn, the practice has grown and evolved steadily from the original firm, which was founded over 60 years ago. Through 30 years of 'organisation building', Murphy/Jahn has succeeded in combining the best of design creativity and corporate professionalism. The firm believes their commitment to this balance is fundamental to the successful translation from architectural concept into building reality. Murphy/Jahn are committed to creating forward-reaching buildings, which will endure the test of time and become a source of pride in the minds of owners, users, communities and ourselves.

The Murphy/Jahn approach to design is both rational and intuitive; it attempts to give each building its own philosophical and intellectual base, and has established an opportunity to exploit its particular elements to achieve a visual and communicative statement. The rational part details with the realities of a problem. The intuitive aspect deals with the theoretical, intellectual aspects – a subconscious ability to sense the intrinsic structure of a problem and establish priorities for the elements of design which deal with space, form, light, colour and materials, and the way architecture communicates through symbol and meaning of architectural language.

NL Architects

NL Architects is an Amsterdam-based office. The four principals officially opened practice in January 1997. All were educated at Delft University while living in Amsterdam. NL's 'commuting' office started while carpooling between these cities (in that sense they like to think of themselves as autodidactic; the recurrent fascination with mobility and tarmac perhaps could be traced back to being 'educated' on the highway). Their projects focus on ordinary aspects of everyday life, including the unappreciated or negative, that are enhanced or twisted in order to bring to the fore the unexpected and positive potential of the things that surround us.

Patel Taylor Architects

Encompassing architecture, urban design and landscape, Patel Taylor's projects include major regeneration such as the Thames Barrier Park, educational buildings, like the Centre for Theatre, Film and TV Studies faculty building in Wales, and small community buildings. Each scale serves to inform the other allowing them the potential to look at related issues from a broad perspective, whilst maintaining a focus on the individual project.

In addition to their architectural projects they have gained international recognition for their skills in urban design, master planning and landscape design. They respond with sensitivity and innovation to a site and brief, to provide outstanding solutions for all their clients, who range from local authorities, lottery applicants, enterprise bodies and the private sector. Many of their projects have been won through international competitions, and these together with their numerous awards (including four RIBA 2001 awards) and a variety of publications, testify to the quality of their work.

Perkins & Will

Perkins & Will, founded in 1935, is a professional service firm staffed with architects, interior designers and planners. The firm, with offices in Chicago, Atlanta, Charlotte, Los Angeles, Miami, Minneapolis, New York and Paris, practices on an international basis, having completed work in 41 countries and in 49 states of the United States.

Perkins & Will first gained national recognition for the design of educational facilities, and since then, hundreds of school, college and university projects have been planned and designed worldwide. Perkins & Will has since expanded the firm's practice to include corporate-commercial-civic projects, along with projects that involve the healthcare and science-technology sector.

Perkins & Will is one of the nation's most respected design firms, both for excellence in design and for services to clients. Through the years, the projects of the firm have received hundreds of awards, and its principals have been honoured for their contributions to their profession. The firm was recently named by the American Institute of Architects as Firm of the Year for 1999. Of equal importance is the adherence to a design process that emphasises commitment, communication and co-ordination, resulting in responsive service and projects that satisfy client goals.

From a modest beginning over 65 years ago, Perkins & Will has grown to become an organisation of more than 300 design professionals, with a dedication to quality that was established by the founders.

Perkins Eastman Architects PC

Perkins Eastman Architects is a knowledge-based design firm offering its clients unique solutions, innovative environments and design excellence in architecture, programming, planning and interior design. The firm's primary practice areas are centers of excellence formulating design solutions predicated on research, expertise and creativity. Our goal is to sustain continuing excellence in design and service based on the unique needs and objectives of each client.

With a staff of over 400, and offices in New York City, Pittsburgh, Stamford, Charlotte and Toronto, Ontario, the firm offers design and planning expertise in a variety of building and project types to private and public sector clients both nationally and internationally. Our practice area specialties have been developed around the knowledge and interests of our principals and senior staff. Since the firm's founding in 1981, its work has been widely published and receives numerous design awards each year.

Polshek Partnership Architects

Located in New York City since the founding of the practice in 1963, the Polshek Partnership is known for architectural excellence and for its longstanding commitment to cultural, educational, governmental and scientific institutions. Projects have been published internationally and recognised with numerous awards for design excellence, for their important contributions to the cultural life of their cities and for the stabilisation of their precincts.

The seven partners and 18 associates proceed from the shared belief that the most elegant architectural responses are both technically and socially relevant to their time and place. Characterised by a collaborative process, the architectural solutions are rooted in extensive research involving the analysis of context, program, public image and environmental and construction technologies. This commitment and the resulting approach have led to the completion of hundreds of projects that in their typological, geographical and formal diversity authentically expresses the individual's client mission.

Pugh + Scarpa

Pugh + Scarpa is an architecture and engineering firm with offices in Santa Monica, California and Charlotte, North Carolina. Founded in 1984, the firm has grown to a staff of 20 professionals and is currently working on a broad range of major commissions for private, public and institutional clients. Pugh + Scarpa's work emphasises formal and material research and innovation with a particular commitment to sustainable design.

Pugh + Scarpa have received numerous design awards, won many design competitions and have been published extensively for their work. Most recently, the have been recognised for outstanding achievement for Colorado Court, a 44-unit single room occupancy housing project that has been developed as a model for sustainable living. Colorado Court will be one of the first affordable housing projects in the United States to be 100 per cent energy independent.

Renzo Piano Building Workshop

The Renzo Piano Building Workshop (RPBW) was established in 1968 by Renzo Piano in Genoa, Italy. The firm has since expanded and now operates offices in

Genoa and Paris. The workshop permanently employs 70 architects together with a further 20 support staff including CAD operators, model makers, and administrative and secretarial staff. The firm's architects are of many nationalities and each is selected for his or her experience, enthusiasm and calibre. The staff has wide experience in working in multidisciplinary teams on building projects in France, Italy and beyond.
RPBW provides full architectural design services and consultancy services during the construction phase. Design skills also include interior design, town planning and urban design services, landscape design and exhibition design.
Works currently in progress include the Harvard University Art Museum in Cambridge, Massachusetts, the Chicago Art Institution expansion, the Nasher Sculpture Center in Dallas, Texas, the Woodruff Arts Center expansion in Atlanta and the New York Times Headquarters.

Rick Joy Architects

The work of Rick Joy Architects has been celebrated for its focus on craft and the holistic integration of the design and construction processes. Functionality and longevity are balanced by a deep commitment to continually search for the generative origins of a contemporary architecture that is derived from the essences of the context and community. In the few years since its inception, the firm has received numerous awards, been exhibited extensively, and has been featured in numerous publications worldwide.
In the work, a great deal of attention is given to the qualities of the sensual experiences. Rick Joy Architects strives for a synthesis of the logical aspects of the design and a visceral understanding of the experiences. The more ethereal aspects of the intimate experiences – the decomposed granite crunching under your feet, the gentle trickle of water, the lacy shadow of a tree, a wall, a framed blue sky – are often more important than the object itself. An architecture develops that, in its deliberate simplicity, gently nudges people on to a more engaging multi-sensory experience and heightens the awareness of actually being there. These are the things that bring our soul and intellect into alignment. The simplest things can evoke the deepest feelings. The silence in great music is often more profound than the sounds.

Santiago Calatrava S.A.

Santiago Calatrava S.A. was founded in 1986, in Zurich, by the Spanish born architect and engineer Santiago Calatrava. In 1989, a second office was opened in Paris in order to work on the increasing number of foreign commissions, and to be as near as possible to the sites of the projects in progress, in particular to the Lyon-Satolas Airport Railway Station project. A further office was set up in Valencia in order to provide the required support within Spain.
In this way, an organisation has evolved which is international in a real sense, and which is always within reach of the next site. The offices are characterised by their cultural diversity and their mostly multilingual staff. Modern communications permit exceptionally decentralised working practices. Experience and ideas from the different regions of Europe can flow in and influence the work of the individual offices, which can be utilised equally by the partner offices.

sauerbruch hutton architects

Matthias Sauerbruch and Louisa Hutton studied at the Architectural Association (AA) in the early 1980s, and taught there for five and two years, respectively, before establishing their practice in London in 1989.
In their work on urban competitions, they were able to continue research into the themes they had pursued with their units at the AA – in particular that of the development of the post-industrial city as an ecologically and sensually sustainable environment. Following their success in competitions in 1990 and 1995, they were commissioned to execute two large projects in Berlin, where they opened a second office in 1993.
The experience of the residential projects in London and the urban-scale buildings in Berlin has led to an architecture which redefines the current notion of ecologically aware building. Their concern for the sustainable use of resources – both natural and urban – is extended into their idiosyncratic spaces at all scales. These are articulated through rich colours, materials and textures that reflect a concern with the well being of the individual and his enjoyment of the physical environment.

Sean Godsell Architects

Sean Godsell was born in Melbourne in 1960 and graduated with First Class Honours from the University of Melbourne in 1984. He spent much of 1985 travelling Japan and Europe and worked in London from 1986 to 1988 for Sir Denys Lasdun. In 1989 he returned to Melbourne and worked for The Hassell Group. In 1994 he formed Godsell Associates Pty Ltd Architects. Godsell obtained a Masters of Architecture degree from RMIT University in 1999 entitled 'The Appropriateness of the Contemporary Australian Dwelling'. In 1999 he was also a finalist in the Seppelt Contemporary Art Awards (Environmental Design) held by the Museum of Contemporary Art in Sydney and his work 'Future Shack' was shown in New York, Paris and London as a finalist in the Architecture for Humanity Exhibition.
He added the RAIA Award of Merit (institutional) for his design of Woodleigh Art School to his list of design awards in 1999.
In 2000 he won the RAIA Award of Merit (residential new) for the Carter/Tucker House and his work was featured in the ABC TV documentary 'In the Mind of the Architect'. In addition, the Carter/Tucker house won a Commendation, the RAIA Robin Boyd national award and won Highly Commended by the jury for the AR + D awards in London – one of 15 winners from over 700 entries in all building types from around the world. This building won Best Building in the region in The World Architecture Awards announced in Hong Kong at the end of June 2001. His work was exhibited in 2000 in Denmark, London and Switzerland and has been published extensively in Europe, USA and Asia. His 'Future Shack' modular house received a commendation award at the 2001 RAIA awards.

SHoP/Sharples Holden Pasquarelli

SHoP/Sharples Holden Pasquarelli is an emerging design firm with five partners whose education and experience encompass architecture, fine arts, structural engineering, finance and business management. Founded in 1996, SHoP was recently awarded the 2001 Emerging Voice Award by the Architectural League of New York and the 2001 Academy Award in Architecture from the American Academy of Arts and Letters.
The firm's broad range of projects includes a university academic building, a civic park, public art institutions, museums, retail shops and mid-rise apartment buildings. With each new design problem, the office uses a combination of digital expertise, in the form of three-dimensional computer form generation, rapid prototyping and model building in their in-house shop, to arrive at an original and buildable solution which only that particular project could have inspired.
SHoP/Sharples Holden Pasquarelli's reputation as architects who can link emerging concepts and theories of the digital age with the tactile fundamentals of design and construction is what sets them apart from other design practices. The office believes that the exploration of new systems of practice is best tested through actual construction using both spatial and non-spatial agendas to reach the point of translation between conceptual and physical solutions. The office uses a mixture of three-dimensional computer

form generation techniques along with rapid prototyping, model building and architectural detailing in their own woodshop to provide spatial solutions that are open, gestural, revealing, precise and unique.

Sidnam Petrone Gartner Architects

Sidnam Petrone Gartner is a 14-person architectural firm based in New York City. Headed by three partners, Sidnam Petrone Gartner is a strong design practice that also provides a comprehensive range of architectural services. These include pre-design feasibility and programming services; design and contract administration; and submittals to the appropriate authorities, including building management and government authorities. The firm has served over 160 clients since its founding by Coty Sidnam in 1980 and its projects have included numerous co-op and condominium apartments, urban townhouses, second homes and suburban free-standing houses, corporate offices and retail establishments.

Although the clients are diverse, they are unified in their desire for architecture that is well conceived and well executed by a team of professionals. Corporate clients include Polo Ralph Lauren, Time Warner, Calvin Klein, COTY Beauty, Hartmann Luggage, Palm Pictures and America Online. Many private clients return to Sidnam Petrone Gartner as they relocate or expand their residential or corporate holdings.

At any one time, Sidnam Petrone Gartner services approximately 12 clients. Projects are designed and managed by the partners, Coty Sidnam, Bill Petrone and Eric Gartner, who lead a team of young, creative design professionals. The partners maintain a strong presence throughout the design and construction process, collaborating with clients, engineers, lighting and audio/visual consultants, and interior designers, and providing the leadership necessary to produce a coherent and comprehensive design.

The work of Sidnam Petrone Gartner has been published many times in *The Architectural Review* and *Interior Design*. Recent publications include *New York Times Sunday Magazine* and *House Beautiful*. In 1997 the Saddle River House was honoured by the New Jersey AIA. The design for America Online received a 1999 Award from the New York City AIA as an outstanding architectural interior. In 2000, the Private Residence, Harrison, NY was awarded a Silver Medal for excellence in architecture by the AIA New Jersey, and more recently The Chicago Athenaeum 2001 American Architecture Award.

Sophie Hicks, SH Architects

SH Architects is the firm behind the Paul Smith flagship stores in London, Milan, and soon, in Paris. Specialising in luxury conversions with high quality finishes, the London-based firm see themselves as perfectionists. Balancing aesthetics with functionality, utilising new materials, and reusing old materials in new ways, they demand the highest quality of workmanship. The firm is committed to the highest standards of design.

Stein Halvorsen AS Sivilarkitekter MNAL

Stein Halvorsen started the office following the competition on the Sami Parliament. It has taken part in competitions leading to commissions in the fields of culture, public buildings, domestic buildings, offices and urban planning. Among the most interesting projects could be mentioned: the Sami Parliament; the Norwegian residence in Berlin; main fire station in Bergen; greenhouse in the botanical garden in Oslo and second prize in the international competition for the new opera house in Oslo.

The office doesn't have a clear recognisable style in architecture, but it has a clear philosophy of the importance of empathy in every task and to be opposed to perishable fashions that continually appear. A basic recognition that the human being is formed by its surroundings is the starting point. Recently the office received Statens Byggeskikkspris – the Norwegian State Prize for Architecture – where the grounds mainly were adaptation to scale and interaction with surroundings.

Steven Ehrlich Architects

Founded in 1979, Steven Ehrlich Architects is a 28-person architectural team whose studio is a converted dance hall in Culver City, California. This award-winning firm is internationally recognised for its distinctive public and residential designs that extend the Los Angeles tradition of architectural innovation, fusing technology with sensitivity to both culture and the environment. Steven Ehrlich Architects is committed to public architecture that encourages a multicultural fusion of people and place and to residential work that creates serene environments that replenish the soul.

The growing international influence of the firm's work is recognised in the Rizzoli International Publications monograph, *Steven Ehrlich Architects* (1998). The firm has won more than 50 design awards including three national American Institute of Architects design awards (1997), the first practice to be so honoured since I.M. Pei in 1974.

Award-winning architectural projects include the Sony Music Entertainment's West Coast Headquarters in Santa Monica (1992), the Robertson Branch Library of the Los Angeles public library system (1997) and the adaptive re-use of Grand Central Arts Building for Cal State University Fullerton in Santa Ana, California (1999). Current showcase projects include a house and mosque in Dubai, UAE; the 65,000-square-foot Art Center for Orange Coast College in Costa Mesa, California; the 75,000-square-foot Southwest Staging Building for UCLA; San Bernardino Valley College's Master Plan & Design of Five Buildings; in addition to the new Kendall Square Bio-tech Building. The firm also has a number of residences in design and construction.

The practice is led by design principal Steven Ehrlich, FAIA, who is joined by principals, Cecily Young, AIA, James Schmidt, AIA and Thomas Zahlten, AIA.

Studio Granda

Studio Granda was established in 1987 in Reykjavík, Iceland.

The partners Margrét Hardardóttir and Steve Christer trained at Edinburgh and Newcastle universities respectively and both later graduated from the Architectural Association in London.

The practice is involved in a wide range of public and private projects including buildings, interiors, infrastructure, landscape, furniture and collaborations with artists. Notable works include the Reykjavík City Hall (1992), 'Aktion Poliphile' residence in Wiesbaden (1992), Supreme Court of Iceland (1996) and the Reykjavík Art Museum (2000).

TEN Arquitectos

TEN Arquitectos – Taller de Enrique Norten Arquitectos S.C. – was founded by Enrique Norten in 1985. Partner Bernardo Gómez Pimienta joined the firm in 1987. Currently, TEN Arquitectos has 20 staff.

TEN Arquitectos is dedicated to creation and investigation in architecture and design. They have been involved in projects of many different types and scales. The work of TEN Arquitectos has been widely recognised in Mexico as well as internationally.

Among its most recognised buildings are the National School of Theatre; the Hotel Habita, the Insurgentes Theater Renovation, the French Youth Center in Lindavista, the Services Building for Televisa; all in Mexico City, as well as several residential and commerical projects of all kinds. Currently, TEN Arquitectos is developing various projects in the United States as well as in several Mexican cities.

UN Studio – Ben van Berkel and Caroline Bos

Ben van Berkel (Utrecht, 1957) studied architecture at the Rietveld Academy in Amsterdam and the Architecture Association in London, receiving the AA Diploma with Honours in 1987. Caroline Bos (Rotterdam, 1959) studied History of Art at Birkbeck College, University of London.

In 1988 they set up architectural practice in Amsterdam. The Van Berkel & Bos Architectuurbureau has realised among other projects the Karbouw office building, the Erasmus bridge in Rotterdam, museum Het Valkhof in Nijmegen, the Moebius House and the NMR facilities for the University of Utrecht. Current projects are a restructuring of the station area of Arnhem, a music theatre for Graz (A) and the design and restructuring of the Wadsworth Atheneum Museum of Art in Hartford, Connecticut.

In addition to Van Berkel & Bos Architectuurbureau Ben van Berkel and Caroline Bos established in 1998 a new firm: UN Studio (United Net). UN Studio presents itself as a network of specialists in architecture, urban development and infrastructure.

Ben van Berkel and Caroline Bos have lectured and taught at many architecture schools around the world. They are currently visiting professors at Princeton University, leading the Public Construction unit. Central to their teaching is the inclusive approach of architectural works integrating virtual and material organisation and engineering constructions. In 2001 Ben van Berkel has been appointed as Dean of Architecture at the Städelschule in Frankfurt.

VIIVA ARKKITEHTUURI OY

VIIVA was established by Rauno Lehtinen, Pekka Mäki and Toni Peltola in June 1996. VIIVA arkkitehtuuri Oy is a limited company that was founded when the principals won an open planning competition for the Finnish Embassy in Berlin.

VIIVA works in the fields of architectural design, interior design, landscape architecture, urban planning, graphic design and exhibition design and is a regular participant in national and international planning competitions.

VIIVA recruits the number of staff it needs to accomplish current projects. The employees are usually young architects or students of architecture with high qualifications in various fields of design as well as computer-aided design.

The Finnish Embassy in Berlin, designed by VIIVA, was awarded with Best Overall Building Award in the 2001 Arup World Architecture Awards in Hong Kong.

Williamson Pounders Architects, PC

Founded in 1990, Williamson Pounders Architects, PC, of Memphis, Tennessee, provides planning, architecture and interior design services to civic, religious, educational and commercial clients. Principals James F. Williamson, AIA, and Louis R. Pounders, AIA, lead WPA's staff of 15 architects and support personnel. Dedicated to design excellence and superior client service, WPA has earned a reputation for being one of the leading architectural firms in the mid-south. Recent projects from WPA include Lichterman Nature Center, Metropolitan Inter-Faith Association Headquarters, The Law Offices of Burch Porter and Johnson, Ballet Memphis and St. Thomas More Catholic Church. WPA's projects have appeared in L'Arca, Chiesa Oggi and Contemporary Stone and Tile. Over the last decade, the firm has received more than 40 design awards including honours from the local, state and regional AIA, the Interfaith Forum on Religious Art and Architecture, the Chicago Athenaeum and the Eugene Potente, Sr. Liturgical Design Competition.

Yabu Pushelberg

Established in 1980 by George Yabu and Glenn Pushelberg, the firm's creative director and managing partner respectively, Yabu Pushelberg has long built its reputation on providing a myriad of design solutions for an eclectic and demanding clientele. A distinctly creative enterprise that views its mission to be one of bringing forth creative strategies for business, Yabu Pushelberg develops content right along side its clients, rather than simply giving form to their ideas. Concepts are custom-developed to suit the client's objectives to ensure successful commerce.

With an in-house staff of over 65, the firm is able to provide its clients with a full scope of design and project administration services for speciality retail and department stores; hotels and spas; leisure and entertainment venues; showrooms; hospitality and select corporate environments. Other creative/design facets of the firm include marketing and communications, graphic design services and visual merchandising concepts. Since 1992, the firm has been engaged in creating a range of furnishings and carpets manufactured and marked under licensing agreements with ICF/Nienkämper.

The firm's headquarters is in Toronto, Canada and recently opened a second studio in New York.

Index

Acknowledgments

In our eighth edition of the International Architecture Yearbook, The Images Publishing Group wishes to thank the contributors who have made this international publication a resounding success.

In particular the publishers, Alessina Brooks and Paul Latham, would like to thank Rod Gilbert, Diane Strong and the rest of the IMAGES team for such a concerted effort.

We wish to extend our grateful thanks to Catherine Slessor for kindly sharing her knowledge and expertise in the writing of the introduction for this book, and for her invaluable assistance in co-ordinating the participants of this edition and advice on projects.

Alessina Brooks & Paul Latham
Publishers

1100 Architect • AC Martin Partners • Adhoc Architects • Alberto Campo Baeza Arquitecto • Antoine Predock Architects • Architectures Jean No
• ARM.RPVHT Pty Ltd • Atelier D'Architecture Franck Hammoutene • Atelier Hitoshi Abe • Axel Schultes Architekten • Azman Owens Architec
Baumschlager & Eberle • Behnisch, Behnisch & Partner • Bernard Tschumi Architects • Bohlin Cywinski Jackson • Bolles+Wilson • Bucholz McE
• Centerbrook Architects • Cesar Pelli & Associates • Claudio Silvestrin Architects • Daly, Genik Architects • Denton Corker Marshall • Design Offic
Dominique Perrault Architecte • Droog Design • Edouard François et Associés • (EEA) Erick Van Egeraat Associated Architects • Eric Owen M
Architects • Fentress Bradburn • Foster & Partners • Gehry Partners • Gluckman Mayner Architects • DEO London • Ingenhoven Overdiek und Part
• Jakob + Macfarlane • Jarmund/Vigsnæs AS • Juhani Katainen Architects • Kisho Kurokawa architect & associates • Kohn Pedersen Fox Associa
• Koning Eizenberg Architecture • Kreykenbohm Architekten • Kuth/Ranieri Architecture • Leers Weinzapfel Associates • Leo A Daly Architects • L
and Space, LLC • Meili Peter • MGT Architects • Michael Hopkins & Partners • Morphosis • Mr Patrick Berger • Mr Santiago Calatrava • Ms Cather
Slessor • Murphy/Jahn • Patel Taylor • Perkins Eastman Architects PC • Perkins & Will • Polshek Partnership • Pugh + Scarpa • Renzo Piano Build
Workshop • Rick Joy Architect • sauerbruch hutton architekten • Sean Godsell Architects • SH Architects • SHoP/Sharples Holden Pasquarelli • Sidn
Petrone Gartner Architects • Stein Halvorsen • Steven Ehrlich Architects • Studio Granda • TEN Arquitectos • The Cox Group • UN Studio van Berkel a
Bos • Viiva Arkkitehtuuri • Williamson Pounders Architects • Yabu Pushelberg • 1100 Architect • AC Martin Partners • Adhoc Architects • Alberto Cam
Baeza Arquitecto • Antoine Predock Architects • Architectures Jean Nouvel • ARM.RPVHT Pty Ltd • Atelier D'Architecture Franck Hammoutene • Ate
Hitoshi Abe • Axel Schultes Architekten • Azman Owens Architects • Baumschlager & Eberle • Behnisch, Behnisch & Partner • Bernard Tsch
Architects • Bohlin Cywinski Jackson • Bolles+Wilson • Bucholz McEvoy • Centerbrook Architects • Cesar Pelli & Associates • Claudio Silves
Architects • Daly, Genik Architects • Denton Corker Marshall • Design Office • Dominique Perrault Architecte • Droog Design • Edouard Françoi
Associés • (EEA) Erick Van Egeraat Associated Architects • Eric Owen Moss Architects • Fentress Bradburn • Foster & Partners • Gehry Partner
Gluckman Mayner Architects • DEO London • Ingenhoven Overdiek und Partner • Jakob + Macfarlane • Jarmund/Vigsnæs AS • Juhani Katain
Architects • Kisho Kurokawa architect & associates • Kohn Pedersen Fox Associates • Koning Eizenberg Architecture • Kreykenbohm Architekte
Kuth/Ranieri Architecture • Leers Weinzapfel Associates • Leo A Daly Architects • Line and Space, LLC • Meili Peter • MGT Architects • Michael Hopk
& Partners • Morphosis • Mr Patrick Berger • Mr Santiago Calatrava • Ms Catherine Slessor • Murphy/Jahn • Patel Taylor • Perkins Eastman Archite
PC • Perkins & Will • Polshek Partnership • Pugh + Scarpa • Renzo Piano Building Workshop • Rick Joy Architect • sauerbruch hutton architekten • Se
Godsell Architects • SH Architects • SHoP/Sharples Holden Pasquarelli • Sidnam Petrone Gartner Architects • Stein Halvorsen • Steven Ehrlich Archite
• Studio Granda • TEN Arquitectos • The Cox Group • UN Studio van Berkel and Bos • Viiva Arkkitehtuuri • Williamson Pounders Architects • Ya
Pushelberg • 1100 Architect • AC Martin Partners • Adhoc Architects • Alberto Campo Baeza Arquitecto • Antoine Predock Architects • Architectu
Jean Nouvel • ARM.RPVHT Pty Ltd • Atelier D'Architecture Franck Hammoutene • Atelier Hitoshi Abe • Axel Schultes Architekten • Azman Owe
Architects • Baumschlager & Eberle • Behnisch, Behnisch & Partner • Bernard Tschumi Architects • Bohlin Cywinski Jackson • Bolles+Wilson • Buch
McEvoy • Centerbrook Architects • Cesar Pelli & Associates • Claudio Silvestrin Architects • Daly, Genik Architects • Denton Corker Marshall • Des
Office • Dominique Perrault Architecte • Droog Design • Edouard François et Associés • (EEA) Erick Van Egeraat Associated Architects • Eric Owen M
Architects • Fentress Bradburn • Foster & Partners • Gehry Partners • Gluckman Mayner Architects • DEO London • Ingenhoven Overdiek und Part
• Jakob + Macfarlane • Jarmund/Vigsnæs AS • Juhani Katainen Architects • Kisho Kurokawa architect & associates • Kohn Pedersen Fox Associate
Koning Eizenberg Architecture • Kreykenbohm Architekten • Kuth/Ranieri Architecture • Leers Weinzapfel Associates • Leo A Daly Architects • Line a
Space, LLC • Meili Peter • MGT Architects • Michael Hopkins & Partners • Morphosis • Mr Patrick Berger • Mr Santiago Calatrava • Ms Catherine Sless
• Murphy/Jahn • Patel Taylor • Perkins Eastman Architects PC • Perkins & Will • Polshek Partnership • Pugh + Scarpa • Renzo Piano Building Worksh
• Rick Joy Architect • sauerbruch hutton architekten • Sean Godsell Architects • SH Architects • SHoP/Sharples Holden Pasquarelli • Sidnam Petro
Gartner Architects • Stein Halvorsen • Steven Ehrlich Architects • Studio Granda • TEN Arquitectos • The Cox Group • UN Studio van Berkel and Bo
Viiva Arkkitehtuuri • Williamson Pounders Architects • Yabu Pushelberg • 1100 Architect • AC Martin Partners • Adhoc Architects • Alberto Campo Bae
Arquitecto • Antoine Predock Architects • Architectures Jean Nouvel • ARM.RPVHT Pty Ltd • Atelier D'Architecture Franck Hammoutene • Atelier Hito
Abe • Axel Schultes Architekten • Azman Owens Architects • Baumschlager & Eberle • Behnisch, Behnisch & Partner • Bernard Tschumi Architect
Bohlin Cywinski Jackson • Bolles+Wilson • Bucholz McEvoy • Centerbrook Architects • Cesar Pelli & Associates • Claudio Silvestrin Architects • Da
Genik Architects • Denton Corker Marshall • Design Office • Dominique Perrault Architecte • Droog Design • Edouard François et Associés • (EEA) Er
Van Egeraat Associated Architects • Eric Owen Moss Architects • Fentress Bradburn • Foster & Partners • Gehry Partners • Gluckman Mayner Architec
• DEO London • Ingenhoven Overdiek und Partner • Jakob + Macfarlane • Jarmund/Vigsnæs AS • Juhani Katainen Architects • Kisho Kurokawa archite
& associates • Kohn Pedersen Fox Associates • Koning Eizenberg Architecture • Kreykenbohm Architekten • Kuth/Ranieri Architecture • Leers Weinzap
Associates • Leo A Daly Architects • Line and Space, LLC • Meili Peter • MGT Architects • Michael Hopkins & Partners • Morphosis • Mr Patrick Berg
• Mr Santiago Calatrava • Ms Catherine Slessor • Murphy/Jahn • Patel Taylor • Perkins Eastman Architects PC • Perkins & Will • Polshek Partnershi
Pugh + Scarpa • Renzo Piano Building Workshop • Rick Joy Architect • sauerbruch hutton architekten • Sean Godsell Architects • SH Architects
SHoP/Sharples Holden Pasquarelli • Sidnam Petrone Gartner Architects • Stein Halvorsen • Steven Ehrlich Architects • Studio Granda • TEN Arquitect
• The Cox Group • UN Studio van Berkel and Bos • Viiva Arkkitehtuuri • Williamson Pounders Architects • Yabu Pushelberg • 1100 Architect • AC Mar
Partners • Adhoc Architects • Alberto Campo Baeza Arquitecto • Antoine Predock Architects • Architectures Jean Nouvel • ARM.RPVHT Pty Ltd • Atel
D'Architecture Franck Hammoutene • Atelier Hitoshi Abe • Axel Schultes Architekten • Azman Owens Architects • Baumschlager & Eberle • Behnisc
Behnisch & Partner • Bernard Tschumi Architects • Bohlin Cywinski Jackson • Bolles+Wilson • Bucholz McEvoy • Centerbrook Architects • Cesar P
& Associates • Claudio Silvestrin Architects • Daly, Genik Architects • Denton Corker Marshall • Design Office • Dominique Perrault Architecte • Dro
Design • Edouard François et Associés • (EEA) Erick Van Egeraat Associated Architects • Eric Owen Moss Architects • Fentress Bradburn • Foster
Partners • Gehry Partners • Gluckman Mayner Architects • DEO London • Ingenhoven Overdiek und Partner • Jakob + Macfarlane • Jarmund/Vigsna
AS • Juhani Katainen Architects • Kisho Kurokawa architect & associates • Kohn Pedersen Fox Associates • Koning Eizenberg Architecture
Kreykenbohm Architekten • Kuth/Ranieri Architecture • Leers Weinzapfel Associates • Leo A Daly Architects • Line and Space, LLC • Meili Peter • MG
Architects • Michael Hopkins & Partners • Morphosis • Mr Patrick Berger • Mr Santiago Calatrava • Ms Catherine Slessor • Murphy/Jahn • Patel Tay
• Perkins Eastman Architects PC • Perkins & Will • Polshek Partnership • Pugh + Scarpa • Renzo Piano Building Workshop • Rick Joy Architec
sauerbruch hutton architekten • Sean Godsell Architects • SH Architects • SHoP/Sharples Holden Pasquarelli • Sidnam Petrone Gartner Architects • Ste
Halvorsen • Steven Ehrlich Architects • Studio Granda • TEN Arquitectos • The Cox Group • UN Studio van Berkel and Bos • Viiva Arkkitehtuu
Williamson Pounders Architects • Yabu Pushelberg • 1100 Architect • AC Martin Partners • Adhoc Architects • Alberto Campo Baeza Arquitecto • Anto
Predock Architects • Architectures Jean Nouvel • ARM.RPVHT Pty Ltd • Atelier D'Architecture Franck Hammoutene • Atelier Hitoshi Abe • Axel Schult
Architekten • Azman Owens Architects • Baumschlager & Eberle • Behnisch, Behnisch & Partner • Bernard Tschumi Architects • Bohlin Cywinski Jacks
• Bolles+Wilson • Bucholz McEvoy • Centerbrook Architects • Cesar Pelli & Associates • Claudio Silvestrin Architects • Daly, Genik Architects • Dent
Corker Marshall • Design Office • Dominique Perrault Architecte • Droog Design • Edouard François et Associés • (EEA) Erick Van Egeraat Associat
Architects • Eric Owen Moss Architects • Fentress Bradburn • Foster & Partners • Gehry Partners • Gluckman Mayner Architects • DEO Londor
Ingenhoven Overdiek und Partner • Jakob + Macfarlane • Jarmund/Vigsnæs AS • Juhani Katainen Architects • Kisho Kurokawa architect & associates
Kohn Pedersen Fox Associates • Koning Eizenberg Architecture • Kreykenbohm Architekten • Kuth/Ranieri Architecture • Leers Weinzapfel Associate
Leo A Daly Architects • Line and Space, LLC • Meili Peter • MGT Architects • Michael Hopkins & Partners • Morphosis • Mr Patrick Berger • Mr Santia
Calatrava • Ms Catherine Slessor • Murphy/Jahn • Patel Taylor • Perkins Eastman Architects PC • Perkins & Will • Polshek Partnership • Pu
+ Scarpa • Renzo Piano Building Workshop • Rick Joy Architect • sauerbruch hutton architekten • Sean Godsell Architects • SH Archite
• SHoP/Sharples Holden Pasquarelli • Sidnam Petrone Gartner Architects • Stein Halvorsen • Steven Ehrlich Architects • Studio Granda
Arquitectos • The Cox Group • UN Studio van Berkel and Bos • Viiva Arkkitehtuuri • Williamson Pounders Architects • Yabu Pushelberg • 1100 Ar